The Children of Africa in the Colonies

ANTISLAVERY, ABOLITION, AND THE ATLANTIC WORLD

R. J. M. BLACKETT AND
JAMES BREWER STEWART
Series Editors

The Children of Africa in the Colonies

FREE PEOPLE OF COLOR IN BARBADOS
IN THE AGE OF EMANCIPATION

Melanie J. Newton

LOUISIANA STATE UNIVERSITY PRESS ✳ BATON ROUGE

Published by Louisiana State University Press
Copyright © 2008 by Louisiana State University Press
All rights reserved
Manufactured in the United States of America
First printing

DESIGNER: *Amanda McDonald Scallan*
TYPEFACE: *Whitman and AIKoch Antiqua*
TYPESETTER: *J. Jarrett Engineering, Inc.*
PRINTER AND BINDER: *Thomson-Shore, Inc.*

Library of Congress Cataloging-in-Publication Data

Newton, Melanie J., 1974–
    The children of Africa in the colonies : free people of color in Barbados in
the age of emancipation / Melanie J. Newton.
        p. cm. — (Antislavery, abolition, and the Atlantic World)
    Includes bibliographical references and index.
    ISBN 978-0-8071-3326-2 (cloth : alk. paper) 1. Free blacks—Barbados—
History—19th century. 2. Slaves—Emancipation—Social aspects—
Barbados. I. Title.
    F2041.N49 2008
    972.981′00496—dc22

                                        2007042882

The paper in this book meets the guidelines for permanence and durability of the Committee on Production Guidelines for Book Longevity of the Council on Library Resources.♾

For keir, lily, alex, and nico

CONTENTS

ACKNOWLEDGMENTS

Growing up in Barbados, away from the Caribbean's major centers of radical state and social experimentation, there was no escaping the excitement of the region in the 1970s and early 1980s. The very air was charged with a sense of possibility that a more humane and people-centered socialist or social democratic path could be forged. In an echo of Grenada's Fedon Rebellion of 1795, the Grenada Revolution of 1979–1983 brought the turbulence of the age almost next door to Barbados. I had a children's book extolling the virtues of the revolution, and I thought Maurice Bishop and Fidel Castro extremely handsome and swashbuckling fellows, whereas Margaret Thatcher, Ronald Reagan, Eugenia Charles, Edward Seaga, and Jean-Claude Duvalier were the devil incarnate. I remember newspaper reports of the final bloody weeks of the People's Revolutionary Government; the mass killing of one faction of its leadership, including Bishop; and the humiliating U.S. invasion of Grenada on October 25, 1983, when about six thousand U.S. troops occupied a country of one hundred thousand people. Even as a child I experienced an acute sense of embarrassment at the fact that the government of Barbados—my government—provided the regional base from which the invasion was launched. The invasion seriously undermined the regional and intellectual cohesiveness of challenges to the new forms of North American and European imperialism asserting themselves in the era of Britain's formal exit from much of the region.

These memories of the Grenada Revolution—and the relationship of Barbados and Barbadians to it—inspired this study of the impact of the Haitian Revolution and transatlantic abolitionism on Afro-Barbadian politics and community formation in the age of emancipation. This book is about Barbados, a country that still bears (somewhat uncomfortably) the nickname Little England for its perceived topographical similarities and steadfast imperial loyalty to the former metropole. Like England, Barbados has been somewhat insulated from the tides of revolution that periodically have swept its neighbors. Instead, it has been an island from which imperial invasions—whether of Spanish Jamaica in 1655, Grenada in 1983, or Haiti in 1994—often have been launched. And yet I grew up with a very strong sense that Barbadians had a far more ambivalent relationship with empire than the moniker Little England would allow. The study is an effort to make sense of my country's complicated place within the former British Empire, the Caribbean, and the Atlantic world. Questions I have always had about the social forces that shape the Caribbean's popular political movements, and the broader regional and transatlantic circuits of Afro-Caribbean radicalism out which the 1979 "Revo" was born, have shaped this book. Hopefully, the book also has something important to say about the English-speaking Caribbean as a whole, a community that, on the surface, can seem as placid as Barbados is supposed to be and yet throughout its modern history has generated popular political movements that have forcefully reminded imperial authorities and local political elites alike that they can never really feel secure in their hold on power.

Writing this book would not have been possible without the assistance and influence of a number of individuals and institutions. I thank the Rhodes Trust for providing the scholarship to Oxford University, where I completed the dissertation on which this book is based. Oxford's Faculty of Modern History and St. Antony's College also awarded grants that facilitated research trips to London and Barbados. The University of Toronto provided me with a generous research grant and a teaching leave to complete my writing. I am indebted to my supervisors, Alan Knight and Colin Clarke, for pushing me to produce good work. I will never submit any work for publication without reading it with what I hope are eyes as constructively critical as theirs. I would especially like to thank Jerry Handler, whose influence on this book is obvious to anyone who knows anything about the history of slavery in Barbados, and whose support and friendship have been invaluable since he first met me as a fresh-faced and pretty clueless graduate student in my first month at Oxford. Woodville Marshall has been an inspiration, an example of how to write thorough and meaningful stories about the past and a source of excellent criticism and support, especially as the reader for Louisiana State University Press. Hilary Beckles's influence also is profound in this book, and I thank him for his scholarship, his support, his perseverance as a committed public intellectual, and his suggestion, many years ago, that I should consider a career in academia. I am grateful to Diana Paton, Sue Peabody, Mary Turner, Gad Heuman, John Gilmore, Megan Vaughan, Alissa Trotz, Honor Ford-Smith, Nigel Bolland, Anne MacPherson, Chandra Bhimull, Richard Drayton, Barbara Todd, Jennifer Mori, and Sean Hawkins for their comments and criticisms of sections of this book. Alissandra Cummins and Janice Whittle, respectively the director of the Barbados Museum and Historical Society and the curator of the Queen's Park Gallery in Barbados, helped me to find the phenomenal Guyanese artist Philip Moore, whose work graces the cover of this book. Thanks also to Jocelyn Dow, Catherine Roberts, Abdel Razzaq al Takriti, and Byron Moldofsky and Mariange Beaudry from the Cartography Department at the University of Toronto. I also would like to thank Richard Blackett, James Stewart, and Rand Dotson from Louisiana State University Press for seeing value in this work and accepting it for this series on abolition in the Atlantic world. I have enjoyed working with the staff of Louisiana State University Press tremendously, especially the editors with whom I had most contact, George Roupe and Karin Kaufman.

Historians could not do their work without the forbearance and expertise of archivists and librarians. The staffs of the Barbados National Archives, the Barbados Public Library, the Main Library and Law Library of the University of the West Indies (UWI) at Cave Hill, and the Barbados Museum were both knowledgeable and enjoyable to work with. In the United Kingdom the staff of Rhodes House Library and the Bodleian in Oxford, the National Archives at Kew Gardens and the British Library have helped shape the work of countless researchers, including myself. I also thank the staff of the National Institute in Kingston, Jamaica, who very patiently provided me with documents that were crucial to my research even though I appeared on the institute's doorstep just before a state of national emergency was declared in the country. My experiences at a number of conferences have been essential to this book. I am eternally indebted to the organizers and members of the Association of Caribbean Historians for their engagement with my ideas over the years. I wish also to thank those present at conferences where I have first presented crucial aspects of my argument. In this regard I am grateful to colleagues at the 2003 conference of the American Historical Association, the 2002 Berkshire Conference of Women Historians and Caribbean Feminisms Workshop, and the 2001 Conference of the Canadian Association of Latin American and Caribbean Studies. Many thanks also to Pedro Welch and Richard Goodridge, who gave me the opportunity, in 1999, to present one of my first papers at the History Department at UWI at Cave Hill.

There are many others whose influence on this book is less straightforward but no less significant. I thank my friends from McGill University in Montréal, especially Dave Austin, Pat Harewood, Ahmer Qadeer, Dan Robins, Anup Grewal, Terna Gyuse, Koni Benson, Astrid Jacques, and Kuda Saburi for their inspiration and indefatigable belief in the possibility of a just future for all people. My close friends in Barbados, especially Rob Leyshon, Risée Chaderton, and Renée Coppin, have sustained me through graduate school and my early academic career. My peers in Oxford, especially Mark Hickford, Damon Salesa, Stephanie Mitchell, and Monike Lutke-Entrup, provided an intellectual environment that forced me to stretch my horizons. My roommates on Lathbury Road and Brewery Street, Katrin Hansing, Emma Westney, Gaelle le Pottier, Sea Ling Cheng, Matt de Bakker, Robert McCaw, Christoph Wilke, and Tilman Ludke, were a source of diversion and excellent discussion. My students at the University of Toronto constantly renew my enthusiasm and love for history and my sense of the Caribbean as a place with enormous lessons to teach the world. Thanks also to Luisa Quinteros, Nova Vaughan-Burnett, and Samantha Hushison.

Last, but of course not least, I wish to thank my family, beginning with my late grandfather, Martin Newton, for his wonderful stories about growing up in Barbados in the early twentieth century. My parents, Velma and Anthony Newton, my sister Lesley, brother-in-law André, and nephews Alex and Nico have given me infinite support and love over the years. My husband Jens Hanssen is an inspiration, a companion, and an intellectual fellow traveler. And finally, I thank my children, Keir and Lily, who made sure that this book took longer to write than I intended but make every day an adventure worth having.

ABBREVIATIONS

ACH	Association of Caribbean Historians
BDA	Barbados Department of Archives
BMBG	*Barbados Mercury and Bridgetown Gazette*
BMHS	Barbados Museum and Historical Society
BPL	Public Library, Bridgetown, Barbados
CO	Colonial Office (records housed in the National Archives, London)
JBMHS	*Journal of the Barbados Museum and Historical Society*
JCH	*Journal of Caribbean History*
JSH	*Journal of Social History*
NCF	National Cultural Foundation, Barbados
PP	Parliamentary Papers
SPG	Society for the Propagation of the Gospel in Foreign Parts
UWI	University of the West Indies

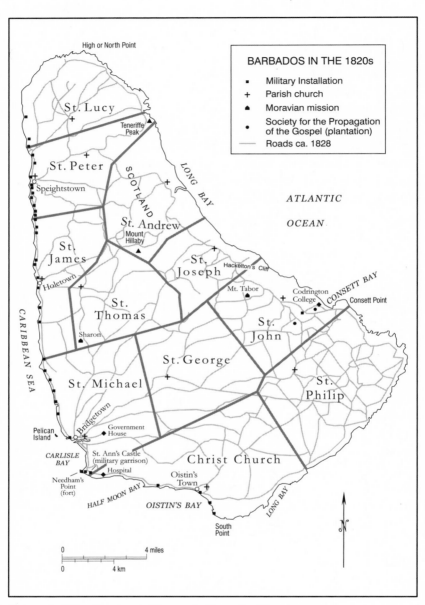

Cartography Office, Department of Georgraphy, University of Toronto

INTRODUCTION

O N August 2, 1838, one day after the act that ended slavery in the British Caribbean came into effect, "a large and respectable party of . . . gentlemen" dined at the Bible Depository of the Barbados Auxiliary Bible Society of the Free People of Color in the island's capital city, Bridgetown. They came to celebrate the arrival of "full" emancipation and the end of apprenticeship—the period of transition from slavery to freedom that commenced on August 1, 1834, and ended on August 1, 1838. The newspaper report of this dinner provides a rich vignette of the expectations and hopes, social and ideological transformations, and socioeconomic and political tensions that slave emancipation in the anglophone Caribbean entailed.

One Thomas Harris Jr., co-owner of the *Liberal*, a newspaper owned and edited by men of color, organized the gathering. His newspaper carried the only report of the event on August 4. Only men of color free before emancipation were invited to attend. According to the *Liberal's* anonymous journalist, the island's "*former free* [!] people . . . with scarcely an exception, have greeted the first of August, as a day that brings them as well as their brethren liberty." If whites, women, or any of the island's more than eighty thousand recently emancipated people were present, their attendance was not acknowledged in the newspaper report. The *Liberal's* other owner, Samuel Jackman Prescod, chaired the meeting, and Harris Jr. delivered the keynote address. Harris viewed British slave emancipation as a harbinger of better things to come for his "class" of society—Afro-Barbadians free before general emancipation:

> I rise with a heart uplifted with gratitude to a merciful Creator, for the inestimable blessing this day vouchsafed me, of meeting to celebrate our Emancipation. I say our Emancipation, gentlemen, because I do assert, and that too, without the fear of contradiction, that this day in which . . . the legislature of this Island has granted freedom to the slave—also made us *free indeed*. For I feel quite certain, that every one present will agree with me

when I assert that we were heretofore only nominally free. . . . Gentlemen, by one Queen, the stain, that disgraceful stain of slavery and its horrors, . . . has been removed from the escutcheon of Britain. Long may she reign to witness the good effects of the blessing she has conferred upon a grateful though calumniated people. . . . Gentlemen . . . we must admit, to use the language embodied in an admirable resolution of the coloured people of America, "That [the late emancipated class] are our brethren by the lieu [sic] of *consanguinity*, of *suffering*, and of *wrong.*

Harris expressed his hope that emancipation would bring the "advancement of our class . . . the colored body," and that "the other class" (namely, whites) would reform the island's laws and grant people of colour equal "rights and privileges."[1]

Despite these lofty sentiments, biographical information about the men who addressed this dinner raises troubling questions regarding why they suddenly and publicly embraced former slaves as their "brethren" and adopted emancipation as the moment of *their* freedom. Four of the men were Afro-Barbadians who had been very active in the civil rights struggle for free people of color during slavery, but none of them appears to have been an active abolitionist before 1834. Three of them—Thomas Harris Jr., William Nunes, and Joseph Kennedy—actually had been slave owners.[2] Although he had not himself owned slaves, Samuel Jackman Prescod's wife, Katherine (née Cruden), was a slave owner who had also been executor of the estate of a deceased female relative, which included more than twenty slaves.[3] The only man whose abolitionist credentials predated emancipation was an Afro-Antiguan named Henry Loving, the editor of Antigua's *Weekly Register*, a newspaper that had promoted the causes of greater civil rights for Afro-

1. *Liberal*, 4 August 1838.

2. Barbadian slave owners had to register their slaves every three years between 1817 and 1832. Afro-Barbadian slave owners were denoted by the abbreviations "fm" and "fn," for "free mulatto" and "free negro," respectively, or less frequently with some variation of "fbw," "fbm," "fcw," or "fcm," for "free black woman [man]" and "free colored woman [man]." In 1817–1829, Thomas Harris Jr. is listed as owning one slave. However, in 1832 the name is listed twice, possibly referring to Harris Jr. and his father Harris Sr. One Thomas Harris owned twelve slaves and the other nine. T 71/520, 533, 546, 552, Barbados Slave Registries, 1817–1832. Nunes owned three slaves in 1832 (T 71/548, 1832); Kennedy owned nine slaves (T 71/533 and 552, 1823 and 1832).

3. T 71/520, 1817, Return of Jane Rose Cruden for herself (twenty-four slaves) and Katherine Rose Cruden, then in Europe (four slaves); T 71/547, 1832, Return of Katherine Cruden of twenty-one slaves, the property of Jane Rose Cruden, deceased.

Caribbean people and the abolition of slavery. Loving had recently completed his appointment as a special magistrate in Barbados during the apprenticeship period.[4]

The men who spoke at this gathering clearly did not view this as an opportune moment to account for their past involvements with slavery. They staged a public refashioning of the past and attempted to set the tone for all future relationships between "*free people*" and former slaves. In this new version of the past and the future there was to be no discussion of Afro-Barbadians as slave owners. The emancipation of slaves was publicly incorporated as a new chapter in the ongoing civil rights struggle of free people of color. That struggle was itself reinvented as unmarked by tensions of any kind or disagreements among free people of color themselves regarding their political goals. Afro-Barbadians were now presented, to themselves and to the *Liberal's* reading public in the Caribbean and Britain, as a political community united by opposition to racial discrimination, regardless of differences of past legal status or socioeconomic position. Afro-Barbadians free before emancipation were being educated about their duty to safeguard the interests of former slaves. Whites were being served notice that emancipation was only the first step in the redefinition of freedom without slavery. They could now expect, so the report implied, to find Afro-Barbadians united behind a common vision of political reform.

The exclusion of the voices of women and the working poor illustrates the degree to which patriarchy and class paternalism defined this new unity between "old" and "new" free people. This movement was to be led by a small group of urban and bourgeois men who assumed for themselves the right to speak for an expanded constituency of Afro-Barbadians, including women and former slaves. Few well-to-do men of color saw the poor as legitimate political actors in their own right and no one raised the possibility of a formal political role for Afro-Barbadian women at this or any other public event. Harris may have indicated the "proper" housekeeping role he thought women of color should play in the civil rights cause when he invited whites to gain "a nearer association with our families. . . . [T]hey

---

4. PP 1831–1832, vol. 20, *Report from select committee on the extinction of slavery throughout the British dominions*, testimony of Henry Loving, Esq., f.c.m [free colored man], Antigua, editor of the *Weekly Register*, 28 June 1832. The special or stipendiary magistrates were appointed under the 1833 imperial emancipation act and the 1834 Barbados emancipation act to arbitrate in disputes between employers and apprentices and chair tribunals that heard apprentices' manumission cases (for further discussion, see chapter 5, pp. 142–144).

will find, upon a closer intimacy, that our Drawing and Dining rooms are not inferior in comfort or refinement to their own."[5]

The abolitionist sentiments expressed at this dinner emerged out of a more complicated history of entanglement with slavery than these men might have liked to admit. Yet these entanglements make it problematic to simply dismiss their antislavery statements as disingenuous. The lives of these four Afro-Barbadian men illustrate how intimate and multilayered relationships were between free people of color and slaves: Many free nonwhites owned slaves *and* counted slaves, former slaves, and slave owners among their kin.[6] These men would have been well aware of the political advantages they might hope to gain from emancipation, as it had long been obvious that British Caribbean free people of color could expect more civil rights concessions from abolitionists than from the proslavery lobby. They had less to lose economically from emancipation than did most whites as few Afro-Barbadians, even former slave owners such as Harris, Nunes, and Kennedy, depended entirely on slave ownership for their economic survival.

The 1838 dinner throws into relief questions that thus far have received relatively little attention from scholars. How did the rise of abolitionism and the lengthy collapse of the system of slavery impact the expectations and experiences that free people of color in the anglophone Caribbean had of freedom? In what ways might emancipation have transformed their conceptions of freedom, their interactions with slaves/former slaves and whites and their relations with one another? Was British slave emancipation a significant moment for the forging of new kinds of diasporic and imperial political consciousness among Afro-Caribbean people, as Harris's references to the British Empire and "the coloured people of America" and the presence at this event of the Antiguan Henry Loving suggest? What became of the effort to forge a unified Afro-Barbadian political collectivity in the years after slavery? Finally, what are the implications of rethinking the role of free Afro-Barbadians and of race as a tool of popular mobilization in the transition from slavery to freedom? These are the questions this book sets out to answer.

Nearly seventy years ago in his classic and groundbreaking study of the Haitian

5. *Liberal*, 4 August 1838.

6. Either Thomas Harris Jr. or his father had been born in slavery, and Samuel Prescod once spoke of a great uncle who was a slave. Jerome Handler, Ronald Hughes, and Ernest M. Wiltshire, *Freedmen of Barbados: Names and Notes for Genealogical and Family History Research* (Charlottesville: Virginia Foundation for the Humanities and Public Policy, 1999), 25; see Prescod's reference to his great uncle in the *Liberal*, 23 January 1839.

Revolution, *The Black Jacobins,* Trinidadian intellectual C. L. R. James alerted his readers to the importance of understanding slave emancipation as a crucial moment in the shaping of popular political consciousness and understandings of freedom in the societies of the Atlantic world, particularly among people of African descent. Despite the foundational place of James's work in the development of studies of slave emancipation, relatively few historians have seriously and consistently taken up his preoccupation with tracing changes in political consciousness.[7] The study of the process of slave emancipation and postslavery society in the British Caribbean has been dominated by debates about the role of abolition in the wider political and economic policy of the empire, the place of slave emancipation in the historical development of capitalism, and studies of postemancipation rural labor relations. These discussions are important, and I have no wish to appear to minimize their significance. However, insofar as questions of political consciousness have entered the debate, they have continued to be framed largely in terms of struggles between the newly freed and their erstwhile owners for the control of land and labor.

This study seeks to reintegrate analysis of popular political consciousness into historical understandings of the political dynamics of the long process of British slave emancipation. The contest between estate authorities and slaves, and laborers and employers—the traditional fault line for studies of struggles for power and personal autonomy in the postemancipation Caribbean—is central to the story told in this book, but I have sought to place examinations of rural labor dynamics within the broader context of insular, regional, and transatlantic intellectual and political currents and socioeconomic changes. I have situated struggles over, first, the future of slavery and, second, the order of things in postslavery society within an intracommunal context, focussing primarily on relations among Afro-Barbadians themselves. In so doing, this book has reexamined the role of free people of color in the development of slavery, challenging historiographical assumptions about the "marginality" of free people of African descent in Caribbean slave societies. Although free people of color were economically and legally mar-

7. C. L. R. James, *The Black Jacobins; Toussaint L'Overture and the San Domingo Revolution* (1938; reprint, Penguin Books, 2001). See also Carolyn Fick, *The Making of Haiti: The Saint Domingue Revolution from Below* (Knoxville: University of Tennessee Press, 1990); Mimi Sheller, *Democracy after Slavery: Black Publics and Peasant Radicalism in Haiti and Jamaica* (London: Macmillan Education, 2000); Monica Shuler, *"Alas, Alas, Kongo": A Social History of Indentured African Immigration Into Jamaica, 1841–1865* (Baltimore: Johns Hopkins University Press, 1980).

ginalized in Barbadian slave society, they were an integral part of the social structure, and crucially shaped conceptions of freedom and slavery in the island. Their presence challenged the planter-state's efforts to clearly delineate boundaries between free and slave and white and nonwhite, while creating avenues through which enslaved people could negotiate and claim spaces of freedom for themselves despite the severe legal limitations imposed by slavery.

This book traces transformations in the political consciousness and material circumstances of free people of African descent in Barbados, Britain's oldest sugar-producing colony, during the years of transition from slavery to freedom in the British Caribbean. Barbadian free people of color were not secondary actors in or passive observers of the drama of slave emancipation.[8] Rather, like their counterparts elsewhere in the Americas, they played a central role in the abolition debate and in the reordering of socioeconomic relations after slavery. Beginning in the 1790s, as Caribbean colonial governments responded to revolutionary upheavals in the French Atlantic world with repressive measures against free people of color, a small group of free Afro-Barbadian men began what would become a long civil rights campaign. In the half-century that followed, their struggle transformed Barbadian public life, challenging both slavery and the principle of white supremacy.

This book focuses on the period between the French and Haitian revolutionary wars of 1789–1815 and the aftermath of the cholera epidemic that swept through the Caribbean in the middle of the century, reaching Barbados in 1854. The analysis encompasses the period of legal reform of British Caribbean slavery known as slave amelioration, the apprenticeship period of 1834–1838 and the economic crisis that struck the older colonies of the British Caribbean after they lost their preferential trade status with Britain in 1846. Beginning in the late eighteenth century, the societies bound together by the transatlantic slave trade were convulsed by a century of struggles over the future of slavery and the meaning of freedom. Abolitionism forever transformed the public sphere of Britain and its colonies and reshaped the way in which people of African descent in the British Caribbean, whether free or slave, conceptualized their sociopolitical position in their individual colonies, in the empire and in the wider world. People of African descent in the Americas and Europe adapted the ideals of liberal freedom and radical democracy in order to formulate new languages of equality with whites and novel ways of challenging slavery. British slave emancipation was a key moment

8. For general and comparative discussion of free people of color and emancipation in the Americas, see Robin Blackburn, *The Overthrow of Colonial Slavery, 1776–1848* (London: Verso, 1988).

in a century-long process through which people in the societies of the Atlantic world contested and redefined race, class, gender, colony-metropole relationships, subjecthood, and citizenship.

The analytical lens I have adopted in this study echoes Nicholas Thomas's observations regarding the study of colonialism. Thomas notes that "only local-ized theories and historically specific accounts can provide much insight into the varied articulations of colonizing and counter-colonial representations and prac-tices. . . . [C]olonialism can only be traced through its plural and particularized expressions."[9] Thus the in-depth study of particular locations is essential to our understanding of the "plural and particularized" dynamics of emancipation and articulations of freedom in the societies of the Atlantic world. An understanding of local circumstances in older British Caribbean colonies such as Barbados, where slavery was largely internally regulated and structures of governance were com-plex, is essential for a grasp of the specific institutional, political, economic, and demographic context that shaped how local actors responded to and influenced emancipation.

Barbados is an important site for historical analysis because as Britain's oldest sugar-producing colony, the second largest exporter of sugar in the British Carib-bean during the late eighteenth and early nineteenth centuries, and the seat of a consolidated governor generalship of the Windward Islands from 1833 onward, de-velopments in Barbados had implications for other areas, especially in the eastern Caribbean. Yet such a study is most illuminating when it is informed by a perspec-tive that highlights the interplay between transatlantic, imperial, regional, and lo-cal factors. The degree of the Caribbean's integration within the Atlantic system makes it impossible to grasp the dynamics of slave emancipation without taking account of the interaction between broader transatlantic connections and the par-ticularities of individual Caribbean societies.

The contest over slavery was a constitutive struggle for free people of color, through which they came into existence as a political community. Yet the pre-cise boundaries and even the existence of that community were neither stable nor the subject of universal consensus, since it was never entirely clear who exactly *was* a free person of color or whether some people, based on gender and property ownership, should have access to greater "freedoms" and privileges than others. As a result, this community-building process was expressed as much through in-

---

9. Nicholas Thomas, *Colonialism's Culture: Anthropology, Travel, and Government* (Cambridge: Polity, 1994), ix–x.

ternal fragmentation, exclusion, and disunity as through claims to a shared identity as free people of color. Inequalities of class and gender, competing claims to authority, disagreements arising from different personal and political relationships with slaves, and profound ambivalence toward both the pro- and antislavery struggles shaped how Barbadian free people of color constantly refashioned the limits of this community.

Free Afro-Barbadian participation in the debate over slave amelioration, through the establishment of missionary, educational and philanthropic institutions, was a key component in transformations that occurred in public life during and after amelioration. By presenting themselves as the agents of imperial reform against an intransigent white creole elite in the 1820s and 1830s, free Afro-Barbadians challenged planter authority and undermined white supremacy. At the same time, tensions between elitist and more democratic approaches to antiracist reform constantly threatened to unravel the community many civil rights campaigners claimed to promote. The 1820s witnessed public confrontations between a populist, mass-based, and democratic vision of freedom among free and enslaved Afro-Barbadians that reflected the more radical potential of the "age of revolution," and a more limited vision of reform that generally appealed to bourgeois and wealthy free people of color. Bourgeois Afro-Barbadian civil rights reformers sought to distance themselves from, and often expressly repudiated, the revolutionary, disorderly, plebian, and antislavery visions of freedom circulating around the Atlantic world. Only in the face of white hostility and inflexibility during the 1830s did well-to-do Afro-Barbadians reluctantly associate themselves with the demotic politics of working-class free people of color and slaves.

Gender was as central to the struggle for greater civil rights and this conflictual process of community building as it was to the experience of being a free person of color.[10] White and Afro-Barbadian men may have fought one another over the civil rights implications of slave emancipation, but they shared a belief in new patriarchal codes of proper Christian conduct for men and women, centered on the suppression of "illegitimate" sexual relations between whites and people of African descent, the restriction of independent economic activity by women, and the

10. On gender, slavery, and slave emancipation, see Pamela Scully, *Liberating the Family? Gender and British Slave Emancipation in the Rural Western Cape, 1823–1853* (Oxford: James Currey, 1997), 2; and Amy Dru Stanley, *From Bondage to Contract: Wage Labor, Marriage, and the Market in the Age of Emancipation* (Cambridge: Cambridge University Press, 1998).

control of free laborers and laboring-class families. After emancipation, privileged white and Afro-Barbadian men viewed unmarried free women of color as a symbol of prostitution, social transgression, and the disorder of slavery. For many Afro-Barbadian men the community cohesion, "respectability," and socioeconomic advancement of free people of color depended upon the "domestication" of nonwhite women. Afro-Barbadian civil rights campaigners and bourgeois families put their domesticity on display in civic organizations such as temperance and friendly societies. They deployed a gendered and sexualized political rhetoric based on notions of Christian respectability and orderly domestic arrangements to illustrate their moral superiority over both the nonwhite working classes and the white creole elite. Even though many women of color continued to exercise their economic independence and laboring-class people in general refused to conform to elitist conceptions of marriage and family life, they had to contend with increasingly repressive laws and social prohibitions that sought to enforce such views.

This study also examines the impact of cultural and political connections between colony and metropole on the politics and world views of Afro-Caribbean people. In recent years, by situating "colony and metropole in one analytic frame" scholars have rethought the social, cultural, political, and economic connections between the Caribbean and its various European metropoles.[11] Mimi Sheller's observation that the political claims of Afro-Jamaicans after emancipation "were clearly grounded on an assertion of membership in the British Empire, and morally grounded in English law and constitutionality" applies equally to Afro-Barbadians.[12] Nevertheless, any examination of the interactions between Afro-Caribbean people and the empires of which they were subjects must take into account the fact that European empires was not the only "imagined communities" that shaped Afro-Caribbean political subjectivities.[13] Emphasizing the ideological impact of the imperial tie on nonwhite political consciousness without exploring the significance of other regional and transatlantic connections replicates imperi-

11. Ann Laura Stoler and Frederick Cooper, *Tensions of Empire: Colonial Cultures in a Bourgeois World* (Berkeley and Los Angeles: University of California Press, 1997), preface, viii, and introduction, 34. See also Christopher Schmidt-Nowara, *Empire and Antislavery: Spain, Cuba, and Puerto Rico, 1833–1874* (Pittsburgh: University of Pittsburgh Press, 1999), and Catherine Hall, *Civilising Subjects: Metropole and Colony in the English Imagination, 1830–1867* (Chicago: University of Chicago Press, 2002).

12. Sheller, *Democracy after Slavery,* 219.

13. Benedict Anderson, *Imagined Communities: Reflections on the Origin and Spread of Nationalism* (London: Verso, 1983).

alist perspectives on the process and meaning of emancipation.[14] Several scholars, notably researchers of the Haitian Revolution, have sought to move beyond the imperial divisions that continue to set the parameters of most scholarly analysis of the nineteenth-century Caribbean.[15]

This study seeks to nuance the analysis of colony and metropole in various ways. First, it highlights the importance of mobility, migration, and communication—within the island, around the eastern Caribbean, and to West Africa—to Afro-Barbadians' conceptualizations of freedom both before and after general emancipation. The study argues that, within the island, interactions and movements back and forth between the rural and urban spheres of life crucially shaped Afro-Barbadian politics and modes of identification in slave and postslave society.[16] Second, it illustrates the political and economic significance of intra- and inter-island labor migration in creating long-distance kinship and communications networks and informing Afro-Barbadian conceptions of freedom. In the early years after emancipation, migration around the countryside to towns or to neighboring territories was vital to laboring-class Afro-Barbadians' efforts to resist the increasingly repressive conditions of the island. These post-1834 migration patterns echoed those of the slavery era, when they were a defining characteristic of freedom for "masterless" people such as free Afro-Barbadians, runaways, urban slaves, and slaves with relatively autonomous or itinerant occupations.[17] The issue of labor migration was also pivotal to Afro-Barbadians' engagement in imperial debates about the distribution of labor in the British Atlantic world. Civil rights cam-

14. Paul Gilroy, *The Black Atlantic: Modernity and Double Consciousness* (Cambridge: Harvard University Press, 1993), 1–40; Julius Sherrard Scott III, "The Common Wind: Currents of Afro-American Communication in the Era of the Haitian Revolution" (Ph.D. diss., Duke University, 1987); John Thornton, "'I Am the Subject of the King of Congo': African Political Ideology and the Haitian Revolution," *Journal of World History* 4, no. 2 (1993): 181–214.

15. Barry David Gaspar and David Geggus, eds., *A Turbulent Time: The Haitian Revolution and the Greater Caribbean* (Bloomington: Indiana University Press, 1997); James, *The Black Jacobins*; Scott, "Common Wind"; Sheller, *Democracy after Slavery*.

16. For recent analysis of the role of towns in the cultural and political life of the nineteenth-century British Caribbean, see Pedro Welch, *Slave Society in the City: Bridgetown, Barbados, 1680–1834* (Kingston: Ian Randle, 2003) and Juanita de Barros, *Order and Place in a Colonial City: Patterns of Struggle and Resistance in Georgetown, British Guiana, 1889–1924* (Montreal: McGill-Queen's University Press, 2003). See also Franklin Knight and Peggy Liss, eds., *Atlantic Port Cities: Economy, Culture, and Society in the Atlantic World* (Knoxville: University of Tennessee Press, 1991).

17. The use of the term "masterless" is taken from Scott, "Common Wind."

paigners of color actively participated in and were deeply divided over Barbadian planters' policy of severely restricting emigration in order to maintain control over the labor force.

The idea of migration as an expression of freedom also informed Afro-Barbadians' political identifications with the African continent and other parts of the African diaspora. Support for the values of the empire was based on a belief in Britain's ability and willingness to follow through on its promises to further the cause of the political empowerment of "the children of Africa in the colonies." Afro-Barbadian imperialists expected the British government to pursue a vigorous antiracist and antislavery policy in the Caribbean and Africa. Prior to the 1820s, many free Afro-Barbadians, particularly those of the bourgeoisie, sought to downplay their skin color and African descent, emphasizing their legal position as free people and their status as property owners in their quest for civil rights reform. By contrast, particularly after 1838, African descent and the experience of racial oppression became bases for claims to equality with whites. Schemes for Afro-Barbadian emigration to Africa as agents for Britain's suppression of the slave trade and the "civilization" of Africa were a key means through which Barbadians of color expressed their sense of imperial and African diasporic belonging and their commitment to an antislavery agenda. During the final decade of slavery and in the years after emancipation, this racial consciousness also served to further the political ambitions of middle- and upper-class people of African descent. This imperialist expression of racial solidarity and African diasporic consciousness illustrates the ease with which the language of liberal freedom accommodated itself to metropolitan British claims to moral and cultural superiority over nonwhites elsewhere in the world.[18] The political right of the British government to maintain colonial power in the Caribbean and to establish it in Africa was assumed to be legitimate and, in fact, necessary in order to further the cause of liberating Africans on the continent and in the diaspora from European oppression and from their own "backwardness."

Immediately after emancipation, tensions of class and political ideology came to the fore over the issues of electoral franchise reform and labor migration, contributing to devastating political factionalism among people of color, and dashing the political and economic dreams of the plebian majority. This intracommunal discord was framed by wider transatlantic currents of debate regarding the con-

18. See Uday Singh Mehta, *Liberalism and Empire: A Study in Nineteenth-Century British Liberal Thought* (Chicago: University of Chicago Press, 1999).

trol of labor and the role of nonwhite "subjects" in the state institutions of the empire and its colonies. As Holt and Sheller has shown, many postemancipation societies experienced a rapid process of "de-democratization" after an initial period of radical reformism, as state authorities reneged on earlier promises to support the aspirations of formerly enslaved people and instead supported an elite backlash against former slaves.[19] Although a tiny group of comparatively wealthy free men of color gained political influence as a result of emancipation, the absence of fundamental change in the distribution of land and wealth after emancipation left most pre-1834 free people of color and former slaves with little hope of political enfranchisement or socioeconomic betterment. In the dire economic climate of the late 1840s and 1850s, many Afro-Barbadians lost hope in the possibility of political reform in the island and came to see emigration to the African continent, as simultaneously agents of British liberal "civilization" and African liberation, as the solution to their difficulties.[20]

The experiences of Afro-Barbadian emigrants in West Africa—whether as missionaries or as parts of communities of migrants from the Americas—reflected the ambiguities of their attitudes about themselves as would-be agents of civilization, opponents of the enslavement of Africans, and defenders of Africa's potential. Some Afro-Barbadians never lost their sense of attachment to their former homeland in the Caribbean or to the British Empire, while others committed themselves entirely to their new environment. As analysis of one especially remarkable family of Barbadian emigrants to Liberia illustrates, the Caribbean origins of these migrants shaped their lives and those of their descendants in crucial ways. The Barclays epitomized the wider phenomenon of the ambivalent yet important role of these first- and second-generation Barbadian West Africans in the aftermath of the "Scramble for Africa." On the one hand, their civilizationalist and paternalistic attitude toward indigenous Africans brought them into conflict with African communities who fought the encroachment of Western cultural standards, laws, and political institutions as migrants from the Americas took over their lands and sought to influence their community structures. On the other hand, as key po-

19. Thomas Holt, *The Problem of Freedom: Race, Labor, and Politics in Jamaica and Britain, 1832–1938* (Baltimore: Johns Hopkins University Press and Ian Randle, 1992), 215–309; Sheller, *Democracy after Slavery*, 6–7.

20. Some Barbadians emigrated to West Africa in the late nineteenth century, including people of color free before emancipation. See Nemata Blyden, *West Indians in West Africa: The African Diaspora in Reverse* (Rochester, N.Y.: University of Rochester Press, 2000), and pp. 277–281 of the present volume.

litical figures in one of Africa's last sovereign states the Barclays in turn fought efforts by Western imperial governments, including Britain, to colonize Liberia and acted as cultural and political brokers between the Liberian state and pan-Africanists from the Americas.

Analysis of the involvement of free people of African descent in the reform of slave society and the abolition of slavery is also central to understanding the manner in which racialized categories of subject and citizen were reconfigured in the period between the Haitian Revolution and the mid-nineteenth century. Free people of color were a topic of great interest in British abolitionist circles at the height of the antislavery debate, when there was much discussion of their possible role as a "buffer" between emancipated people and planters. However, by the mid-1840s they all but disappeared from metropolitan discussions of postemancipation British Caribbean society, except in reference to contexts, notably Jamaica, in which the possibility of political power devolving onto the Afro-Caribbean majority loomed large in the imperial imagination. A similar pattern is evident in the historiography of emancipation.[21] With the exception of Samuel Jackman Prescod, editor of the *Liberal* and the first man of color elected to the colonial assembly, other people of color free before apprenticeship are seldom mentioned in the literature on postemancipation Barbados.[22]

This vanishing act stems from sources less mundane that the fact that every Afro-Caribbean person was, de facto, a "free person of color" following slavery's abolition. Rather, it is a manifestation of problematic notions about the position of free people of African descent in slave and postslave societies. Free people of color have long been represented as either marginal and somewhat out of place in slave societies, or as a group occupying the middle tier between free whites and enslaved blacks. Such depictions of marginality or inbetween-ness frequently in-

21. For exceptions, see Mavis Campbell, *The Dynamics of Change in Slave Society: A Socio-political History of the Free Coloreds of Jamaica, 1800–1865* (London: Associated University Presses, 1976); Gad Heuman, *Between Black and White: Race, Politics, and the Free Coloreds of Jamaica, 1792–1865* (Oxford: Greenwood Press, 1981); Susan Lowes, "The Peculiar Class: The Formation, Collapse, and Reformation of the Middle Class in Antigua, West Indies, 1834–1940" (Ph.D. diss., Columbia University, 1994); and Susan Lowes, "'They Couldn't Mash Ants': The Decline of the White and Non-White Elites in Antigua, 1834–1900," in Karen Fog Olwig, ed., *Small Islands, Large Questions: Society, Culture and Resistance in the Post-Emancipation Caribbean* (London: Frank Cass, 1995), 31–52.

22. Alana Johnson, "The Abolition of Chattel Slavery in Barbados, 1833–1876" (Ph.D. thesis, Cambridge University, 1994); Claude Levy, *Emancipation, Sugar, and Federalism: Barbados and the British West Indies* (Gainesville: University Presses of Florida, 1980).

volve a conflation of legal status, skin color, and class, with the "typical" free non-white subject assumed to be mixed-race and bourgeois—neither white nor black, rich nor poor, slave nor free.[23]

These assumptions have occasionally led to problematic representations of brownness and "free colored" identity as a state of racial indeterminacy with almost socially pathological repercussions. Some modern scholars have echoed the views of earlier generations of writers in suggesting that brown people in the Caribbean lacked a "complete" sense of identity because they were neither fish nor fowl. An 1820s novel on plantation life in Jamaica asserted that "brown man hab no country . . . only de neger and de buckra [white man] hab country," because mixed-race Jamaicans lacked an ancestral focus in either Europe or Africa, unlike "pure" whites or blacks. Mavis Campbell reasserted such sentiments in her 1976 study of Jamaican "free coloreds," stating that they strove for the impossible dream of being "white" and "by the nature of their birth [and] their phenotypic imprecision" lacked "identity focus" and "any self-conception or self-confidence they might have had."[24]

Many European travelers and white creole writers from the eighteenth and nineteenth centuries found the liminal position of free Afro-Caribbean people deeply troubling. Free people of color embodied the tensions of slavery and empire, representing a "liminal site of mixtures and crossings produced by the exercise of colonial power [on which] boundaries were redrawn and the colonizer/colonized divide was reordered."[25] Europeans and creole whites wrote derisively and fearfully about their unpredictable political allegiances, their "imitation" of "European" cultural practices, their "anomalous" legal status as "unappropriated people" or the racial and sexual transgressiveness of "mulattoes."[26] Such writings expressed imperial and white creole anxieties about the long-term repercussions of slavery and colonial rule over Africans and their descendants. On one hand, the presence

23. For a similar observation see Lowes, "Peculiar Class," 119–120.

24. Quote from anon., *Marly, or The Life of a Planter in Jamaica* (Glasgow: Richard Griffin, 1828), 94, cited in Richard D. E. Burton, *Afro-Creole: Power, Opposition, and Play in the Caribbean* (Ithaca: Cornell University Press, 1997), 35–36 and 42; Campbell, *Dynamics of Change*, 368, see also 49. See also Hilary Beckles, "On the Backs of Blacks: The Barbados Free-Coloureds' Pursuit of Civil Rights and the 1816 Slave Rebellion," *Immigrants and Minorities* 3, no. 2 (July 1984): 167–188.

25. Quote from Gyan Prakash, *After Colonialism: Imperial Histories and Postcolonial Displacements* (Princeton: Princeton University Press, 1995), 3.

26. Jerome S. Handler, *The Unappropriated People: Freedmen in the Slave Society of Barbados* (Baltimore: Johns Hopkins University Press, 1974).

of free African Americans actually confirmed the principle of white freedom and black enslavement. The power to manumit slaves was a central aspect of slave owners' authority, confirming their patriarchal power to confer rights on the "deserving" and withhold them from the "undeserving." On the other hand, free people of color embodied the possibility that slavery's race, class, and legal boundaries would be overturned, either because more and more of the descendants of Africans would be born free or would acquire freedom or because free Afro-Caribbeans would unite with slaves and violently overthrow the slaveholding order. Events in late-eighteenth-century Saint Domingue, where *gens de couleur* outnumbered whites and eventually allied with slave rebels, first against white counterrevolutionary colonists and then against the French empire, fueled white fears of "race war" across the Caribbean.

Brown, or "mixed-race," people were particularly disturbing to many Europeans, as a sign of the threat that slavery and prolonged encounters with nonwhite colonial subjects posed to white purity. As Catherine Hall argues, "[I]n a world in which sexuality was locked into racial and class thinking, with their complex logics of desire, the boundaries between rulers and ruled were necessarily unstable. Mixed-race children were particularly problematic, for how was the in between to be categorized?"[27] Brown people simultaneously titillated and terrified Europeans. The most dangerous of all, some argued, were free brown women, who were alleged to subvert all boundaries of class, legal status, and race by prostituting themselves to white male lovers, taking over the proper role of white women through these "illegitimate" relationships and reproducing the free brown population.[28] This obsession with so-called miscegenation continues, as Stephen Small has noted, to dominate the scholarly literature.[29]

The freedom of people of African descent challenged the national myths that

27. Hall, *Civilising Subjects,* 10. See also Ann Laura Stoler, *Race and the Education of Desire: Foucault's History of Sexuality and the Colonial Order of Things* (Durham, N.C.: Duke University Press, 1995), 46.

28. See, for example, Médéric-Louis-Elie Moreau de Saint-Méry, *Description topographique, physique, civile, politique et historique de la partie francaise de l'isle Saint-Domingue . . .* (1797), quoted in Susan Socolow, "Economic Roles of the Free Women of Color of Cap Français," in Barry David Gaspar and Darlene Clark Hine, eds., *More than Chattel: Black Women and Slavery in the Americas* (Bloomington: Indiana University Press, 1996), 279. On the centrality of women's "reproductive identity" to the perpetuation of slavery and its socioeconomic relationships, see Jennifer L. Morgan, *Laboring Women: Reproduction and Gender in New World Slavery* (Philadelphia: University of Pennsylvania Press, 2004), 3.

29. Stephen Small, "Racial Group Boundaries and Identities: People of 'Mixed Race' in Slavery

divided the boundaries of Europe and metropolitan freedom from the "racially im-pure" colonies and colonial subjugation. Many Europeans who wrote about the colonial Americas in the eighteenth and nineteenth centuries alternately repre-sented free people of color, particularly brown women, as objects of sexual danger, desire, and distrust, with descriptions slipping back and forth between "*mimicry*—a difference that is almost nothing but not quite . . . to *menace*—a difference that is almost total but not quite."[30] Free people of color symbolized what was most troubling about the Caribbean: The black and brown colonial population could not simply be categorized as "natives," and white creoles seemed increasingly too alien to be considered European. They were emblematic of an uncomfortable sense that the Caribbean was an alarming extension of Europe, disturbingly close and familiar and yet irretrievably separate and different. This interplay between imperial power and anxiety about its implications is evident in the passage of dis-criminatory laws against free people of color at the height of the slave trade from the late seventeenth to late eighteenth century, notably laws outlawing interracial marriage, preventing free people from exercising a range of civil liberties, limiting their ability to travel to the metropole or restricting their opportunities for socio-economic advancement.[31] But the law was an unreliable ally in the struggle to keep blackness in chains and out of Europe: In the absence of explicit legal prohibitions, what was there to distinguish free people of African descent from whites? Why could not a free man of color of property and education from the colonies move from being a subject to being a citizen?[32]

After emancipation each colonial power found different solutions to the "problem" of whether or not to include Afro-Caribbean people within the limits of the imperial nation. British Caribbean emancipation delegitimized the principle of using the law to enforce the boundary between black subordination and white

---

across the Americas," *Slavery and Abolition* 15, no. 3 (1994): 17. Carl Campbell's *Cedulants and Capitu-lants: The Politics of the Coloured Opposition in the Slave Society of Trinidad, 1783–1838* (Port-of-Spain: Paria Publishing, 1992), Campbell's *Dynamics of Change,* Heuman's *Between Black and White,* and Beckles's "On the Backs of Blacks," for example, are predominantly studies of mixed-race free people.

30. Homi Bhabha, "Of Mimicry and Man," in Stoler and Cooper, *Tensions of Empire,* 158.

31. Fick, *Making of Haiti,* 20–21; Sue Peabody, *"There Are No Slaves in France": The Political Culture of Race and Slavery in the Ancien Régime* (New York: Oxford University Press, 1996), 111–119; Stoler, *Race and the Education of Desire,* 47.

32. The 1685 French Code Noir, the law regulating slavery throughout the French empire, granted full citizenship to free men of color who met the franchise qualification. Herbert S. Klein, *African Slavery in Latin America and the Caribbean* (New York: Oxford University Press, 1986), 238.

liberty but it did not eliminate the assumption that maintaining such a boundary was a valid political imperative. In the aftermath of abolition the political and ideological work of containing the danger posed by liminal categories of colonial subjects, like educated and propertied free people of color and brown people, was quickly taken over by a discourse about the inherent, scientifically indisputable and biological inferiority of people of African descent. Particularly after the 1865 Morant Bay Rebellion in Jamaica, free people of color in the Caribbean, previously distinguished in the minds of colonizers by their legal status, property ownership, light skin color, and/or education, could be dismissed as lazy and unimportant at best or violent and ungrateful at worst.[33]

This study sheds light on the ways in which the activities of free people of color in the colonies informed and challenged these changing discourses of subjecthood and citizenship. In Barbados free people of color fought white supremacy by laying claim to forms of civic engagement and cultural practices that previously had been the markers of whiteness, one of the island's most basic citizenship requirements. Simply reducing the civil rights debates between Afro-Caribbean people and whites between the 1790s and 1850s to skin color misses the ways in which "race" and phenotype were informed by class, education, and certain cultural and gendered practices, notably forms of public religious expression, marriage practices, and household organization. By examining the interplay of these factors, this study nuances conflicts between free Afro-Barbadians and other sociolegal groups, as well as among free Afro-Barbadians themselves regarding who among them had a legitimate claim to citizenship.

I avoid the problematic language of free black and colored marginality and inbetween-ness, instead focusing on the diverse ways in which free Afro-Barbadians were integral to the society, intellectual life, and economy of the island before and after 1838. These multiple forms of participation complicated divisions of race, class, gender, and legal status. Additionally, I seek to examine how and why color hierarchies shaped the experiences, kin relationships, and social and political allegiances of Afro-Barbadians in late-eighteenth- to mid-nineteenth-century Barbados in *some* contexts but not, it seems, in others. I prefer this approach to attempts to draw a clear fault line between brown or "colored" and black free people, a perspective that misses the important subtleties and particularities of racial identification during this period.

This raises the important issue of terminology and I would like to offer expla-

33. Thomas Eudell, *The Political Languages of Emancipation in the British Caribbean and the U.S. South* (Chapel Hill: University of North Carolina Press, 2002), 107–120; Hall, *Civilising Subjects*, 338–379.

nations and guidelines regarding some of the terms used in this book. The inconsistent manner in which terms describing Afro-Barbadians were used in this period makes it difficult to be conclusive regarding how phenotype, class, and legal
status related to each other. It is often unclear from documentary sources whether
terms such as "colored," "black," "Negro," "mulatto," and "person of color" are references to the legal status, class position, or phenotype of the person or group being discussed.[34] This lack of clarity itself illustrates that, even in Barbados, where
the line between white and nonwhite was considered to be impassable, percep-
tions of skin color were highly susceptible to social rather than physical charac-
teristics.[35] Analysis of the slave registration returns of 1817–1832, which stated the
phenotype of Afro-Barbadian slave owners, reveals great variations. In one case, a
very wealthy and possibly extremely light-complexioned planter of Afro-Barbadian
descent was "whitened" in the slave registries, and was never listed as a "free mulatto" by the registrar of slaves.[36] The *Barbadian*, a nineteenth-century newspaper
used extensively for this study, occasionally referred to all free people of color, regardless of phenotype, as "colored," as opposed to "negro," a term the newspaper
usually reserved for slaves. Yet the same newspaper often referred to any apparently working-class Afro-Barbadians of whose legal status the editor was uncertain
as "Negroes," employing this term, therefore, as a description of working-class status and blackness.[37] In his will, the wealthy merchant of color London Bourne is
described as "coloured," yet during his lifetime various observers noted that he had
an extremely dark complexion.[38]

I have elected to use the terms "free people of color," "free Afro-Barbadians,"
and "free people of African descent" most frequently throughout this study. "Free

34. See, for example, an 1824 advertisement for a domestic in the newspaper the *Barbadian* requesting a "steady, middle-aged Coloured Woman." *Barbadian*, 10 January 1824.

35. See discussion of race as a socially defined rather than simply phenotypic category in the Saint
Domingue context in Stewart King, *Blue Coat or Powdered Wig: Free People of Color in Pre-revolutionary
St. Domingue* (Athens: University of Georgia Press, 2001), 159.

36. This was Jacob Belgrave, the owner of the large Ruby plantation in St. Philip with 238 slaves.
The registrar of slaves probably "whitened" him on account of his wealth and social prominence. See,
for example, T71 520, Barbados Slave Registries, 1817.

37. *Barbadian*; see, for example, 8 October 1824 and 4 June 1834.

38. *Liberal*, February 9 1859, cited in Cecilia Karch, "A Man for All Seasons: London Bourne,"
JBMHS 45 (1999): 19; J. A. S. Thome and J. H. Kimball, *Emancipation in the West Indies: A Six Months'
Tour of Antigua, Barbados and Jamaica in the Year 1837* (New York: American Anti-Slavery Society, 1838),
75; Will of London Bourne, 3 February 1869, RB4, BDA.

people of color" themselves often used this term in petitions and other documents, and the term "Afro-Barbadian" encapsulates the element of diasporic thought and experience. Both terms also seem to reflect the terminology current in the era of the writing of this book and are, I hope, therefore more meaningful and less offensive to the reader. I also use the expression "free coloreds and blacks," a term that appeared on petitions. Occasionally, when all of the above terms seem cumbersome and repetitive, I use the term "nonwhite," the chief merit of which is brevity. I have avoided the terms "freedmen" or "freedwomen" because not all free people of color had been born in slavery and many would not have seen themselves as "freed" people.

This study is divided into nine chapters and three sections and is organized chronologically, although there is some overlap in the time periods discussed in each section. The first section (chapters 1–4) concentrates on the period from the 1790s to the beginning of apprenticeship, section 2 (chapters 5–7) concentrates on apprenticeship and the very first years of "full" freedom, and section 3 (chapters 8 and 9) concentrates on the period from 1838 to the 1850s.

Free people of color remain an intensely charged subject in the modern Caribbean, as a metaphor for continuing entanglements with empire and the contradictions of our complex racial subjectivities. This book is an attempt to understand the experiences and perspective of the men and women who are the subject of what follows, even those aspects of their thought that do not sit comfortably with a twenty-first-century audience. It is also an engagement with current debates about race and racial tension in the Caribbean and the legacy of slavery and emancipation. It is my hope that exploring such complexity will offer readers material for thinking through the implications of the ways in which debates about race, gender, class, and empire from this era remain salient in our own time and to consider how, and to what ends, histories of slavery and emancipation are mobilized in politics and public life in the contemporary Caribbean.

PART ONE

SLAVES, SUBJECTS, AND CITIZENS

People of African Descent in Barbadian Slave Society

After the Egyptian and Indian, the Greek and Roman, the Teuton and Mongolian, the Negro is a sort of seventh son, born with a veil, and gifted with second sight in this American world,—a world which yields him no true self-consciousness, but only lets him see himself through the revelation of the other world. It is a peculiar sensation, this double-consciousness, this sense of always looking at one's self through the eyes of others, of measuring one's soul by the tape of a world that looks on in amused contempt and pity. One ever feels his twoness—an American, a Negro; two souls, two thoughts, two unreconciled strivings; two warring ideals in one dark body, whose dogged strength alone keeps it from being torn asunder.

—W. E. B. DU BOIS, *The Souls of Black Folk*

1 / DEFINING FREEDOM IN
THE INTERSTICES OF SLAVE SOCIETY

Iɴ the two centuries between the establishment of the earliest British Caribbean colonial settlements and emancipation in 1834–1838, the slavery-based societies of the Caribbean evolved into intricate networks of relationships within and across legal and racial boundaries. The rural and urban spheres were intertwined and equally important aspects of slavery's development, a relationship that shaped daily existence for all members of society.[1] The eastern Caribbean island of Barbados, described by one scholar as "effectively one vast sugar plantation" by the nineteenth century, developed an extensive network of highways and byroads connecting hundreds of large plantations, smaller farms of intermediate size, and minuscule landholdings to the urban centers of the capital city of Bridgetown as well as the smaller towns of Oistins, Holetown, and Speightstown.[2] These connections developed to facilitate the economic exploitation of land and labor on rural estates, but subaltern groups in Barbadian slave society used them for their own

1. Hilary Beckles, "Slaves and the Internal Market Economy of Barbados: A Perspective on Nonviolent Resistance," paper presented at the 20th ACH conference, University of the Virgin Islands, U.S. Virgin Islands, 1988; Barry Higman, *Slave Populations of the British Caribbean, 1807–1834* (1984; reprint, Kingston: Press, University of the West Indies, 1995); Christine Hünefeldt, *Paying the Price of Freedom: Family and Labor among Lima's Slaves, 1800–1854* (Berkeley: University of California Press, 1994); Roderick A. McDonald, *The Economy and Material Culture of Slaves: Goods and Chattels on the Sugar Plantations of Jamaica and Louisiana* (Baton Rouge: Louisiana State University Press, 1993); Sidney Mintz and Douglas Hall, *The Origins of the Jamaican Internal Marketing System,* Yale University Publications in Anthropology 57, New Haven, 1960; Philip Morgan, *Slave Counterpoint: Black Culture in the Eighteenth-Century Chesapeake and Lowcountry* (Chapel Hill: University of North Carolina Press, 1998); Michael Mullin, "Slave Economic Strategies: Food, Markets and Property," in Mary Turner, ed., *From Chattel Slaves to Wage Slaves: The Dynamics of Labour Bargaining in the Americas* (London: James Currey, 1995), 68–78; Richard Wade, *Slavery in the Cities: The South, 1820–1860* (London: Oxford University Press, 1964); Welch, *Slave Society in the City;* Knight and Liss, *Atlantic Port Cities.*

2. Quote from Higman, *Slave Populations,* 52.

purposes, creating interstitial spaces through which they shaped and subverted a system in which they were officially powerless.[3]

As Hilary Beckles and Karl Watson have argued, Barbadian slavery was the product of "unique geographic, demographic and economic forces, which tended towards compromising rather than confrontationalist social attitudes."[4] Throughout the eighteenth century, Barbados was notable for the absence of armed slave insurrection, with no plots having been uncovered since the 1780s. Nevertheless, for local authorities this relative calm went hand in hand with enormous difficulties in policing the interactions between slaves and free people. As Sidney Mintz and Richard Price have argued, while the legal code of slavery theoretically assigned everyone a place in the social hierarchy based on race and legal status, the "conception of a society divided into two hermetically sealed sectors can be seen for what is [sic] really was: the masters' ideal, never achieved."[5] Everyday interactions blurred the boundaries between those who were enslaved and those who were free. As Barbadian slave society matured in the eighteenth century, many owners gradually conceded a degree of independence without which slave ownership would have been difficult. Slaves used such arrangements to carve out areas of personal freedom for themselves that undermined distinctions between slavery and freedom.[6]

This background shaped the growth of the island's free population of color, informing relations among free Afro-Barbadians and with other sociolegal groups. This chapter analyzes the relationship between free people of color and slavery, examining the interstitial freedoms made possible by the space of identification they shared with slaves. It also explores their ambivalent position within slave society and their attitudes toward a system that simultaneously oppressed and privileged them.

People of African and African European descent who were legally free existed

3. Sidney Mintz and Richard Price, *An Anthropological Approach to the Afro-American Past: A Caribbean Perspective* (Philadelphia: Institute for the Study of Human Issues, 1976), 18.

4. Hilary Beckles and Karl Watson, "'Social Protest and Labour Bargaining: The Changing Nature of Slaves' Responses to Plantation Life in Eighteenth-Century Barbados," *Slavery and Abolition* 8, no. 3 (1987): 273.

5. Mintz and Price, *Anthropological Approach*, 13 and 18.

6. Elsa Goveia, *The West Indian Slave Laws of the 18th Century* (Barbados: Caribbean Universities Press, 1970), 52. For discussion of the idea of the negotiations of freedom in everyday life, see María Elena Díaz, *The Virgin, The King, and the Royal Slaves of El Cobre: Negotiating Freedom in Colonial Cuba, 1670–1780* (Stanford: Stanford University Press, 2000).

early in Barbados, even while the legal system that entrenched firmly the relationship between bondage and race was being refined.[7] Free people of color were neither a clearly "separate and distinct entity" nor an easily categorized "social group," as some historians have termed them.[8] Their interactions with slaves and whites helped to sustain various kinds of interstitial freedoms that colonial authorities found difficult to suppress and that conflicted with the colonial state's legal definition of the category "free person of color." By the early nineteenth century, slaves and free Afro-Barbadians shared a space of identification based on residential patterns, kinship ties, occupation, and cultural practices. As Saidiya Hartman has argued in the U.S. context, this "common set of identifications," which has emerged among people of African descent in slave societies, "[e]xceed[s] the parameters of resistance in creating alternative visions and experiences of subjectivity, though they do indeed challenge the dominant construction of blackness. This shared set of identifications and affiliations is enacted in instances of struggle, shared pleasures, transient forms of solidarity, and nomadic, oftentimes illegal, forms of association."[9]

THE RISE OF THE SUGAR PLANTATIONS

Prior to the 1640s, when it became the first major sugar producer in the British Empire, Barbados was a struggling colonial outpost producing a variety of crops for export, principally tobacco and cotton but also ginger and indigo.[10] The representative assembly established in 1638–1639 gave extensive self-governing powers to the small landowning male elite. In the early seventeenth century the plantoc-

7. Goveia, *West Indian Slave Laws;* Neville Hall, "Law and Society in Barbados at the Turn of the Nineteenth Century," *JCH* 5 (1972): 20–45; Arnold Sio, "Marginality and Free Coloured Identity in Caribbean Slave Society," in Hilary Beckles and Verene Shepherd, *Caribbean Slave Society and Economy: A Student Reader* (London: James Currey), 1991, 150–151.

8. Karl Watson, *The Civilised Island Barbados: A Social History, 1750–1816* (Bridgetown: Graphic Printers, 1979), 189–190; Beckles, "On the Backs of Blacks," 185.

9. Saidiya V. Hartman, *Scenes of Subjection: Terror, Slavery and Self-making in Nineteenth Century America* (New York: Oxford University Press, 1997), 61.

10. Sidney Mintz, *Sweetness and Power: The Place of Sugar in Modern History* (New York: Penguin Books, 1985), 37; David Watts, *The West Indies: Patterns of Development, Culture and Environmental Change since 1492* (Cambridge: Cambridge University Press, 1987), 146; Gary Puckrein, *Little England: Plantation Society and Anglo-Barbadian Politics, 1627–1700* (New York: New York University Press, 1984), 3–65; Larry Gragg, *Englishmen Transplanted: The English Colonization of Barbados, 1627–1660* (Oxford: Oxford University Press, 2003), 88–98.

racy accounted for at most a few hundred individuals out of a population of about nine thousand, of whom an estimated two thousand were European indentured laborers and two hundred were African slaves. The majority of colonists were white farmers and former indentured laborers, most of whom owned too little property to have much influence, since the electoral franchise requirement was freehold tenure of ten acres of land. The shift to plantation-based sugar production in the mid-seventeenth century enhanced the exclusivity and power of the Barbadian plantocracy. The capital outlay required for plantation agriculture and the oligarchic system under which land was granted to colonists during the period of transition to sugar favored already wealthy planters and aristocratic émigrés with the right political connections. An influx of well-connected royalist English émigrés during the English Civil War further consolidated the plantocracy and pushed smaller farmers off their land.[11]

Barbados was difficult to capture and well protected by the British navy, and, after Restoration in 1660, the island enjoyed a degree of sociopolitical stability that was unrivaled in the British Caribbean. By the late seventeenth century, with a low rate of planter absenteeism in comparison with other Caribbean plantation colonies, the Barbadian plantocracy had developed a well-defined, insular character with stable patriarchal family structures and inheritance patterns. About 120 planter families could trace their roots back to the settlement of the island before and during the civil war. The planter elite also had a deeply rooted local political culture, controlling both houses of the island's legislature and all of the island's eleven parochial governmental boards, called vestries.[12] These factors helped to

11. Hilary Beckles, *White Servitude and Black Slavery in Barbados, 1627–1715* (Knoxville: University of Tennessee Press,1989), 3 and Hilary Beckles, *A History of Barbados: From Amerindian Settlement to Nation-State* (Cambridge: Cambridge University Press, 1990), 11–12; Robin Blackburn, *The Making of New World Slavery: From the Baroque to the Modern, 1492–1800* (London: Verso, 1997), 230; Hume Wrong, *Government of the West Indies* (Oxford: Clarendon Press, 1923), 28; Puckrein, *Little England,* 31.

12. Richard S. Dunn, *Sugar and Slaves: The Rise of the Planter Class in the English West Indies, 1624–1713* (Chapel Hill: University of North Carolina Press, 1972), 76; Jack Greene, "Changing Identity in the British Caribbean: Barbados as a Case Study," in Nicholas Canny and Anthony Pagden, eds., *Colonial Identity in the Atlantic World* (Princeton: Princeton University Press, 1987), 240–242; Puckrein, *Little England,* 24 and 39; Beckles, *History of Barbados,* 42–46 and 160; Gragg, *Englishmen Transplanted,* 66–69; Karl Watson, "Salmagundis vs. Pumpkins: White Politics and Creole Consciousness in Barbadian Slave Society, 1800–34," in Howard Johnson and Karl Watson, eds., *The White Minority in the Caribbean* (Oxford: James Currey, 1998), 17–19; Watts, *West Indies,* 286–300 and 332.

ensure that no one who lacked wealth or connections could easily ascend to the ranks of the white elite.[13]

African slavery was initially an institution of minor importance compared with indentured and free white labor. The first slave law was passed in 1636, proclaiming that, from then on, all blacks and Indians brought to the island, and their descendants, were slaves for life unless contracts had previously been made to the contrary.[14] The expansion of the sugar economy led to the rapid decline of white indentureship and massive imports of Africans. Toward the end of the 1640s planters and British traders seeking a large-scale supply of labor turned to the slave trade, and by the late 1600s few Europeans emigrated willingly to Barbados as indentured laborers.[15] Largely as a consequence of the slave trade, Barbados became the most densely populated island in the Caribbean, with an estimated 362 people per square mile in 1690. During the next fifty years the slave population soared while the indentured servant population shrank to fewer than 1,000. By 1789 no white bondservants remained in Barbados, by which time there were at least 62,115 slaves, 16,167 whites, and 838 free people of color in the island.[16]

Wherever sugar reigned in the seventeenth- and eighteenth-century Caribbean, whites quickly became the minority.[17] Nevertheless Barbados was peculiar for having had a period of intense, predominantly white immigration before and during the early years of the "sugar revolution." Throughout much of its colonial history Barbados maintained a higher ratio of whites than any other island

13. Beckles, *White Servitude*, 16; Puckrein, *Little England*, 23–24; Otis Starkey, *The Economic Geography of Barbados: A Study of the Relationship between Environmental Variations and Economic Development* (New York: Columbia University Press, 1939), 83.

14. Handler, *Unappropriated People*, 12; Robert H. Schomburgk, *The History of Barbados* (London: Longman, Brown, Green and Longmans, 1848), 266.

15. Beckles, *White Servitude*, 42–44 and 115–127; Hilary Beckles and Andrew Downes, "The Economics of the Transition to the Black Labour System in Barbados, 1630–1680," in Beckles and Shepherd, *Caribbean Slavery in the Atlantic World*, 239–252; Blackburn, *Making of New World Slavery*, 230; Noel Deerr, *The History of Sugar*, vol. 1 (London: Chapman and Hall, 1949), 160; Starkey, *Economic Geography*, 61.

16. Carl Bridenbaugh and Roberta Bridenbaugh, *No Peace Beyond the Line: The English in the Caribbean, 1624–1690* (New York: Oxford University Press, 1972), 29; Greene, "Changing Identity," 216; Beckles, *White Servitude*, 10; William Dickson, *Letters on Slavery . . . to which are added, Addresses to the Whites, and the Free Negroes of Barbadoes* (London: J. Philips, 1789), 44–45; Handler, *Unappropriated People*, 18–19.

17. Of the Caribbean's major sugar exporters, only Barbados, Martinique, Guadeloupe, Trinidad, and Cuba never developed slave-to-free ratios of at least 10:1. Watts, *West Indies*, 325.

in the Caribbean. In 1790 the ratio of whites to nonwhites in Barbados was 1:4, compared with 1:10 in Jamaica, 1:18 in Antigua, and 1:16 in the French colony of Saint Domingue. From the 1780s until the end of slavery the white creole population remained stable at about sixteen thousand.[18] This pattern was atypical in the anglophone Caribbean, where white population decline was generally precipitous throughout the eighteenth century.[19] These demographic patterns, coupled with the difficulty of upward mobility into the ranks of the plantocracy, meant that smallholders and landless people, rather than wealthy planters, constituted the majority of the white population. By the mid-eighteenth century a distinctive "poor white" group had become a permanent feature of the Barbadian social landscape, absorbing ever more victims of downward social mobility. According to estimates, poor whites consistently accounted for 40 to 60 percent of the white population by the time of slave emancipation in 1834.[20]

THE MARGINALIZATION OF WHITE WAGE LABOR

In the mid-eighteenth century Barbadian planters began to experiment with cost-cutting measures in estate management designed to encourage slave population growth through natural increase rather than imports and replace most white employees with slaves.[21] A skilled stratum of slaves replaced white artisans, petty managers, and head drivers. The occupational diversification of estate slave labor

---

18. Orlando Patterson, *The Sociology of Slavery: An Analysis of the Origins, Development and Structure of Negro Slave Society in Jamaica* (London: MacGibbon and Kee, 1969), 15; Watson, *Civilised Island*, 61–62; Beckles, *History of Barbados*, 32; Edward Brathwaite, *The Development of Creole Society in Jamaica, 1770–1820* (Oxford: Clarendon Press, 1971), 80; Jill Sheppard, *The "Redlegs" of Barbados: Their Origins and History* (New York: KTO Press, 1977), 43.

19. Dunn, *Sugar and Slaves*, 237; Watts, *West Indies*, 311–312.

20. Hilary Beckles, "Black over White: The 'Poor White' Problem in Barbados Slave Society," *Immigrants and Minorities* 7, no. 1 (1988): 4; Sheppard, *"Redlegs" of Barbados*, 43 and 63; Watson, *Civilised Island*, 108; Beckles, *History of Barbados*, 42, and Hilary Beckles, "Land Distribution and Class Formation in Barbados, 1630–1700: The Rise of a Wage Proletariat," *JBMHS* 36, no. 2 (1980): 129; Handler, *Unappropriated People*, 18–19; J. McCusker and R. Menard, *The Economy of British America, 1607–1789* (1985; reprint, Chapel Hill: University of North Carolina Press, 1991), 153.

21. J. R. Ward, *British West Indian Slavery, 1750–1834: The Process of Amelioration* (Oxford: Clarendon Press, 1988), 13; Watts, *West Indies*, 312; Marietta Morrissey, "Women's Work, Family Formation, and Reproduction among Caribbean Slaves," in Beckles and Shepherd, *Caribbean Slavery in the Atlantic World*, 674–676.

accelerated the decline of white estate employment and led to an increase in the proportion of slaves who did not work as field hands.[22]

Slave population growth and estate labor policies contributed to "extensive unemployment among white labourers, with the consequences of their increased material impoverishment and loss of technical skills—a process, if anything, that was the obverse of that experienced by a significant section of the slave and free non-white population."[23] Work associated with enslavement and blackness was out of the question for a socially "respectable" white person. Estates' hiring policies reinforced this view: In 1744 the manager of Codrington estate noted that plantation managers refused to hire white estate laborers.[24] European travelers frequently commented on Barbados's noticeably large population of poor whites, stating that many of this "degraded class" lived on the charity of enslaved neighbors and friends.[25] The situation was particularly acute for white women, who were already proscribed by accepted social norms from most labor and business activity. Plantation slavery made white female poverty an endemic feature of the Barbadian social landscape. By the end of the eighteenth century, work as midwives, seamstresses, cooks, maidservants, and nursemaids, which had once been the preserve of white women, was usually performed by slave women. White women outnumbered and tended to outlive white men in many British Caribbean colonies, making for poor marriage prospects and a high rate of widowhood. These factors explain why white women apparently constituted a significant percentage of impoverished whites in Barbados.[26]

22. Beckles and Watson, "Social Protest," 284; Mary Butler, "Mortality and Labour on the Codrington Estates, Barbados," *JCH* 19, no. 1 (May 1984): 48–67; Watson, *Civilised Island*, 140; J. Harry Bennett, *Bondsmen and Bishops: Slavery and Apprenticeship on the Codrington Plantations of Barbados, 1710–1838* (Berkeley and Los Angeles: University of California Press, 1958), 12–20; on diversification of labor in early modern plantation societies, see Morgan, *Laboring Women*, 146.

23. Quote from Beckles, "Black over White," 3.

24. Manager Abel Alleyne to the SPG, 4 April 1744, Codrington Plantation Correspondence, cited in Beckles, "Black over White," 4.

25. See for example H. N. Coleridge, *Six Months in the West Indies, in 1825* (London: N.p., 1826), 286–287.

26. Dickson, *Letters on Slavery*, 42. The transition from free to skilled slave labor was complete on plantations by 1700. By 1680, 49 percent of the households in Bridgetown had no white maid servants and 92 percent had domestic slaves. Beckles, *White Servitude*, 138–139; Cecily Forde-Jones, "Mapping Racial Boundaries: Gender, Race, and Poor Relief in Barbadian Plantation Society," *Journal of Women's History* 10, no. 3 (Autumn 1998): 11–13 and 21–23; Trevor Burnard, "A Failed Settler Society: Marriage and Demographic Failure in Early Jamaica," *Journal of Social History* 28, no. 1 (Fall 1994): 63–83.

Paradoxically slavery, the very system that had entrenched such stark class and gender hierarchies among creole whites, also provided a means through which economically marginal whites sustained themselves. For most whites, the only respectable way to survive was to own slaves. Indeed, owning at least one slave became the sine qua non of white respectability, and many who could not afford to buy or hire slaves starved because they either would not or could not engage in work associated with enslavement.[27] The lack of economic opportunities and possibilities for land ownership led to the emergence of a parallel system of slave ownership, with many whites owning small numbers of slaves but little or no land and surviving by hiring out their slaves to others, including plantations.[28] Hilary Beckles has illustrated that a significant number of white women in Barbados survived by establishing themselves in urban areas and hiring out the labor of slaves, mainly women, as domestic workers and prostitutes.[29] The practice of "hiring out" was already significant enough in 1688 to be discussed in the "Act for the governing of Negroes," the most important law of the Barbadian slave regime. One of the act's clauses, which was repealed in 1706, prohibited the island's Jews from keeping large numbers of slaves for the purpose of hiring out their labor. The specific targeting of Jews indicates that this clause was meant to preserve the practice for Christian slave owners, rather than outlawing it entirely.[30]

An 1824 Barbados government report concluded that, out of 5,206 slave owners in the island, 3,671 had no land, and most of that number possessed a handful of slaves. Two years later, a representative in the House of Assembly described Barbados as a colony in which "there are many Slave Owners in low-circumstances of life."[31] In 1832, about 80 percent of Barbadian slave owners owned between one and twenty slaves, accounting for nearly 28 percent of the slave population. While this was a common pattern in sugar-producing colonies, where frequently more than 70 percent of owners had fewer than twenty slaves, no other colony had such a high percentage of slaves concentrated in the small slave-owner cate-

27. *BMBG*, 11 December 1821 and 23 September 1822.

28. Handler, *Unappropriated People*, 151.

29. Hilary Beckles, "White Women and Slavery in the British Caribbean," in Beckles and Shepherd, *Caribbean Slavery in the Atlantic World*, 659–669.

30. "An Act for the governing of Negroes" was passed on 8 August 1688. Richard Hall, *Acts, passed in the island of Barbados . . .* (London: R. Hall, 1764), 112–121; Goveia, *West Indian Slave Laws*, 25.

31. Barbados Council, *Report of a Committee of the Council of Barbadoes, appointed to inquire into the actual condition of the Slaves in this Island . . .* (London: N.p., 1824), 77–78 and 151 (CO 31/50, Barbados, Sessional Papers, 1816–1863, 7 March 1826), National Archives, London.

gory. Furthermore, in most other colonies, many small-scale slave owners were still landholders, which was less common in Barbados.[32]

Owners were supposed to assume total control over hired out and itinerant slaves, bargaining over wages and making sure that their slaves turned over their earnings.[33] However, hired slave labor—from the hire of domestics and artisans by individuals to plantations' regular use of hired gang labor—evolved into a practice whereby some slaves acquired a significant degree of personal autonomy. Owners hired out labor for pecuniary gain, but hiring out was also a convenient means of devolving responsibility for the care of slaves for whom they had no work, since those who hired slaves were responsible for their food and clothing during the period of hire.[34] In exchange for a fixed monthly rate, sometimes as low as one dollar, some owners would even issue passes to their slaves granting permission for them to seek employment where they liked and generally to do more or less as they pleased.[35] Despite frequent efforts by the legislature to condemn unregulated self-hires, hiring such slaves was a widely accepted means of procuring labor. Newspaper advertisements for hired labor occasionally made it clear that those advertising expected to negotiate the terms of employment with the slave, not the owner.[36] Hiring out illustrates that, despite owners' efforts to maintain total control over their slaves, the smooth functioning of slavery required that slaves have a certain amount of autonomy. In theory, according to the 1688 slave law, slaves were not supposed to leave their owners' places of residence without written permission. In reality, slaves regularly traversed the island without passes to attend weekend dances, to go to market on Sundays, and to hire themselves out.

The decline of white wage labor, the stratification of the estate labor force according to skills and widespread slave ownership by landless free people had several consequences for the working lives of slaves. In 1789 William Dickson, an Englishman who worked for a time as the governor's private secretary, observed that "some slaves live and are treated so very differently from others, that a super-

32. Higman, *Slave Populations*, 102–103.

33. O. Nigel Bolland, "Proto-Proletarians? Slave wages in the Americas," in Turner, *Chattel Slaves*, 126–138.

34. Bennett, *Bondsmen and Bishops*, 13; Barry Higman, *Slave Population and Economy in Jamaica, 1807–1834* (1976; reprint, Kingston: Press, 1995), 41–42. See also Paul D. Lack, "An Urban Slave Community: Little Rock, 1831–1862," *Arkansas Historical Quarterly* 4, no. 3 (1982): 258–287.

35. CO 28/119, Barbados, Original Correspondence, 1816–1854, No. 116, MacGregor to Glenelg, 24 May 1837, enclosing case of the classification of an apprentice named Rebecca as a domestic.

36. See, for example, *BMBG*, 29 June 1816.

ficial observer would take it for granted, they belong to classes of men, who hold distinct ranks in society, so to speak, by tenures essentially different."[37] He was referring mainly to the labor hierarchy of the estates, which had large numbers of favored and skilled slaves such as drivers and other estate "officers," boilers, watchmen, and artisans.[38] Enslaved women were excluded from nearly all occupations in the officer and skilled categories on Caribbean plantations. Although certain skilled and favored occupations were gendered as female—particularly domestic work, huckstering, and seamstressing—women were disproportionately concentrated in field labor throughout much of the Caribbean by the early nineteenth century.[39]

By the 1800s, while the majority of slaves spent much of their lives in the fields, many performed other kinds of labor and a growing percentage lived and worked off of the plantations. Even after the abolition of the slave trade Barbados had a surfeit rather than a shortage of estate laborers and the majority of hired-out slaves in the nineteenth century performed nonagricultural labor.[40] At the same time, urban development and a high rate of white residency in the island ensured that there was a market for nonplantation work. Barbados had one of the highest levels of demand for domestic slaves in the anglophone Caribbean. In 1788 a committee of the House of Assembly found that a quarter of slaves labored in some kind of domestic capacity as butlers, doormen, maids, washers, nurses, carriage postilions, and so on.[41] The island also sustained a large number of skilled artisans, creating stiff competition among enslaved, free Afro-Barbadian, and white craftspeople for paid work.[42] The 1834 compensation records show that more than 44 percent

37. Dickson, *Letters on Slavery,* 6.

38. Hilary Beckles, *Black Rebellion in Barbados: The Struggle Against Slavery, 1627–1838* (Bridgetown: Antilles Publications, 1984), 62; Dickson, *Letters on Slavery,* 14 and 53; Edwin Lascelles, James Colleton, Edward Drax, Francis Ford, John Brathwaite, John Walter, William Thorpe Holder, James Holder, and Philip Gibbes, *Instructions for the Management of a Plantation in Barbadoes and for the Treatment of Negroes, &tc.* (London: N.p., 1786), 22 and 26.

39. Higman, *Slave Populations,* 189–192; Hilary Beckles, *Natural Rebels: A Social History of Enslaved Black Women in Barbados* (London: Zed Books, 1989), 31–38; Janet Henshall-Momsen, "Gender Roles in Caribbean Agricultural Labour," in Malcolm Cross and Gad Heuman, eds., *Labour in the Caribbean: From Emancipation to Independence* (London: Macmillan Caribbean, 1992), 142–143; Bernard Moitt, *Women and Slavery in the French Antilles, 1635–1848* (Bloomington: Indiana University Press, 2001).

40. Watson, *Civilised Island,* 141; Ward, *British West Indian Slavery,* 13.

41. Watson, *Civilised Island,* 142.

42. Higman, *Slave Populations,* 81 and 140.

of Barbadian slaves were employed in areas other than field labor, and about one-quarter did not live on estates. By comparison, more than 70 percent of Jamaica's slaves were field laborers, and about 92 percent lived on agricultural units.[43]

URBAN SLAVERY AND RURAL LIFE

Cities and towns were crucial to the development of these complex and dynamic patterns of slave ownership and slave labor.[44] They had a significant impact on population distribution, residential patterns for slave owners and slaves and the development of extensive systems of internal marketing and itinerant slave labor. In Barbados, a small island of 166 square miles or just over one hundred thousand acres, a web of constant social and economic interaction between rural and urban areas brought the socioeconomic dynamics of plantations into the towns and, simultaneously, brought the towns to the countryside.

By the early nineteenth century Barbados had a highly urbanized population. Free people who owned little or no land tended to be concentrated in cities, while about 17 percent of slaves in the island lived in Bridgetown by the end of the 1820s.[45] With little need for field labor, towns had a completely different labor hierarchy from that of rural areas, with domestics, tradespeople, and artisans constituting a large majority of urban slaves. Barbados's 1817 slave registration returns showed that domestic slaves were by far the largest category of all urban slave laborers, accounting for 50 percent of Bridgetown's 9,254 slaves. Significantly, the second largest category of urban slaves in the 1817 slave registry was the 28 percent listed as having no occupation, which might reflect the large numbers of urban slaves who were hired out to perform a variety of different types of work as well as slaves whose owners hired them out over long periods and had little idea how their slaves earned a living. "Skilled tradespeople" were a distant third at 11.8 percent, with a wide variety of other categories—"stockkeepers," "transport workers,"

43. Higman, *Slave Population and Economy in Jamaica*, 42; Higman, *Slaves Populations*, 550.

44. See, for example, Hünefeldt, *Paying the Price of Freedom*; Mary Karasch, *Slave Life in Rio de Janeiro, 1808–1850* (Princeton: Princeton University Press, 1987); Welch, *Slave Society in the City*.

45. See Higman, *Slave Populations*, 226–259; Welch, *Slave Society in the City*, 95. Higman suggests that the percentage of urban slaves was declining between 1817 and 1834 in most British Caribbean islands, which Welch speculates might have been the result of slave owners' decision to redistribute slaves into rural areas after the abolition of the slave trade. See Higman, *Slave Populations*, 87, and Welch, *Slave Society in the City*, 95.

"fishermen," "sellers," "laborers," and "nurses"—accounting for just over 8 percent of the physically able slave population. Bridgetown had no slaves in the category of "drivers," and only 0.1 percent were listed as "field laborers."[46]

Connections between rural and urban life facilitated patterns of slave mobility through hiring out as well as the development of relatively autonomous spaces and networks of Afro-Barbadian cultural and economic activity. By 1800 Sunday was firmly established as market day across the British Caribbean, and Barbadian slaves routinely traveled from all but the most remote areas of the island to the four principal towns, particularly Bridgetown, to sell their produce. Barbadian estate slaves lived on food imported and dispensed by the estates but they turned the small "garden plots" attached to their homes into the basis of a vibrant system of intraisland marketing. The population of Barbados, particularly in urban centers, depended upon slaves' garden plots for several basic dietary staples, as well as poultry and livestock products.[47]

Urbanization, the slave-dominated internal marketing system and the practice of self-hire facilitated the development of one of the most independent slave occupations and one of the few skilled jobs dominated by slave women— huckstering. The most widespread type of huckstering was that of itinerant "petty hucksters," who traversed town and countryside selling perishable and nonperishable goods.[48] Owners often permitted especially skilled hucksters to ply their trade on their own, on the understanding that a share of the profits would be turned over to the owner at agreed upon intervals. Perhaps more than any other form of slave labor, huckstering came to symbolize the internal paradoxes of Barbadian slave society's heavy reliance on semi-independent and itinerant laborers. On one hand, many slave owners, consumers, and employers depended on hired out slave labor for economic survival and the provision of essential goods and services. On the other hand, hucksters and other skilled, self-hired slaves were unwanted competition for free merchants and wage workers, and were perceived to be a threat to public order because of the degree of personal independence they enjoyed.

In the eighteenth century the colonial government tried several times to outlaw huckstering and control the practice of hiring out but failed because few free

46. Higman, *Slave Populations,* 228.

47. Beckles, "Slaves and the Internal Market Economy," 2–3; Handler, *Unappropriated People,* 70 and 125–130; McDonald, *Economy and Material Culture,* 16; Mintz and Hall, *Origins,* 23;

48. Beckles, "Slaves and the Internal Market Economy," 13. Jennifer Morgan cautions against overemphasizing the opportunities enslaved women had for mobility. See Morgan, *Laboring Women,* 169.

people could afford to obey the laws and there was no political will to enforce them.[49] In 1784 the legislature admitted the centrality of slave marketing to the island's internal economy, and passed an act restricting huckstering to a particular market in Bridgetown. The attempt to confine hucksters to one place, which had little impact, was a tacit recognition of hucksters' economic importance as well as the threat that competition from hucksters posed to free urban merchants.[50] In 1818 a group of white men from St. George parish published a notice threatening owners who permitted the island's "many idle Negroes . . . to traffic and huckster, to the great injury of the owners of property in general" that in future they would have "all such Negroes brought to Justice."[51] In response to such outcries and frequent petitions from Bridgetown merchants, the legislature passed an act in 1819 outlawing itinerant huckstering, which, like all previous attempts, was ineffective.[52]

By the early nineteenth century, then, some hired out and itinerant slaves lived an interstitial existence, facilitated by divergence between the letter of the law and the actual needs of everyday life. Even though these people were legally categorized as slaves their lives were often indistinguishable from those of legally free people of color. The free population of color grew in part out of this group of comparatively autonomous slaves. In turn, the presence of a sector of society legally categorized as free people of color increased the dangers that the quasi-freedom of many slaves posed to the social order. Furthermore, the similarities and close ties between the lives of free people of color and relatively independent slaves provided such slaves with the space to pass as free and created fertile ground for sociopolitical solidarity between free and enslaved Afro-Barbadians.

MANUMISSION AND THE GROWTH OF
THE FREE AFRO-BARBADIAN POPULATION

A combination of legal tradition, custom, economic circumstances, and social attitudes shaped manumission practices in American slave societies. The earliest

---

49. Hall, *Laws of Barbados*, No. 116; Fortunatus Dwarris, *Substance of the Three Reports of the Commissioner of Inquiry into the Administration of Civil and Criminal Justice in the West Indies, extracted from the Parliamentary Papers* . . . (London: Joseph Butterworth and Son, 1827), 20–21.

50. Watson, *Civilised Island*, 147–148.

51. *BMBG*, 11 August 1818.

52. See CO 31/47, petition from Bridgetown merchants, 21 January 1818; CO 30/20, No. 381, Barbados, Acts, 1814–1856, "An Act to prohibit Goods from being carried about from House to House or about the Roads or Streets . . . ," passed 25 May 1819, National Archives, London.

free populations of color in the British Caribbean may have been Africans who gained freedom in the early seventeenth century at the end of terms of indenture-ship, similar to white indentured servants. It is also possible that the Roman law principle that dictated that legal status derived from mothers was not universally applied in this early period and that the offspring of relationships between white men and enslaved African women were sometimes freed.[53]

Anglo-Saxon traditions of slavery had no precise equivalent for the Ibero-American practice of *coartación* or gradual manumission, which had its roots in the medieval legal principle that enslavement was an "unnatural" and transitional human condition through which outsiders and their descendants could be inte-grated into society.[54] The absence of such a tradition in English legal practice may have facilitated the decision by colonial authorities in Barbados to equate en-slavement with African or Indian ancestry in 1636, even before the transition to sugar cultivation provided an economic incentive to develop a large, captive la-bor force. The rapid transition to large scale sugar cultivation and imports of Af-rican slaves in the second half of the seventeenth century sealed the association between African descent and enslavement. Barbados's 1688 "Act for the governing of Negroes," which became a legal model for the establishment of slave codes else-where in the British Caribbean, justified the enslavement and importation of Af-ricans on two grounds. The first argument rested on economic necessity, as "the Plantations and Estates of this Island, [could not] be fully managed and brought into use, without the labour and service of great numbers of Negroes and other Slaves." The second argument was cultural, asserting that the laws of the English "nation" could not apply to "Negroes and other Slaves brought unto the People of this Island for that purpose [cultivating the estates]" because such people were "of barbarous, wild and savage nature, and such as renders them wholly unqualified to be governed by the Laws, Customs and Practices of our Nation." Except in in-stances of capital crime, slaves were permanently placed outside the common law, and the 1688 act established special slave courts with juries composed of three freeholders—themselves planters and slave owners—which functioned until the end of slavery in 1834. The act also included clauses that punished slave owners who failed to uphold the boundaries that it established, suggesting that these early

53. Handler, *Unappropriated People,* 13. For a comparative discussion of manumission in the Americas, see Klein, *African Slavery,* 217–241.

54. Klein, *African Slavery,* 194–195.

planter-legislators understood that white settlers might have to be trained in the habits of white supremacy.[55]

Such economic and cultural justifications for placing "Negroes and other Slaves" under the jurisdiction of a special slave code did not negate the importance of preserving the limited possibility of manumission from slavery. Manumission was essential to the perception of legitimacy for slave owners and slaveholding states, but if not severely restricted and rigorously controlled, manumission could lead to the emergence of a large free population of color and call into question the separation between "Negro" enslavement and "English" freedom that was enshrined in the 1688 law. Barriers such as high manumission costs were used to preserve the freeing of slaves as a privilege for a small, white, wealthy elite. Although the price of freedom could be worked out privately between an owner and slave, manumission fees were set by law, and had to be paid to the vestry of the parish in which the slave was manumitted. An annuity was then supposed to be paid out of the fee to the freed person for her/his support. While there were legal means through which the fees could be evaded, it involved either the owner or the slave going to England to effect the manumission under a 1732 British act that made it possible to free a slave from the colonies without paying any fees. Many owners did make use of this act but for those without the financial means of traveling to the metropole it was obviously impossible. In 1801 manumission fees were raised from fifty pounds (which could be waived if the owner was impoverished) to a nonnegotiable three hundred pounds for women and two hundred pounds for men. The change was made in response to several trends: More women were being manumitted than men, slave owners tended to manumit old or infirm slaves so as not to have to take care of them, and manumission numbers in general had risen significantly in the last decades of the eighteenth century.[56]

Varying combinations of such economic and legal restrictions made manumission extremely difficult in most American plantation-based slave societies. Although tradespeople and domestics were disproportionately represented among the free population of color, few slaves, skilled or not, had any realistic hope of earning enough to procure freedom for themselves or family members. Slave owners' dependence on the hiring out system, particularly owners who had little or no property other than their slaves, made them reluctant to give up this

55. Hall, *Acts,* 112–121; Goveia, *West Indian Slave Laws,* 25.

56. Handler, *Unappropriated People,* 44–47.

steady income, and most could not afford the manumission fees. These factors contributed to low manumission rates in Barbados, which rose from 157 individuals (0.2 percent of the slave population) in 1817 to only 363 individuals (0.4 percent of the slave population) in 1832, typical rates for the British Caribbean.[57]

In many slave societies the majority of those manumitted were women, although enslaved women were underrepresented among skilled slaves, and few therefore had the means to earn the money to buy their freedom and the freedom of their children.[58] Women consistently accounted for over 60 percent of Barbadian manumissions during the nineteenth century. For example, between 1809 and 1811, 168 men and 263 women were freed.[59] Some female slaves, like their male counterparts, managed to earn enough money to purchase their freedom and that of their family through their own labor. The will of Phoebe Ford, a free Afro-Barbadian shopkeeper from Holetown who was probably a huckster during her bondage, shows that she had first earned the money to buy her freedom and set up a small retail shop then purchased and manumitted her three children.[60] It was also not uncommon for women to be manumitted as a "gift" for years of service as domestics or for women to be manumitted by male partners or bought out of slavery by other freeborn or freed family members. Domestic work and huckstering were the two areas of work that offered the greatest opportunities for women to achieve manumission by hiring themselves out and earning money or receiving freedom from their owners without having to pay.[61]

57. Ibid., 51–52; Watson, *Civilised Island*, 140. Manumission rates did not vary much until the mid-1820s, when, as part of its amelioration policy, the imperial government insisted that barriers to manumission be removed.

58. Ira Berlin, *Slaves without Masters: The Free Negro in the Antebellum South* (New York: New Press, 1974), 151.

59. Manumission figures from Handler, *Unappropriated People*, 49. Jane Landers, Kimberley Hanger, and Herbert Klein all caution against placing too much emphasis on the role of white male manumitters in the growth of free populations of color in slave societies. They argue that free family members of color tended to be more significant as manumitters. See Jane Landers, "Introduction," and Hanger, "Patronage, Property and Persistence," in Jane Landers, ed., *Against the Odds: Free Blacks in the Slave Societies of the Americas* (London: Frank Cass, 1996), viii and 50; and Klein, *African Slavery*, 230.

60. CO 28/92, No. 16, petition of Sam Gabriel, Catherine Abel Duke, and William Collins, 8 March 1823. Also cited in Handler, *Unappropriated People*, 57 and 133.

61. Beckles, *History of Barbados*, 52; Handler, *Unappropriated People*, 22–25. For comparison, see Berlin, *Slaves without Masters*, 151; Hanger, "Patronage, Property and Persistence," 50.

As in much of the Caribbean, Barbados's free population of color began to increase rapidly after the 1780s. As table 1 shows, the most dramatic growth took place during the last forty years of slavery, when free people of color constituted the fastest growing segment of the island's population. Nevertheless, low manumission rates throughout much of the eighteenth century ensured that the free population of color in Barbados always remained much smaller, both in absolute numbers and as a percentage of the total population, than in many other islands, and Afro-Barbadians always remained a minority of the free population, with whites still outnumbering free people of color by a ratio of 2:1 in 1833.[62] By contrast, the populations of whites and *gens de couleur* in Saint Domingue were almost equal on the eve of the revolution, and by 1831 free people of color outnumbered whites 4:3 in Jamaica, 3:1 in St. Kitts, and 4:1 in Trinidad.[63] In this respect, Barbados resembled the free population of color in parts of the southern United States more than other Caribbean islands.[64]

There is insufficient census information to make any conclusive statements about the composition of the free Afro-Barbadian population. Manumission was the major factor driving the growth of the free black and colored population, making it likely that the proportion of *freed* people, as opposed to *freeborn* people, was high. However, the importance of natural increase—the freeborn children of free women of color—should not be discounted and might explain why there was almost gender parity in the free population of color, although women still outnumbered men. The role of natural increase likely grew as the free population of color grew.

The presence of free people of color made it possible for the enslaved to subvert slave law and carve out extralegal forms of freedom within the interstices of Barbadian slave society. At the same time, despite significant commonalities, the legal distinction between free people of color and slaves created points of tension and conflict that limited the possibility of turning this shared space of identification into a basis for political collectivity.

62. Handler, *Unappropriated People*, 18–19.

63. Arnold Sio, "Race, Colour and Miscegenation: The Free Coloured of Jamaica and Barbados," *Caribbean Studies* 16, no. 1 (1976): 7; Edward L. Cox, *Free Coloreds in the Slave Societies of St. Kitts and Grenada* (Knoxville: University of Tennessee Press, 1984), 12; Carl Campbell, "Trinidad's Free Coloureds in Comparative Caribbean Perspectives," in Beckles and Shepherd, *Caribbean Slavery in the Atlantic World*, 600; Fick, *Making of Haiti*, 118–134; Higman, *Slave Populations*, 19.

64. Berlin, *Slaves without Masters*, 136 and 398; Cox, *Free Coloreds*, 12; Heuman, *Between Black and White*, 7; Fick, *Making of Haiti*, 77.

TABLE 1. WHITE, FREE PEOPLE OF COLOR, AND SLAVE POPULATIONS IN BARBADOS, 1748–1834

Year	Whites	Free people of color	Slaves	Total population	Total free population	% of total population free people of color	% of free population people of color	Manumissions per year
1748	15,192	107	47,025	62,324	15,299	0.2	0.7	
1768	16,139	448	66,379	82,966	16,587	0.6	2.7	
1773	18,532	534	62,548	81,614	19,066	0.65	2.8	
1786	16,167	838	69,115	86,120	17,005	1.0	4.9	
1801	15,887	2,209	69,196	87,292	18,096	2.5	12.2	
1809	15,566	2,263	69,369	87,198	17,829	3.0	12.7	
1810	15,517	2,526	69,119	87,162	18,043	2.9	13.9	
1811	15,794	2,613	69,132	87,539	18,407	3.0	14.2	
1812	15,120	2,529	68,569	86,218	17,649	2.9	14.3	
1813	15,561	2,412	65,995	83,968	17,973	2.9	13.4	
1814	15,920	2,317	66,663	84,900	18,237	2.7	12.7	
1815	16,145	3,319	69,280	88,744	19,464	3.7	17.1	
1816	17,072	3,007	71,286	90,365	19,079	3.3	15.7	157[a]
1825	14,630	4,524	78,096	97,251	19,150	5.2	24.0	
1826	14,584	4,777	80,551	99,912	19,361	4.8	25.0	107
1827	14,687	4,896	79,383	98,966	19,556	4.9	25.0	
1828	14,824	5,020	80,050	99,894	19,844	5.0	25.3	
1829	14,959	5,146	81,902	102,007	20,105	5.0	25.6	223
1833–34	14,592	6,584	82,807	103,983	21,176	6.3	31.1	363[b]

Source: Compiled from Handler, Unappropriated People, 18–19, 49, 51.

[a] Manumissions in 1817.

[b] Manumissions in 1832.

FREEDOM OUTSIDE THE LAW

The social and working sphere that was shared by most people of African descent, slave and free, made it difficult for slave owners and the state to maintain control over slaves and prevent the growth of the free Afro-Barbadian population. By the eighteenth century Barbados no longer had extensive forests or
rugged countryside to which slave maroons could escape and establish large autonomous communities, but slave society itself provided spaces for slaves who
chose to make a run for freedom to reinvent themselves as free people of color.[65]
As the slave population exploded in the mid-seventeenth century, the island's legislature quickly identified free Afro-Barbadians as a social aberration whose presence subverted efforts to regulate contact between free and slave. The first known
reference to free people of color in Barbados is a law of 1652 prohibiting anyone
from "entertain[ing] any man or woman, White or Black, above one night, if he
doth not know him to be a Free-man."[66] This law indicates that there were already
people of color who were legally free and authorities were worried slaves would
use this fact to pass as free themselves. The reference to whites also indicates the
propensity of white indentured servants to abscond from service and possibly
reflects fears that extremely light-complexioned slaves and free people of color
might be passing as whites.

The difference between being a slave away from one's owner with leave, being legally free and being a fugitive was extremely obscure. Urbanization, the poor
regulation of itinerant and self-hired slaves and the friends and family of runaways
around the island colluded to confound colonial authorities' efforts to cope with
the problem of slave marronage. Particularly toward the end of the eighteenth
century, when the rapid growth in the size of the free population of color was noticeable to any casual observer, the presence of large numbers of "legitimately"
free Afro-Barbadians made it easier for slaves to abscond from their owners. It is
impossible to know how many runaways there were at any given time in Barba-

---

65. Hilary Beckles, "From Land to Sea: Runaway Barbados Slaves and Servants, 1630–1700,"
Slavery and Abolition 6, no. 3 (1985): 79–94; Jerome Handler, "Escaping Slavery in a Caribbean Plantation Society: Marronage in Barbados, 1650–1830s," *New West Indian Guide/Nieuwe West-Indische Gids*
71 (1997): 183–225; Gad Heuman, "Runaway Slaves in Nineteenth Century Barbados," *Slavery and Abolition* 6, no. 3 (December 1985): 95–111.

66. John Jennings, Acts and Statutes of the Island of Barbados, 2nd ed. (London, 1656), 20–21,
cited in Handler, *Unappropriated People*, 13.

dos, but in 1833, the governor estimated that the free nonwhite population, officially less than seven thousand, was in reality about twelve thousand. This estimate likely reflects the significant numbers of "free" people whose manumissions were improperly recorded or downright illegal, the number of nonagricultural and hired slaves whom any stranger might have assumed to be free, and the numbers of runaways passing for free.[67]

Often, owners who hired their slaves out for long periods and depended upon them to return with the money they had earned only realized that their slaves had absconded once the appointed day for payment had passed. Maroons could slip into the world of slaves and free people of color, taking advantage of their connections in the towns and around the island.[68] Like the legally free, runaways gravitated toward urban areas where they could more readily find work and where they were least likely to have their freedom questioned. Bridgetown was known to be teeming with runaways, particularly its ever-expanding slum areas. The Bay Street and Nelson Street districts in the south of the town were crowded collections of small wooden houses largely inhabited by free people, slaves living apart from their owners and hiring themselves out, and, it was well known, a sizable fugitive population.[69]

Escaping the island altogether was another possibility, particularly after the capture of nearly all the Windward Islands by the British during the wars against France. There was a particularly close relationship between Barbados and the more recent British acquisition of Trinidad, as well as the former Dutch colonies of Demerara and Berbice on the coast of South America, where many Barbadian planters owned property. Numerous Barbadian slaves and free people of color lived in these neighboring colonies or had family and friends there. Due to chronic labor shortages wages for hired slaves and skilled workers were better in some neighboring colonies than in Barbados, and skilled Barbadian slaves whose owners hired them out sometimes went as far as British Guiana to find work.[70] Runaway slaves were often suspected of having gone to other islands to reunite with

67. CO 28/111, No. 22, Governor Lionel Smith to Stanley, 29 October 1833.

68. See, for example, advertisements for the runaway Betsy Lemon, in *BMBG*, 30 March, 3 and 12 September 1816.

69. Heuman, "Runaway Slaves," 95–111; Handler, "Escaping Slavery," 183–225. For comparison, see Wade, *Slavery in the Cities,* 214–225.

70. Beckles, "From Land to Sea"; Deerr, *History of Sugar* 1:161–162; see, for example, CO 28/101, n.d, alphabetized correspondence, Petition of Richard Walden, native of Bridgetown, Barbados;

free family members already there, and runaways from elsewhere in the Wind-wards and the Guianas were sometimes discovered passing for free in Barbados.[71]

The French revolutionary and Napoleonic wars also led to the presence of large numbers of British troops, garrisoned at St. Ann's to the south of Bridge-town. A black regiment in the imperial army, formed of Africans liberated from enemy slave ships at the end of the eighteenth century, was garrisoned at Adam's Castle near the capital. Imperial troops, particularly those of African descent posted in Caribbean cities, undermined the segregation of slave and free.[72] In 1813 an advertisement for a runaway named James, a tailor, mentioned that he had been the property of an army captain in the Third West India Regiment and had, since his disappearance, "repeatedly been seen at St. Ann's, where he has much connection, having formerly been messman to the 6th W.I. [Regiment]."[73] Sev-eral notices appeared for slave women suspected of having left the island as the wives of black soldiers.[74] Slave men could escape under the cover of interisland military maneuvers. In June 1816 an advertisement announced the capture of a "Barbadian Negro" in St. Lucia who had gone with the military to Martinique in 1808 and Guadeloupe in 1809 and had used this military experience to pass for a free man.[75]

Pretending to be a slave out on a written pass from his/her owner was also an alternative to passing for free. For example, Toney, a slave who had in the past hired himself out in Bridgetown and Christ Church, was "seen with a forged Pass, and no doubt has deceived many, and, as he can read and write, he may renew his pass."[76] Many runaways hid in the homes of their family and friends on planta-tions or the slave "yards," which adjoined the homes of slave owners who did not

---

D. Graham Burnett, *Masters of All They Surveyed: Exploration, Geography, and a British El Dorado* (Chi-cago: University of Chicago Press, 2000), 20; Pedro Welch, "'Crimps and Captains': Displays of Self ex-pression among Freed Coloured Women, Barbados, 1750–1834," *Journal of Social Sciences IV* 2 (Decem-ber 1997): 106; Minutes of the St. Michael Vestry, 11 November 1847, notice for sixteen pounds' worth of manumission annuities due to Sarah Lane, living in Demerara; Higman, *Slave Populations*, 84.

71. *BMBG*, 19 April 1817, 31 January 1818, and 27 July 1822; *Barbadian*, 22 July 1825; See also Heu-man, "Runaway Slaves," 101.

72. Brathwaite, *Development of Creole Society*, 106; Roger Norman Buckley, *Slaves in Red Coats: The British West India Regiments, 1795–1815* (New Haven: Yale University Press, 1979).

73. *BMBG*, 30 January 1813.

74. See, for example, the notice for Celia, in ibid., 4 August 1818.

75. Ibid., 15 June 1816.

76. Ibid., 20 July 1819.

own large tracts of land, particularly in towns.[77] Slaves would frequently run away when they thought they might be separated from friends and family through sale, as was the case with Hester, who, after being advertised for sale, was suspected of being hidden by her husband, a tailor living in Nelson Street.[78] Free people of color frequently participated in hiding their own relatives or those of their friends. An 1822 notice for Penelope stated that "she is supposed to be harboured by her mother, Mary Barrow (passing herself as a free woman), living in Nelson-street; or by Mary Johnson, a free coloured woman also a resident in Nelson Street."[79] The owner of Hamlet, a black slave fisherman, suspected after he had run away that "he may pass himself off as a free man, having two sisters who are free subjects," one of whom lived in Bay and the other in Nelson Street.[80]

RELATIONS BETWEEN FREE PEOPLE OF COLOR AND SLAVES

As in other slave societies, free Afro-Barbadians were heavily concentrated in urban areas. Between 1809 and 1829 about 63 percent of the free population of color lived in Bridgetown, and Speightstown, the island's second largest city, had a sizable free population of color.[81] It is likely that, in Barbados as elsewhere, manumission favored skilled urban slaves, who were more likely than rural field laborers to have the capital to buy their freedom or have social connections with free people who could afford and were willing to pay for manumission.[82] Opportunities for them in the countryside were few: Free people of color were excluded from plantation work, and there was little hope for them to own land, let alone plantations.[83] Life as a free person of African descent in rural areas must have been dangerous, with the constant possibility of racist attack, being mistaken for a ma-

77. Heuman, "Runaway Slaves"; Handler, "Escaping Slavery," 209.

78. *BMBG*, 1 January 1814.

79. Ibid., 30 July 1822.

80. Ibid., 6 September 1817.

81. Higman, *Slave Populations*, 96. An 1825 description of Speightstown observed that the "population of the place is colored in a very large proportion, and you may walk some time in the street before you will meet a white or black man or woman." Coleridge, *Six Months*, 48. It is unclear whether the distinction between "colored" and "black" in this statement is one of legal status between slaves and free people of color, or phenotypically between people of lighter and darker skin color.

82. Klein, *African Slavery*, 229.

83. Handler, *Unappropriated People*, 121 (Handler found clear evidence of only four Afro-Barbadian plantation owners between 1780 and 1834); Watson, *Civilised Island*, 201–202.

roon, or being seized and illegally clapped into bondage. There was also an element of choice—like landless whites, free people of color apparently had no desire for work as plantation field laborers, which was considered by all free people to be degrading.[84]

Many free Afro-Barbadians had either themselves begun life as slaves or were barely a generation removed from slavery, and slaves' kinship networks therefore frequently included free people of color.[85] This further encouraged the mobility of slaves, and owners had to accommodate in some measure slaves' need to maintain their family connections. Visiting or permanently reuniting with free and enslaved kin elsewhere in the island influenced decisions about recreation, slaves' own-account economic activities, and marronage. The presence of free people of color and slaves in towns deepened personal ties between country and town and served to make the town a place to which one could escape from plantation life.

Spirituality provided another realm in which free people of color and slaves tended to identify with one another. Some free Afro-Barbadians, and most slaves, practiced or believed in Obeah, an African-derived term for "the control or channelling of supernatural/spiritual forces by particular individuals or groups for their own needs, or on behalf of clients who come for help."[86] Two nonconformist Christian sects that had been active in Barbados since the late eighteenth century—the Methodists and the Moravians—had congregations almost entirely composed of free Afro-Barbadians and slaves. The Methodist Church built a chapel in Bridgetown in 1819, and its membership grew rapidly. Although the congregation was composed of both free people and slaves, most Methodists in Barbados were free people of color and few if any of the white people who occasionally worshiped in Methodist churches were creoles.[87]

West Indian planters considered the Methodists' teachings and methods particularly subversive of slavery and the established church. The fact that free men of color could be ordained and that Methodists proselytized among slaves without

84. James S. Handler and Arnold A. Sio, "Barbados," in David Cohen and Jack Greene, *Neither Slave Nor Free: The Freedmen of African Descent in the Slave Societies of the New World* (Baltimore: Johns Hopkins University Press, 1972), 216–217.

85. Higman, *Slave Populations,* 81 and 396.

86. Quoted from Kenneth Bilby and Jerome S. Handler, "Obeah: Healing and Protection in West Indian Slave Life," *JCH* 38 (2004): 154; J. W. Orderson, *Creoleana: or social and domestic scenes and incidents in Barbados in days of yore* (London: Saunders and Otley, 1842), 37. Orderson claimed that obeah had its "nucleus" in Bridgetown.

87. Noel Titus, *The Development of Methodism in Barbados* (Bern: Peter Lang, 1993), 28.

the permission of owners did nothing to improve Methodists' relations with local whites.[88] The Methodists were confined to Bridgetown and Speightstown, where they had chapels and schools for slaves and free people of color. The Moravians, by contrast, found more favor with planters, since they conducted missionary activity only with slave owners' permission and distanced themselves from abolitionism. They were given access to plantations, establishing a mission station at Sharon in the central parish of St. Thomas in the 1790s and another at Mount Tabor in the eastern parish of St. John in 1825. While the majority of their congregations were enslaved people, there were some free Afro-Barbadians and a few whites.[89]

In towns, slaves and free Afro-Barbadians formed the majority of the laboring-class population and created a vibrant street-oriented working-class culture that colonial elites and authorities found threatening. By the late eighteenth century the towns' itinerant hucksters, small shopkeepers, artisans, and manual laborers were largely Afro-Barbadian and the shared social and working sphere of free and enslaved Afro-Barbadians created immense policing problems for slave owners and colonial authorities.[90] A law passed in 1820 to regulate the fares of porters and boatmen in Bridgetown referred to the "notorious fighting, quarrelings, and other evil and pernicious practices of the Porters and Boatmen openly carried on in the public Streets, Wharfs and landing places in Bridge Town to the disturbance of the general quiet of the Inhabitants." The law illustrates the legislature's concern that the rowdiness of these men was evidence of an Afro-Barbadian working-class urban culture that crossed legal boundaries. One of the act's clauses explicitly sought to preserve legal distinctions by prescribing a punishment of flogging for slaves and imprisonment for free boatmen who were "complained against for . . . refusing to work when called upon in [sic] giving abusive language."[91] The pro-planter *Barbadian* frequently published letters calling for a strengthened Bridgetown police force that could put a stop to "the blasphemous and obscene

88. Handler, *Unappropriated People*, 158.

89. Ibid., 154–161; A. K. O. Lewis, "The Moravian Mission in Barbados 1816–1886: A study of the historical context and theological significance of a minority church among an oppressed people" (Ph.D. thesis, University of Birmingham, 1983), 1–28; Titus, *Development of Methodism*.

90. F. W. N. Bayley, *Four Years' Residence in the West Indies, during the years 1826, 7, 8 and 9* (London: William Kidd, 1833), 60–61.

91. CO 30/20, No. 403, "Act passed to regulate the fares to be taken by the porters and boatmen in Bridgetown," passed 9 August 1820.

language of the slaves, and 'the degraded part of the free population' . . . which al-most daily is heard in our streets."[92]

Whites constantly feared that the urban Afro-Barbadian "crowd" might turn on them. Such discomfort was illustrated during an 1827 legal case, when a white Bridgetown resident named John Staunton successfully appealed his conviction for refusing to help two white Bridgetown policemen as they were trying to ar-rest an Afro-Barbadian man outside Staunton's business. The slave was accused of theft, and when the police confronted him, he refused to say who he was or where he was from. As the police tried to drag him away, a large crowd of "colored per-sons" of unspecified legal status gathered in front of Staunton's counting house. They followed the action, "shouting and hooting & exciting the Slave to escape if he could, & advising him to lie down & not to go." The policeman claimed they asked several "slaves" standing nearby to bring a cart and help them, but none moved. When they saw Staunton and his assistant, two white men, the constables asked them for help, and they refused. During the inquiry Staunton was adamant that, had he helped, "[he and his assistant] should have been exposed to the hoot-ings and vituperations" of the Afro-Barbadian crowd, whom he claimed the con-stables did not, in fact, dare to ask for assistance.[93]

Free Afro-Barbadians and slaves mingled openly at dances, which free people of color often hosted. The fact that such mixed social activities were illegal under the 1688 law was increasingly irrelevant, since by the nineteenth century those provisions of the law were ignored or misinterpreted. In 1821, after a white man was murdered when he intervened to stop such a dance at the home of a "free coloured person," a letter writer to the *Mercury* voiced many whites' sense of impo-tence in the face of such flagrant violations of their authority. He observed, "These illegal gatherings are becoming every day more frequent; the time was, when they (the negroes and coloured people) considered it a mark of favour if they were per-mitted to meet occasionally on a Saturday or Sunday afternoon to amuse them-selves, provided they dispersed at the close of evening." The author noted that, in another recent case, when a "gentleman's coloured servant" was wounded at such a dance, the gentleman had sought a warrant for the arrest of the "free coloured person, at whose house the negroes had been permitted to assemble" with "a view of doing away with a nuisance which had become so frequent." The magistrate

92. *Barbadian*, 10 August 1830.
93. CO 31/50, 2 and 30 January 1827.

who heard the case ruled that no crime had been committed, as the 1688 act only "prohibited the meeting of negroes on *Plantations*, and no where else." The magistrate's interpretation reflects how far whites' own understanding of the law now diverged from its original meaning. According to the author, the legal decision had given free people of color and slaves the impression "that they cannot be legally prevented from assembling when and where they please."[94]

Despite the legal stratifications of slave society, the close connections between slaves and free people of color constantly challenged and redefined social boundaries, and free people of color actively collaborated in this process of subversion. At the same time, free people of color were not the unqualified allies of slaves. They tended to oppose slavery insofar as it affected them and their families but support its existence as a legitimate legal and social institution.

SLAVERY, SLAVE OWNERSHIP, AND FREE AFRO-BARBADIAN IDENTITY

Being free and of African descent in a society based on black slavery and white freedom inherently produced situations of personal insecurity and political ambivalence. No free Afro-Barbadian enjoyed the legal privileges accorded to even the poorest white person or was ever fully safe from the possibility of having her or his free status challenged. While many were determined to defend their freedom and that of their families, or obtain freedom for slave relatives, such desires could coexist with support for slavery as an institution. Slave ownership was a mark of social status and an economic asset for all free people, and even those who did not own slaves were indirectly economically dependent upon the plantations and slavery for their survival. Table 2, based on data compiled for this study from the Barbados Slave Registries, illustrates patterns of slave ownership among free Afro-Barbadians between 1817 and 1832.

The data in tables 2 and 3 illustrate key trends with regard to how gender informed patterns of Afro-Barbadian slave ownership. The vast majority of slave owners of color—between 60 and 70 percent each year—were female, the ma-

---

94. *BMBG*, 18 June 1821. See also discussion in Jerome Handler and Charlotte Frisbie, "Aspects of Slave Life in Barbados: Music and Its Cultural Context," *Caribbean Studies* 11, no. 4 (January 1972): 5–46; Handler, *Unappropriated People*, 123 and 172.

TABLE 2. GENDER DISTRIBUTION OF BARBADIAN SLAVE OWNERS OF COLOR AND THEIR SLAVES, 1817–1832

	1817	1820	1823	1829	1832
Female slave owners of color	400	479	234	413	413
Male slave owners of color	232	195	221	217	198
Total slave owners of color	632	674	445	630	611
% of free people of color slave owners	21.0[a]	22.4[a]	9.8[b]	12.2[c]	9.3[d]
Slaves owned by females of color	1,626	1,778	847	1,580	1,542
Slaves owned by males of color	791	673	830	872	764
Total slaves owned by people of color	2,417	2,451	1,677	2,452	2,306

Sources: Barbados Slave Registries, Records of the Colonial Office, National Archives, Kew Gardens, London, T71/523, 528, 533, 546, 552.

[a]Based on 1816 population data.

[b]Based on 1825 population data.

[c]Based on 1829 population data.

[d]Based on 1833–34 population data.

jority resident in St. Michael parish, most likely in and around Bridgetown.[95] This imbalance might correlate with the proportion of women in the free population of color or it might represent financial choices made by Afro-Barbadian women who had the means to invest their capital in slaves, since slaves were a source of marketable labor, financial independence and social respectability. This pattern was also typical for other societies in the Americas.[96] Both sexes tended to own very small numbers of slaves—between three and four on average—but many women of color appear in the slave registers as owners of unusually large numbers of slaves, sometimes more than twenty, which was comparatively rare for men. Often, these women bore the same surname as prominent Afro-Barbadian merchants who appeared as owners of far fewer slaves. This could suggest that

95. Only in 1823 did the number of female slave owners of color registered for St. Michael dip below that of men, an exception that seems to reflect errors in the registration process for St. Michael that year.

96. Handler, *Unappropriated People*, 55; Kimberley Hanger calculated that women bought 77.8 percent of the slaves purchased by free people of color in eighteenth-century New Orleans (Hanger, "Patronage, Property and Persistence," 46); Heuman, *Between Black and White*, 14.

TABLE 3. GENDER DISTRIBUTION OF SLAVE OWNERS OF COLOR IN ST.
MICHAEL AND OTHER PARISHES, 1817–1832

	1817	1820	1823	1829	1832
St. Michael Parish					
Female slave owners of color	369	417	171	384	402
Male slave owners of color	200	157	175	202	189
Total slave owners of color	569	574	346	586	591
Slaves owned by females of color	1,518	1,581	666	1,483	1,505
Slaves owned by males of color	655	526	680	814	739
Total slaves owned by people of color	2,173	2,107	1,346	2,297	2,244
Other parishes					
Female slave owners of color	31	62	63	29	11
Male slave owners of color	32	38	46	15	9
Total slave owners of color	63	100	109	44	20
Slaves owned by females of color	108	197	181	97	37
Slaves owned by males of color	136	147	150	58	25
Total slaves owned by people of color	244	344	331	155	62

Sources: Barbados Slave Registries, Records of the Colonial Office, National Archives, Kew Gardens, London, T71/523, 528, 533, 546, 552.

women in these elite families tended to invest in slaves, probably their own personal servants and slaves whom they hired out, while men perhaps had a wider variety of investment possibilities open to them. Both men and women displayed a marked preference for owning women rather than men—analysis of the sex of slaves owned by Afro-Barbadians for the year 1829 shows that female slaves accounted for 63 percent of the total. Owners with only one slave tended to own a female, probably because women and girls were cheaper, could be exploited for personal use or hired out as domestic workers, manual laborers, or sexual slaves, and their children belonged to the owner.[97]

With the exception of the data for 1823, when there appears to have been underrecording of the numbers of female Afro-Barbadian slave owners in St. Michael, the overall number of nonwhite slave owners and the numbers of slaves they owned remained remarkably constant between 1817 and 1832, even though the population of free people of color grew significantly. The registers do not give

97. T 71/546, return for 1829.

an indication that free people of color in Barbados either manumitted more slaves or traded slaves more aggressively than their white counterparts. This suggests that most free people of color who owned slaves at the time of emancipation already owned them a decade and a half earlier. The newly recorded free Afro-Barbadians being counted in this period either lacked the capital to purchase slaves or chose not to expend their financial resources on slave ownership. As table 2 shows, this trend translated into a rapid decline in the numerical significance of free people of color as slave owners. Thus, by 1832, fewer than one free Afro-Barbadian in ten owned slaves, down from one in five in 1817. While slavery remained vital to certain individuals and families, fewer and fewer free Afro-Barbadians had an immediate stake as slaveholders in the maintenance of the system.

The overall constancy in the size of the Afro-Barbadian slave-owning population also belies another noticeable shift toward increasing levels of urban concentration that took place between 1817 an 1832. The proportion of free people of color registered as rural slave owners was never large, but it dwindled from 244 in 1817 to 62 in 1832. This may indicate a wider trend toward the increasing urbanization of free people of color in Barbados during the final decades of slavery. Again, the reasons why are not clear, but the result would have been that fewer free people of color had direct day to day contact with rural plantation life, and slaves owned by free people of color were probably even less likely to be employed regularly, if at all, in agricultural labor.

While free people of color sometimes bought their own kin in order to free them, they also owned slaves for their services and do not appear to have been more inclined to manumit their slaves than white owners, either in Barbados or other New World slave societies. Upon her death in 1823, Phoebe Ford, the previously mentioned manumitted slave and Holetown shopkeeper, left behind two slaves and a house worth five hundred pounds.[98] When Coobah Gibbs died in 1830 one of her sons, a daughter and her granddaughter were free, but she died before she could manumit her brother, and her remaining son and two daughters. She left two slaves for her two free children.[99] William Bourne, the father of a wealthy slave-born merchant of the early to mid-nineteenth century named London Bourne, owned three slaves himself before manumitting his wife and

98. CO 28/95, Barbados 1650, President Skeete to Bathurst, 6 July 1825, enclosing papers relating to the petitions of Sam Gabriel Ford and W. C. Ford.

99. Handler, Hughes, and Wiltshire, *Freedmen of Barbados,* 21.

adult children in England in 1818. His son London owned three slaves in right of his wife, but went to great lengths to manumit slave family members.[100]

Free people also rented their relations from their owners in exchange for the privilege of having them live with them. Most references to such rental arrangements relate to free men of color renting their enslaved kin. In response to a question from the 1831–1832 House of Commons commission on slavery as to how a free man of color could survive in the West Indies, a Jamaican plantation manager stated that one option was for such men to

> form connections with slave women, and establish themselves in villages; and in right of their wives occupy lands belonging to the owners of the estates. I knew one of them . . . who rented two acres of land, and he paid 30s. for an acre of land; so that his ground rent was £3. He was a married man, but his wife was a slave, and he had to pay a rent for her; he paid £18 a year for her; that was in order to ensure her living with him; and besides that he supported himself, and in a great measure his wife. She was occasionally with her mistress, but when she was with him he supported her, and himself and the children, and did militia duty; and I believe he had nothing but those two acres of land, because he came down to borrow money from me to manumise [sic] his wife, and a certain sum was wanted to make up the balance; he could not accomplish the freedom of his wife.[101]

Others who were unable to buy their kin out of freedom used such rental arrangements as a means to help them run away. In late 1832 a newspaper advertisement from the owner of a slave named Nanny Flora stated that she was probably being harbored by her husband, a free black tailor, who had pretended to hire her but never paid the rent for her and was now in debt to her owner.[102]

People who used legal channels to save themselves or their relatives from slavery often found themselves embroiled in complicated legal battles that only made the possibility of freedom more tenuous. A frequent cause of legal disputes and loss of freedom was the discovery that manumission fees had not been paid. Upon such a discovery, people who had believed they were free might find them-

100. Karch, "Man for All Seasons," 2–3.
101. PP 1831–1832, vol. 20, *Report from select committee*, 18.
102. *Barbadian*, 24 December 1832.

selves escheated to the Crown as public property to be sold at auction or, worse, confronted by the next of kin of a deceased owner who claimed a legal right to inherit them.

In the early nineteenth century several free people of color appealed to colonial and imperial authorities to spare them from reenslavement. Such cases reveal the precariousness of freedom and the determination with which people fought to secure that status for their relatives. In 1823 a free Afro-Barbadian woman named Harriet Burke, who had been living as a free woman for twenty-seven years, appealed to the crown via the secretary of state for the colonies, Lord Bathurst, when the freedom of one of her children was threatened. Four of her children had been born after her manumission, making them legally free from birth, but in 1804 her second child was "when an infant, seized by a relation of her former mistress, and conveyed into the Country." The governor at the time of the abduction gave her permission to reclaim him, which she did, but he was stolen again and sold. Harriet found herself in worse difficulties in 1823, when in response to her latest petition for her son's freedom, the governor and the attorney general ruled that her deceased owner had committed various legal errors, as a result of which neither Harriet nor her children had ever been legally free. Although the Crown apparently found in her favor, she was nevertheless removed from the St. Michael Vestry almshouse list and lost her manumission annuity. When she appealed again in 1833 for ten years' retroactive manumission payments, the vestry prosecuted her.[103]

Sarah Stewart, a woman who claimed that her owner Margaret Stewart had manumitted her in 1794, fought to her dying day to save her children from enslavement. When Margaret Stewart died in the 1810s, her son-in-law, John Francis Gill, tried to claim Sarah and her children as his slaves. Sarah's appeals against his claim spanned the administrations of four governors between the 1810s and 1829. In reviewing Sarah's last appeal before she died, Acting Protector of Slaves John Mayers stated that he suspected her case was invalid because Margaret only had a life interest in Sarah and therefore had no legal right to manumit her.[104] Furthermore, Margaret had never paid the required manumission deposit. Mayers also suspected that Sarah's manumission documents were forged. The slave registra-

103. CO 31/4, 10 June 1823; Minutes of the St. Michael Vestry, 5 August 1833.

104. The office of protector of slaves was created under the Consolidated Slave Act of 1826 and is discussed in chapter 3, pp. 97–98, and chapter 4, pp. 125–126.

tion records of 1820 to 1829 listed Sarah and two of her sons as the property of John Francis Gill, and Sarah died shortly after the 1829 return was taken. Because she was a woman, Sarah's legal predicament endangered every generation of her family, as Mayers noted that "it is alleged [Sarah] has left other Children and Grand Children not yet met with by John Francis Gill so as to be taken into possession."[105]

Manumission battles could become even more complicated when the slave owners involved were Afro-Barbadians who died intestate and whose slaves had constituted their principle form of property. One such manumission battle offers hints of the messy interpersonal relationships that developed between slaves and impoverished Afro-Barbadian slave owners. Jane Denny and her children were owned by a free woman of color, Agnes Charlotte Denny, who died intestate. Upon her death in 1829, they were escheated to the crown, whereupon Jane Denny petitioned for their freedom on the grounds that, as Agnes's children were illegitimate and there were no debts to be settled on Agnes's estate, there was no reason for them to continue in slavery. The board decided the case in their favor, however, Agnes's daughter, Hannah Maria Denny, intervened and argued that Agnes's children needed the Denny slaves in order to sell them and settle their mother's outstanding debts. They argued that, if the board's manumission order were to be carried out, "[Agnes's children] will want food & a shelter, as their mother owes more than the house is worth." Upon hearing of the intention of Agnes's daughter, Hannah Maria, to claim and sell her and her children, Jane Denny sent a desperate petition to the Board of Treasury in which she alleged that "through the influence of the said Hannah Maria Denny, and her Friends, your Memorialist with her Children and Grand Child, may be doomed to a state of perpetual Slavery, and thereby fall into the hands of the said Hannah Maria Denny who is her inveterate Enemy." Jane claimed that Hannah Maria was lying to the acting protector of slaves and that she only wished "to obtain the possession of your Memorialists, Children, and Grand Child, by any Means whatever, to render their future existence wretched and miserable." Jane sought to strengthen her case by claiming a respectable connection with a white free man, the children's father, stating that "[Jane's] children are by one father, a Gentleman descended from one of the first families in this Island, but now reduced by Misfortune to the greatest Adversity,

105. CO 28/105, No. 71, Governor James Lyon to Sir George Murray, 30 April 1830, enclosing documents relating to the petition of Sarah Stewart.

and not in his power to render any service to his Children, much less to emancipate them from the Cruel Yoke of Slavery."[106]

Even if far more women than men of color were slave owners, slavery was also central to the expression of free Afro-Barbadian masculinity. All free men, regardless of color, had to serve in the militia, a military institution that existed throughout the British West Indies for protection against both external invasion and slave rebellion. Established in Barbados in the 1630s, militia duty was mandatory for all free men between fifteen and sixty years of age. The militia system was also an attempt by slave-owning states to preserve white population numbers and the economic viability of the white patriarchal family. Every estate was responsible for providing one militia tenant for a certain number of slaves or acres of land that the estate owned and had to provide that man with a small amount of land for the support of himself and his family.[107] However, joining the militia became a rite of passage through which Afro-Barbadian men who were maroons or newly freed from slavery asserted their free status. In 1814, one hundred dollars was offered for a Barbadian tailor named Daniel Lewis, who "absconded" from Fort Royal in Martinique during its time under British administration, where he now

passed himself off as a free man, and as such, actually served in Mr. David's company of militia, Fort Royal, whereby establishing his freedom there, having a paper or certificate in his possession (which was sworn to by a white person) purporting to be the freedom of Barbados, signed John Lucomb, Church Warden; that £300 had been lodged for that purpose, which proves to be a forgery. Daniel is generally well known in and about Fort Royal and St. Pierre, and all the Barbadian people there know him to be the Slave of Mrs. Lewis above-mentioned, although he associated with free people of color at Martinique, who are now supposed to secrete [sic] him.[108]

106. CO 28/106, Treasury correspondence 21220 29/12 S. 75, Lord Commissioners of the Treasury to Horace Twiss, 6 January 1830, enclosing documents relating to the petition of Jane Denny in behalf of herself and Children . . . and her Grand Child . . . 26 March 1830. The imperial Board of the Treasury was the final arbitrating body in disputes over the property of the deceased. The outcome of this case is discussed in chapter 3, p. 98.

107. James Handler, "Freedmen and Slaves in the Barbados Militia," *JCH* 19 (1984): 7.

108. *BMBG*, 7 June 1814. Martinique was captured and held by the British from 1803 until the end of the war.

Men of color were barred from positions as commissioned officers in the militia, but by 1816 there were 1,726 white and 473 enlisted Afro-Barbadian men.[109] Although no records were kept of their numbers, some free men of color also held militia tenancies by the nineteenth century.[110] At the beginning of the post-emancipation period in 1838 a writer to the *Liberal* newspaper described Barbados as a place "where the ingenuity of our legislators can hardly even *now* preserve the preponderance [of white men] in our Militia."[111]

CONCLUSION

By the nineteenth century, free people of color were an integral part of the Barbadian social fabric, simultaneously challenging and reinforcing the sociolegal inequalities on which slavery was built. The majority of free Afro-Barbadians shared their social and working lives with slaves but a significant minority of them was also directly implicated in the slave system as owners of human property. The number of slave owners of color remained stagnant in the final decades of slavery, however, meaning that, while there was a stable group of nonwhite slave owners, the overall economic stake of free Afro-Barbadians in the maintenance of slavery was decreasing with time. The period of the most rapid growth in the size of the island's free population of African descent coincided with the upheavals of the French and Haitian revolutions. These events transformed the Atlantic world, creating a new political climate within which free people of color in many Caribbean territories, including Barbados, would begin to redefine both their sense of their own identity and their relationships with slaves and slavery.

109. Handler, "Freedmen and Slaves"; Nathaniel Lucas Mss., "General Return of the Militia of Barbados," 24 April 1816, 405, Microfilm 17, BPL (hereafter cited as Lucas Mss.). For comparison see Herbert Klein, "The Colored Freedmen in Brazilian Slave Society," *JSH* 3 (1969): 31–33.

110. CO 31/47, 21 January, 8 February, and 31 March 1818.

111. *Liberal,* 1 August 1838.

2 / RACE AND POLITICS IN AN AGE OF INSURRECTION

I N 1789 the French Revolution exploded onto the political scene of the Atlantic world. In Saint Domingue, the only successful antislavery revolution in Caribbean history began in 1791 and drew on traditions of African and Afro-creole slave resistance, the wealth, education, and determination of the largest free population of color in the Caribbean and the democratic ideals of the French Revolution. By 1804 former slaves and free people of color in the former French colony, which was now renamed Haiti, had succeeded in forming a fractious but powerful alliance that overthrew both slavery and French colonial rule. The revolutionary wave also swept the French-speaking territories of the eastern Caribbean, with uprisings in Martinique, Guadeloupe, and the British-ruled but predominantly francophone island of Grenada.[1] These uprisings and conspiracies brought radical conceptions of freedom, democratic governance, and universal equality almost to the shores of Barbados, the oldest bastion of entrenched planter power and white supremacy in the British Caribbean.

If most of the eighteenth century was marked by the widespread consolidation of slave regimes, the final decades were notable for the emergence of the first significant metropolitan challenges to slavery's legitimacy. In the 1770s and 1780s, opposition to the slave trade and slavery grew, fueled by landmark legal cases that undermined slavery on metropolitan soil, concerted political efforts to outlaw the slave trade and by the appearance of abolitionist societies, notably

1. Laurent Dubois, *A Colony of Citizens: Revolution and Slave Emancipation in the French Caribbean, 1787–1804* (Chapel Hill: University of North Carolina Press, 2004); David Geggus, "The Slaves and Free Coloreds of Martinique during the Age of the French and Haitian Revolutions: Three Moments of Resistance," in Robert L. Paquette and Stanley L. Engerman, eds., *The Lesser Antilles in the Age of European Expansion* (Gainesville: University Press of Florida, 1996), 280–301; Anne Pérotin-Dumon, "Free Coloreds and Slaves in Revolutionary Guadeloupe: Politics and Political Consciousness," in Paquette and Engerman, *Lesser Antilles in the Age of European Expansion*, 259–279; Gaspar and Geggus, *Turbulent Time.*

in Britain and France. With the help of antislavery lawyers, enslaved people resident in Europe sued their owners for their freedom, drawing on traditions that discouraged slavery in several European states. The question of civil rights for free people of color was one of the earliest flashpoints of the French and Haitian Revolutions. Noted free people of color, such as Olaudah Equiano and Vincent Ogé of Saint Domingue, agitated against slavery and racial discrimination in the colonies. Finally, the growing presence of free populations of African descent in Europe and the Americas—such as London's "black poor" and black loyalist refugees who fled the thirteen colonies of the United States after the defeat of the British in the 1780s—raised fundamental civil rights questions. Should these people be allowed to settle wherever they chose, including the metropole? Should they be given the same rights and privileges as whites? Could they be "citizens"?[2]

Just as major attacks on their civil rights propelled Saint Domingue's *gens de couleur* into the fray of revolutionary politics, free people of color in the British Caribbean responded to the climate of revolution and repression with collective efforts to defend and expand their civil rights. The response of free Afro-Barbadians to the reformist and revolutionary movements of the late eighteenth and early nineteenth centuries reflected this group's rapid growth and increasing internal socioeconomic stratification. By the 1790s, a clearly identifiable socioeconomic elite of color, distinct from laboring-class free blacks and coloreds, had appeared in several anglophone Caribbean colonies. Strictly speaking, the Afro-Barbadians who had the greatest social, cultural, and economic capital, who were overwhelmingly merchants, small propertyholders, and tradesmen, constituted a part of the island's bourgeoisie. However, they were the socioeconomic elite among the nonwhite population, and for the purposes of this study they will be referred to as the "Afro-Barbadian elite." In terms of the racial order in the colony and in the Atlantic world, they were very much subaltern.

Elite Afro-Barbadians sought to distinguish themselves from the majority of people of African descent by emphasizing their class superiority over other free Afro-Barbadians and identifying themselves with the institutions of slavery and planter rule. A well-to-do minority of free men of color asserted its right to be included in areas of public life reserved for white men.[3] They said nothing, however,

2. Blackburn, *Overthrow of Colonial Slavery*; Dubois, *Colony of Citizens*, 98–104; Lawrence C. Jennings, *French Anti-Slavery: The Movement for the Abolition of Slavery in France* (Cambridge University Press, 2000); Peabody, *There Are No Slaves in France*.

3. Handler and Sio, "Barbados," 254–257; Sio, "Marginality," 153.

about civil rights either for the less well-to-do or free women of color. Yet even as these men sought to gain rights by repudiating many of the democratic ideas and possibilities of the French and Haitian Revolutions, their challenge to the principle of racial exclusion laid the groundwork for a new kind of antiracist politics and Afro-Barbadian political collectivity, helping to generate other, far less conciliatory countercurrents of political thought among lower-class Afro-Barbadians, free and slave.

THE EMERGENCE OF THE FREE AFRO-BARBADIAN ELITE

The Barbadian legislature had a poor track record when it came to successfully enforcing laws that directly restricted the economic activities of free people of color. In the spheres of formal politics and judicial rights, however, state repression against free Afro-Barbadians was far more effective. A 1721 law limited the qualification for the vote, holding of elective office, and jury duty to white males who were at least twenty-one years old, British subjects, Christians, and the owners of at least ten acres of land or a house with an annual taxable value of at least ten pounds. The law also specified that "no person whatsoever . . . whose original extraction shall be proved to have been from a Negro" could testify in a court of law. As Handler states the 1721 law deprived free people of color "of a major device that protected against assault, theft, and similar offenses against property and person." The loss of the right to testify "made it more difficult to win cases and to validate claims to free status."[4]

A 1739 law permitting slaves to testify against free people of color increased the legal vulnerability of free Afro-Barbadians since it did not permit them to testify. The act recognized that, given the close relations between free and enslaved people of color, a slave might be the only witness to crimes allegedly committed by free people of African descent. Rather than being an act for the amelioration of slavery, this law "made it less cumbersome for whites to recover stolen property or press charges against freedmen" accused of engaging in illegal trade with slaves. Slaves could not testify against whites, and free people of color could not testify at all, thereby ensuring that, without the assistance of white witnesses, no Afro-Barbadian, slave or free, had any effective means of legal defense against whites.[5]

There were some rights free people of color shared with whites but it is likely

4. Handler, *Unappropriated People*, 67–68.
5. Ibid., 69.

that the exercise of these rights was severely restricted in practice. Laws of 1649 and 1688 made it illegal for slaves to strike or use any "insolent language or gesture" against a free person, regardless of color. However, it is difficult to see how this right could have been defended once free Afro-Barbadians lost the right to testify in court.[6] Unlike Jamaica and Antigua, there were no legal restrictions on their right to own property, but this reflected the fact that the Barbadian plantocracy's monopoly of most of the island's arable land made it impossible for the island to develop an equivalent to the large and powerful "colored" planter classes of Jamaica, Saint Domingue, and other islands of the Lesser Antilles.[7] There were no laws, such as those passed in Saint Domingue, barring free Afro-Barbadians from the professions, although social discrimination was enough to prevent qualified people of color from practicing any profession in Barbados.

This repressive social, economic and legal apparatus was sufficient to limit the development of a self-sustaining free Afro-Barbadian elite of planters and merchants. There were always a few comparatively privileged free Afro-Barbadians but they appear to have been extremely rare before the end of the eighteenth century.[8] The earliest group of prosperous free people of color was likely composed of the mistresses and the mixed-race offspring of wealthy white men but we cannot be certain what chances these women and their children had of inheriting property or gaining long-term financial security as a result of these relationships. Some extremely light-complexioned people of African descent may have achieved social "whiteness" and entered the ranks of white society rather than becoming the nucleus of an Afro-Barbadian elite.

Only in the latter half of the eighteenth century did the number of wealthy free people of color become a noticeable feature of the island's socioeconomic landscape, especially in towns. In Barbados, as elsewhere in the British Caribbean dur-

6. Ibid., 70–72; Heuman, *Between Black and White,* 5–6.

7. In 1831, only 75 free people of color in Barbados had taxable property worth more than thirty pounds a year. By contrast, in St. Domingue on the eve of the revolution, free people of color owned one-third of the land and one-fourth of the slaves. Handler, *Unappropriated People;* Laura Foner, "The Free People of Color in Louisiana and St. Domingue," *JSH* 3, no. 3 (1970): 425. And in 1826, the Jamaican legislature classified 400 of the island's 28,800 free nonwhites as "rich," found 5,500 living in "fair circumstances," and described the remainder as "absolutely poor." Sio, "Race, Colour and Miscegenation," 12. On laws restricting Afro-Antiguan property ownership, see Lowes, "Peculiar Class," 130.

8. Jerome Handler, "Joseph Rachell and Rachael Pringle-Polgreen: Petty Entrepreneurs," in D. G. Sweet and G. B. Nash, eds., *Struggle and Survival in Colonial America* (Berkeley and Los Angeles: University of California Press, 1981), 276–291.

ing the same period, some free women of color established themselves as urban hoteliers and madams, both significant economic sectors in Caribbean port cities. By the last decade of the century a small number of Afro-Barbadian hucksters and shopkeepers, often former slave women, accumulated wealth, sometimes enough to buy family members out of slavery and bequeath significant amounts of property. During the 1790s, the symbol of nonwhite business success in Barbados was the female hotelier, most vividly commemorated in a 1796 engraving of Bridgetown innkeeper Rachael Pringle-Polgreen. The mistress of a white man who had bought her freedom, Pringle-Polgreen became one of the richest businesswomen of the 1780s and 1790s. She died in 1791, leaving property that included nineteen slaves.[9] In the early nineteenth century free Afro-Barbadian women such as Betsy Austin, Sabrina Brade, Hannah Lewis, and Susannah Ostrehan ran the most popular taverns in Bridgetown.[10]

By the end of the eighteenth century the number of free people of color had increased sufficiently for their presence to attract attention from William Dickson, the governor's private secretary and an early commentator on West Indian slavery. Dickson specifically addressed a section of his work *Letters on Slavery* to "the Free Negroes of Barbadoes and to the more enlightened and regular of the Slaves." The growth of the free population of color worried the colonial legislature. In contrast to 1744, when the House of Assembly overwhelmingly voted down a bill to raise the cost of manumitting female slaves, a bill to raise manumission fees by 600 percent for women and 400 percent for men passed with little opposition in 1801.[11] One might surmise that, as in Saint Domingue during the same interval, white lawmakers' desire to limit manumissions was inspired by the appearance of a distinct black and mixed-race bourgeoisie, many of them the children of free women of color who had come into property through relations with wealthy white men.[12] An Afro-Barbadian male merchant elite of color, some of whose businesses were fairly substantial enterprises, also established itself in the island's towns. One of

9. Handler, "Joseph Rachell"; Handler, Hughes, and Wiltshire, *Freedmen of Barbados,* 43.

10. Bayley, *Four Years' Residence,* 27–28, 149–150; Handler, *Unappropriated People,* 33–37; William Lloyd, *Letter from the West Indies, During a Visit of 1836, and the spring of 1837* (London: N.p., 1839), 7. For comparison, see Paulette Kerr, "Victims or Strategists? Female Lodging-House Keepers in Jamaica," in Verene Shepherd, Bridget Brereton, and Barbara Bailey, *Engendering History: Caribbean Women in Historical Perspective* (Kingston: Ian Randle, 1995), 197–212.

11. Handler, *Unappropriated People,* 33–34, 40. See chapter 1, p. 37, of the present volume.

12. John D. Garrigus, "Redrawing the Color Line: Gender and the Social Construction of Race in Pre-Revolutionary Haiti," *JCH* 30, nos. 1–2 (1996): 28–50.

the wealthiest Afro-Barbadian merchants of the early nineteenth century, London
Bourne, owned three stores in Bridgetown, a large house, and had assets worth
between twenty and thirty thousand dollars.[13] With the exception of only four
planter families of African descent identified for the period between 1780 and
1834, such men and their families became the most affluent group of color in the
island.[14]

While some children of color were sent to school abroad to receive a classical
education, most boys and girls of color would have had at most vocational training in Barbados. Some men of color were extremely well educated, either through
the agency of a family member or their own efforts.[15] Boys had a better chance of
receiving a sound education than girls who, like their white counterparts, probably had only such instruction as was considered necessary to make them "ladylike," including singing, dancing, reading, writing, and training in the "domestic
arts." Descriptions of the lifestyles of free people of color in the British Caribbean
are rare, but in 1837 American abolitionists James Thome and Horace Kimball met
Joseph Thorne, a prominent free man of color, his wife and two other "coloured
gentlemen"—the Methodist minister Joseph Hamilton and the Bridgetown merchant Thomas J. Cummins—at Thorne's home. Thorne, who had been a slave until
he reached the age of twenty sometime around the turn of the century, afterward
became a Bridgetown merchant and shoemaker. At some point in his early life
Thorne had been exposed to a good education, which must have included vocational training, reading, and writing, and a thorough knowledge of the Bible, as he
became a highly respected Anglican lay catechist. Given that the Anglican Church
in Barbados never ordained black and colored men as clergy, Thorne's theological
knowledge probably far exceeded what one might expect of a lay catechist. Thome
and Kimball's description of his parlor is valuable as a unique glimpse into the domestic life of a privileged free person of color in Barbados during the nineteenth
century. They were struck by the "scientific appearance" of the room:

> On one side was a large library of religious, historical, and literary works,
> the selection of which displayed no small taste and judgment. On the op-

13. Thome and Kimball, *Emancipation in the West Indies*, 75.

14. Bayley, *Four Years' Residence*, 27–28, 149–150; Handler, *Unappropriated People*, 33–37, 84, 121;
Lloyd, *Letter from the West Indies*, 7; Pedro Welch and Richard Goodridge, *"Red" and Black over White:
Free Coloured Women in Pre-Emancipation Barbados* (Bridgetown: Carib Research and Publications,
2000), 72–78.

15. Watson, *Civilised Island*, 213.

posite side of the room was a fine cabinet of minerals and shells. In one corner stood a number of curious relics of the aboriginal Caribs, such as bows and arrows, etc., together with interesting fossil remains. On the tops of the books-cases and mineral stand, were birds of rare species, procured from the South American Continent. The centre table was ornamented with shells, specimens of petrifactions, and elegantly bound books. The remainder of the furniture of the room was costly and elegant.[16]

But for the largely Caribbean and South American origins of his artefacts and curios, Thorne's parlor would not have seemed out of place in a typical bourgeois, mid-nineteenth-century metropolitan British home. It was a display of middle-class colonial values, a demonstration of a "respectable" education and taste, as well as a constant, and—in the eyes of Victorians—"manly" quest for self-improvement and amateur curiosity about the natural world.

Mixed-race people may have been somewhat more likely than those of darker complexion to be wealthy.[17] The slave registries certainly suggest that they owned more slaves, with slave owners classified as "mulatto" far outnumbering those listed as "negro." However, Barbados lacked the finely graded distinctions of color that led to the development of a coherent mixed-race or colored sense of identity in several other Caribbean territories. Mixed-race people in Barbados did not enjoy special legal privileges, nor was the enmity that characterized social and political relations between free blacks and free coloreds elsewhere such a significant feature of social relations.[18] Winthrop D. Jordan has argued that different attitudes among whites toward "miscegenation" made mixed-race people more acceptable to whites in Jamaica than in Barbados. Arnold Sio challenges this claim, saying that mixed-race people faced less severe legal discrimination in Jamaica than in Barbados only because Jamaican whites were less secure in

16. Thome and Kimball, *Emancipation in the West Indies,* 73.

17. Neville Connell, "Hotel Keepers and Hotels in Barbados," *JBMHS* 33, no. 4 (1970); Handler, *Unappropriated People,* 41–42, 56–59, 130–133; Higman, *Slave Populations,* 192.

18. For information about relations between people of mixed race and those of darker color, as well as free nonwhite property ownership, see Campbell, "Trinidad's Free Coloureds," 603–604; Foner, "Free People of Color," 425; Handler and Sio, "Barbados," 247–248; Heuman, *Between Black and White,* 36 and 46; Harry Hoetink, "Surinam and Curaçao," in Cohen and Greene, *Neither Slave nor Free,* 64–84; Lennox Honeychurch, *The Dominica Story: A History of the Island* (London: Macmillan Education, 1995), 100–102; Levy, *Emancipation, Sugar, and Federalism,* 31; Sio, "Race, Colour and Miscegenation," 12; Watson, *Civilised Island,* 190.

their position than their Barbadian counterparts and sought to "co-opt" mixed race people to preserve their own position.[19] Prevailing color stereotypes among whites, reflected both in their preference for mixed-race women as domestics and as mistresses, meant that mixed-race Barbadian women likely significantly outnumbered black women among the mistresses of white men. However, the color imbalance would have been less stark among independently wealthy businessmen and women.[20]

Although free people of color as a group owned far fewer slaves than did whites, slave ownership was important to the economic advancement and survival of elite Afro-Barbadians. By the 1820s the prominent Belgrave family owned sugar estates and numerous slaves in the southern parishes of St. Philip and Christ Church.[21] Successful black and colored entrepreneurs used slave labor in their businesses. Tavern keepers used slave chambermaids and prostitutes in their establishments. Many of the island's wealthiest Afro-Barbadian merchants were both slave owners and counted rural plantations among their most valued customers.[22]

Thus, around the turn of the century, a stratum of economically privileged, male, and sometimes well educated Afro-Barbadian entrepreneurs was consolidating itself in the island's towns, particularly Bridgetown. Men such as the planter Jacob Belgrave and the merchants Joseph Thorne, John Montefiore, Thomas J. Cummins, and William Bourne must have suffered numerous indignities at the hands of whites. They would have seen white men no more clever than they were gaining access to influential political circles and using the courts to defend their interests, exercising privileges of which the wealthiest Afro-Barbadian woman or man could only dream. Free people of color in Barbados must have bitterly resented their legal disadvantages long before the 1790s, but the revolutionary up-

19. Winthrop D. Jordan, *White Over Black: American Attitudes towards the Negro, 1550–1812* (Chapel Hill: University of North Carolina Press, 1968), 174–178; Sio, "Race, Colour and Miscegenation," 21.

20. For example, Thome and Kimball described Joseph Thorne as being "of dark mulatto complexion, with the negro features and hair" and London Bourne and his wife as being "of the glossiest jet." Thome and Kimball, *Emancipation in the West Indies,* 74–75.

21. In 1817 Jacob Belgrave owned the Ruby estate in St. Philip with 238 slaves (T71 520, Barbados Slave Registries, 1817). In 1829 his son owned 29 slaves (T71/546, Barbados Slave Registries, 1829); Handler, Hughes, and Wiltshire, *Freedmen of Barbados,* 4–5.

22. On Afro-Barbadian slave owners and merchants John Montefiore, Thomas J. Cummins, and William Bourne, see *BMBG,* 29 November 1823; Newcastle and Bissex Hill Plantation Journals, n.d. [early 1820s], BMHS; Handler, Hughes, and Wiltshire, *Freedmen of Barbados,* 15; *Barbadian,* 8 July 1825; Karch, "Man for All Seasons."

heavals of the late eighteenth century lent both opportunity and a sense of urgency to those well-to-do men who wished to challenge racial segregation.

THE BEGINNING OF THE CIVIL RIGHTS STRUGGLE

The ideas of "liberty, equality, and fraternity," once in the hands of people of African descent, represented a danger potentially more threatening to the Caribbean's white minorities than any invading European navy. During the 1790s, free Afro-Barbadians came under a cloud of increasing suspicion as whites received news of insurrections involving free Afro-Caribbean people elsewhere. Besides the Haitian Revolution, the antislavery rebellion of 1795–1796 in Grenada, led by the wealthy free colored planter Julien Fedon, struck terror into the hearts of white Barbadians. White reactionary sentiment reached fever pitch in 1796, when a Barbadian free man of color named Joe Denny was accused of murdering his white neighbor, John Stroud. Although it was obvious that the murder had been an accident, Denny was sentenced to death. The case became a focal point for whites' deep-seated racial hostilities, with powerful popular pressure exerted to have Denny executed. Whites responded to news that the imperial government had commuted Denny's sentence to transportation for life by rioting. The fact that Governor Ricketts had a free colored mistress, who had accompanied him from Tobago and lived openly with him as his common law wife, dramatically increased white outrage. The mistress, Betsy Goodwin, was cast as something of a Marie Antoinette figure, exerting too much power over the throne, and it was widely rumored that she had influenced the governor's decision. The Denny case highlighted free Afro-Barbadians' legal vulnerability, since, as people of color, neither Denny nor any of the witnesses to the murder could testify.[23]

The case led a group of fifty-eight free men of color to write to the governor asking for the civil right to testify in court. The tone of these petitioners stood in stark contrast to the more radical expressions and activities of their counterparts elsewhere in the Lesser Antilles during the 1790s. This petition, like those that would follow it for many years to come, was phrased in deferential terms. The authors stated that they accepted the necessity of their "subordinate state" within Barbadian slave society, thereby distancing themselves from the more democratic concept of universal civil rights. The signatories to this petition, some of whom

23. Neville Hall, "Law and Society in Barbados at the Turn of the Nineteenth Century," *JCH* 5 (1972): 32–38; Handler, *Unappropriated People*, 73–74.

were slave owners, expressed enthusiastic support for slavery. They pressed their claim by arguing that "if a white man may murder a Free Coloured man, and escape the punishment of such laws, then we have no security for our lives, and we are in a much worse condition than our slaves."[24]

In 1803 the House of Assembly received an equally proslavery petition, allegedly signed by over three hundred free men of color, asking it to reject a bill that would have limited their rights to acquire and bequeath land and slaves. The planter who proposed the law stated that it was intended to preempt the possibility of an insurrection like Grenada's Fedon Rebellion. It was probably not coincidental that the bill surfaced shortly before the final desperate battle by free people of color and slaves against Napoleon's efforts to reimpose slavery in Saint Domingue. In opposing the bill the Afro-Barbadian petitioners were at pains to distance themselves from any antislavery radicalism and to make their support for slavery clear:

> Although we have all our lives been accustomed to the assistance of slaves, we must immediately deprive ourselves of them and perform every menial office with our own hands. . . . Many of our children who are now grown almost to the years of maturity have from their earliest infancy been accustomed to be attended by slaves; if this bill should pass into law, when we are no more, these children cannot possess a single slave. What will then be the meaning of their condition? Surely death would be preferable to such a situation![25]

This was followed by a petition to the House of Assembly in 1811, signed by 172 free men of color, and a memorial to the governor in 1812, both requesting the right to testify in court.[26]

It is instructive that, of all these early petitions, that of 1803, the only petition appealing for equal rights of slave ownership, carried the most signatures. The three hundred people who signed the petition probably accounted for most of the

24. Lucas Mss.; Minutes of the Barbados Council, 15 October 1799, "The Humble Memorial and Remonstrance of the Free Coloured People . . . ," 14 October 1799, cited in Handler, *Unappropriated People*, 76.

25. "The Humble Petition of the Free Coloured People, Inhabitants of the Island," cited in ibid., 147; Beckles, *Black Rebellion*, 82–83.

26. Handler, Hughes, and Wiltshire, *Freedmen of Barbados*, v.

Afro-Barbadian slave owners in the island at the time. Of the petitions requesting the right to give testimony, that of 1811 was the largest, and it is probable that only the most affluent Afro-Barbadian men were invited to sign it. The signatories included the most prominent men of color in the island, such as the planter Jacob Belgrave Jr. and the merchant William Bourne Sr. The issues of property bequests and the threatened limits to acquisition of property were irrelevant to the majority of free people of color, few of whom left written wills or possessed enough property to be affected by the proposed law. It is highly unlikely that the majority of free people of color had any part in the preparation of these documents and they cannot be assumed to represent the views of all or even most free Afro-Barbadians.

A PERNICIOUS INFLUENCE

As long as the Haitian Revolution and the wars with France raged across the Caribbean, Barbadian planters were unwilling to consider the requests made in these petitions from the Afro-Barbadian elite and either ignored them or dismissed them as impertinent. But as the revolutionary wars drew to a close, voices of dissent began to resurface. When the wars ended, aristocrats on both sides of the British Atlantic found themselves facing new levels of organized public opposition to their authority in the form of violent demands for political reform and mass anti-slavery organizing. The resurgence of abolitionism in Britain and a slave insurrection in Barbados provided the catalyst for the male Afro-Barbadian elite's political breakthrough. In the face of these greater threats, by the latter years of the 1810s, the Barbadian plantocracy would find legislative concessions to the proslavery and pro-planter elite of color to be a far more attractive political option than a few years before.

Abolitionists had hoped that the end of the slave trade would force British Caribbean slave owners to encourage natural population increase and improve slaves' living conditions. By 1811, however, there were suspicions that the slave populations of the West Indies were declining without imports and that slave trading continued illegally within the Caribbean. As a result of these concerns, in 1812 the abolitionist lobby in the British Parliament succeeded in getting the imperial government to pass an act in the crown colonies forcing slave owners to register their slaves and self-governing colonies such as Barbados were pressured to pass similar laws. The establishment of slave population registers in the 1810s revealed that, with the exception of Barbados, the slave populations of all of the sugar colonies were declining without slave imports.[27]

Toward the end of 1815 there was a highly public debate between the Barbadian legislature and the imperial government over the establishment of a slave registry in Barbados. The legislature claimed that the bill's abolitionist supporters harbored the "ultimate object" of slave emancipation. Throughout the island planters openly expressed their fear that, particularly after recent events in Haiti, the registration bill would raise slaves' hopes of emancipation and incite them to rebel. Finally, in November, the legislature rejected the imperial registration bill.[28] The substance of the debate reached enslaved and free working-class Afro-Barbadians in fragmented form. By the end of 1815, slaves and some free people of color were convinced the registry bill was in fact an imperial emancipation bill, which the local assembly was blocking.[29] Believing that they had imperial support, slaves followed the example of Saint Domingue and carried out the island's first and only armed slave uprising in April 1816.[30]

Prior to the night of April 14, 1816, no slave conspiracies had been uncovered in Barbados for more than a century.[31] The 1816 rebellion's timing was directly connected to the changing political climate of the post–Napoleonic era. It was the first of three major slave insurrections to take place in the British Caribbean in the last two decades of slavery, with increasing intensity, the second occurring in Demerara on 1823 and the last and most extensive in Jamaica in 1830–1831. Each rebellion illustrated growing social instabilities as the enslaved added their voices

27. Barry Higman, *Slave Populations,* 72–75. Crown colonies were recently captured colonies, mostly taken from the French, Spanish, and Dutch at the end of the eighteenth century, which were ruled directly by the Colonial Office through a governor rather than via a colonial legislature.

28. Beckles, *Black Rebellion,* 92–93; *BMBG,* 18 November 1815; CO 28/85, Miscellaneous, unnumbered, G. W. Jordan, agent for Barbados to Bathurst, 27 March 1816, enclosing petition from the Council and Assembly of Barbados to the Prince Regent, 17 January 1816.

29. Michael Craton, *Testing the Chains: Resistance to Slavery in the British West Indies* (Ithaca: Cornell University Press, 1982); Craton, "Proto-Peasant Revolts: The Late Slave Rebellions in the British West Indies, 1816–32," in Michael Craton, *Empire, Enslavement, and Freedom in the Caribbean* (Kingston: Ian Randle, 1997), 282–305.

30. See references to Saint Domingue in Barbados House of Assembly, *Report of a Select Committee of the House of Assembly appointed to enquire into the origin, causes, and progress, of the late Insurrection* (Barbados: T. Cadell and W. Davies, 1818), 7, 33–34 (hereafter cited as *1818 Report*).

31. John Poyer, *The History of Barbados, from the First Discovery of the Island, in the year 1605, till the Accession of Lord Seaforth, 1801* (London: Printed for J. Mawman, 1808), 174; Beckles, *Black Rebellion,* 52–85. Poyer cites the year of this last conspiracy as 1702, whereas Beckles gives the year as 1701.

to the debate over slavery's future. The 1816 rebellion is the least documented of the three major uprisings of the late slavery period. Unlike the Demerara and Jamaica rebellions, no parliamentary inquiry was conducted. An 1818 report from the Barbados House of Assembly is the only document containing slave testimony, and the only source providing information on the internal organization of the rebellion. However, the report is a problematic document, since, despite its stated aim, uncovering the root of the rebellion was not really its primary purpose. First and foremost, the legislature was refuting an abolitionist publication that asserted that slaves had rebelled because of poor treatment. Second, it was designed to convince the British public of the danger of championing abolition.[32]

The rebellion confirmed whites' fears about the potentially incendiary effects of the freedom with which slaves and free people of color moved about the island and engaged in close daily contact with each other. An estate physician interviewed for the 1818 report attributed the rebellion to "the great and rapid increase of the free coloured population; in so far as the slaves . . . might easily be led to conceive themselves to be as much entitled to freedom as the great number of their own colour who were free."[33] According to the report, slaves' "vague hope (and uncertain prospect) of freedom" was "strengthened by the information, imparted by some free People of Colour, as well as by some of the most daring of the Slaves (who had gained an ascendancy over their fellows by being enabled to read and write), and stated to have been obtained from the English Newspapers, which were occasionally produced and read . . . to enforce conviction on the minds of the hearers."[34]

Although most of the island's population was illiterate, information about the registry bill debate traveled around the island via the extensive network of links among free people of color and slaves. During the debate, whenever ships carrying the mail from England arrived, slaves and free people of color in Bridgetown would crowd around, eager to know the news. Slave and free hucksters, artisans, and other itinerant Afro-Barbadian workers transmitted information and details of newspaper reports along the island's internal trading routes.[35] In his deposition, King Wiltshire, a rebel slave from Bayley's plantation in St. Philip parish, where

32. The publication was the anonymously authored "Remarks on the Insurrection in Barbadoes, and the Bill for the Registration of Slaves," *Christian Observer* 15, no. 6 (June 1816): 403–414.

33. *1818 Report*, 52–54.

34. Ibid., 6–7.

35. Lucas Mss.,19 June 1816, 447–448.

the rebellion began, mentioned that the plantation's butler, Sampson, returned from the capital on Saturday, April 13, and said, "Well, this day's Newspaper has done our business,—for the Packet [mail from London] has arrived, and brought our freedom."[36] A letter that appeared in the *Mercury* newspaper a month after the rebellion called for strict regulation of "the vast swarms of coloured people who infest our streets and public roads, from one end of the Country to the other." The author blamed the "pernicious bias which was given to the minds of the slaves on the Plantations" by free people of color for the revolt.[37]

Hilary Beckles argues that free Afro-Barbadians were more active during the rebellion as militiamen helping to suppress the outbreak. He sees this as evidence of the immense social and political distance between slaves and free people of color: "Unlike the free-coloureds in other islands whose ideological expressions in relation to slaves and whites show much ambivalence, in Barbados their leadership was firmly pro-planter."[38] Nevertheless, the evidence of the role of free Afro-Barbadians in the rebellion suggests a more ambivalent political and social relationship between slaves and even elite free people of color. The role of free people of color in the revolt, as rebels or suppressors, was limited. Planters typically assumed that slaves were incapable of conceiving and plotting an event of such proportions without assistance from outsiders.[39] The report accused four free men of color—Cain Davis, John Richard Sarjeant, a man with the surname Roach, and Joseph Franklyn—of leading the revolt. Davis had slave children and Franklyn was the illegitimate son of a St. Philip planter who had freed him at fifteen and tried to leave him property in his will, which magistrates declared illegal on the dubious grounds that it was written under the influence of alcohol.[40] Davis, Sarjeant, and Roach seem to have lived in the St. Philip area, and according to a slave from Bayley's plantation, they spread rumors that freedom was "to be given to [the slaves] through a black woman who was a Queen, for whom Mr. [William] Wilberforce acted in England."[41] The report also alleged that a free man of color who lived near

36. *1818 Report*, 28. See Andrew Lewis, "'An Incendiary Press': British West Indian Newspapers during the Struggle for Abolition," *Slavery and Abolition* 16, no. 3 (December 1985): 359.

37. *BMBG*, 15 May 1816.

38. Beckles, "On the Backs of Blacks," 182.

39. *1818 Report*, 35–36.

40. Beckles, *Black Rebellion*, 180; Handler, *Unappropriated People*, 86. Five other free people of color were taken prisoner but released without trial. See Lucas Mss., Colonial General Orders, 10, 19, and 22 June 1816.

41. *1818 Report*, 33–34.

to the Thicket and River estates was seen helping to plan the rebellion, although the slave who testified to this said he could not remember the man's name.[42] In January 1819 an unknown number of slaves and free people of color, among them Cain Davis, were transported from the island as punishment for their alleged involvement in the insurrection. They were sent first to Honduras and then to Belize, but eventually eighty-eight survivors, including Davis, were shipped to Sierra Leone.[43]

The evidence of Franklyn's involvement in the rebellion is particularly shaky. A slave testified that Franklyn held frequent meetings with Jackey, the driver at Simmons plantation in St. Philip and an organizer of the rebellion, and was to be made governor of the island in the event of success.[44] However, this is the only evidence produced against him in the report, and it hardly supports claims that he was a rebel leader. Colonial authorities seem to have singled Franklyn out for reasons not directly connected to the revolt. In his journal, Nathaniel Lucas, a magistrate, assemblyman, and inspector of prisons during the uprising's suppression and the subsequent months of martial law, made special note of Franklyn's execution, which suggests that his death was an especially sweet victory for the plantocracy.[45] Both Franklyn and James Sarjeant had signed the 1811 petition requesting the right to testify in court, but Beckles speculates that "Franklyn's personal life experiences seemed to have driven him away from the 'moderate' politics of the free-coloured community and into the ambit of slave radicalism."[46]

The military tribunal's eagerness to implicate Franklyn despite all evidence to the contrary lends itself to speculation that Franklyn was indeed involved in what planters viewed as radical political activity, even if he had no direct connection to the revolt. Information on the political activities of slaves and free people of color was often ignored or suppressed by the governor, legislature, and the local press. It is possible that Franklyn and the other two men executed expressed political views that earned them the wrath of the legislature. A claim made many years later,

42. Ibid., 29–31.

43. Eighty-five of those transported to Sierra Leone survived. Although these Barbadians were initially subject to severe restrictions in terms of movement and labor in Sierra Leone, they eventually gained full freedom to move around the colony. Many became quite successful, such as Cain Davis, who enjoyed a career as a village superintendent by the 1840s. See Blyden, *West Indians in West Africa*, 35–37.

44. *1818 Report*, 26.

45. Lucas Mss., 29 June 1816, 392–393.

46. Beckles, *Black Rebellion*, 95; Handler, Hughes, and Wiltshire, *Freedmen of Barbados*, 20 and 47.

in 1838, by the *Liberal,* whose owners, Thomas Harris Jr. and Samuel Jackman Prescod, were men of color free before general emancipation, lends weight to this speculation. A *Liberal* editorial defiantly stated:

> There are some very respectable people who believe, to this day, that Frank-lyn was no more concerned in the rebellion of 1816 than the man in the moon. He was a man of bold independent spirit and therefore greatly dis-liked by those who then ruled the country with rods of iron—the oppor-tunity to get rid of him was too good a one to be lost, so he was hung [*sic*]. Had we, too, been [men] in those days, we, too, and dozens of others whom we can *now* point to with pleasure and with pride as co-operators in a good cause, would have been hung for the same reason that hung Franklyn—*We are too troublesome* to the Great. But, praised be God! those days of ram-pant iniquity are for ever flown—and to hang a man in these days, *with the semblance of law,* some better evidence must be found than that which hung Franklyn.[47]

Unable to build a case against Franklyn for insurrection, the legislature executed him on the vague charge of inciting others to revolt.[48] The hanging of Franklyn suggests that, even as some free Afro-Barbadian men sought to placate the planter assembly, others were giving voice to an altogether different brand of antiracist political thought.

While they were busy crushing the insurrection white colonial authorities praised the loyalty of "good" free men of color who supported the slave-owning cause during the rebellion. Contemporary reports made much of the devotion and courage of Afro-Barbadian militiamen who helped to suppress the insurrection and the free men of color in the Christ Church militia were singled out for spe-cial mention. In a private letter one militia colonel stated that the "free colour'd" in his regiment "behaved admirably. . . . They would dash singly into a house full of rebels without looking behind for support and dig out the fellows. It was this in-trepid courage that appalled the Blacks."[49] Such behavior would be entirely consis-

47. *Liberal,* 7 March 1838.

48. Hilton A. Vaughan, "Joseph Pitt Washington Francklyn, 1782–1816," *Democrat,* January 1971, cited in Beckles, *Black Rebellion,* 95.

49. Colonel John Rycroft Best to Abel Dottin, 27 April 1816, cited in Hilary Beckles, "The Slave-Drivers' War: Bussa and the 1816 Barbados Slave Rebellion," *Boletín de estudios latinoamericanos y del Caribe* 39 (December 1985): 97.

tent for people who for two decades had been desperately trying to prove their loyalty to powerful whites. But most free Afro-Barbadians, like the majority of slaves, played no part in the events of April 1816. Only two militia regiments fought in the rebellion, those of St. Michael and Christ Church.[50] Even if St. Michael accounted for 50 percent of the total number of free militiamen of color, there were only 463 "colored" militia privates in 1816 out of an estimated 3,007 free people of color. This number is too low to account for the entire Afro-Barbadian adult male population. The rebellion's organizers probably anticipated that most free people of color would not participate, and do not seem to have expected assistance from them, despite their role in providing information. They had no illusions that local free people of color, whatever their social ties to the enslaved, would translate such ties into armed solidarity. At the same time the organizers wrongly assumed that black imperial soldiers would support the rebellion, because they believed that the imperial government would back a slave uprising to obtain freedom that local white authorities were illegally withholding.[51]

ELITE AFRO-BARBADIANS AND
THE AFTERMATH OF THE REBELLION

After the rebellion the legislature looked at the free elite of color with new eyes. The assembly interviewed four free Afro-Barbadians for the report because "[f]rom the nearer approximation which existed between the Free People of Colour and Slaves, arising frequently from original connection or previous acquaintance . . . the conversations of the latter might have been less guarded when mixing with others of their own colour." They selected only men "of the most respectable of that class whose, conduct, with scarcely any exception, at the period of the Insurrection, had been highly meritorious." In other words, they selected only the most prominent Afro-Barbadian men, who had demonstrated their commitment to slavery during the uprising.[52]

The testimony of these men provides insight into the dynamics of relations between slaves and free Afro-Barbadians. Particularly instructive is the testimony of

---

50. Beckles, *Black Rebellion,* 97–102.

51. CO 318/52, West Indies, Original Correspondence, 1816–1833, Windward and Leeward Islands Correspondence, Leith to the Duke of York, 14 May 1816; see also CO 28/85, Civil No. 5, Leith to Bathurst, 30 April 1816, enclosing Colonel Codd to Leith, 25 April 1816.

52. *1818 Report,* 11.

Jacob Belgrave, the wealthiest man of color in the island, who owned plantations in St. Philip and Christ Church at the time of the insurrection. In mid-December Belgrave was returning from Bridgetown to his plantation, and as he was passing by a neighboring estate he "heard a great noise amongst the negroes who were at work in the field." His servant called to him and said "that the negroes were very abusive towards [Belgrave], complaining that they were free, and that he was one who prevented them from having it." Belgrave had a similar experience on the Good Friday before the insurrection, at an estate on the border between St. Philip and Christ Church. On that occasion "he was attacked by a black woman there, who (to his face) abused him, and said, he was 'one of those fellows who prevented the slaves from having their freedom—that it had been sent out to them, and they would have it.'"[53] Belgrave was among the planters whose property sustained the worst damages—£6,720 worth—possibly indicating that he had been specifically targeted.[54]

William Yard, Thomas Harris, and Thomas Brewster were the other men of color interviewed. All had signed the 1811 petition on court testimony.[55] Brewster, a tailor and shopkeeper, stated that as he was returning to Bridgetown from a plantation in Christ Church he passed Searle's plantation in Christ Church, "one of the slaves there asked him if he had any good news for them, and he said he did not."[56] In his testimony Yard alleged,

That some time previous to the Insurrection on the fourteenth of April, he heard the slaves, as *"commonly as a penny loaf for a penny,"* say that they were to be free. . . . [A] short time before the Insurrection, he went (being a Taylor by trade) to General William's estate, in the Parish of St. Thomas, on business; that, on his way there, he met a man driving cattle, who asked him if there was any good news for them? and if the Governor was come? . . .—to which Deponent answered, that he had not. That, on his return from General Williams' to Town, he saw, at *Ayshford's* Plantation, the gang of negroes receiving their allowance: that one of them (a woman) asked him if he had heard any thing of the Governor, and if he had brought news for them, and could tell any thing about their freedom?—upon which

53. Ibid., 38–39.
54. Ibid., 59–63; Watson, *Civilised Island*, 256.
55. Handler, Hughes, and Wiltshire, *Freedmen of Barbados*, 24.
56. *1818 Report*, 40–41.

Deponent, putting his finger on his mouth, advised her to be quiet: to which she answered, she understood him. . . . [O]ne Sunday, on coming from his house (a little way out of Town) to his shop, he heard that one of his boys, having been questioned by some negroes from the country, whether he knew any thing about their freedom? had pretended to read to them, from a Newspaper, that they were to be free; and he rebuked the boy for attempting to impose on the negroes.[57]

None of the whites interviewed spoke of having "heard" slaves say anything, or having been directly asked by them for news or confronted about their views. The verbal attacks on Belgrave are especially revealing. As far as the slaves who abused him were concerned, as a man of color *and* a member of the plantocracy, he was a traitor who could be condemned publicly to his face for betraying a cause that they perhaps felt should have been his own.

In late 1816, as a reward for their loyalty, the House of Assembly considered a bill to allow certain free people of color to give evidence in court. The legislature specified that the measure should apply only "to the most enlightened class of the free people of colour" and not "to the vulgar class, many of whom have no idea of the nature or Solemnity of an Oath."[58] In March 1817 a group of prominent free Afro-Barbadian men sent a letter to the house "for ourselves, and in behalf of the free people of Colour in general," expressing gratitude for the bill. Without it, they stated, "our lives and properties were not secure, and . . . our condition was little, if anything, better than that of Slaves." Once again they distanced themselves from any association with the concept of inalienable and universal rights. They reaffirmed their support for slavery and for the necessity of "a distinction" between white and Afro-Barbadian free inhabitants and assured the assembly that they understood "there are privileges which the latter do not expect to enjoy." The privilege of testifying in court, they stated, was all they wanted, and having obtained that "thro' the Justice and Wisdom of the Legislature, we are perfectly satisfied." Finally, they expressed their pleasure that their conduct "upon a late unfortunate occasion, has met with the approbation of the Legislature" and promised the House of Assembly "that we shall be ready at all times to give proofs of our Loyalty, and sincere attachment to the King and Constitution, and to risk our Lives in the defence and protection of our Country and its Laws." The letter was signed by

57. Ibid., 39–40.
58. CO 31/47, 8 October 1816.

Jacob Belgrave, William Yard, and Thomas Harris, along with nine other free men of color. Among the signatories, Thomas Harris was himself a former slave, and William Bourne had several family members who had been born slaves, connections that apparently did not hamper their support for slavery as an institution.[59] The house was pleased by the letter's deferential tone, and it passed the testimony bill in May 1817. The bill did not specify any property qualification; however, it applied only to those who had been baptized as Christians—a tiny percentage of the free population of color—and those free before the passage of the act. No one freed after 1817 could expect the same privileges.[60]

Immediately after the rebellion, the house also repealed the 1801 act setting manumission fees at three hundred pounds for women and two hundred pounds for men, which might appear to be a sign of gratitude to free people of color for support during the rebellion. However, like a similar act passed in Grenada the following year, it was passed under pressure from the imperial government to reduce restrictions on manumission and was more a recognition of reality than an act of generosity. Since 1801 manumission fees had been evaded by having manumission deeds effected in England or, more commonly, by simply never paying the fees. The lowering of the fees did not result in an increase in the number of recorded manumissions, indicating that high fees were not the main factor limiting manumissions, of which the legislature was probably aware when it passed the bill.[61]

The passage of the 1817 testimony act did not mean that the planter-state now trusted free Afro-Barbadians. The specter of Haiti dogged free people of color in all of their interactions with the colonial state and the rebellion heightened already intense fears that free people of color might plot revolution in connivance with slaves. This was illustrated in 1818, when a new militia bill was passed. The house decided that current Afro-Barbadian militia tenants could keep their tenements, but in future no man of color would be allowed to hold a militia tenancy.[62] White hostility was made clear again in 1819 when an Afro-Barbadian soldier in the imperial army returned to the island and was almost immediately imprisoned

59. CO 31/47, 4 March 1817, "Letter from Free People of Colour to the Assembly." The address was also signed by Charles S. Beckles, Samuel F. Collymore, T. Belgrave, Samuel Cowse, William Bourne, T. B. Collymore, T. Jordan, J. Collymore, and J. Montefiore. See also Handler, *Unappropriated People*, 86–87.

60. CO 31/47, 21 January, 8 February, and 31 March 1818.

61. Handler, *Unappropriated People*, 49; Cox, *Free Coloreds*, 53.

62. CO 31/47, 21 January, 8 February, and 31 March 1818.

by magistrates who accused him of being a Haitian spy. His crime was to have had the audacity to wear his military uniform in public and openly challenge a white slave owner whom he saw beating a slave in the street. According to the soldier, the news of his case spread throughout the island and "caused a great sensation among the Slaves . . . who now seemed to think the Magistrates had reason for what they did, & I was repeatedly warned by People of Colour, that my life was in danger. . . . From the time that I was apprehended as an Emissary from St. Domingo, an opinion seem'd to prevail among the Slaves that my arrival was in some measure connected with them."[63] That same year the legislature debated an act for establishing an "Alien Office," specifically intended to prevent the immigration of free people of color from elsewhere in the Caribbean, especially Haiti. The Alien and Census Act forced ships docking in the island's harbor to report the presence of any free nonwhites on board and gave magistrates the power to jail any foreigners or natives "of a Suspicious Character," clauses aimed at controlling the entry of people of color.[64]

The bill helped to galvanize a sense of political consensus among free Afro-Barbadians. During the debate the gallery of the House of Assembly was packed with "Coloured People" displeased by the measure, and some free Afro-Barbadians later organized a public meeting at which four hundred of their number were present.[65] At the meeting a committee of prominent Afro-Barbadian men was formed to petition against the bill. Among them were the individuals interviewed for the 1818 report, and the chairman was Jacob Belgrave Jr. This affirmed his self-appointed position as the spokesman and leading political figure among free people of color. The community authority of those elected to the 1819 Alien Bill Committee very likely derived from the fact that they came from among the small number who received the right to testify in 1817 and were individuals whom the legislature might take seriously. Nearly all of them were merchants and planters, some of whom, such as John Montefiore, Thomas Cummins, and Jacob Belgrave, were extremely wealthy. Thus for what was destined to be a brief period, individuals such as Belgrave would enjoy popular support as elected leaders of the free

---

63. CO 28/86, Index, correspondence of the Commander-in-Chief, unnumbered, Captain Elton, King's Dragoon Guards to Lt. Col. Teesdale, Commander of the King's Guards, Manchester Barracks, 22 July 1817, Teesdale to the Prince Regent, 26 July 1817, and Loveless Overton to Teesdale, 30 June 1817. Overton was freed after Teesdale wrote to the Prince Regent about his case.

64. CO 30/20, "An Act for establishing an Alien Office . . . ," passed 29 June 1819.

65. CO 31/49, 10 April 1821.

community of color. However, 1819 would mark the last time that the role of the proslavery elite, as the self-appointed voice of the interests of free people of color, would go uncontested.[66]

THE CHALLENGE TO THE OLD ELITE, 1823–1824

Franklyn's execution might have sent a chill through those who had more radical hopes for change than the established elite but it did not remove the context within which radicalism could thrive. Even as the Afro-Barbadian elite rose above the ranks of the majority of laboring-class and impoverished free people of color, the size of that underprivileged majority was growing at an unprecedented rate. Elite petitioners thus claimed to be acting "in behalf" of the entire free population of color at precisely the moment when they could never have been less certain that their views were shared by the majority.

The petitions sent by elite Afro-Barbadians from the 1790s to 1820s made them the most politically visible among the free population of color. The election of these elite men to the 1819 Alien Bill Committee seems to suggest that, at least in the eyes of several hundred other free Afro-Barbadians, their presumed community leadership was then considered legitimate. However, by excluding the overwhelming majority from its benefits on the basis of religious distinctions, the 1817 testimony bill confirmed the socioeconomic chasm that had been growing among free people of color since the late eighteenth century. As Handler has noted, the law applied "primarily to those who demeanor and life style reflected the values that whites considered appropriate and nonthreatening."[67] Thus this legislative concession, which secured the pro-planter loyalty of a privileged few, also alienated the Afro-Barbadian elite politically from the majority of free people of color. During the 1820s these divisions came to the surface in the form of demands from the underprivileged for more far-reaching changes than the black and colored elite had hitherto envisioned.

A pivotal moment for free Afro-Barbadian politics occurred in 1823, and, as

66. The members of the 1819 Alien Bill Committee were Jacob Belgrave, Samuel and Renn Jordan, Thomas Harris Jr., John Montefiore, Thomas J. Cummins, Nathaniel Alsop, Thomas Jordan, William Roach, Joseph Kennedy, John Durant, Benjamin Partridge, John Wilson, Christopher Serjeant, Joseph Collymore and Thomas Harris (probably Sr.), see CO 31/49, 4 February 1824.

67. Handler, *Unappropriated People*, 87.

in 1816, external events related to the imperial debate over the future of slavery provided the catalyst. In May 1823 the imperial Tory government compromised with abolitionist ministers of Parliament (MPs) and adopted a "gradual emancipation" policy. When news of the decision reached Barbados in June, many slaves again believed that freedom would shortly be at hand.[68] Then, in August 1823, a massive slave rebellion swept nearby Demerara, rumored to have been aroused by the teachings of a Methodist and abolitionist missionary whose congregation included many of the slaves who led the revolt.[69] In the aftermath of the parliamentary debate and events in Demerara, racial and religious tensions ran high in Barbados. In September, the *Mercury* newspaper carried a letter from an anonymous correspondent whose color is not known but whose language was unusually bold in its public condemnation of racism. Under the pseudonym "Y," the author of the letter compared two recent murder cases; in one, two white men were accused of the murder of a slave, and in the other, two slaves were accused of murdering a white man. The writer alleged that the white men were not even brought to trial, whereas the slaves were sentenced to death. The writer argued that the deciding factor in the two cases was the race of the defendants and the victim.[70]

A few weeks later, in October, in response to the revelations about the Demerara revolt, a white mob demolished the Bridgetown Methodist chapel and the missionary, William Shrewsbury, and his pregnant wife had to flee to safety. The destruction of the chapel followed weeks of sporadically violent tension between whites and the congregation, which was overwhelmingly composed of free Afro-Barbadians. White mobs stoned the church during services and assaulted Jacob Belgrave's son as well as the slave of a British Methodist army officer. According to the governor a deputation of free people of color from the Methodist Bible Society told him that they feared for their lives.[71] In a letter to Governor Warde the members of the society stated that, immediately prior to the chapel's demolition, a "large body" of armed free people of color had gathered to protect it. On that oc-

---

68. CO 28/92, No. 24, Governor Henry Warde to Lord Bathurst, 14 June 1823; Claude Levy, "Barbados: The Last Years of Slavery, 1823–1833," *Journal of Negro History* 44, no. 4 (October 1959): 311.

69. Emilia Viotti da Costa, *Crowns of Glory, Tears of Blood: The Demerara Slave Rebellion of 1823* (New York: Oxford University Press, 1994).

70. *BMBG*, 30 September 1823. This is the only reference I found to these cases.

71. CO 28/92, No. 57, Warde to Bathurst, 23 October 1823, enclosing Warde to Attorney General Hinds, 20 October 1823.

casion Belgrave's son was beaten, which, as he was "a Son of the most respectable Coloured Person in the Island . . . caused a very unpleasant sensation."[72] Governor Warde nervously informed the Colonial Office that "great Apprehension is entertained here that a Conflict may take place between the white Inhabitants and Free People of Colour, the horrible consequences of which, would be beyond all Power of calculation."[73]

Immediately after the chapel was torn down, a group of free Afro-Barbadian men, the same individuals who had been elected to the 1819 Alien Bill Committee, sent a nervous letter to the House of Assembly, professing as usual to speak "in behalf of the free colored community at large." Jacob Belgrave's name headed the list of signatures. The authors expressed their support for the island's institutions and stated their "willingness to resist, to the best of our ability, any innovations in the present form of the society, which may appear likely to be productive of consequences injurious to the well-being of the Colony." They denounced the "ill-directed, but too successfully conceived efforts" of British abolitionists and expressed their "pleasure" regarding the "the efforts which are now making in every part of the Country, to impart religious instruction to the Slaves . . . by teaching them to be contented and happy in their present highly improved condition." They assured the house that they had no intention of taking advantage of the unsettled political climate to press the legislature for increased rights, and stated that "such report, by whomsoever circulated, is entirely void of foundation."[74]

Previous petitions claiming to represent the entire community had not elicited public disavowal from among other free people of color, but this time was different. The Belgrave address provoked a mass meeting of hundreds of other free people of color, who decided to formulate their own address to show their opposition to its contents. The counteraddress was published in a newspaper in January 1824 and was signed by 373 free men of color. Like the first address, this one also promised that demands for civil rights would be deferred until the colony was in a less agitated state.[75] However, it was addressed to the governor, not, as had hitherto been the norm, to the legislature. In other words, the petitioners were go-

72. Handler, *Unappropriated People*, 160.

73. CO 28/92, No. 59, Warde to Bathurst, 25 October 1823.

74. CO 31/49, 21 October 1823, "The Humble Address of the free coloured Inhabitants . . . ," 20 October 1823.

75. Handler, *Unappropriated People*, 90–97.

ing over the heads of the colonial assembly straight to the Crown. The challeng-
ers' message to the British government, the local legislature, and the group led by
Belgrave was clear. In light of the British government's new position on gradual
emancipation, they would no longer publicly endorse slavery in order to curry
favor with local whites:

> Politically situated as we are, it is our ardent wish to pursue that peaceable
> demeanour and strict *neutrality* which has ever been the characteristic of
> the Free Coloured Inhabitants . . . nor do we conceive an exposition of our
> sentiments on any political question by any means necessary. But should it
> be requisite to remove any unfavourable impression which might arise . . .
> from our *neutrality* . . . we will endeavour to prove . . . our unshaken at-
> tachment to his Majesty's Government and the interests of our Country,
> and that we are worthy of that kind consideration which we shall solicit at
> a future period.[76]

The term "political question" was an oblique reference to the debate over slavery.
The emphatic claim that political "neutrality" had always characterized their
views on slavery was patently untrue. Some of the men who signed the 1824
counteraddress had signed previous petitions in which they wholeheartedly expressed their support for slavery. However, by claiming that they had always been
neutral regarding slavery, the authors of the address were carefully trying to distance themselves from the proslavery cause and illustrate their loyalty to the imperial government without openly defying the legislature.

The House of Assembly, which until recently had accorded little value to support from free Afro-Barbadians, now viewed this act of apparent political defec-
tion as rebellion. The assembly launched an inquiry in February 1824 into the
counteraddress, effectively putting those who had signed it on trial. The testimony indicates that the 1823 parliamentary debate had caused a schism among
the Afro-Barbadian elite over the issue of slavery. Several people opposed the anti-
abolitionist tone of the Belgrave address, not necessarily because they were abolitionists but because, in the wake of the 1823 parliamentary debate, they recognized that the growing influence of abolitionism in British politics might provide

76. *Globe*, 22 January 1824, cited in ibid., 94–95.

them with powerful allies in the imperial Parliament. Others were apparently motivated by heartfelt outrage at the legislature's insubordination toward the imperial government. They expressed a deep loyalty to the crown and a perception of
the imperial government as the ultimate source of justice and arbitration—a conviction very similar to slaves' belief that the monarchy and Parliament were their
defenders against the tyranny of local slave owners. Still others seem to have acted
on the basis of agreement with the gradual emancipation policy and anger at being associated with proslavery political opinions. The pro-planter *Barbadian* later
accused some of the instigators of the counteraddress of being members of something called the "Radical Party," but this is the only instance in which this name
is documented, and there is no evidence that Afro-Barbadian "radicals" actually
grouped themselves together as a political faction.[77]

All of these tensions surfaced during the investigation into the counteraddress.
The inquiry revealed that Samuel Collymore, a prominent man of color who had
himself signed the 1799, 1811, 1812, and 1817 memorials and petitions and had
been elected to the Alien Bill Committee in 1819, was one of the main instigators
of the counteraddress. Thomas J. Cummins, who also sat on the 1819 committee
and had signed the Belgrave address, testified that Collymore had denounced the
address for its obsequiousness to the local legislature and its open disagreement
with the abolitionist language emanating from the imperial Parliament. Cummins
stated that Collymore "had said they [the free people of color] should not look to
the legislature but to the 'Mother Country' for their rights." He also alleged that
Collymore dismissed the reference in the Belgrave address to the improved condition of the slaves, saying that "there was no improvement in their condition."
If these accusations were true then they represented a new level of public defiance from free Afro-Barbadians against white supremacy and the slaveholding regime. Collymore's rebellious attitude even converted some of the most conservative Afro-Barbadians. For example, William Yard, one of the "respectable" men of
color interviewed for the 1818 rebellion report, a member of the 1819 Alien Bill
Committee and a signatory to the Belgrave address, confessed under questioning
that, after speaking to Collymore, he "wished his arm had dropped off before [he]
signed that [the Belgrave] address." He alleged that Collymore had told him that
"the Governor with tears in his eyes had objected to the Address because it con-

77. *Barbadian*, 29 July 1825.

tained expressions about [Secretary of State for War and the Colonies] Earl Bathurst and the People at home [in Britain]."[78]

Thomas J. Cummins also accused Collymore of openly stating that people of color should be allowed to sit in the House, the first time a demand for the political enfranchisement of Afro-Barbadians was documented.[79] John Callaird, a black man originally born in either St. Vincent or Grenada, expressed even more militant views on the subject of political enfranchisement. Callaird was symptomatic of the growing impatience among free people of color with the lack of legal reform in Barbados, particularly since similar reform campaigns by free Afro-Caribbean people in neighboring islands had recently met with some success. Although Callaird did not sign the counteraddress, the house nearly ordered him deported for saying that Afro-Barbadian men should be allowed to sit in the legislature, which they were allowed to do in Grenada. The legislature found it especially ominous that he urged Barbadian free men of color to "fight" for this political right.[80]

The testimony also illustrated the development of an interisland Afro-Caribbean political network, an example of a much wider transatlantic phenomenon.[81] Witnesses referred to the existence of correspondence networks in the eastern Caribbean, through which free people of color in different colonies kept each other informed of local developments and exchanged political advice. The constant movement of slaves and free people of color between the islands of the eastern Caribbean would have facilitated the development and maintenance of such correspondence networks. The correspondence revealed embryonic efforts by some free people of color across the eastern Caribbean to build an interisland opposition to racial segregation. In this case, Afro-Caribbean correspondents from nearby islands urged their counterparts in Barbados to refute the Belgrave address and show their support for the British government. One young Afro-Barbadian man named Renn Collymore mentioned that, when news of the

78. CO 28/93, No. 20, Warde to Bathurst, 31 March 1824, enclosing "Examination of Witnesses . . . relative to the Publication . . . purporting to be the production of 373 of the free black and coloured inhabitants . . . expressive of their disapprobation of the loyal and respectful Address which was presented to the Legislative Bodies on the 21st October last by a Committee or free coloured and black persons," 3 and 4 February 1824.

79. CO 31/49, 4 February 1824.

80. CO 28/93, No. 20, Warde to Bathurst, 31 March 1824, enclosing "Examination of Witnesses . . ."; Handler, Hughes, and Wiltshire, *Freedmen of Barbados,* 10.

81. Scott, "Common Wind."

address reached other islands, his uncle received letters from free people of color in Tobago, St. Vincent, and Antigua "requesting [us] to do something to show that it was not the general feeling."[82]

The men who signed the Belgrave address—all of whom were members of the 1819 committee—apparently considered it their right to assume the role of a political oligarchy and were unapologetic in the face of widespread discontent with their leadership. No elections had been held among free people of color to choose their political representatives since the Alien Bill Committee was elected in 1819. According to Thomas Harris Jr., one of the signatories of the original address and a member of the Alien Bill Committee, when they drew up the address, "he was fully impressed, as were those who acted with him, that they were justified in doing so from the opinion that they entertained of the feelings generally of all the enlightened, respectable and wealthy part of their Body. . . . There was not a general communication but we communicated it partially with the most respectable."[83]

However, one taste of democratic decision making in 1819 followed by several years of community oligarchy was apparently not enough for other free Afro-Barbadians. As far as they were concerned, the Alien Bill Committee no longer had any political mandate. The counteraddress was not the first act of popular defiance against the elite: Early in 1823, when a royal commission on West Indian legal reform toured the British Caribbean, another group of free Afro-Barbadians had complained to the commission about racial discrimination in the island without the permission of the Alien Bill Committee, whose members felt they should have been consulted.[84] The Alien Bill Committee seems to have ignored this first act of mutiny, but by October it was impossible to disregard the growing frustration of less privileged free people of color with the wealthy clique who presumed to speak on their behalf. The organizers of the Belgrave address practically admitted that, like whites, they now recognized and feared the political potential of Bridgetown's free black and colored laboring-class crowds. They confessed to having sent the address in large part to silence opposition to their community leadership and to prevent an increasingly alienated laboring-class of free people of color from breaking ranks and voicing more radical demands for change. Thomas Jordan, one of the

82. CO 28/93, No. 20, Warde to Bathurst, 31 March 1824, enclosing "Examination of Witnesses . . ."

83. Ibid.

84. Ibid.

prime movers behind the Belgrave address, stated that he decided to call a meeting of the Alien Bill Committee to draw up the address, noting that

> in consequence of . . . the Mobs assembling about the Town and particularly at the Free Coloured School, where there was a large collection of coloured persons, not wishing to let there be any improper Construction to be put upon our Silence;—I suggested to Mr. [Thomas J.] Cummins not to let there be any assembling, but to prepare a Draft of an address and bring it to me and that if I approved of it I would sign it—He asked who should prepare it I told him to call together a few of the most discreet.[85]

There was a clear difference in the class backgrounds of those who signed the two addresses. Aside from one man for whom no other records have been found, all who signed the October address were men of means whose names appear as taxpayers and significant property owners. Most were members of the 1819 committee and had signed previous petitions. By contrast, there are no other records of the existence of most of the men whose names were appended to the counteraddress, indicating that many were not taxpayers and were of low socioeconomic status.[86] Most of the men who signed the counteraddress were probably of the so-called vulgar class, deliberately excluded by the legislature from the 1817 extension of civil rights. The 1817 testimony bill had also opened up a generational rift among free men of color, with less affluent and younger free people of color harboring resentment against the fortunate few who benefitted from the 1817 testimony bill. The wave of dissent was also distinctly urban, marked by great hostility toward Jacob Belgrave, who, as a rural planter, was increasingly seen as a political outsider.[87]

In February a public apology for the counteraddress was published in the *Barbadian*, carrying twenty signatures, including those of some men who signed the counteraddress. Among the names were many leading free men of color, distinguished by wealth and public prominence. The apology expressed support for the Belgrave address, claiming that "we should have felt most happy and willing to have signed the same, had the short time allowed for its preparations admitted of

85. Ibid. For more on the "Free Colored School," see chapter 3, pp. 102–104, of the present volume.
86. Handler, *Unappropriated People*, 97.
87. CO 31/49, 4 February 1824.

us being called upon."[88] That same month the house passed a resolution explicitly rejecting the notion that there were universal and inalienable rights to which free people of color were entitled and denying that free Afro-Barbadians had a "right" to any privileges not granted to them by the legislature for good conduct. The resolution also expressed approval of the original address. The assembly's unequivocal statement was an attempt to close off the intensifying debate about the role of race in determining the limits of the political community. They saw, as did free blacks and coloreds, that the assembly's power to grant individual rights to a select group of Afro-Barbadian oligarchs—much like the power of slave owners to confer or deny freedom upon individuals—was central to the maintenance of the racial order. Acknowledgment that rights might be conferred on the basis of a principle of universality would open the door to more democratic demands and, ultimately, might bring the issue of slavery to the center of the political agenda in the developing struggle over racial discrimination.[89]

CONCLUSION

Although this was the first public political illustration of how divisions of class, age, and culture shaped politics among free people of color in Barbados during this turbulent period, it was neither the beginning nor the end of political divisions among them. The case of Joseph Franklyn and the other Afro-Barbadian men who joined him on the gallows in 1816 suggests that even before 1823 the conservative political views expressed in the petitions were not the only ones being voiced publicly among free people of color. Other voices, from less privileged quarters and representing different ideological positions, were emerging to question who had the legitimacy to speak "for" the community, what civil rights should be demanded, and even the basic meaning of "rights." Particularly after 1823, the imperial policy of "slave amelioration" and growing pressure from abolitionists would open up new spaces for the expression and debate of these diffuse political ideas, transforming the public sphere of Barbadian society in ways which would shape Afro-Barbadian politics well beyond the end of slavery.

88. *Barbadian*, 25 February 1824. The signatories were Edward Jordan, Thomas G. Hope, Joseph Jordan, Joseph H. Cummins, Hamlet Lynch, Charles Falkland, Francis Wood, William Oatley, John S. Manning, Anthony Barclay Sr., Charles Phipps, Richard Beck, Isaac Carvallo, Lovelace Ovleton (likely the aforementioned Loveless Overton), James J. Ince, James T. Mapp, Walter S. Gordon, James Massiah, Philip Walcott, and Charles Grasett.

89. CO 31/49, 18 February 1824.

I N 1823 the British government adopted a policy of pursuing the "amelioration" of slavery as, in theory, part of the process of slavery's "gradual extinction." Amelioration consisted of a range of legal and social reforms whose objec-
tive was the improvement of the "moral" and physical condition of slaves and free
people of African descent. This reform process was intended as a compromise that
would indefinitely preserve the status quo in the British Caribbean. Yet even before 1823, years of what planters viewed as Colonial Office meddling had begun to
effect enormous changes in Britain's Caribbean slaveholding colonies. Amelioration had a profound impact on slaves and free people of color, their relations with
whites, and the institutions that regulated their lives.

Through amelioration policy, the imperial government sought to Christianize slaves and transform the legal environment of slave society by reforming slave
and common law in order to give slaves and free people of color greater legal protection. But the Colonial Office left the responsibility for framing such policies in
the hands of predominantly white West Indian slave owners who did everything
they could to subvert the amelioration process and reinforce the legal apparatus of
racial segregation. As a result, amelioration's effects were contradictory. On one
hand, free people of color in Barbados found themselves struggling against new
forms of public segregation. On the other hand, debates over amelioration policy
created space for free people of color and slaves in the British Caribbean to establish new roles for themselves in public life, and provided them with a new political language in which to articulate claims to equality with the empire's white
subjects.

The proselytizing aspect of amelioration encouraged missionary activity and
philanthropic work among slaves and numerous missionary societies, some with
explicitly abolitionist mandates, sprang up in Britain and the Caribbean in the late
eighteenth and early nineteenth centuries. Philanthropy quickly became another
terrain on which whites and Afro-Barbadians battled over racial segregation and

civil rights.[1] For elite Afro-Barbadians, Christian philanthropic organizing provided a platform to further their demands for political reform, since philanthropy
was a form of civic involvement that planters could not easily suppress as subversive. Through philanthropy, free people of color challenged the state's racial segregation policies, creating their own outlets for the provision of such services as education and poor relief.

Afro-Barbadian philanthropy also helped to forge and articulate a sense of
community among people of African descent while ensuring that socioeconomic
inequality would be one of that community's organizing principles. Even if the
Afro-Barbadian elite did not view the enslaved as their equals, they did not entirely
exclude them as outsiders. The charities established by free people of color were
notable for not being segregated by legal status—slaves as well as lower-class free
people of color were designated as the beneficiaries. This community organizing
illustrates Arnold Sio's point that "the continuation of relations with slaves was not
a barrier to a free coloured identity."[2]

AMELIORATION AND RELIGIOUS REFORM

West Indian planters had been pursuing what they termed amelioration measures
since the late 1700s, largely as a means to increase estate productivity and maintain the size of the estate labor force without such heavy reliance on the slave
trade.[3] Abolitionist MPs were not convinced by these efforts, and the battle in the
1810s over the establishment of slave registries was among the first in a long series
of struggles between the imperial government and West Indian legislatures over
slave amelioration. The Colonial Office wanted legislatures to extend greater common law protection to slaves and free people of color in order to decrease the arbi-
trary power of slave owners. Imperial officials also wanted creole elites to support
missionary activity with legislative reforms in order to counter the abolitionist argument that slavery was incompatible with Christianity. Amelioration was predominantly intended to "modernize" the laws relating to slavery and Christianize
slaves but the reforms also had implications for free people of color. In 1818 the

1. For comparison, see Lowes, "Peculiar Class," 131–132, on philanthropy and elite free black and
colored identity in Antigua.
2. Sio, "Marginality," 153.
3. Robert Luster, *The Amelioration of the Slaves in the British Empire, 1790–1833* (New York: Peter
Lang, 1995); Ward, *British West Indian Slavery*.

new governor of Barbados advised the House of Assembly to reform laws relating to both free people of color and slaves. He saw these ameliorative reforms as essential in order to build up "a Constitutional Force for the security of the Colony" in the aftermath of the Haitian Revolution and the 1816 rebellion.[4]

In 1823, British abolitionist MP Thomas Fowell Buxton succeeded in getting the Tory government to adopt a policy of using amelioration measures to reform the morals of West Indian societies and effect the "gradual extinction" of slavery in the West Indies, albeit at some unspecified point in the future, rather than viewing amelioration simply as a means to "mitigate" slavery.[5] Reform of the Caribbean's religious institutions, particularly of the Church of England, was central to this agenda. The majority of West Indian planters refused to allow missionaries to preach to their slaves, viewing Christian teachings and literacy as inherently subversive of slavery. The Anglican clergy in the West Indies came mainly from the planter class and supported the planters' right to determine whether or not their slaves had access to Christian teachings. In 1817, the Colonial Office requested a survey of Anglican Church membership, which revealed that about twenty-six hundred people were baptized in Barbados in the period from 1812 to 1817, very few of whom were slaves or free people of color. Few Afro-Barbadians, slave or free, were baptized Christian before 1834.[6]

Although a law had been passed outlawing Obeah in 1806, it was designed to arrest the practice of cursing and poisoning enemies rather than to suppress African-derived creole spiritual practices, and it was poorly enforced. In 1818, under imperial pressure, the legislature passed a new act against Obeah, and a handful of people were actually transported from then until the end of slavery for "practicing obeah." The debate over the act shows that Obeah was understood to cross legal boundaries. The original bill agreed to by the House of Assembly specifically referred to "slaves," but the council changed the wording to "persons," acknowledging that Obeah's adherents were both slave and free.[7]

4. CO 31/47, 6 August 1818.

5. Blackburn, *Overthrow of Colonial Slavery,* 421–422; Holt, *Problem of Freedom,* 18.

6. CO 28/86, unnumbered, Governor Lord Combermere to Secretary of State for the Colonies Lord Bathurst, 20 August 1817, enclosing "General Return of the Clergy of Barbados"; A. Caldecott, *The Church in the West Indies* (London: Society for Propagating Christian Knowledge, 1898); Handler, *Unappropriated People,* 154; Jerome Handler, Frederick Lange and R. V. Riordan, *Plantation Slavery in Barbados: An Archeological and Historical Investigation* (Cambridge: Harvard University Press, 1978), 175.

7. CO 31/47, 30 June and 28 July 1818.

The absence of free people of color and slaves from the Anglican Church was not surprising. Even the few who joined knew they were unwelcome in what was very much the planters' church. The island's churches were racially segregated, with slaves and free people of color seated in the most distant and uncomfortable sections. In the Anglican survey of 1817 the rector of St. Thomas parish was exceptionally honest, admitting that the church deliberately excluded slaves and free Afro-Barbadians. Although many people of color came to him to be baptized, he always turned them away.[8] Subsequent baptism and burial returns for the 1820s showed that Christian marriage among slaves and free people of color was extremely rare. Although slaves could have Christian marriage ceremonies, there were only two such weddings between 1808 and 1820. In 1811, in St. Joseph parish, there was one marriage between a slave man and a free woman of color, the only Anglican marriage across legal boundaries for the next decade.[9]

Particularly after the 1823 imperial policy shift, missionary societies promoting education and Christianity in the Caribbean sprang up throughout Britain. In 1825 the Anglican Church responded to the competition from nonconformist missionaries by establishing two dioceses in the West Indies, one based in Barbados for the eastern Caribbean and the other in Jamaica.[10] Barbadian planters, who had largely sought to preserve Anglican worship as a key marker of whiteness, now sought to take control of the amelioration process by determining what kind of Christian message would reach slaves and free Afro-Barbadians, and some planters began to accept missionaries they considered to be nonthreatening.

The Society for the Propagation of the Gospel's Codrington plantation took the lead in planter-initiated religious reform. In 1825 the Codrington chaplain reported in the newspaper that the estate's seventy-one children now always attended chapel regularly, "seats in a particular part of the chapel being provided for them" and many "free-coloured persons" and slaves from neighboring areas were now "in the habit of frequenting this Chapel."[11] By the late 1820s there were

8. CO 28/86, unnumbered, Combermere to Bathurst, 20 August 1817.

9. Ibid; CO 28/90, unnumbered, Skeete to Bathurst, 24 February 1821 and CO 28/91, No. 4, Warde to Bathurst, 20 March 1822, enclosing baptism and burial returns.

10. See John Gilmore, "Episcopacy, Emancipation and Evangelization: Aspects of the History of the Church of England in the British West Indies" (Ph.D. thesis, Cambridge University, 1984).

11. *Barbadian*, 22 July 1825, "Statement of the Plan Observed on the Society and College Estates in Barbados."

several Anglican lay catechists, one of whom was the free man of color Joseph Thorne.[12] An 1827 letter from an anonymous planter to the *Barbadian* spoke of Thorne in glowing terms as a "humble, but meritorious individual, who, for his great and unostentacious [sic] services" had "done much good upon several estates" during a decade as a lay catechist.[13]

The impact of the Church of England's new activity, particularly the establishment of the new diocese, was immediate. People of African descent were cognizant of the practical benefits and social respectability Christian conversion could bring. Unmarried free mothers of color in particular responded to the opportunity to legitimate the status of their children. For example, nearly all baptisms recorded in the parish of St. Thomas in 1825 were family members of planters and militia tenants, whereas in 1826 alone, there were sixty baptisms of illegitimate Afro-Barbadian children.[14] Estate chapels provided new venues for social interaction and diversion and, in some cases, church attendance became part of the dynamics of estate labor bargaining. The Codrington chaplain reported that, in order to encourage estate slaves' attendance, those who came to church on Sundays were given tickets proving that they had come to church. When these were presented to the estate manager, he gave them the afternoon of the following Saturday off from work. He noted that, as a result of this incentive, "attendance is now regular and full from the adult estate Negroes."[15]

The imperial government and the church sought to use amelioration to enforce a particular vision of the family. The 1824 Consolidated Slave Act implemented in the Crown Colony of Trinidad linked the issue of compulsory manumission to the patriarchal Christian family. The law made it easier for a slave man who had acquired enough money to "have the power of purchasing his own manumission, or that of his wife and child; and thus the father may become, as it is fit he should, the Instrument of liberty for his offspring."[16] Despite their apparent interest in Christianity, slaves and free people of color often resisted Christianity's

12. Handler, *Unappropriated People*, 165–166. See also chapter 2, pp. 62–64, of the present volume.

13. *Barbadian*, 17 August 1827.

14. "Baptisms solemnized in the Parish Church of St. Thomas . . . in the Years 1825–1829," RL 1/50A, BDA.

15. *Barbadian*, 17 August 1827.

16. *Barbadian*, 20 April 1824. On gender, family, and the amelioration process, see Scully, *Liberating the Family?*

emphasis on monogamy and patriarchy, largely due to a belief that such marriages would limit their freedom. In 1829 the chaplain at the Codrington estate illustrated how gender shaped slaves' reluctance to enter Christian marriage contracts. He was not surprised that "men who have lived in a state of polygamy, or even have seen others live in such a state, may be unwilling to restrict themselves to a single wife, or to take her for better or worse." The Codrington attorney observed that a man who had more than one female partner considered them all to be his "wives," rather than just informal sexual dalliances. While women of African descent may not have been fully versed in the intricacies of nineteenth-century marriage law, they recognized that such laws demanded their subordination to their husbands, exposing them to violence and limiting their personal freedom. The chaplain noted that "women also object to Christian matrimony, thinking that it gives them, as it were, a second master, and ties them for life to a man who may neglect or ill use them."[17] The Moravians also found that women's resistance restricted the effectiveness of their struggle against polygamy.[18] The Codrington estate chaplain attributed the endurance of polygamy despite the growing influence of Christianity to the bad example set by free people of color and slaves of comparatively high status. He expressed the paternalistic hope that "[w]hen Christian instruction has had longer time to operate; when the free-coloured class universally apply to the minister for ratifying the sacred bond; when the domestics and tradespeople on estates, who form the intermediate link, do the same; the lower ranks of slaves will naturally follow the example."[19]

The church and the colonial state also tried to eliminate Sunday markets and ban Sunday dances, an important part of the social and economic lives of slaves and free Afro-Barbadians, in order to encourage slaves to observe Sunday as the Sabbath. An 1825 act made Sunday markets illegal and encouraged slave owners to make a different day of the week available for slaves to go to market. Despite the act, Sunday dances and market trade continued and few people of color used the day for church attendance. In 1827 the *Barbadian* reported, "Shops frequented by

17. Reverend Anthony Hamilton, Codrington estate chaplain, "Progress of Religious Instruction in the West Indies," *Barbadian*, 9 June 1829.

18. Diary of the Negro Congregation at Mount Tabor Moravian Church, St. John, 31 October 1830, Microfilm BS 59, BPL (hereafter cited as Moravian Diary).

19. John Forster Clarke, manager of Codrington, "Progress of Religious Instruction in the West Indies," *Barbadian*, 9 June 1829.

blacks and coloureds opened, but kept their windows closed." In 1828, "in certain places at a distance from town, the Sunday trafficking between plantation slaves and town-hucksters still [went] on briskly, in daring contempt of the law." A little more than a year before emancipation, a *Barbadian* reporter complained about the continuation of Sunday huckstering in Bridgetown, claiming to have counted eighty-one slaves on one of the roads leading into Bridgetown on their way to the market.[20]

Thus slaves and free Afro-Barbadians responded to religious reform policies in ways not always foreseen by the authorities, incorporating useful or appealing aspects of Christianity into existing cultural practices and, frequently, resisting others. At the same time that the imperial government sought to reengineer the religious practices of people of African descent imperial policy makers also attempted to overhaul the legal framework of slavery. Imperial government intervention in relations between the colonial authorities and nonwhite British subjects opened up new possibilities for slaves and free people of color to try to gain some advantage in their struggles with local state authorities.

RACIAL IDENTITY AND LEGAL STATUS DURING AMELIORATION

The imperial government's interest in ameliorating slavery seemed to offer slaves and free people of color a means to circumvent local political and judicial authorities who were perceived to be more hostile. Immediately after the May 1823 debate, Secretary of State for the Colonies Lord Henry Bathurst published a list of recommendations for amendments to laws on the treatment of slaves and dispatched a royal commission of enquiry to the British Caribbean to examine the legal and administrative structures of the colonies.[21] News of the visit spread around Barbados, and free people of color took the opportunity to bring their complaints before the commission. Although the commission had no binding powers, many

---

20. *Barbadian* 18 December 1827, 1 and 13 June 1828, 27 March 1833.

21. Bathurst's most significant suggestions were that manumission fees be abolished and increased facility be made for slaves to purchase their freedom; that the whip be outlawed as a form of punishment; that slaves be allowed to own property, and that it be made illegal for families to be separated by sale. See Beckles, *History of Barbados*, 86. On gender and the debate about the outlawing of the whip, see Diana Paton, "Decency, Dependence and the Lash: Gender and the British Debate over Slave Emancipation, 1830–34," *Slavery and Abolition* 17, no. 3 (December 1996): 163–184.

free people of color saw it as a higher authority that might overrule local magistrates or make their cases known to the crown. Complaints from individuals whose free status was threatened because their manumission fees had allegedly not been paid constituted the majority of cases recorded in the final report on Barbados.[22]

The 1823 commission was followed a year later by the imperial Consolidated Slave Act, implemented in the crown colony of Trinidad, and the Colonial Office insisted that self-governing colonies such as Barbados pass similar legislation. Consolidated slave acts brought together all previous legislation on slavery into one act and eliminated some of the more brutal provisions of the slave laws. The debate over the Consolidated Slave Act in Barbados illustrates another unintended side effect of the amelioration process. Amelioration provoked a sense of crisis among the plantocracy about the preservation of the legal barriers between slave and free status upon which the system rested. Among other things, the act promoted manumission, which one British legal advisor to the 1823 commission viewed, in terms that must have sounded ominous to planters, as "the best, or certainly the least objectionable mode, of getting rid of slavery, safely and by imperceptible degrees."[23]

The legislature's first discussions of the bill were turbulent because of disagreements between the Legislative Council and the House of Assembly. In defending the first draft of the bill against claims that it compromised the rights of free people of color, the speaker of the assembly was unapologetic about his own view that amelioration's reforms necessitated defining legal rights more explicitly along racial lines. In his opinion, given "that intercourse, that intimate association which exists between the Slave and the free colored and free black People: is it not then unjust that the latter should in a moral point of view, be so far elevated above this unfortunate class of our fellow creatures, who are peculiarly entitled to legislative protection?"[24]

When the act was finally passed, it provoked a storm of protest from free Afro-Barbadians because it racialized laws that formerly had referred only to free people, regardless of color, and thereby imposed "new and unmerited grievances

---

22. PP 1825, vol. 15, *First report of the Commissioner of Inquiry into the administration of civil and criminal justice in the West Indies*, 62; CO 318/60, Commissioners of Legal Inquiry, vol. 5: Barbados, Tobago and Grenada," Barbados case of Mary Cooper, December 1823–September 1824.

23. Dwarris, *Substance of the Three Reports*, 20–21.

24. CO 31/49, 25 May 1824.

and disabilities" upon them. One clause made it illegal for slaves to strike white people, whereas the original law had referred simply to free people. Another clause made it legal for the first time for slaves to cultivate and market aloes and cotton but stipulated that only whites could inspect slaves' crops. These crops were important for small-scale farmers and this clause made it impossible for free Afro-Barbadian farmers to sell their crops legally or inspect crops grown on their property using slave labor. The clause was probably intended to prevent slaves and free people of color from colluding in selling stolen produce, since aloes and cotton sold well in the markets.[25] The imperial government disallowed the first Barbados Consolidated Slave Act of 1825 but reluctantly assented to the amended 1826 version, which removed most of the newly stated racial distinctions between whites and free people of color. However, the legislature refused to repeal clauses stating that any person of color who could not provide proof of freedom was presumed to be a slave.[26]

Despite planters' apparent retreat from the most explicit forms of racial segregation in the 1826 act, their total political hegemony at all levels of government provided ample opportunity for a newly invigorated racial segregation policy to seep into public life as the shadowy companion of the amelioration process. In 1823 the legislature and the parish vestries began to enforce old laws, which had long ago fallen into disuse, prescribing racial segregation in public spaces. The earliest example of this renewed commitment to segregation was an apparently minor dispute over access to church pews. Most of the island's churches had been rebuilt after a devastating hurricane in 1780, at which time, to assist with the rebuilding, pews were made available for purchase to members of the congregations. Having a pew set aside for oneself and one's family was a sign of high social standing, and white planters and wealthy merchants were the only people to whom vestries would sell pews. By the 1820s, however, the system was in disarray, with many people renting out their pews to others. In 1823 the issue of pew rents came to the fore as the vestry of St. Michael parish, which maintained the island's largest Anglican church, sought to regulate the practice. The vestry grudgingly agreed to meet Secretary of State Lord Bathurst's 1823 demands that it increase the pew space available for slaves and free people of color in Anglican churches, but planters were determined to maintain strict racial segregation and public observation of class hierarchy. According to the vestry, pews had been illegally transferred to

25. Handler, *Unappropriated People*, 97–100.
26. Beckles, *History of Barbados*, 87; Handler, *Unappropriated People*, 97–98.

others, and "some [were] transferred even to Coloured person's [sic], who did not contribute to the rebuilding of the Church." The vestry now moved to put an end to this practice.[27]

Activities that brought slaves, free people of color, and whites into close so-cial contact on relatively equal terms and had long been accepted as "respectable" were also proscribed. Clauses in the 1826 Consolidated Slave Act that made it il-legal for slaves to drink, gamble, or cockfight—three areas of social activities in which men of all social and legal backgrounds had interacted on terms of relative equality—were veiled racial segregation measures. After the act was passed, the local authorities, the press and the police condemned gambling and cockfighting as pastimes in which no "respectable" white man would participate. As recently as 1818, the *Mercury* could advertise a cockfight at the home of "a very old and re-spectable Inhabitant of the Parish of St. Joseph . . . under the direction of a party of Gentlemen." By 1827 the *Barbadian* triumphantly reported that, under the terms of the Consolidated Slave Act, the Bridgetown Night Watch was engaging in a campaign of "putting down" gambling houses kept by free people of color. The newspaper added that a white man was about to be brought up in court for "keep-ing a house of this infamous description." The editor demanded that "the nests of cockfighters" be broken up, but noted that "if GENTLEMEN will go to those places, there will be no end to them," indicating that some upper-class white men were not so keen to compromise their amusement even for the sake of preserving white supremacy.[28]

The legislature also strenuously resisted Bathurst's demands that the Consoli-dated Slave Act make it mandatory for slave owners to manumit slaves who had enough money to buy their freedom and that the cost of buying freedom be set by a committee of appraisal rather than by private agreement. Planters' opposition to compulsory manumission was not rooted in any serious concern that the mea-sures would lead to an increase in the number of manumissions. At stake, rather, was the future of master-slave relations. The right to decide whether or not to free one's enslaved property was a treasured aspect of slave-owning culture and the as-sembly argued that whites would never accept a measure that "invest[ed] slaves with the power, at their own will, and against the will of their owners, of pur-

27. Minutes of the St. Michael Vestry, 26 May 1823.

28. *BMBG*, 14 March 1818; *Barbadian*, 20 February 1827.

chasing their freedom."[29] Second, enforcing compulsory manumission laws would mean granting enslaved people direct access to state institutions whose primary purpose was the defense of slaves' individual rights rather than the property rights of slave owners. Such a policy represented a fracturing of the bond between the interests of propertied white men and the apparatus of the colonial legislature and judiciary. In 1831 the legislature finally passed an act eliminating manumission fees, but it would not consent to any fundamental change to the principle that manumission was a "gift" from owners.[30]

In spite of the Barbadian regime's efforts to subvert amelioration, the reforms stealthily undermined slavery in subtle but important ways. In 1827, the legislature reluctantly agreed to create an Office for the Protection of Slaves under the direction of a protector of slaves. The position was never firmly established, being filled only by an acting protector of slaves from 1828, but this office, combined with imperial pressure to facilitate manumission, had a vital impact on amelioration.[31] The acting protector of slaves was certainly not the unqualified ally of Afro-Barbadians who sought to validate the free status of themselves or their kin, but the position helped to further a tendency on the part of the Crown to rule in favor of manumission petitions based on the principle of the right to freedom alone, without considering other factors.

A comparison of three manumission cases that reached the imperial government between 1825 and 1831 illustrates this shift as well as the role played by the acting protector of slaves in helping enslaved people or free Afro-Barbadians to gain or keep their freedom. It would be a misreading of these cases to see in them the gradual triumph of the idea of inalienable universal human rights for all. Nevertheless, they did represent a shift from the planter legislature's view that increases in rights for slaves and free people of color were "gifts" rather than matters of impersonal legal interpretation. In 1825, after the death of a free woman of color of some property, her slave Sukey and Sukey's small daughter were given to the woman's sons, who were on bad terms with each other. They took out their frustrations on Sukey to such a degree that the parish clergyman wrote to the presi-

29. CO 28/102, Speaker of the House of Assembly Robert Haynes to Warde, 1826, cited in Handler, *Unappropriated People*, 43.

30. Handler, *Unappropriated People*, 48–49.

31. See notice of the appointment of John Mayers, attorney-at-law, to the post of Acting Protector of Slaves, *Barbadian*, 25 January 1828.

dent of the Legislative Council, who recommended her manumission to the imperial Board of Treasury. The board ordered that she and her child should be set free only if it were proved that she could support herself and her child. If not, then they should be escheated to the Crown.[32] In this case, the decision hinged upon Sukey's ability to support herself financially.

By contrast, at the end of the 1820s, the board appeared more willing to rule in favor of manumission when slaves petitioned for freedom or their legal status was in doubt. In the 1829–1830 case of the Denny family of slaves mentioned in chapter 1, which was supported by the acting protector of slaves, the Board of Treasury made no enquiries into the issue of how the Denny family had been treated as slaves. The board also ignored claims made by the free people of color who claimed ownership of the Dennys that the slaves were required to settle debts. The board decided that the Denny family should all be freed immediately, along with two other members of the family who were not even mentioned in the petition.[33] After a devastating hurricane in 1831, Susanna Prescod, a free woman of color, applied for title to the slaves of her deceased sister, who had been killed in the hurricane. Since her sister had died intestate, all her property was escheated to the Crown. Whereas the Board of Treasury had found in favor of similar requests in the early 1820s, in this case they ordered instead that the slaves be manumitted immediately. They also ordered that Prescod be compensated for them if her claim was found to be valid, prioritizing the manumission of the slaves over Prescod's property rights.[34]

Amelioration forced an issue that Barbadian planters wished to avoid to the center of the debate about slavery's future, namely, whether or not there was any legitimate basis for denying free people of African descent the legal freedoms that whites enjoyed. As such, amelioration placed a question mark over the legal, social, and political position of free people of color as well as slaves. It was therefore

32. CO 28/95 1650, Barbados, Skeete to Bathurst, 6 July 1825, enclosing papers relating to the petitions of S. G. Ford and W. C. Ford, free colored men; CO 28/99, Treasury correspondence Lord Commissioners of the Treasury to J. Wilmot Horton, 14 March 1826, re: petitions of W. C. Ford and S. G. Ford.

33. CO 28/106, Alphabetized correspondence, unnumbered, Petition of Jane Denny in behalf of herself and Children . . . and her Grand Child . . . , 26 March 1830; CO 28/106, Treasury correspondence 21220 29/12 S. 75, Lord Commissioners of the Treasury to Horace Twiss, 6 January 1830, relating to memorial of Jane, Sarah Denny et al. See discussion of this family's case in chapter 1, pp. 54–55.

34. CO 28/109, No. 68, Governor James Lyon to Secretary of State Viscount Goderich, 7 February 1832, enclosing petition of Susanna Prescod.

not a coincidence that both the imperial government and the Barbadian legislature increasingly framed discussions of the amelioration process in terms of race, or that free people of color throughout the British Caribbean sought to link their quest for greater civil and political rights with amelioration. By the middle of the decade, the problem of racial discrimination against free blacks and coloreds had become a major issue in the debate over slavery in the British Caribbean. Perhaps the biggest single factor contributing to this was the alliance between abolitionist MP Stephen Lushington and the Afro-Jamaican elite's well-organized civil rights movement.[35]

Additionally, stories reached the British abolitionist press and parliamentary lobbyists about the increasing levels of persecution being meted out against free Afro-Caribbean people, as whites took out their rage about the antislavery debate and fears of slave resistance on free blacks and coloreds. The first such instance was the destruction of the Bridgetown Methodist chapel in 1823, which was followed by whites' ongoing persecution of Barbadian Methodists.[36] After missionary William Shrewsbury was run out of the island in 1823, a free woman of color named Sarah Ann Gill, described by Methodist church officials as a "respectable coloured Woman," continued to hold Methodist services at her Bridgetown home, which slaves and free people of color attended. Whites threatened to destroy her house because her congregation included slaves, and the governor and the Bridgetown magistrates allegedly tried to force her to stop the meetings. According to the secretary of the British Wesleyan Methodist Society, many people of color who did not attend the services "considered the threats and demonstrations of the Riotous Whites against Mrs. Gill's house as marks of hostility to them, the People of Colour, as a body." When the magistrates told Gill not to invite slaves she replied that "rather than exclude the poor Slaves I will have no Meetings at all."[37] The description of Gill as a "respectable" widow and the fact that she was doing

35. Campbell, *Dynamics of Change*, 108–109 and 118–119.

36. Parliament, House of Commons, *An Authentic Report of the Debate in the House of Commons, June 23, 1825, on Mr. Buxton's Motion Relative to the Demolition of the Methodist Chapel and Mission House in Barbadoes* (London: J. Hatchard and Son, 1825); Levy, "Barbados," 312–313.

37. Handler, *Unappropriated People*, 157; CO 28/96, Miscellaneous Offices Correspondence, No. 174, Barbados Secretary of the Methodist Missionary Society Richard Watson to Bathurst, 15 January 1825; CO 28/95, Government Executive, No. 84, Warde to Bathurst, 26 March 1825, and Government Executive No. 88, Warde to Bathurst, 29 March 1825, enclosing "Report of a Committee of the Privy Council on an Investigation of the Conduct of the Acting Magistrates of Bridge-Town . . . ," 5 May 1825; CO 31/49, 5 April 1825.

Christian missionary work were crucial to the political interest the case generated in the Colonial Office. She had the social attributes—"respectability" and Christian faith—abolitionists wished to encourage.

PHILANTHROPY, RACE, AND THE POLITICS OF AMELIORATION

Despite their proslavery views even some of the most conservative upper-class Afro-Barbadians recognized that the climate of imperial reformism and antislavery lent legitimacy to struggles against racial discrimination. The strong religious emphasis of British amelioration policy and the growing popularity and influence of imperial missionary philanthropy in Britain offered free people of color a way to express their "respectable" status, demonstrate their loyalty to Britain, and circumvent segregation laws. Abolitionism sparked a rapid growth in the number of philanthropic organizations in the British Caribbean during the early nineteenth century. In Barbados philanthropic activity was intimately tied to local struggles against racial discrimination. Free Afro-Barbadians embraced charitable work as politics by other means, since philanthropy was the only area of civic life in which all groups, regardless of race, were allowed to participate without restriction. Afro-Barbadian philanthropy was also part of the process of the consolidation of the free community of color, a sign both of group consciousness and increasing class stratification.[38]

Poor-relief provisions in Barbados, whether state sponsored or as the result of private initiative, had always been profoundly racialized and elitist. During the seventeenth and eighteenth centuries the Barbadian state used poor relief to ensure that the socioeconomic status of poor whites remained above that of Afro-Barbadians.[39] Neither the planter legislature nor individual whites established any state or private philanthropic societies for slaves or free people of color. Despite the doctrine of white supremacy, poor relief, education, and health provisions for indigent whites were in a sorry state. As Beckles has noted, while the principle of racial supremacy of whites was enshrined in all public institutions, "planter elitism was not offended, but confirmed, by the existence of a white working-class

38. Melanie Newton, "Philanthropy, Gender and the Production of Public Life in Barbados, c1790–c1850," in Pamela Scully and Diana Paton, eds., *Gender and Slave Emancipation in the Atlantic World* (Durham, N.C.: Duke University Press, 2005), 225–246.

39. Forde-Jones, "Mapping Racial Boundaries,"10 and 26–27.

culture of poverty on the periphery of the plantations."[40] Elite whites rarely displayed concern for the island's large and growing population of impoverished whites. Through parish vestries the state provided minimal services in a half-hearted attempt to maintain the superior social status of whiteness. By the early nineteenth century the government supported one free school for poor white boys. Although white girls could attend parish schools, there were no charity schools or scholarships for poor white girls. There were also no charitable societies run by white women in eighteenth-century Barbados that dispensed relief for white women and girls.

In the late 1700s missionary and philanthropic organizations began to spring up in Britain and the Caribbean seeking to conduct work among slaves and free Afro-Caribbean people. Frequently free people of color, both men and women, initiated or responded to the missionary call. Having been marginalized in the sphere of public life, they were now eager to use the new opportunity to play an unprecedented public role.[41] In Barbados, as the free Afro-Barbadian elite consolidated itself in the 1790s, philanthropic activity provided a means for members of this group to affirm their social position and demonstrate that they deserved civil rights increases. In 1798, just one year before a group of free men of color first petitioned for the right to testify in court, many of these same individuals formed the Samaritan Charitable Society of the Free People of Colour, a poor-relief organization. Although the society's mandate was allegedly nonpolitical, all known members of the charity were Afro-Barbadian men, many of whom were also active in the civil rights campaign from 1799 onward. The Samaritan Charitable Society remained active well into the postemancipation era, and by the 1820s it was the oldest philanthropic society in the island.[42]

At the end of the eighteenth century such organizing by free men of color posed no fundamental threat to either the social hierarchy or the power of the

40. Beckles, *History of Barbados*, 48–49.

41. Moira Ferguson, *The Hart Sisters: Early African Caribbean Writers, Evangelicals, and Radicals* (Lincoln: University of Nebraska Press, 1993); Mary Turner, *Slaves and Missionaries: The Disintegration of Jamaican Slave Society, 1787–1834* (Urbana: University of Illinois Press, 1982), 105 and 198.

42. *Barbadian,* March 25 1828, notice of a ball at the Samaritan Charitable Society's mansion; 19 September 1849, notice of celebration of Samaritans' fifty-first anniversary; Handler, Hughes, and Wiltshire, *Freedmen of Barbados,* names of members of the Samaritans in March 1820 (John Alsop, Francise Bootman, George Thomas Dolrond, John Durant Sr., Richard Durant, Benjamin Crofts Eversley Jr., Cato Roach, and Francis Wood).

white planter elite, and planters ignored it, as they ignored antidiscrimination petitions from Afro-Barbadian men. However, the growth of movements to reform or
abolish slavery transformed the political significance of philanthropy in the British Caribbean. For Caribbean planters and the British aristocracy, abolitionism—
with its network of extraparliamentary committees, societies, mass meetings, and
petitions—was more than just a threat to the institution of slavery. It was part of
a new public culture that attacked the foundations of aristocratic governance.[43]
Abolitionism was one aspect of a widespread demand for the reform of public
life unleashed in the Atlantic world in the aftermath of the American and French
revolutions. It was similar to what American historian Mary Ryan has termed the
"proliferation of publics" in the early-nineteenth-century United States, as groups
marginalized because of race, class, or gender sought to "constitute themselves
as a public" and began to use different forms of civic activity—such as philanthropic and cultural societies, newspapers, and mass meetings—to participate in
American political life.[44]

The philanthropic challenge to the white Barbadian elite began in earnest in
1818, when, as an amelioration measure, the new governor acted as patron for the
Colonial Charity School, making it the first publicly supported school for children of color, both enslaved and free, in the British Caribbean.[45] Whites were
outraged by the school's plan to teach mixed classes of free children of color and
slaves and by the possibility that slave children would be taught to write. In December 1818 an anonymous letter in the *Mercury* expressed whites' popular fears
that educating free colored, black and slave children together would "tend to produce between them correspondent feelings and sentiments. . . . The distance between their ranks is the widest in the scale of society, and the institutions of that
community in which slavery exists, should prevent their distance from being too
much contracted." Such teaching, so the argument went, interfered with slave

43. See David Brion Davis, *The Problem of Slavery in the Age of Revolution, 1770–1823* (Ithaca: Cornell University Press, 1975); J. R. Oldfield, *Popular Politics and British Anti-Slavery: The Mobilisation of
Public Opinion against the Slave Trade* (Manchester: Manchester University Press, 1995).

44. Mary Ryan, "Gender and Public Access: Nineteenth-Century America," in Craig Calhoun, ed.,
Habermas and the Public Sphere (Cambridge, Mass., MIT Press, 1992), 267–268. See also Sheller, *Democracy after Slavery*, 41–68.

45. Handler, *Unappropriated People*, 173–176. The school's name was eventually changed to the National School for Coloured Children.

owners' control of their slaves and slaves educated with free people might be incited to rebel against their bondage.[46] In 1819 Thomas Harris, a man of color and the junior secretary of the Colonial Charity School Committee, informed the public that the schools' trustees would separate slave and free children once sufficient funds were available, would only accept slave children with the written permission of their owners and planned to limit the curriculum for slave children to learning the Bible and Church of England doctrines.[47] Public indignation at the mixing of slave and free children of color in the school seems to have died out quickly and it does not seem that the school committee ever built a separate schoolroom.

White opposition to the project had little to do with the specifics of the school's educational policy. The Colonial Charity School was not the only school where Afro-Barbadian teachers taught groups of slave and free children. Men and women of color made a living teaching mixed classes of free children of color and the children of skilled and officer slaves, particularly in Bridgetown and Speightstown. An American sailor who spent time in Barbados during the War of 1812 noted that "coloured" women "of every shade," usually the mistresses of white men, taught music and singing, probably to girls of color.[48] In 1827, two years after the founding of the Anglican diocese of Barbados, no objections were raised when the bishop and a prominent white planter-clergyman established a "coloured Sunday school" for free people and slaves, which does not appear to have been internally segregated along legal lines.[49] The Colonial Charity School was controversial because it was the direct result of imperial slave amelioration policies, had gubernatorial sanction, and its administrative board was composed entirely of men of color—the first time that Afro-Barbadians had held such important positions.[50] The school was therefore a symbol of collaboration between the imperial government and local free people of color, lacking the approval of the Barbadian legislature. Neither the governor's support nor the applications of the school committee moved the legislature to give the Colonial Charity School financial support in the early

46. *BMBG*, 1 and 8 December 1818.

47. *BMBG*, 6 February 1819.

48. Nathaniel Hawthorne, ed., *The Yarn of a Yankee Privateer* (New York: Funk and Wagnall's, 1926), 12.

49. *Barbadian*, 30 October 1827.

50. *BMBG*, 6 February 1819.

1820s, although, according to the governor some of the island's "more opulent Inhabitants" made private donations.[51]

The school added to whites' unease about amelioration and the maintenance of racial hierarchies in public life. Two years after the school was founded a white music teacher felt compelled to publish an angry disclaimer in response to rumors that he had provided the music for a "Mulatto Dance": "[I]t is most true, I gave my services at a coloured Concert, for the benefit of the Charity School, which, as a Christian, I could not refuse; and shall do the same whenever requested."[52] "Mulatto dance" was a term used to refer to private parties given by mixed-race prostitutes for the entertainment of men, usually elite white planters, merchants, and army or navy officers and soldiers.[53] The use of references to illicit interracial sex to discredit a fund raiser for the school indicates the depth of public hostility and fear. At the same time, the rumor conjured up a familiar sexualized image of free people of color that whites perhaps found less politically threatening than that of pious Afro-Barbadians working with the imperial government to provide a Christian education for the nonwhite poor.

In 1819, the Colonial Charity School was joined by the Barbados Auxiliary Bible Society of the People of Colour, a colonial offshoot of the British Bible Society that distributed Bibles to the lower classes in Britain and throughout the empire and had strong abolitionist connections. The St. Mary's Society for the Education of the Coloured Poor in the Principles of the Established Church and for other Charitable Relief, which also had a British equivalent, was formed in the mid-1820s.[54] The philanthropic societies that sprang up in Barbados did not have abolitionist mandates but their executive committees consisted of Bridgetown's Afro-Barbadian merchant elite. Thomas Harris and Thomas J. Cummins, both secretaries of the Colonial Charity School Committee during the 1810s and 1830s, and Richard Durant, the secretary of the Samaritans in 1830, were prominent figures in the struggle for increased rights, with Harris and Cummins having been members of the 1819 Alien Bill Committee. The first committee of the St. Mary's Society in 1827 was a who's who of the free Afro-Barbadian merchant community. Among its twenty-nine members were the prominent businessmen Joseph Ken-

51. CO 31/47, 30 May 1820.

52. *BMBG,* 16 May 1820.

53. Hawthorne, *Yarn of a Yankee Privateer,* 104.

54. *Barbadian,* 16 May 1826; Clare Midgley, *Women against Slavery: The British Campaigns* (London: Routledge, 1992), 46.

nedy, Thomas J. Cummins, John Montefiore, Benjamin Massiah, Joseph Thorne, Joseph Shurland, Isaac Carvallo, and London Bourne.[55]

Several of the societies formed by free people of color during the 1820s also had female auxiliaries, which were responsible for female pupils or recipients of benefits and subordinate to the primary boards composed of men. These committees consisted of prominent Afro-Barbadian women, most of whose surnames indicate a family relationship to the men on the main committees. In 1827, the president of the Ladies' Branch Association for the Education of Female Children of the Coloured Poor—the auxiliary of the St. Mary's Society—was Mary Montefiore, whose husband, merchant of color John Montefiore, was on the St. Mary's committee. Mrs. (Thomas) Cummins, Mrs. (Joseph) Shurland, Mrs. (Benjamin) Massiah, and Mrs. (Charles) Phipps were among the nine auxiliary members whose husbands were either on the main committee of the St. Mary's Society or were prominent in other Afro-Barbadian charities.

While such philanthropic work was a new public role for women of color, it reinforced gendered hierarchies in public and family life and established the "respectability" of women of color with kin relationships to elite men at the expense of single and financially independent women. The first names of most female philanthropists of color are not known—their family names and marital status provide the sole guide to who they were. The public presence of these women served to establish the social respectability of the family name they carried, thereby emphasizing the role of their male relatives as patriarchal household heads. Furthermore, by highlighting their married status and family connections, these women distinguished between the respectability of their social circle and that of the Afro-Barbadian "concubines" of white men who, although sometimes wealthy, were not "respectable" married women. These elite married women of color were also separating themselves from working women of color in the public view who were usually not married, such as lodging-house keepers and hucksters. In the lists of names for the Ladies' Branch Association, married members were listed before unmarried members, further elevating the status of marriage within their own socioeconomic circle. It is likely that many of the unmarried members of the association were also the kin of politically active Afro-Barbadian men. Miss Lynch, for example, was probably the sister-in-law of Mrs. (Hamlet) Lynch, who was also a committee member and whose husband sat on the St. Mary's Society commit-

55. "First annual report of the Society for the Education of the Coloured Poor," *Barbadian*, 14 September 1827.

tee. Hamlet Lynch had signed civil rights petitions and addresses in 1799, 1811, and 1823.[56]

Free women of color did not form philanthropic organizations independently of men in their community such as those that flourished in the United States during the Jim Crow era.[57] Elite free women of color in Barbados were surely as invested in the struggle to end racial discrimination as men but they used philanthropy to define and make public their social position as morally upright and privileged women while channeling their political agency through men. The women of color who established these charities may have calculated that women's charitable work under the direction of men would present a united and "respectable" impression of the free Afro-Barbadian community. Such a strategy may have made it difficult for white opponents to mobilize the stereotype of the "loose" and dangerously independent free woman of color, thereby shielding female philanthropists from accusations of being immoral "public" women.

Never before had so many Afro-Barbadian men and women assumed such public civic roles. What was more, their charities provided services for slaves and free Afro-Barbadians that the government could not even competently provide for whites. By the early 1820s the Colonial Charity School was the fourth largest school in the country. In the first year of its existence the St. Mary's Society and its Ladies' Branch Association, which sought to educate, clothe, and feed the hungry and provide Christian burials for the dead, claimed to have 87 free boys, 60 free girls, 112 slave boys, and 70 slave girls attending their school, making a total of 329.[58] By the mid-1820s there were numerous schools for slaves and free children of color, most of them in Bridgetown and many of them run by free people of color. In 1823 there were at least twenty-five schools in St. Michael operated by free people of color, teaching a total of 583 pupils, of which the largest by far was the Colonial Charity School with 150. Most of the others had fewer than 20 pupils and eighteen such schools were run by women.[59] This list is almost certainly incomplete, and it does not give information on schools in other parishes. Commenting

56. *Barbadian*, 18 September 1827; Handler, Hughes, and Wiltshire, *Freedmen of Barbados*.

57. See Deborah Gray White, *Too Heavy a Load: Black Women in Defense of Themselves, 1894–1994* (New York: W. W. Norton, 1999).

58. *Barbadian*, 14 September 1827.

59. CO 28/93, Miscellaneous No. 23, Warde to Bathurst, 6 May 1824, enclosing "Total of Schools in the Parish of St. Michael in the Island of Barbados," 16 December 1823. By 1833, the School had 222 pupils. Handler, *Unappropriated People*, 175.

on Bridgetown schools in 1825, a British observer noted, "These schools are scattered about the parts of the town principally inhabited by the colored people, who are by these means more readily induced to send their children. These children are chiefly of the lowest order of the free colored and of the domestic and mechanic slaves in Bridge Town and the immediate vicinity." He also mentioned that, for the most part, the children were not taught to write.[60] In Speightstown there were several schools for slaves and free people of color, and by 1830 there were eleven charity schools scattered around the island for free Afro-Barbadian and slave children, although it is not known how many were run by people of color.[61]

Free Afro-Barbadians also formed community social institutions in the 1820s specifically for themselves, such as the Library Association, which was founded about 1824. A notice of a Library Association meeting in November of that year mentioned that a postmeeting dinner would be held at the establishment of leading Afro-Barbadian hotelier Hannah Lewis, which could suggest that free people of color were using their business networks to sustain and promote their community activities.[62] The Lyceum, a theater for free people of color, was established in 1830, as the few theaters in the island either had segregated seating or were for whites only. The Lyceum was funded by a subscription from the free Afro-Barbadian population. The advertisement for the first performance at the theater listed the names of seven stewards, including Thomas J. Cummins and Samuel Jackman Prescod, who would shortly become key figures in the struggle for civil rights.[63]

While this organizing illustrated a growing sense of responsibility on the part of the Afro-Barbadian elite toward slaves and free people of lower economic status, it also served to establish the elite's public respectability and social superiority while dividing Afro-Barbadians into dispensers and recipients of charity. The directorial committees of these societies were entirely composed of free people of color who were either wealthy or comparatively well-to-do, and who were for the most part baptized Christians.[64] Similarly, membership in Afro-Barbadian social

---

60. Coleridge, *Six Months*, 51–52.

61. PP 1831–1832, vol. 47, *Incorporated Society for the Conversion and Religious Instruction of the Negro Population, Annual Reports for 1828 and 1833*, cited in Handler, *Unappropriated People*, 178.

62. *Barbadian*, 11 May, 1824.

63. *Barbadian*, 18 February 1830; Handler, *Unappropriated People*, 214.

64. Some elite families, like the Montefiores, Carvallos, and Pinheiros, were of Portuguese-Jewish and African descent.

organizations was only for those who were considered "respectable." For example, the 1830 performance at the Lyceum cost subscribers one dollar per ticket, which was beyond the means of most slaves and free people of color. No one would be admitted without a ticket, but "[p]ersons of respectability not subscribers, may be admitted to see the performance with the consent of the Stewards on paying 1 1/4 dollar for each ticket." Shut out of politics because of their race, the free Afro-Barbadians who organized such events and societies were consolidating their public role by establishing a parallel social hierarchy to that of whites.[65]

ELITE WHITES AND THE RACIALIZATION OF PHILANTHROPY

White Barbadians responded to the challenge from nonwhite philanthropists and abolitionists by immediately founding organizations for poor whites and strengthening state support for whites-only charitable institutions. In 1819, in response to the establishment of the Colonial Charity School, local planters and clergymen set up a Barbados branch of the aristocratic and conservative British Society for Promoting Christian Knowledge (SPCK). In an early speech, the chairman of the Barbadian SPCK, a planter, made it clear that the society's purpose was to maintain white supremacy in the face of threats from uppity free people of color. He observed that "the poor white people of this Community do not fill that rank in Society to which they properly belong" and reminded his audience that it was "in [their] interest as much as [their] duty" to address the problem of white poverty. He then proceeded to dismiss Afro-Barbadian philanthropy as an "emulation" of white charity, an obvious attempt to seize the moral high ground that planters felt Afro-Barbadians had captured.[66]

The Barbados SPCK founded the Bridgetown Central School for indigent white boys in 1819, and a girls' Central School was established in 1826. The society's committee was all white, and the subscription fee was a minimum of £1.10s, or up to £5, which automatically excluded even whites who were not affluent. In 1822 the

65. Quote from *Barbadian*, 18 February 1830. In a similar contemporaneous phenomenon in Britain, philanthropic and social institutions were an important means by which middle-class and nonconformist men established public roles. See, for example, Leonore Davidoff and Catherine Hall, *Family Fortunes: Men and Women of the English Middle Class* (London: Routledge, 1987), 416–449; and Catherine Hall, *White, Male, and Middle Class: Explorations in Feminism and History* (Cambridge: Polity, 1992), 255–295.

66. *BMBG*, 2 March 1819.

legislature assumed financial responsibility for the Central School, a degree of support and responsibility that it never considered extending to similar organizations run by free Afro-Barbadians while slavery lasted.[67] An 1826 petition from the SPCK to the assembly proposed that the Central School should be a means of establishing a "core" of white teachers for the parochial schools and schools for children of color, which implies that they hoped the school would help limit the number of Afro-Barbadian teachers. In 1825 the Anglican clergy founded the St. Peter's Benevolent National School in Speightstown for the children of slaves and free people of color. Planters dominated the school committee, and its 1829 report mentioned that a Central School graduate was already installed as teacher at St. Peter's.[68] In 1829 the Barbados Society for the encouragement of Arts and promoting Mechanical Trades and General Industry was formed, which was also a planter, merchant, and clergy initiative to improve the lot of poor whites.[69]

Particularly after the imperial government's 1823 adoption of its amelioration policy Barbadian planters tried to wrest control of the amelioration process away from the Colonial Office. After mid-1823 there was a noticeable change in planters' public rhetoric, as they sought to legitimate themselves as the proper protectors of slaves' interests. It was the beginning of a shift away from the blatant language of proprietary rights to a romanticized and patriarchal discourse in which slaves were constructed as dependent vassals, almost members, of the planter's extended family. In August 1823 the local clergy and the General Agricultural Society, a planter organization, held a meeting at the Central School and resolved to pursue a policy of Christianizing slaves.[70] Shortly after the meeting the attorney for one large St. Andrew plantation wrote to the estate's absentee owner informing him of the recent resolution passed by planters and clergy and reported that most large estates had immediately appointed their own lay catechists. The manager offered the assurance that he, like all of the other planters, had gath-

67. CO 31/49, 20 March 1821; CO 30/20, "An Act for the better management and support of the Central School established . . . by the Barbados Society for Promoting Christian Knowledge," 18 January 1822.

68. CO 31/51, 18 July 1826, petition from the Central School to the House of Assembly; *Barbadian*, 26 October, 6 November 1827, 14 November 1828, and 8 December 1829.

69. CO 31/51, 17 March 1829, petition from the Barbados Society for the encouragement of Arts and promoting Mechanical Trades and General Industry; *Barbadian*, 29 November and 8 December 1829.

70. *BMBG*, 8 August 1823.

ered the slaves on the estate together and "candidly told [them] what has passed & what we are willing and even desirous to do for the amelioration of their condition."[71]

An 1824 letter to the *Barbadian* from "A Master of a Family," titled "Family Religion," instructed other planters about the best means of Christianizing slaves. First, he recommended paying special attention to domestic servants, since, having been raised in the master's family, they had "acquired better habits—more civilized feelings—and a moral frame of temper: here is the soil, then, most ready for Christianity. Were these persons instructed in Christian principles, and practice, by family worship, as they often have parents or brothers, sisters or children, amongst the laboring class, the leaven would be much sooner spread." The same writer called out to his fellow planters, stating, "Christian! are you a father and a master? Remember, I beseech you, that you do not stand alone in the world—that you have others to take care of, and to answer for, as well as for yourself."[72]

As planters expanded their private educational and missionary activities among slaves, they also aggressively strengthened racial segregation. In the late 1820s the parish vestries, which were responsible for overseeing parochial schools and whose members were all clergymen and landowners, increased funding for parochial schools. These schools were for whites only, and the vestries sought to improve the attendance of poor white children. They restated the racial segregation policy, making it clear that no free children of color would be admitted. By the early 1830s, St. Philip and Christ Church were the only parishes that funded schools for free children of color, who were educated separately from whites.[73]

Planters and the clergy also worked together to establish mutual benefit clubs for slaves, called friendly societies. Bathurst had recommended that slave owners form such societies in order to teach slaves, who were assumed to be spendthrifts, to save their money. Friendly societies promoted patriarchal Christian social values, accepting only baptized Christians, while drunks, "polygamists," and people in common law unions were not admitted. Unlike the later friendly so-

71. D239M/E20579, Fitzherbert Papers, Sir Reynold Alleyne to Messrs. Nelson and Adam, 4 December 1823, BDA.

72. *Barbadian*, 24 September 1824.

73. Minutes of the St. Philip Vestry, 25 March 1830; *Barbadian*, 8 June 1830; Minutes of the Christ Church Vestry, 30 August 1832.

cieties of the twentieth-century anglophone Caribbean or the *cabildos de nación* of Cuba during and after slavery, which were grassroots initiatives by Africans and people of African descent, the Barbadian societies of the 1820s and 1830s were created by elites and state authorities, formed to enforce the social and behavioral norms prescribed by the Anglican Church and improve planters' image in Britain.[74] Even, here, however, free people of color stole the march on the plantocracy—by the end of slavery the largest friendly societies in the island were the sex-segregated St. Mary's Male and Female Friendly Societies, which were attached to the free black and colored St. Mary's Society and had three hundred members in 1835.[75]

In contrast to Afro-Barbadian women, white Barbadian women established their own independent charities during the 1820s. Philanthropy gave white women new opportunities to play a responsible and influential public role while also strengthening the bonds of white community and white supremacy. In 1825, the Ladies' Association for the Relief of the Sick and Indigent Poor of Bridgetown and its Environs was founded, its members all wealthy white women, whose charity was initially for poor whites only. Planters turned the Ladies' Association into the showpiece of a reinvigorated sense of white moral leadership. In contrast to poor-relief organizations run by free people of color, the Ladies' Association received generous grants from the island's legislature. An 1828 "amateur exhibition of the fine Arts," directed by a leading member of the council to raise funds for the Ladies' Association, would only allow people of color to view the exhibit on Sundays.[76]

Through philanthropy upper-class white women invented a new public image of themselves to replace the typically derogatory representations of them in the local press. The *Barbadian* newspaper, which printed several editorials and satirical articles during the 1820s implying that wealthy white women were ignorant, spoiled, and a nuisance, patronizingly praised the "perseverance" of white female philanthropists in the 1830s, stating that had their societies been run by men,

74. *Barbadian*, 13 October 1832; A. F. Wells and D. Wells, *Friendly Societies in the West Indies: Report on a Survey by A. F. and D. Wells* (London: HMSO, 1953); Beckles, *History of Barbados*, 151–152; Rebecca Scott, *Slave Emancipation in Cuba: The Transition to Free Labor, 1860–1899* (Princeton: Princeton University Press, 1985), 9 and 66.

75. *Barbadian*, 6 and 10 June 1835.

76. *Barbadian*, 26 December 1826 and 22 January 1828.

"they should have folded long before."[77] This quote might be an indication that most of the charities established and run by wealthy white men were not effective in their operations. This seems likely given that few if any of them published annual reports of their activities, in contrast to the Ladies' Association and the largest Afro-Barbadian charities.

Elite white female philanthropists took on a maternal public role that coincided with the language of male planter paternalism. The Ladies' Association first began to provide charitable relief to slaves and the Afro-Barbadian poor about 1829, dispensing poor relief and distributing Bibles and religious books with the stated aim of rescuing young people "from the contagion of vice."[78] Often, such undertakings were an extension of the domestic role of female members of planter families as the mistress of the house, in contrast to the grandiose and highly publicized acts of charity conducted by the planters and the clergy. The Moravian mission at Mount Tabor in St. John was opened in 1826 under the auspices of a planter's wife, Mrs. Haynes, who gave the Moravians land for the mission station and who herself became involved in teaching the slave children on her husband's plantation. In letters, Haynes maternally and condescendingly referred to the mission school children as "her Negro children."[79]

CONCLUSION

Amelioration transformed the cultural and political terrain of Barbados, opening up channels beyond the narrow and formal institutional method of petitions to state officials, allowing slaves and free people of color to challenge planter authority. Afro-Barbadians met amelioration's religious reforms with strategies of both accommodation and popular cultural resistance. In many areas of public life, amelioration stimulated competition between Afro-Barbadians seeking to expand their access to state institutions and whites who were determined that any such concessions would come only at the behest of individual planters or the planter state. Elite people of color also used amelioration to develop an Afro-Barbadian social hierarchy that was both patriarchal and unequal, with a small group of well-

77. See *Barbadian,* letter from "Amelia Sobersides," 9 August 1825, letter from "Patty Lackbrain," 20 January 1829, and editorial on the Ladies' Association and the St. Michael Clothing Society, 7 January 1835.

78. *Barbadian,* 12 October 1829.

79. Moravian Diary; see, for example, the entry for 5 August 1827.

to-do men taking the lead as self-appointed political representatives and moral guardians. However, elite views about reform and the organization of the non-white community did not go unchallenged from below. If the antislavery debate legitimized activities such as philanthropy as a new means for elite free men and women of color to press their demands for reform and display their respectability, it did the same for hundreds of other people of color, slave and free, who used other public venues to express more radical visions of what change should mean.

I n the final decade of slavery, various strands of antielitist and largely plebian Afro-Barbadian populism emerged, primarily through street protests, mass meetings and, perhaps most dramatically, organized physical occupations of segregated whites-only public spaces. This populist trend grew as much out of resentment at the Afro-Barbadian elite's proslavery views and claims to represent the nonwhite majority as out of opposition to white supremacy. Slaves and working-class free people of color frequently protested together against people and institutions associated with white supremacy. This popular antisegregationism reflected and was rooted in a proimperial Afro-Caribbean political sentiment, which was very different from and, in fact, represented a fundamental challenge to whites' traditional attitudes toward the empire. For working-class Afro-Barbadians, abolitionism and the new antislavery and reformist trend in imperial politics represented a redefinition of "Britishness" and imperial identity that offered the best hope of bringing about meaningful political change in the Caribbean. As the antislavery struggle reached its climax, some free Afro-Barbadians began to acknowledge publicly that their fight against racism could not be separated from the struggle against slavery.

The Afro-Barbadian merchant elite's relationship to popular reformism was ambivalent. While elite Afro-Barbadians moved away from the more explicitly proslavery statements of earlier years they were still reluctant to embrace emancipation. In fact, Afro-Barbadian merchants often sought political alliances with whites *against* former slaves, demanding reform to protect their business interests from former slave competition. However, the colonial government remained firmly opposed to desegregation and imperial officials began to imagine an expanded political role for free people of color, assuming that they were the natural representatives and protectors of the newly freed. In response many politically ambitious men of color who had previously ignored the free Afro-Barbadian ma-

jority sought to reinvent themselves as the leaders of a mass-based political constituency of people of color.

THE POLITICS OF THE STREETS

In contrast to elite men of color, who preferred to use formal and established political channels to make their case, public spaces were the only platform available
to Afro-Barbadians of lower-class background. The poor and underprivileged—
the supposed objects of elite benevolence—quickly recognized the potential usefulness of free black and colored charities as places to gather and discuss politics.
The well-to-do authors of the 1823 Belgrave address admitted nervously that they
wrote it in order to put an end to meetings by what they described as "mobs" of
"coloured persons" who assembled at the Colonial Charity School to discuss the
political situation during the tense period before the destruction of the Methodist chapel. The signatories' eagerness to assure the legislature of their support
for slavery suggests that proabolitionist sentiments were voiced at these meetings.[1] Such goings-on confirmed Barbadian government officials' worst suspicions
about the possible political overtones of Afro-Barbadian charitable organizing. In
March 1824 the St. Michael vestry asked the rector of the parish not to permit free
people of color to use the church for any philanthropic purposes, since the recent
House of Assembly inquiry into the January 1824 counteraddress had revealed that
"a certain class of free coloured people have formed Societies and . . . under the
Mark of Religion they [might] project Schemes dangerous to the legal Establishment of the Colony."[2]

Grassroots Afro-Barbadian rebellion against people and institutions associated with the state's racial discrimination policy intensified in the 1820s, and
the victims of their outrage were not only whites or segregated spaces. The Afro-
Barbadian planter Jacob Belgrave Jr. was again selected as a target of popular dis-
like, as he had been in 1816. In 1824 a large crowd of people of color subjected Belgrave and several other upper-class Afro-Barbadian men to a very public verbal
assault. The protest occurred when Belgrave was leaving for England, where he in-

1. CO 28/93, No. 20, Warde to Bathurst, 31 March 1824, enclosing "Examination of Witnesses. . . ."
See previous reference in chapter 2, p. 85. In 1827, a group of free people of color also met at the school
to compose a petition against the discriminatory clauses of the second Consolidated Slave Act. *Barbadian*, 25 December 1827.

2. Minutes of the St. Michael Vestry, 25 March 1824.

tended to take on the unofficial role of agent for free Afro-Barbadians and present himself to the secretary of state for the colonies on the community's behalf.[3] According to the *Barbadian*, a crowd of free black and colored people and slaves assembled at the wharf

> for the express purpose, as it would appear, of hissing Mr. Jacob Belgrave, and a few other coloured men, of the most respectable class, who accompanied him when he took boat to embark aboard the ship *Lancaster*, bound for Liverpool. And to give the greater degree of atrocity to the conduct of these rioters, they waited on the wharf until the boat returned with the party of Mr. Belgrave's friends, who, we understand, were pelted and hissed, and annoyed in every disagreeable way—For the greater part of the evening the Town was in an uproar with the noise of these riotous men, followed by mobs of slaves, who are at all times ready to join in any such disturbance, and who, it appears, the owners—tyrants, as we are represented to be— cannot keep in doors.[4]

The presence of slaves at this protest recalls the two occasions in 1816 just before the rebellion, when slaves accosted Belgrave and accused him of being responsible for denying them their freedom. Despite being a planter, Belgrave experienced a degree of personal vilification to which whites were not subjected. The demonstration can be read as an act of political solidarity between slaves and free Afro-Barbadians against men such as Belgrave, who were seen as traitors against their own color.

The 1824 protest against Belgrave and his friends was only the first in a series of public demonstrations through which working-class free Afro-Barbadians and slaves intervened in debates about racial segregation and challenged or ignored the authority of the free black and colored elite. In early 1825 Afro-Barbadians mounted a protest during a public service at the parish church of St. Michael in honor of the whites-only Central School. According to the *Barbadian*'s probably exaggerated report, during the service a large group of people of color swept into the area reserved for whites and blocked the aisles.[5] The *Barbadian* rebuked all free

3. CO 28/96 527, Barbados, agent for Barbados George Carrington to Bathurst, 10 July 1825. It does not seem that Bathurst ever met with him.

4. *Barbadian*, 8 October 1824.

5. *Barbadian*, 18 February 1825.

people of color for the conduct of those in the church and argued that they should be grateful for the privileges granted to some of them by the legislature in 1817. In response, the editor received an angry letter from someone who claimed to be a member of the "coloured gentry" and signed himself "Justice and Order." "Justice and Order's" extraordinary letter was the first published statement by an individual free person of color to be so openly defiant of white supremacy:

> Is it not . . . natural Mr. E[ditor] that [the ceremony] should xcite great curiosity amongst all classes of persons but more particularly amongst those who from local circumstances are precluded from participating in the injoyment of those social refinements which in the Western World appear to be the exclusive right of the whites ought it then to be wondered at that they should so exceed the more refined etiquete of polite manners as merely to intrude in those spaces in the church which were not previously occupied by whites it is also very likely [too] some of them were slaves as many persons of that description go there for the purpose of attending on their owners. . . . I anticipated a hope sir that time and the benevolent spirit of the age might have made some impression on you I however feel some regret on being disappointed with respect to those feelings for rich and poor bond and free which you wish to insenuate [sic] that you possess . . . in regard to those previliges which you have trumpted to the World that the free [colored] people injoy not from the philonthropic feeling of the legeslature towards them but from the tolerateing & benevolent spirit of the age . . . the enlightened part of the free people of Colour do most sincerely feel the degraded state under which they labour nor do they require to be reminded of it by you as they rest fully satisfied that it is their situation alone which gives full scope not only to the [Editor of the *Barbadian*] but to all such reptiles of the tipe to animadvert on thier conduct with impunity.[6]

"Justice and Order" regretted that the editor's bigotry had not been softened by "the benevolent spirit of the age," a concept soon to be made fashionable by William Hazlitt's 1825 collection of political biographies called *The Spirit of the Age; or, Contemporary Portraits.* The idea of "the spirit of the age" became popular in British abolitionist and reformist circles as a term identifying them, not their

6. *Barbadian*, 1 March 1825.

conservative opponents, with liberal intellectual and political trends. "Justice and Order" sarcastically expressed the hope that "the period may not be far remote when the legislature in their wisdom will see the utility of granting [free people of color] an extension of previliges [sic] and by a spontanious & benevolent act worthy of their great and dignified minds grant them relief." The references to "rich and poor, bond and free" and "the liberal spirit of the age" were a subtle expression of support for the amelioration process. The author also brazenly attributed any improvements in the circumstances of free Afro-Barbadians and slaves to the "liberal" imperial political climate, rather than any pretense of "philonthropic [sic] feeling" on the part of the legislature. "Justice and Order" finished by dismissing the Barbadian's editor as a "reptile" and warning him that he was being watched.[7]

The incident again brought class-based political divisions among Afro-Barbadians to the fore, as a week later there was a response from a different writer, also allegedly a free man of color, who proclaimed himself to be "a *real* lover of Justice and Order." This correspondent identified himself as one of the few beneficiaries of the 1817 testimony act, whereas, he stated, the original "Justice and Order" probably spoke for the majority who were not. According to the author, who had been at the church service for the Central School, the protest had been launched by two black men, possibly slaves, who had occupied seats in a public seating area traditionally reserved for whites. The author alleged that "there are a great many *(there are exceptions)* who would do the same the next Sunday, if they could with impunity." This "*real* lover of Justice and Good Order" went on to distinguish himself as a "free-born coloured man" who had been granted the legal right to testify in court in 1817, and he echoed the sentiments of Jacob Belgrave, noting that "he wanted no oath [the right to testify in court], so long as his *word* would pass with every white Gentleman in the Island." Although white observers invariably lumped all free people of color together regardless of phenotype, this writer obviously attached great importance to the fact that the protesters were "black" whereas he was "coloured." He also emphasized the fact that he was free born. At least for some free people of color, both phenotype as well as whether one was born free or a slave were socially significant attributes. The correspondent con-

7. Ibid. William Hazlitt, *The Spirit of the Age; or, Contemporary Portraits*, ed. E. D. Mackerness (1825; reprint, Plymouth: Northcote House, 1991). Hazlitt's language would be echoed a decade later by Edward Stanley, then secretary of state for the colonies, when he informed the imperial parliament that the emancipation bill before them reflected the "liberal and humane spirit of the age." Holt, *Problem of Freedom*, 21.

cluded by warning the white public about the inflammatory views that other Afro-Barbadians voiced in their "private meetings" and stating his hope that the social and legal hierarchy of slave society would always be preserved.[8]

"A *real* lover of Justice and Order's" letter, which contained a far more credible description of the incident than the *Barbadian's* initial report, indicated that the two protesters had taken pains to dress well in preparation for occupying seats reserved for whites. By wearing impeccable Sunday attire and entering a section of the church restricted to them, these two men made a statement about their right to sit anywhere in the church as long as they were respectably dressed. Given that white supremacy was so entrenched in Barbados, the fact that no one made the men leave reveals the fragility of racial segregation in the island. Despite the racist nature of Barbadian slave society many of the rules governing social hierarchies were based on custom rather than written law. Once amelioration placed these customs in doubt, individuals such as these two men took the opportunity to launch a public attack on the everyday practices of racial segregation, a challenge for which whites had no legal response. As these were public seats rather than privately owned pews, church officials had no legal grounds for removing them.

Whether or not church officials had law on their side they were more than ready by December 1831 to manipulate statute law in the interests of preserving segregation. The demonstration began when two Afro-Barbadian apprentice tailors occupied seats in the whites-only section of the church reserved for whites. When church officials tried to remove them, "a mass" of people of color left the galleries reserved for slaves and people of color and "made a stand" in the whites-only area. After the incident it emerged that the protest had been planned ahead of time, and the protesters intended to do the same again the following Sunday. In response, the St. Michael Vestry prosecuted the two tailors (on what charges it is not clear), launched an investigation into the matter, and, to maintain the pretense of fairness, called in a select committee of Bridgetown's most prosperous Afro-Barbadian merchants to discuss the issue.[9] The merchants, none of whom had taken part in the apparently subaltern protest, sought to placate the vestry,

8. *Barbadian*, 8 March 1825.

9. The merchants summoned were John Montefiore, Thomas Harris, Joseph Kennedy, Thomas J. Cummins, William B. Massiah, and Henry Brathwaite (Minutes of the St. Michael Vestry, 7, 13, and 19 December 1831). Given the striking similarities between these two incidents and the fact that the date of the second protest is unclear, it is possible that they were the same, and that the two men were simply not prosecuted until 1831.

claiming without consulting any of the protesters that the events had not been planned and that the protest happened because free people of color were forced to sit with slaves during the service. The merchants recommended that the vestry make "limited" provision for free people of color—presumably themselves—to sit in the whites-only section. After allegedly giving the suggestion its "fullest consideration," the vestry resolved that the pews in the white area were actually the communal property of the island's white inhabitants and it was therefore a violation of white property rights to allow anyone else to sit there. Although this ruling was not challenged, its legality was doubtful, especially in the new political and legal climate of the amelioration period.[10]

RACE, BOURGEOIS "RESPECTABILITY," AND FRANCHISE REFORM

As part of the amelioration process in most colonies during the 1820s, propertied free people of color at last won the right to vote on the basis of a property-restricted franchise qualification. By the 1830s, Barbados, Bermuda, and the Bahamas were the only territories where free people of color still could not testify in court.[11] In 1829, with the encouragement of members of the island's legislature, fifteen merchants of color sent a petition to the Barbadian House of Assembly requesting that the electoral franchise be extended on a limited basis to free people of color. This was the first petition from free people of color in the island demanding the right to vote and hold public office. The authors' tone was extremely deferential; nevertheless, the petition's demands and the language in which they were framed suggest that the even the most cautious and elitist Afro-Barbadian civil rights campaigners were influenced by the liberal political and intellectual trends of the time.

First, the petitioners dismissed the law that denied them the vote as outdated, arguing that as "respectable" Afro-Barbadian men they had earned the right to be "citizens" on an equal footing with their white counterparts. They requested that the property requirement for free men of color be freehold ownership of property with an annual taxable value of ten pounds, the same as it was for white men. This deployment of the concept of citizenship as an earned rather than an inalienable right was a far cry for radical republican ideas of universal manhood suffrage, but this petition was the first from Barbadian free people of color to employ the word

10. Minutes of the St. Michael Vestry, 7, 13, 19 December 1831, and 2 January 1832; *Barbadian*, 17 December 1831.

11. Cox, *Free Coloreds*, 107; Heuman, *Between Black and White*, 33–34.

"citizens," a term of political belonging reminiscent of the French and Haitian Revolutions. Barbadian planters always referred to themselves as the subjects of the English monarchy and "citizenship," with its republican and antimonarchist connotations, was a notion antithetical to their political culture. The petition is also notable for the absence of any reference to the debate about slavery, whether in support of slavery's preservation or abolition. It is likely that, since slavery's long-term survival was seriously in doubt by the end of the 1820s, the petitioners elected not to antagonize the imperial government or, perhaps, one another by raising such a thorny issue.[12]

This petition was first publicly discussed at a February 1829 meeting in the Colonial Charity School, called by the old guard of the free black and colored community, most of them the increasingly unpopular members of the 1819 Alien Bill Committee. The new and more forthright tone of this petition reflected the influence at this meeting of a twenty-one-year-old man named Samuel Jackman Prescod, who, over the course of the next decade, would emerge as the most controversial and, eventually, most influential member of the free Afro-Barbadian community. Born in 1807, the son of a free woman of color and a white planter, Prescod grew up in a time when the political universe of free Afro-Caribbean people was rapidly being transformed, not least by their own struggles for social and political change. Although Prescod was not a member of the free black and colored elite and was largely self-educated, his intelligence and energy were recognized early on, as was illustrated by the effectiveness of his intervention at this meeting and his selection as the manager of the first Afro-Barbadian theater just one year later.[13]

In 1831 the Barbadian legislature finally passed an act extending the electoral franchise and the right to testify to free Afro-Barbadian men. Whereas the 1817 enfranchisement bill had used religious affiliation as the basis for establishing which free men of color could testify, the 1831 "Brown Privilege Bill," as it was popularly known, explicitly used class to determine which free black and colored men were enfranchised. The act extended the vote and the right to testify in court to men of color with thirty pounds' worth of annual taxable property, a requirement fewer than seventy-five men of color could meet in 1831. Moreover, the legislature passed an act preserving the ten-pound property qualification for white men, as well as a bill removing all constraints on slaves' ability to testify against free people

12. CO 31/51, 14 July 1829.

13. Vaughan, *Democrat*, 5 January, 5 and 12 February 1971.

of color in order to further counter the effects of the Brown Privilege Bill.[14] The planter who introduced the latter bill argued that slaves now required greater legal protection against "the freed man [who] may now become the judge of those very acts which his associates have perpetrated against the slaves." The planter made it clear that, as far as he was concerned, slaves and free people of color were equally lacking in principles, noting that there was no grounds for thinking that freedom gave "the slave of yesterday" better moral judgment.[15] Thus a reform that should have been an amelioration measure for free Afro-Barbadians once again benefited the few while excluding the majority and gave the legislature the opportunity to demonstrate its distrust of lower-class people of color.

Even those fortunate few who were enfranchised by the Brown Privilege Bill found their hopes frustrated because the legislature inserted a one-year suspending clause into the bill in order to delay its implementation. In July 1832 a group of men of color who should have been enfranchised under the act petitioned the Crown, complaining that they were still unable to exercise their right to vote and testify because of the clause.[16] The petitioners expressed frustration at the prevalence of legalized racial discrimination and for the first time publicly made connections between their political disenfranchisement, the legal oppression of slaves and, in a concession born of the necessity of the moment, women. In their petition the men referred to an 1831 case of a white man who had shot a free black man in full view of his wife, a group of free Afro-Barbadians and several slaves. None of the free people of color could testify, presumably because of the suspending clause in the 1831 act; the slaves could not testify because slaves were prohibited from testifying in capital trials where the defendant was white; and the man's wife could not testify because a married woman could not testify against her husband.[17]

Bourgeois Afro-Barbadian men pursued other avenues of reconciliation with whites, forging informal alliances with white urban merchants based on common business interests. White Bridgetown residents were no less racist than planters—

---

14. CO 30/21, No. 538, "An Act to remove certain restraints and disabilities imposed by Law on His Majesty's Free Coloured and Free Black Subjects of this Island," passed 9 May 1831. No. 541, "An Act the better to equalize the value of freehold property within this Island," passed 12 May 1831, maintained the qualification for white men. Handler, *Unappropriated People*, 103.

15. CO 31/51, 26 April 1831.

16. The 1831 bill came into effect on 22 November 1832. Handler, *Unappropriated People*, 103.

17. CO 28/109, No. 99, Lyon to Goderich, 4 July 1832, enclosing address from a deputation of free colored persons.

for example, the Bridgetown Commercial Hall, a merchants' club, did not admit men of color, even though it rented its rooms from the wealthy merchant of color London Bourne.[18] Nevertheless, white merchants and tradesmen resented the fact that colonial fiscal policy favored rural landowners at their expense. They were also excluded from the highest levels of politics and the colonial civil service because they were not planters.

White and Afro-Barbadian merchants agreed on the necessity of electoral reform as a means of defending merchants' interests, and saw separate representation for Bridgetown in the House of Assembly as a way to gain political influence. Both groups also feared that emancipation would only increase the competition they faced from slave hucksters. In the early 1830s Afro-Barbadian and white merchants began to cooperate politically, lobbying the legislature to restrict the activities of street hucksters.[19] In 1833, while the first imperial act of emancipation was being debated in the British Parliament, a group of Bridgetown merchants again petitioned the House of Assembly, demanding that, in the event of emancipation, the terms of compensation to planters should prioritize repayment of the estates' debts to local merchants over mortgages or other encumbrances. John Montefiore and Company and William B. Nunes, two merchant houses owned by men of color, were among the firms listed on the petition, together with a list of white-owned merchant establishments.[20]

Philanthropy provided another avenue for class to mitigate the effects of racial tension between the urban Afro-Barbadian and white bourgeoisies. By the later 1820s, white opposition to free black and colored philanthropy was giving way to a paternalistic tolerance. An 1827 editorial in the pro-planter *Barbadian* commended the "Free Coloured people" for their efforts "to create and diffuse generally among their fellow-creatures a religious and moral sense, and to relieve distress of every description." In contrast to the outrage with which many whites greeted the founding of the Colonial Charity School eight years earlier, the *Barbadian*'s editor gave its approval to elite free black and colored philanthropy among slaves and impoverished free people of color. He pointed with condescending approbation to their "general deportment for some time past—to their peaceable, inoffensive, and respectful demeanor—to their liberality in aiding *our* charitable institutions—and to their exertions to spread the knowledge of the Gospel amongst their own class,

18. Karch, "Man for All Seasons," 5.

19. CO 31/51, 27 November 1832.

20. CO 31/51, 27 August 1833, "Petition from Merchants and others. . . ."

as well as amongst Slaves."[21] In 1829 the St. Mary's Society for the Education of the Coloured Poor received state support for the first time in the form of a fifty-pound grant from the vestry of St. Michael parish, which had some white merchant representation, to help build a new poorhouse for the nonwhite poor, the elderly, and invalids. The society's petition displayed a class elitism of which the vestry must surely have approved, stating that the erection of a poor house would ensure that "many unseemly exhibitions of human suffering [would be] removed from the public eye." In 1832 the society petitioned successfully for a grant of one hundred pounds from the vestry.[22] By the 1830s the white Ladies Association and the Afro-Barbadian Ladies Branch Association for the Education of the Coloured Poor were occasionally working together.[23] There was even talk of a possible merger between the Barbados Auxiliary Bible Society of the People of Colour and the whites-only Barbados Auxiliary Bible Society.[24]

White conservatives used their increasingly friendly relations with elite Afro-Barbadians to silence or discredit free people of color with more far-reaching anti-segregationist and antislavery views. In late 1832 a prominent Antiguan free man of color, Henry Loving, visited Barbados on his way back from Britain, where he had spoken out publicly in favor of slave emancipation before an imperial royal commission. Loving, the editor of the *Antigua Weekly Register,* was one of the most important Afro-Caribbean advocates of racial equality and abolition, and he regularly contributed articles to the *Anti-Slavery Reporter,* one of British's leading abolitionist publications.[25] According to the *Barbadian* newspaper, thirty-six "coloured and black gentlemen" threw a party for Loving during his brief stay in Barbados. None of the island's newspapers, which were all owned and edited by whites, would cover the event because it "pertained to free coloured entertainment." However, the *Barbadian* broke its silence on the affair in order to report to the public that Loving had submitted a letter, in which, according to the editor, he described West Indian whites as being disloyal to the imperial government, whereas people of color would support imperial policy. The editor asserted that no "reasonable" man of color could support such an "inflammatory" letter, "put forward at the precise time when long cherished prejudices against them had given way, and

21. *Barbadian,* 2 January 1827.

22. Minutes of the St. Michael Vestry, 25 March 1829 and 25 March 1832.

23. *Barbadian,* 11 September 1833.

24. *Barbadian,* 18 September 1833.

25. *Barbadian,* 14 November 1832; PP 1831–1832, vol. 20, *Report from select committee,* 156–167.

the two classes [whites and free people of color] were approximating nearer and
nearer to each other in Christian fellowship, and love, and harmony, and in almost
every colony the law had placed all free men on a footing of political equality."[26]

BETWEEN THE EMPIRE AND THE PLANTER STATE

Even as upper-class Afro-Barbadian civil rights campaigners dropped the overtly
proslavery and antiradical language and tactics of earlier years, they sought to
distance themselves from the working-class Afro-Barbadian majority. They also
avoided any association between their antiracist struggle and plebian radicalism or
antislavery politics. Ultimately, however, as the crisis over slavery reached its ze-
nith in the 1830s, it became increasingly difficult for elite Afro-Barbadians to pre-
tend that their political fortunes were not tied up with the future of slavery.

Clashes between the Colonial Office and the Barbadian judiciary over the interpretation of slave law brought free Afro-Barbadians into open confrontation
with the planter state, forcing some of them to choose sides between the imperial government and local planters on the issue of slavery. Matters came to a
head as a result of two especially controversial legal cases in 1829 and 1833.[27] In
the first, three slave men were condemned to death for hiring a white man to kill
their owner. In a dramatic turn of events, the prosecution's case fell apart when
it emerged that the key witness—a slave—was not baptized, as only baptized
slaves could testify under the new amelioration laws. To the outrage of the local
magistrates and the white public, the governor pardoned the three men. At this
point, a new scandal developed, because, having been sentenced to death then
pardoned, the three slaves were now, to all intents and purposes, free men. Once
a condemned slave was pardoned, he or she effectively had no owner, since the
state had already compensated the previous owner for the loss of the slave. Magistrates threw the men in jail anyway, but Acting Protector of Slaves John Mayers
intervened and had the men freed. Mayers enlisted the help of Afro-Barbadian lay
preacher Joseph Thorne, who agreed to act as security once they were freed. Find-
ing himself the target of the legislature's wrath for his actions, Thorne defended
himself by saying he only became involved because he had believed the men to be

26. *Barbadian*, 10 October 1832.

27. For more detailed discussion of these cases, see Melanie Newton, "The King v. Robert James,
A Slave, for Rape: Inequality, Gender and British Slave Emancipation, 1823–1834," *Comparative Studies
in Society and History* 47, no. 3 (2005): 583–610.

free. The legislature petitioned the governor to have the men arrested on the dubious legal grounds that their freedom set a bad example to other slaves but to no avail—legal authorities in London eventually upheld the pardon and the three men were released as free people.[28]

The scandal had barely abated when, in 1832, the Barbadian legal system delivered another example of racist justice in the case of an enslaved man accused of having raped a poor white widow and mother. Whether the man was guilty or not, the transcripts of the case clearly show that the chief justice, the solicitor general, the jury, the acting protector of slaves, and the slave's own defense attorney had conspired to send him to the gallows. The president of the Legislative Council, who was then serving as acting governor because the previous governor had been recalled, recognized that the trial had been unfair and surprised everyone by staying the man's execution and referring the matter to imperial legal authorities. Given the example of the 1829 case, he was careful to advise the Colonial Office not to pardon the man, and they obliged by commuting the sentence to transportation for life.

For whites around the island, the alleged violation of this woman's body and the prisoner's reprieve symbolized the future awaiting them all after emancipation, and they were furious. In letters to the editor and at public meetings, whites in almost every parish condemned the decision, even going so far, at one meeting chaired by the slave's own lawyer, as to suggest that both the president and the accused deserved to be lynched.[29] The House of Assembly passed a resolution that argued that, as a result of the 1829 and 1833 cases, slaves could now expect "pardon and reward as the price of the most atrocious crime." The house alleged that there were several "felons" who, "after having been convicted of capital offences have obtained their pardon, and are now at large living in this island as free subjects."[30] These were direct references to the three slave men who had been pardoned and

28. For discussion of the legal implications of pardoning slaves condemned to death, see CO 137/167, Jamaica, Original Correspondence, No. 31, Keane to Huskisson, 9 February 1828, cited by Diana Paton, *No Bond but the Law: Punishment, Race, and Gender in Jamaican State Formation, 1780–1870* (Durham, N.C.: Duke University Press, 2004), 48; CO 28/103, No. 2310, Lyon to Sir George Murray, 22 July 1829, enclosing documents relating to case of John Hurley et al for attempted murder; CO 31/51, No. 2, February 1830; CO 28/104, Law Offices correspondence, No. 5197, Herbert Jenner et al. to Murray, 13 November 1829; and CO 28/105, No. 53, Lyon to Murray, 12 January 1830, No. 740, 8, 9 and 7 February 1830.

29. CO 28/111, No. 1, Skeete to Goderich, 4 January 1833; *Barbadian* 16, 19, and 30 January 1833.

30. *Barbadian*, 26 January 1833.

freed, as well as the 1796 case of Joe Denny, the free man of color whose sentence was commuted to transportation after he was condemned to death for having accidentally murdered his white neighbor. The reference to the Denny case was an expression of intense hostility toward free Afro-Barbadians, insinuating that all free people of color were associated with criminality.[31]

The documents in which details of the public scandal are recorded only hint at the violent nature of whites' reaction and the fear of many Afro-Barbadians. A group of free people of color tried to meet to prepare an address to the Colonial Office to support the president but their meeting was violently dispersed by whites. They prepared the petition anyway, stating that most free people of color shared their views but some had been "convinced or scared over to the opposite Camp" and others "were deterred from showing their opposition to the dominant class."[32] A few days later another Afro-Barbadian delegation presented the president with another petition. For the authors of this document, the situation created by the rape case was a political turning point. Their petition contains the first surviving statement by free people of color that explicitly attributed the oppression of free nonwhites and slaves to common racial background or identified slave emancipation as a possible solution to this problem.[33]

The petitioners asserted their willingness to support the British government, "in the furtherance of any measure" for "the impartial distribution of justice to all classes . . . and the permanent welfare of the Island." This was a veiled but obvious statement of hope that the emancipation bill, shortly to be presented in Parliament, would finally eliminate racism from the island's public institutions. They condemned the legislature's disregard for the president's authority, supported the

31. House of Assembly resolution reprinted in the *Barbadian*, 26 January 1833; CO 31/51, House of Assembly speech by Benjamin Eversley; Handler, *Unappropriated People*, 73–74. See reference to the Denny case in CO 31/51, House of Assembly speech by Benjamin Eversley.

32. CO 28/111, Government Executive No. 12, Skeete to Goderich, 24 March 1833, enclosing "Address of the Free Coloured and Black deputation to President Skeete," 19 March 1833. A mere handful of Afro-Barbadian merchants supported whites who called for the president's resignation, a fact that was played up by the president's opponents to make it appear as though the free population of color shared their views. Four free men of color were elected to the St. Michael parish committee that called for the president's resignation. There are no references to free people of color at any of the other seven parish meetings held to condemn Skeete's decision. CO 28/111, Government Executive No. 2, Skeete to Goderich, 20 January 1833, enclosing extracts from the *Globe*, 12 January 1833.

33. CO 28/111, Government Executive No. 12, Skeete to Goderich, 24 March 1833, enclosing "Address of the Free Colored and Black deputation to President Skeete," 19 March 1833.

accused's right to a fair trial and accused whites of racist hypocrisy.[34] They observed that although they detested "as much as any other portion of this community, the crime with which the said felon stands charged . . . white criminals, of every denomination, are let loose upon the community without producing any feeling of resentment." Under those circumstances, the petitioners stated, "we must necessarily attribute the present ferment, in the particular case, to but one cause," namely, the skin color of the accused and the defendant.[35]

Like the wider contest over the future roles of slavery and race in shaping British Caribbean societies, these events illustrated whites' and Afro-Barbadians' competing visions of their place in the empire. For many white Barbadians the impending catastrophe of emancipation, challenges to racial segregation and the outcome of this rape case were all signs of their declining significance in imperial politics and culture.[36] The first elections after the 1832 reform of the British Parliament, in which most West Indian interest MPs lost their seats, gave concrete political expression to the view that white West Indians were now seen to represent an archaic form of national identity. As David Lambert has noted, the British abolitionist movement represented a redefinition of "Englishness" that reduced white West Indians to an "off white imitation" that was at odds with their sense of themselves as an integral part of the English "nation."[37] At stake in the contest over the Englishness of white West Indians was also the future of their particular conception of *Englishness* in the future of a multiracial and postslavery *British* Empire. Larry Gragg has argued that white identity in the old self-governing territories of the Caribbean was forged around a strong identification with a sense of "English localism" in which "priority [was] given to the apparent needs of a community smaller and more intimate than the state or nation."[38] By contrast, the most committed abolitionists and missionaries in the British Caribbean envisioned that

34. Ibid.

35. CO 28/111, Government Executive No. 12, Skeete to Goderich, 24 March 1833, enclosing "Address of the Free Coloured and Black deputation to President Skeete," 19 March 1833; CO 31/51, 22 January 1833.

36. CO 31/51, 25 January 1833; CO 28/111, Government Executive No. 2, Skeete to Goderich, 20 January 1833, enclosing *Mercury, Barbadian,* and *Globe* newspapers for 12–19 January 1833.

37. David Lambert, "'True Lovers of Religion': Methodist Persecution and White Resistance to Anti-Slavery in Barbados, 1823–1825," *Journal of Historical Geography* 28, no. 2 (2002): 218.

38. Gragg, *Englishmen Transplanted,* 57, citing Ivan Roots, "The Central Government and the Local Community," in E. W. Ives, ed., *The English Revolution, 1600–1660* (London: Barnes and Noble, 1968), 37.

emancipation would mean that Christian Afro–West Indians "could think of themselves and be thought of as black Britons, a term that has come in and out of the
language of nation and empire."[39]

IMPERIAL INTERMEDIARIES

Afro-Barbadians' expressions of imperial loyalty found willing listeners in official
circles on the eve of emancipation. Many white abolitionists increasingly spoke of
free people of color as a potential buffer between white planters and black former
slaves, a position for which many abolitionists believed this group was perfectly
suited because of its presumed position as a racial and socioeconomic "middle
class" in slave society. As people of the same color as the slaves, yet as loyal British subjects who were educated and had absorbed the influence of British culture,
propertied free people of color might potentially be the natural local representatives of the interests of former slaves and a check on the excesses of whites.

Sir Lionel Smith, the new governor sent to Barbados in 1833 to oversee the
transition to emancipation and bring the legislature to heel, epitomized this view
of propertied free people of color as racial, class, and cultural intermediaries.[40]
Smith believed that "the balance of refinements, morals, education and energy
is chiefly in favor of the brown and black—and the Whites have nothing but old
Rights and prejudices to maintain their illiberal Position against their own original
kindred." Smith was also an example of how heavily imperial policy in the Caribbean during this period was influenced by the British experience with other nonwhite and allegedly intermediate subject "races," especially in India, where imperial governance was undergoing a process of significant political transformation.
He saw the recent reform of the Indian government, which was designed to create an indigenous civil service, as justification for a similar reform to benefit free
people of color in Barbados. Smith observed that, in contrast to the newly enfranchised in India, who were "Parsees, Hindoos, Mussulmen, and Mahrattas [sic] . . .
none of them professing Christianity," free Afro-Barbadians were "well-deserving
christians." Smith imported British conceptions of caste in India to describe the
racial hierarchies of the Caribbean, professing his determination to follow a policy

39. Quote from Hall, *Civilising Subjects*, 120. See also 338–379.

40. Sir Lionel-Smith was the first governor general of an administrative consolidation of Barbados
and the Windwards. The islands retained their separate legislative structures, and each had lieutenants
governor, but the governor of Barbados was the governor-in-chief from 1833 to 1876.

of "bringing these Castes [free people of color] forward." He planned to do so by placing them in positions of civil and military administration, particularly as magistrates and militia officers, posts he saw as crucial for both protecting and maintaining control over former slaves.[41] Privately, however, Smith believed that free people of color and former slaves should be subordinate to Europeans. In a particularly bizarre list of suggestions that the Colonial Office never published, Smith argued that, rather than remain with their former owners as apprentices after emancipation, all former slaves should become the apprentices of the Crown and be turned into "military labourers" supervised by "European" army officers with free men of color, "selected for intelligence," as corporals.[42]

In the early months of his tenure Governor Smith publicly supported electoral reform to increase the size of the free black and colored electorate as key to ensuring that the Barbadian legislature would abolish slavery. He supported demands from free people of color that the franchise requirements for whites and Afro-Barbadians be equalized at ten pounds—which was what elite men of color hoped for—arguing that "emergency" might require the election of a new House of Assembly that would pass an emancipation act.[43] He estimated that a ten-pound franchise qualification would enfranchise about 125 free people of color, whereas only 75 were enfranchised under the thirty-pound franchise.[44] Given that the total electorate of the island in 1833 was 1,016, of whom 336 were in St. Michael, increasing the size of the Afro-Barbadian vote, even by a small number, would have had some impact on the political landscape of the country. Smith hoped that electoral reform would lead to "the election of liberal Members from among Merchants and others, less addicted to old Colonial prejudices."[45]

In May 1833, Smith issued a public address to Barbadian free people of color, telling them that they were, in his opinion, "not only fully entitled and qualified to be raised also to confidential civil employment, but I consider it very desirable, at this moment, that you should be appointed Magistrates in particular." In a threatening aside obviously meant for the ears of the legislature, which controlled civil service appointments, Smith promised that, if necessary, he was ready to overrule

41. *Barbadian*, 15 May 1833; CO 28/111, Confidential Barbados No. 3, Smith to Stanley, 23 May 1833, and No. 17, 27 September 1833.

42. CO 28/111, General, unnumbered, Smith to Stanley, 8 July 1833.

43. CO 28/111, No. 22, Smith to Stanley, 29 October 1833.

44. Handler, *Unappropriated People*, 103.

45. CO 28/111, No. 17, Smith to Stanley, 27 September 1833.

the Legislative Council if it refused to appoint free men of color to government posts, possibly thereby establishing a legal precedent for usurping local politicians' authority in the future.[46]

THE AFRO-BARBADIAN ELITE AND POPULIST POLITICS

Smith advocated the political enfranchisement of elite Afro-Barbadian men in part because of his racially paternalistic supposition that these voters would represent the interests of former slaves. In other words, he saw the soon-to-be-emancipated slaves as the racial constituency of the Afro-Barbadian elite, a view that at the time was different from the way in which wealthy free black and colored men viewed their struggle. Smith's intensely racialist understanding of politics offered the Afro-Barbadian elite a new way to promote their own political agenda. Under Smith's governorship the elite began to see the potential usefulness of appealing to popular Afro-Barbadian sentiment, although they still refused to associate them-selves in any way with former slaves.

Governor Smith's public support for the political advancement of propertied free men of color both raised their hopes and antagonized the legislature, who blocked Smith's early attempts to appoint men of color to high office. In May 1833 he tried to make the Afro-Barbadian merchant Thomas J. Cummins an officer in the St. Michael militia, which Smith described as "a good deal composed of Free people of color and Free Blacks who have long been in a state of dissatisfaction, at not being allowed to be Commissioned Officers, no qualification whatever, being required for white Officers, up to the Rank of Captain."[47] Ultimately, however, de-spite his grandiose public declarations in support of desegregation, Smith backed down in the face of opposition from the legislature and discontinued his efforts to make Cummins an officer.

Cummins does not appear to have been a particularly popular figure among free people of color and had always been among the elite clique of civil rights cam-paigners who excluded the majority of free Afro-Barbadians from their reform agenda. Nevertheless, hundreds of free people of color attended a mass meeting in Bridgetown, likely organized by Cummins's merchant friends, to support him.

46. *Barbadian*, 15 May 1833.

47. Ibid.; CO 28/114, No. 35, Smith to Spring Rice, 26 September 1834, papers relating to the "Me-morial of Freeholders of St. Philip on the appointment of Mr. Gaskin as Colonel of Militia." Smith wanted Cummins to replace Gaskin as an officer in the St. Michael militia.

The meeting represented an attempt to show both Smith and the legislature that the elite's demands had widespread appeal. For the first time since the 1819 election of the Alien Bill Committee the Afro-Barbadian elite sought the support of the majority of free people of color as a constituency and decisions were taken at the meeting by popular vote.

Appealing to the popular voice was an uncertain political game, and during the meeting events took a turn that Cummins and his friends apparently did not expect. Samuel Jackman Prescod, who had first challenged the elite publicly four years earlier, quickly took control of the discussion. He stated that the continued exclusion of free men of color from positions of public trust was "disgraceful to the community, " adding that the 1831 franchise reform was "a dead letter" and that the legislature had made that reform more out of "*necessity* than from a conviction of the *justice* of our claims." He produced the text of an address, which he had already prepared for presentation to the governor, clearly illustrating his belief that the legislature's rejection of Cummins exemplified the plantocracy's dismissal of all principles of racial equality:

> We verily believe—indeed, we have indubitable proof—that there are some individuals of the opposite class, who never contemplated that [the 1831 Brown Privilege Bill] which acknowledged our rights, was to be more than nominally beneficial; and who will, therefore, view with displeasure, any attempt of the Executive to raise the most worthy individual of our body. . . . We beg to assure your Excellency, that only the certainty that no individual of our body will ever be officially recommended to your Excellency for public situations, could have induced us to bring our claims to your Excellency.[48]

The address placed explicit emphasis on political representation, demanding full equal rights and accusing the legislature of dishonesty. The petition recognized that the relative impoverishment and lack of education of free people of color in comparison to whites were rooted in a history of unjust "disadvantage." Still, it accepted that property ownership and the right kind of education should be the basis of citizenship, and that only the few who could meet the restricted criteria deserved to be enfranchised.[49] In addition, Prescod's address made no refer-

48. *Barbadian*, 15 May 1833.
49. Ibid.

ence to the issue of emancipation, focusing exclusively on the right of propertied free men of color to the same political privileges as "the other free class." Prescod wrote of free people of color as a "body" whose political identity was defined by both skin color and free legal status, an emphasis that implicitly excluded slaves from their body politic. The fact that so many free Afro-Barbadians considered positions of rank in the militia, one of the institutions most associated with slavery, as appointments that would naturally lead to the "exaltation of our whole body"[50] also suggests that, whatever individuals might think, as a group they prioritized racial equality among free subjects above slave emancipation.

Several of those present thought the resolutions were too confrontational and proposed amendments, but the overwhelming majority was in favor of them and they were passed "amidst loud cheering." Prominent merchants such as Joseph Kennedy and Thomas Harris Jr., who had previously displayed no interest in the views of lower-class Afro-Barbadians, bowed to majority opinion, and Kennedy, Harris, Prescod, Cummins, and a shopkeeper named Anthony Barclay Jr. signed the address.[51] The decision of elite men like Kennedy and Harris to accept the audience's vote as a democratic mandate and sign their names to the address, as well as the decision to have Barclay Jr.—a relative unknown of little wealth but perhaps a popular choice at the meeting—sign with them, represented a significant rapprochement between civil rights campaigners of different class backgrounds. The meeting was also a political breakthrough for free Afro-Barbadians in another way. Their local opponents could not easily dismiss the meeting as illegitimate because it was called to support the political policy of no less a figure than the island's governor. The island's newspapers felt compelled to end their practice of ignoring free black and colored political activities and report the gathering's proceedings, with the *Barbadian* devoting much of the front page to an almost verbatim account of the speeches, resolutions and even reactions of the crowd. Smith sent copies of these reports to the Colonial Office, probably eager to demonstrate his popularity with the island's Afro-Caribbean majority to his superiors.

Despite such pressure the approach of emancipation brought no sign that the legislature had any intentions of further amending discriminatory laws. In the face of such intransigence even the Afro-Barbadian elite embraced a method of public

50. Handler, *Unappropriated People*, 106–109.

51. *Barbadian*, 15 May 1833. Barclay's father had signed the February 1824 apology for the counter-address of January 1824 (see chapter 2, this volume). See further reference to Barclay and his family in chapter 9, this volume, 277–291.

protest—the physical occupation of whites-only spaces—that had previously been associated with more radical Afro-Barbadian reformism. In December 1833 four free men of color from the southern parishes of St. Philip and Christ Church "invaded" the whites-only section of Christ Church parish church, announcing to the vestry board that "nothing could compel them to leave . . . [and] that they did not intend to come again to molest [the vestry board], but on that day they had come and were determined to sit there in defiance of all opposition." The vestry prosecuted the four men.[52]

In contrast to the previous demonstrations in the St. Michael parish church in 1825 and 1831, when elite Afro-Barbadians did not support the protesters, the Christ Church incident became a rallying point for Bridgetown's free black and colored elite electoral reformers, who held it up as a symbol of the need for political reform and collective resistance against racial segregation. In February 1834 a group of Bridgetown merchants, including Thomas J. Cummins, organized a public meeting at the St. Mary's Society's boys' school to demand the lowering of the thirty-pound franchise requirement, and a resolution was passed that invoked the Christ Church protest as an example of bad faith on the part of the local authorities. In a continuing attempt to widen the appeal of his political campaign, Cummins spoke at this meeting and recommended that the property requirement for enfranchisement be lowered to "5 acres and a house value of £10."[53]

THE BRIDGETOWN REFORM
MOVEMENT AND THE 1834 ELECTION

The tensions in Afro-Barbadian politics between commonalities of interest based on race and competing political agendas based on class and legal status were never more evident than in the final House of Assembly elections to occur during the slavery era. Aside from its symbolic significance this election was important because one of the issues at stake was the creation of a separate constituency for Bridgetown, which was still part of the constituency of St. Michael parish. Both white and Afro-Barbadian Bridgetown merchants advocated this reform as it would give them a chance to send their own representatives to the House of Assembly and decrease the power of rural landowners over urban affairs. Three can-

52. Minutes of the Christ Church Vestry, 31 December 1833 and 8 December 1834. The four men were Thomas and Edward Weekes, Benjamin G. Nurse, and James E. Williams.

53. *Barbadian,* 12 February 1834.

didates competed for the parish's two legislative seats: the liberal attorney general, Henry Sharpe, and the two incumbent planter candidates, George Taylor and the solicitor general, Robert Bowcher Clarke. Although all three candidates were white, they represented opposing political camps among the white elite. Clarke had become the plantocracy's most outspoken representative against imperial emancipation policies, and Governor Smith considered him the greatest obstacle to imperial interests in the assembly.[54] Sharpe, by contrast, was the ally of Smith and the Colonial Office, a Bridgetown lawyer planters considered a social outsider and political opponent.[55]

As the governor's candidate and a reformer who dared to challenge two staunch conservatives, Sharpe was extremely popular among free people of color and slaves, even though few Afro-Barbadians could vote. At a meeting of his supporters in May 1834, Sharpe announced that he stood for the education of the laboring classes and equalization of the franchise qualification for white and Afro-Barbadian voters. Furthermore, although he had himself been a slave owner, he declared his support for emancipation.[56] Civil rights agitators of color, including people who had previously appeared hostile to emancipation, rallied behind Sharpe's platform, endorsing both his candidacy and his abolitionist views. At this meeting, Thomas J. Cummins, who had signed many petitions affirming his support for slavery, for the first time referred explicitly to franchise reform as an emancipation measure. He stated that it was particularly necessary now that "a long constituted state of one class of our island society [will be dissolved], advancing it into a higher order."[57]

Cummins still stopped short of claiming that men such as himself sought the vote in order to represent the interests of former slaves. White and Afro-Barbadian Bridgetown merchants where united in their terror of the shortly-to-be-liberated rural slave population, fearing that slaves posed a serious threat to their economic interests and the maintenance of public order and morality in Bridgetown. As emancipation loomed urban merchants began to reimagine Bridgetown as a bourgeois civic space, where policies should reflect mercantile mores and inter-

54. CO 28/113, General No. 11, Smith to Spring Rice, 26 August 1834.

55. CO 28/111, No. 20, Smith to Stanley, 12 October 1833, and CO 28/116, No. 31, Smith to Glenelg, 8 August 1835.

56. In June 1826 Sharpe imported a slave from Grenada. See PP 1846, vol. 28, *Papers . . . Relating to the Labouring Population of the British Colonies*, 21.

57. *Barbadian*, 31 May 1834.

ests and protect them against both the plantocracy and teeming hoards of former slaves. In March 1834 over one hundred Afro-Barbadian and white merchants demanded separate political representation for Bridgetown, stating explicitly that the change was necessary if they were to protect their interests from former slaves. They wanted political control over the city in order to be able to pass regulations to more effectively police the urban laboring classes and control the former slaves who were expected to flood into the city. The first signature on the petition was that of Attorney General Henry Sharpe. Among the merchants who signed were Edmund Haynes, Henry Wilkins, William B. Nunes, Benjamin Massiah, the brothers London and Edward W. Bourne and Thomas Harris Jr., all men of color.[58]

Henry Sharpe's political campaign also fired the imaginations of poorer free people of color and slaves. Whereas merchant elites saw emancipation as an opportunity for very limited political reforms, the underprivileged black and colored majority, both slave and free, saw Sharpe as the political embodiment of all that emancipation promised in terms of their own political and socioeconomic enfranchisement. The intervention of lower-class people of color and slaves into the sphere of formal politics in support of Sharpe made the June 1834 St. Michael election a de facto referendum on the future of the island's political hierarchy. The *Barbadian* described the unprecedented and memorable scene at the June hustings in the St. Michael Cathedral, noting that the

> irreverent behaviour of many, of *all* colours, of political partisans, exceeded all former profanations of the House of God. . . . It is our duty to animadvert more especially on the shameful, indecent, and insulting behaviour of the crowd of negroes and coloured persons—of the lowest degree we are aware—who filled up the pews, and made the walls of that sacred place re-echo with their profane "hurras," several times. The uproar and tumult in the street, and in the churchyard, where the graves of the dead were indecently trampled upon. . . . [I]t was reserved for Monday last to furnish a specimen of the insolence, and utter contempt of all decency, and all respect for their superiors, and all reverence for the House of God, which the negroes and coloured people, some of them probably free persons, dis-

58. CO 31/51, 24 March 1834, "Petition from inhabitants of St. Michael's Parish, praying for an augmentation of their representation." On 27 March 1834 the House of Assembly dismissed the petition as "disrespectful."

played within the very walls of the church. Could any thing be more disgusting than to see negro women, dirty trollops, swaggering up and down the aisles of the cathedral, with their bows of blue ribbon on their arms, the distinguishing badge of those, respectable as well as vulgar, who professed to be the supporters of Mr. Sharpe. In, or out of, the church, we know not which, we have been informed that some of Mr. S's coloured and black friends were extremely insulting to the other candidates, Messrs. [Robert Bowcher] Clarke and [George N.] Taylor, even *hissing* them several times. We are quite sure that the respectable individuals of the coloured class who were, as it might be reasonably expected, anxious for the success of their avowed friend, Mr. Sharpe, are as much disgusted as we are at the intemperate conduct of their brethren. There has been much censure cast on the honorable gentleman for having been the cause of all this excitement, and all this vulgar, impertinent, and tumultuous bearing of the slaves and lower orders of free people.

In the end, Sharpe lost by a landslide to Clarke and Taylor, but the popular response to his campaign transformed the rituals of politics in the island. To the horror of the *Barbadian,* the plantocracy and the merchant elites, such politically illegitimate groups as slaves, lower-class free people of color, and black and colored women were participating in electoral politics, even though they could not vote. In the eyes of the plantocracy and urban merchants the raucous support of Sharpe's campaign by slaves and lower-class free Afro-Barbadians foreshadowed the chaos emancipation would bring to urban affairs. The sight of black women appropriating and wearing party ribbons, the symbol of electoral participation, particularly horrified the *Barbadian,* since their presence represented emancipation's revolutionary potential. On the eve of emancipation, their eagerness to squeeze into the church grounds and be part of the proceedings was a spontaneous act of desegregation and a political statement whose significance went far beyond even of the antisegregationist demonstrations that had taken place in the St. Michael parish church. In turning out en masse for the election, subaltern Afro-Barbadians showed their awareness that emancipation made them a political force, a new public, to be reckoned with.[59]

59. *Barbadian,* 4 and 7 June 1834. On former slave women and postemancipation politics, see Mimi Sheller, "Quasheba, Mother, Queen: Black Women's Public Leadership and Political Protest in Post-Emancipation Jamaica, 1834–65," *Slavery and Abolition* 19, no. 3 (December 1998): 90–117.

The *Barbadian*'s editor recognized that Sharpe's popular appeal derived from the fact that many working-class people of color, both slave and free, had misunderstood him to be, essentially, a democrat. The editor pointed out that it was unfair to "throw the blame of all the blackguardism which distinguished the day of the election, on Mr. Sharpe" just because "an unthinking and ignorant mob of negroes have misunderstood Mr. S's professions, and have fancied that he had proclaimed liberty and equality among all ranks."[60] Nevertheless, the scene on election day was the main reason why several councilors actually threatened to resign when Governor Smith tried to appoint Sharpe to the council, where he could act more effectively as an imperial ally. As usual, Smith caved in, but he asserted that he did so only because they were influential planters and "their retirement would be likely to create a violent Party Spirit in the Island, and occasion much trouble and an excitement among the colored and Black Population ill suited to the Times."[61]

CONCLUSION

By 1834, as the British Caribbean was poised to begin a new era without slavery, the climate of revolution and reform that was reshaping the societies of the Caribbean had also wrought significant changes in the public culture of Barbados. The planter elite, for so long accustomed to governing the island without opposition, now faced challenges on both sides of the Atlantic. In Britain, the antislavery lobby had finally managed to negotiate the end of slavery, assisted by slave rebellions and unrest in the Caribbean. In Barbados, urban merchants, free people of color, and slaves challenged the plantocracy's monopoly on public life.

These new publics were themselves internally fragmented as the merchant elite and the plebian majority struggled to determine the limits of reform and the meaning of freedom. The previously uncoordinated urban street politics of slaves and working-class free Afro-Barbadians found a new cohesion in the 1820s and 1830s, as subaltern people of African descent took advantage of the tensions between the imperial government and the local plantocracy to press for more far reaching civil rights reforms and forcibly brought the desegregation struggle into the streets and other public spaces of the island.

60. *Barbadian*, 4 June 1834.
61. CO 28/113, No. 33, Smith to Spring Rice, 23 August 1834.

PART TWO

The history of the American Negro is the history of this strife,—this longing to attain self-conscious manhood, to merge his double self into a better and truer self. In this merging he wishes neither of the older selves to be lost. He would not Africanize America, for America has too much to teach the world and Africa. He would not bleach his Negro soul in a flood of white Americanism, for he knows that Negro blood has a message for the world. He simply wishes to make it possible for a man to be both a Negro and an American, without having the doors of Opportunity closed roughly in his face.

—W. E. B. DU BOIS, *The Souls of Black Folk*

5 / DISCIPLINE AND (DIS)ORDER
Apprenticeship and the Meaning of Freedom

ON May 14, 1833, Edward Stanley, the new secretary of state for the colonies, presented the slave emancipation bill to the imperial Parliament, and three months later the bill became law, scheduled to take effect on August 1, 1834. The Barbadian legislature was among the last colonial governments to pass a version of the bill in April 1834. With the exception of Antigua, the emancipation acts passed in Britain and the Caribbean established an "apprenticeship" period to allow former slaves and slave owners to "adjust" to freedom. The act granted slave owners twenty million pounds as compensation for the loss of their human property. The second phase of emancipation began with apprenticeship's early end in 1838, two years before the stipulated time.[1] Apprenticeship's intricate system of categorizing former slaves and complicated manumission provisions created marginal groups of free people of color between 1834 and 1838. Former slave owners manipulated the system to prevent apprentices from gaining freedom, disrupting relations between slaves and their free kin in the process. For landless or smallholding slave owners, including a number of Afro-Barbadian women, who had survived by hiring out their slaves' labor, emancipation represented a loss of livelihood and social status.

While ownership of land was highly prized by the newly freed as a means of securing real independence from estate dominance, in Barbados, where the possibilities for an independent peasant livelihood were limited, mobility had always been central to former slaves' ability to exercise freedom.[2] Former slaves' alterna-

---

1. See "An Act for the Abolition of Slavery throughout the British Colonies; for promoting the Industry of the Manumitted Slaves; and for compensating the persons hitherto entitled to the Services of such Slaves," *The Statutes of the United Kingdom of Great Britain and Ireland*, 3 and 4 William IV (London: Parliament Commons, 1833); Holt, *Problem of Freedom*, 48–49.

2. On the importance and difficulties of acquiring land in emancipation-era Barbados, see Woodville Marshall, "Rock Hall, St. Thomas: A Free Village in Barbados," *Journal of Caribbean History* 41, nos. 1 and 2 (2007): 1–50; on mobility and the exercise of freedom in the Caribbean see Sheller, *Democracy after Slavery*, 92.

tives to field labor and rural poverty were usually the more mobile or urban occupations of free people of color and skilled slaves. For Afro-Barbadians free before 1834, apprenticeship brought the freedom of enslaved kin, but it also entailed
increased job competition from former slaves, particularly in cities. As increased
numbers of former slaves migrated to towns, the government responded with repressive regulatory measures. These measures, designed to control former slaves'
social and economic activities, impinged upon the lives of free people of color. Ultimately, government regulations did little to stop the flow of rural-urban migration, and working-class urban residents organized to protest the most offensive
anti-immigration laws.

Emancipation also unleashed a sense of panic among whites and elite Afro-
Barbadians about the social, economic, and moral order. Former slaves and
laboring-class free people of color were the subjects of intense debates about morality. Local elites, both white and Afro-Barbadian, continued their struggles over
racial segregation on this new terrain of public morality, competing to display
their Christian respectability. Elite free people of color used their own counter-
interpretations of respectability as a tool to challenge white supremacy, but they
helped to disseminate an elitist concept of "respectable" behavior against which
former slaves' cultural practices were dismissed as inferior and that preserved
class and gender hierarchies. Plebian Afro-Barbadians refused to accept elite definitions of Christianity and respectability, converting en masse but retaining their
own definitions of respectable worship, community, and family life.

THE INSTITUTIONAL FRAMEWORK OF APPRENTICESHIP

The apprenticeship system was based on a system for classifications of former
slaves, the stipendiary magistracy and committees of appraisal for manumissions. Former slaves were divided into three categories with different dates at
which full freedom would be granted. Children under six years old on August 1,
1834, were declared completely free on that date and could only be apprenticed
with their mothers' consent. Slaves over that age were divided into "nonpraedial"
apprentices—those who had not performed work directly related to agricultural
production—and "praedial" apprentices or agricultural laborers, by far the largest
category. Nonpraedials were to be freed on August 1, 1838, while praedials would
remain apprentices until August 1, 1840. Praedials were further subdivided into
"praedials attached to the soil," consisting of estate laborers who had lived and
worked on one estate and were not hired out as a matter of course and "praedials

not attached to the soil," that is, agricultural laborers who had been hired out.[3] In total, there were 66, 637 Barbadian apprentices on August 1, 1834, of whom more than 80 percent were classified as praedial.[4] In addition, there were 14,732 children who were automatically free and 1,780 elderly, ill, or disabled people not classified for apprenticeship, making a total former slave population of 83,149, the second largest in the West Indies (after Jamaica).[5] All apprentices were to continue to work for their former owners without pay but retained the right, during apprenticeship, to receive rations of food and clothing, to use the houses and land to which they had access as slaves, and to receive medical attention.

The act also created the position of "stipendiary" or "special" magistrates, who took over the judicial functions of slave owners and the slave courts. These magistrates answered to and were paid by the imperial government and could only be removed from office by the governor, in the hopes that this would keep them out of the pockets of employers. Apprentices and employers had to bring labor disputes that they could not resolve to the special magistrates.[6] Barbados was divided into first six and later seven districts for the purposes of administering apprenticeship, each presided over by a stipendiary magistrate during the apprenticeship period, but maintained afterward, with minor alterations, as policing districts.[7] The emancipation acts also included measures for compulsory manumission, designed to enable apprentices to buy the remainder of their time from their former owners or to be awarded it as compensation for ill treatment. Therefore, another crucial duty of the stipendiary magistrates was to chair the appraisal committees, which

3. William Mathieson, *British Slavery and Its Abolition, 1823–1838* (London: Longmans, Green, 1926), 299–300.

4. The act regulated the working hours of praedials, whereas no limits were placed on the working hours of nonpraedials, on the grounds that, since most of them were domestics, their owners would require their services all the time. The Colonial Office reasoned that it was therefore more equitable to free nonpraedial apprentices earlier. See *Barbadian*, 22 January 1834.

5. Barry Higman, *Slave Populations*, 550.

6. John Bowen Colthurst, *The Colthurst Journal: Journal of a Special Magistrate in the Islands of Barbados and St. Vincent, July 1835–September 1838*, ed. Woodville Marshall (New York: KTO Press, 1977), 8–10. The stipendiary magistrates had to be "respectable persons wholly unconnected with the colonies" and "men uninfluenced by the local assemblies, free from local passions." Edward Stanley, quoted in W. L. Burn, *Emancipation and Apprenticeship in the British West Indies* (London: Jonathan Cape, 1937), 197. On the "civilizing mission" of the special magistrates, see Eudell, *Political Languages*, 69–100.

7. In 1836, District E, encompassing St. Peter, St. Lucy, St. Andrew, and St. Joseph parishes, was divided into two, creating District F. District A, which encompassed St. Michael and part of northwestern Christ Church, was administered as one district but had a subdivision for Bridgetown, District A (Town Division).

determined the monetary value of an individual's apprenticeship. Three local magistrates also sat on these committees. Apprentices could also be freed by private arrangement with their employers.[8]

The Colonial Office hoped apprenticeship would ease the transition to freedom but the complicated system of classifications, manumission procedures and staggered dates for full emancipation produced an unequally distributed freedom whose benefits were often nullified by other provisions in the emancipation act. Apprenticeship's classification system also introduced restrictions, created lines of division among apprentices that had not been features of slavery, and produced new bases for tension between former slaves and free Barbadians.

THE MARGINAL FREEDOM OF FORMER SLAVE CHILDREN

Planters were disappointed in their hope that circumstances would force parents to apprentice their free children so that children would receive the basic necessities. Throughout the Caribbean, parents almost universally resisted the apprenticeship of their children; in Barbados, only one child was ever apprenticed.[9] Former slaves were determined that their children should avoid estate labor, and their preferred alternatives were the areas of nonagricultural work that were the livelihood of skilled apprentices and free Afro-Barbadians.

Imperial emancipation policy toward slave families proceeded from ethnocentric and misogynistic assumptions about people of African descent. The 1834 act placed primary legal responsibility for children with mothers, on the presumption that Afro-Caribbean fathers played little role in the care of children. Slave families were seen as dysfunctional, with overly dominant mothers undermining the patriarchal order of society and producing disorderly, lazy children. Local authorities and the press blamed Afro-Barbadian mothers for the withdrawal of children from agriculture. In 1837, the island's chief justice claimed that the prejudice of mothers against field labor was "so strong . . . that they will not allow their children to assist them even in their own gardens, their desire being manifest, where they permit them to be employed, to make them Domestics or Mechanics."[10] The

8. "An Act for the Abolition of Slavery throughout the British Colonies"; CO 30/21, No. 555, "An Act for the abolition of Slavery . . . ," passed 5 April 1834.

9. Holt, *Problem of Freedom,* 66; CO 31/52, n.d., "Report of the Committee appointed to enquire into the condition of the Free Children of Apprenticed Labourers."

10. *Barbadian,* 13 December 1837.

Barbadian railed against mothers for "resisting every advance by their employers to bring them up in honest and industrious pursuits . . . declar[ing] their preference to *trades* for their children. But if the *boys* are to be all tradesmen, what do they design for their girls? These, we presume, are all to be hucksters."[11]

Planters responded to the loss of child labor with particular harshness. At Drax Hall, one of the oldest estates in the rural parish of St. George, the manager ordered that the "[w]oman [is] to be called on to pay the Doctor for their free children or to work 4 Saturdays for each Child & to be told that if the Child falls ill without a Doctor, it shall be bound out [evicted] on its Recovering."[12] Estate nurseries, which had existed on most large plantations, where very young children were looked after while their parents worked, were closed.[13] After his 1837 tour of the West Indies, British MP and antiapprenticeship campaigner Joseph Sturge claimed that Barbadian planters had taken children whose parents refused to apprentice them and "put them out in the road."[14]

The fate of children, both those freed in 1834 and those older than six, depended greatly on the financial position of their parents. Only comparatively economically privileged parents, whether apprentices or free people, had the skills to teach their children a trade or could afford to buy their children's freedom and send them to school. The official number of children in school in the island was 13,869 in 1837, of whom only 2,430 were the free children of apprentices.[15] In 1836 one stipendiary magistrate reported, "Many of the first-class apprentices send their free children to school, but the ordinary field people have neither time nor means, and they [the children] are generally wandering about the Negro huts, shunning their parents' employers."[16] Another magistrate estimated that as many as twenty-five thousand children in the island were neither working nor being educated.[17]

11. *Barbadian,* 8 February 1837. See also 20 September 1834 and 24 February 1836.

12. Records of Drax Hall Plantation, BDA, C. Barrow, "Rules for the uniformity of conduct, c1834–1838."

13. Thome and Kimball, *Emancipation in the West Indies,* 63.

14. CO 28/119, No. 133, MacGregor to Glenelg, 12 June 1837, enclosing extracts from the *Antigua Herald,* 13 and 29 May 1837.

15. PP 1837–1838, vol. 48, *Report on Negro Education, Windward and Leeward Islands,* 228–229.

16. CO 28/117, No. 4, President Beckles to Glenelg, 21 September 1836, enclosure 4, Monthly report of the stipendiary magistrates for August 1836, District F.

17. CO 28/119, No. 15, MacGregor to Glenelg, 26 January 1837, enclosing monthly reports of the stipendiary magistrates, December 1836, No. 2, District A, Rural Division.

Providing adequate care for free children was only possible on most estates if the mother or another female relative or neighbor was free. In 1837, the Moravian missionary at Mount Tabor in St. John met an old woman whose master "had given her free," but she now lived in a gully near the estate. Apprenticed parents had taken her in to look after their children during the day, "but she having been careless about them, the father of the children would allow her no more to stop there. I [the missionary] endeavored to reconcile them to one another, in [which] as it appeared to me, I did succeed."[18] Such an arrangement was possible because the elderly woman had been freed by her former owner, and needed shelter. Employers frequently manumitted apprentices who could no longer work by private agreement. Once free, elderly or ill former slaves could find themselves dependent upon family and community.

APPRENTICESHIP AND MANUMISSION

A similar bias in favor of nonpraedial apprentices was reflected in patterns of manumission. The decreased cost of buying freedom and the abolition of manumission fees made it easier for nonpraedial former slaves to buy themselves out of apprenticeship, but freedom remained too costly for most agricultural laborers. There was an enormous disparity between the price of freedom for praedials and nonpraedials; the average appraisal by stipendiary magistrates of praedial men in 1837 was thirty pounds and, for a woman, twenty-four pounds, while the average for nonpraedials was twelve pounds and three shillings for a man and ten pounds and seven shillings for a woman. Local magistrates generally appraised male and female praedial apprentices at thirty-two pounds and six shillings and thirty-three pounds respectively, and male and female nonpraedials at twelve pounds and seven shillings and ten pounds and nine shillings. Even the stipendiary magistrates' average appraisal rate was too high for most agricultural workers, and stipendiary magistrates frequently deferred to the judgment of local magistrates in appraisal cases.[19]

Manumission also favored nonpraedials who resided in a town. Of 808 manu-

18. Moravian Diary, 2 August 1837.

19. Governor's circular to special magistrates, 25 November 1837, BPL. Stipendiary magistrates considered male praedial apprentices more valuable because they assumed that females were less productive physical laborers. By contrast, local magistrates, themselves planters, were aware that most field laborers were women and girls and that female slaves were the backbone of the rural labor force.

missions recorded in Barbados during the first year of apprenticeship, 531 were nonpraedials and 277 were praedials.[20] It is unlikely that many praedials manumitted were field hands—large numbers of skilled craftsmen were classified as praedials and they probably accounted for a disproportionate number of manumitted praedials. The imbalance between urban and rural patterns of manumission was also stark: 661 of those freed in apprenticeship's first year were from District A, the parish of St. Michael, where Bridgetown was located. In his diary the stipendiary magistrate for rural St. Michael, John Bowen Colthurst, noted that the highest concentration of manumission cases were "in Bridgetown and its neighborhood, where almost the whole of the apprentice population are of that description [nonpraedial]" and that most rural apprentices could not afford to buy their freedom.[21] His claims are corroborated by the monthly reports from stipendiary magistrates from other rural areas. In August 1836, 24 men and 24 women were manumitted in Bridgetown, and between December 1836 and January 1837, the number was 17 men and 18 women, the majority of them tradesmen and domestics.[22] By contrast, the stipendiary magistrate for St. Joseph and St. Andrew, two impoverished rural parishes, stated that there had been no manumissions in August 1836 because the apprentices were too poor.[23]

Apprentices tried to manipulate the system in order to elicit lower appraisals. It was a common tactic to appear at an appraisal hearing dressed in rags and looking infirm.[24] However, former slave owners had the advantage of legal knowledge and the collusion of local magistrates when it came to manipulating the appraisal process. Colthurst complained that "the owners of the services of the apprentices . . . extol the qualifications of the apprentice wishing to purchase his discharge to the skies . . . and by so doing appear determined, if possible, to inflict a penalty upon him for so being a good man."[25]

Despite the Colonial Office's insistence that the different dates for full freedom for praedials and nonpraedials were not a means of "advantaging one class of ap-

20. CO 31/52, Sessional Papers, 18 August 1835.

21. Colthurst, *Colthurst Journal*, 115–116.

22. CO 28/117, No. 4, Beckles to Glenelg, 21 September 1836, enclosing monthly reports of the stipendiary magistrates for August 1836, District A, Town Division; CO 28/119, No. 15, MacGregor to Glenelg, 26 January 1837, monthly reports for December 1836, District A, Town Division.

23. CO 28/117, No. 4, Beckles to Glenelg, 21 September 1836, monthly reports, District F.

24. *Barbadian*, 7 September 1836; Thome and Kimball, *Emancipation in the West Indies*, 67.

25. Colthurst, *Colthurst Journal*, 114.

prentices over another," this was precisely how the difference functioned in prac-tice. Owners deliberately misclassified nonagricultural workers as praedials in order to force them to work until 1840 and receive a higher rate of compensation for them.[26] Between July 1837 and June 1838 the imperial compensation commis-sion changed the classifications of 1,166 Barbadian apprentices from praedial to nonpraedial after intentional misclassification by their former owners.[27]

Apprenticeship also encouraged slave owners to renege on private agreements that had allowed some slaves to live as though they were free people. In May 1837, the Colonial Office and one of the stipendiary magistrates overturned the ruling of the Barbadian solicitor general in the case of a domestic named Rebecca, ap-prenticed to Colleton estate in St. John, who challenged her classification as a field hand. Colleton's proprietor admitted that Rebecca could have been a nonpraedial, because as a slave she had hired her own labor from the estate for a dollar a month and worked on her own account as a domestic, effectively living as a free person. In his deposition a former manager of the estate admitted that a number of Col-leton's slaves had similar arrangements. The proprietor argued that Rebecca's ar-rangement was "an act of kindness" and she should now be able to use it to claim "a title injurious to his interests." Secretary of State Glenelg ruled in Rebecca's favor, stating that her monthly rent of a dollar was probably more than she would have earned her owner working in the fields.[28] Many owners whose slaves had ar-ranged to work on their own account in exchange for a monthly fee had little or no other means of support. For such people, emancipation was a financial catas-trophe, and, during apprenticeship, relations between landless or smallholding employers and their skilled apprentices deteriorated, as owners tried to squeeze every last bit of profit out of their apprentices.[29]

MIXED FAMILIES OF FREE PEOPLE OF COLOR AND APPRENTICES

The harshness of employers' labor policies during apprenticeship was detrimental to the family lives of former slaves who had lived like free people of color. In 1836

26. Ibid., 111–113.

27. Kathleen Mary Butler, *The Economics of Emancipation: Jamaica and Barbados, 1823–1843* (Chapel Hill: University of North Carolina Press, 1995), 33.

28. CO 28/119, No. 116, MacGregor to Glenelg, with enclosures, 24 May 1837.

29. CO 28/119, No. 32, MacGregor to Glenelg, 13 February 1837, enclosing monthly reports from the stipendiary magistrates for January 1837, No. 1, District A, Town Division.

a free man named Robert Cox, who described himself as "a poor Labouring Black Man," sued the planter who owned his four children and their mother. Although Cox had previously paid rent to the owner so that the children could live with him in Bridgetown, the planter illegally classified three of the children, who were over six years old on August 1, 1834, as field laborers and took them back to his St. Thomas estate in January 1836. In his petition to the governor, Cox said that his children were born and raised in Bridgetown and he had regularly paid for the children's hire ever since they became "serviceable" to the estate, probably in order to save them from the fields. The oldest child was a trained seamstress, whereas the two youngest, too little to work before emancipation, were "given voluntarily up to their father, on condition of his feeding and clothing them." Cox was convicted of harboring runaways and jailed by the Bridgetown magistrates. A friend eventually helped Cox by paying for the remaining apprenticeship of one child but the other children remained apprentices because Cox could not afford to free them.[30]

Former owners pursued other policies that were hostile to former slaves' families. During slavery, despite laws to the contrary, estate authorities frequently turned a blind eye when relatives of slaves joined their relations as residents. Apprenticeship witnessed an increase in the numbers of slaves, frequently couples, one of whom was free and the other an apprentice, choosing to live together on the estate where the apprentice worked. The free partner might have become free during apprenticeship, or may have been free before 1834. Planters responded to this trend with evictions, as they did when parents refused to apprentice their free children. In a particularly extreme case from 1838, nine free members of one family— five women and four children—were evicted simultaneously from Walker's estate in St. George. When the women refused to take their children and leave, the manager filed a complaint with the local magistrate, who fined them and imprisoned them when they could not pay. One of the women, Margaret Rose, had hired herself out from her owner and lived with her husband at Walker's for seventeen years, buying her freedom in 1834.[31]

Many praedials who managed to acquire freedom were women manumitted

30. CO 28/123, No. 264, Governor Evan MacGregor to Lord Glenelg, 22 September 1838, enclosing petitions of Robert Cox of St. Michael, 21 January and 23 February 1837, 9 January 1838. Case also mentioned in Colthurst, *Colthurst Journal*, 68–69.

31. *Liberal*, 28 February 1838 and 7 March 1838. Since they were free people the case was under the jurisdiction of regular rather than special magistrates.

through the financial assistance of male kin who were estate headmen or free or enslaved craftsmen. In the case of the evictions from Walker's estate, for example, Margaret Rose's husband, King Green, was a carpenter and had probably helped to pay for her manumission.[32] In 1836 a stipendiary magistrate reported, "Those discharged in general follow their former occupations, except some of the women, who take to domestic work in their own families, and generally quit the occupation of field labour."[33] This was a gendered family survival strategy, because, although buying the freedom of a praedial woman could be more expensive, a manumitted praedial woman could leave field labor and either look after children or take up a more lucrative occupation, like huckstering.[34] The potential impact of the withdrawal of women from field labor posed a particularly serious economic threat to planters. Thus the trend of targeting women for eviction was also rooted in planters' economic self-interest.

MARRONAGE AND RURAL-URBAN MIGRATION

For apprentices and their free relations, the most accessible and attractive freedom to exercise was that of personal mobility. Former slaves had few opportunities to establish themselves as peasant farmers, since the little land available for purchase in Barbados during and immediately after apprenticeship cost between sixty and two hundred pounds an acre, compared with four to twenty pounds in Jamaica and forty to eighty pounds in Antigua.[35] Jobs such as huckstering, domestic and artisanal work, and seamstressing offered both some possibility for upward socioeconomic mobility and the freedom to move around the countryside, or from rural to urban areas, in search of work or to be with family. Postemancipation internal migration patterns in Barbados were reminiscent of marronage trends during slavery, as many former slaves fled the harsh rural estate labor environment for greater freedom in towns or as itinerant laborers.

32. *Liberal*, 28 February 1838.

33. CO 28/117, No. 4, Beckles to Glenelg, 21 September 1836, enclosing monthly reports for August 1836, District B.

34. Bridget Brereton, "Family Strategies, Gender and the Shift to Wage Labour in the British Caribbean," in Bridget Brereton and Kevin Yelvington, eds., *The Colonial Caribbean in Transition: Essays on Post-emancipation Social and Cultural History* (Gainesville: University Press of Florida, 1999), 77–107.

35. O. Nigel Bolland, "Systems of Domination after Slavery: The Control of Land and Labour in the British West Indies After 1838," in Beckles and Shepherd, eds., *Caribbean Freedom*, 107–123.

During apprenticeship, field laborers had Saturday afternoons off by law, and the weekend movement of apprentices back and forth between countryside and towns increased. The *Barbadian* complained, "Every Saturday since the 1st August, 1834, agricultural labourers, stout, able fellows, have been in the habit of coming into town to get portering jobs, rather than hire themselves out to field labour."[36] Although no official statistics on runaways were maintained during apprenticeship, the stipendiary magistrate for rural St. Michael reported that an average of ten runaways who had been caught fleeing rural estates for Bridgetown were sent to his office each morning.[37] By early 1838, stipendiary magistrates and the governor recognized that the freeing of nonpraedials on August 1, while the majority remained apprentices, could occasion a total breakdown in public order, since praedials would probably respond with mass marronage. In January, based on the reports of the stipendiary magistrates for December 1837, Governor Evan MacGregor, Lionel Smith's successor, wrote to the Colonial Office recommending that apprenticeship end for praedials on August 1. MacGregor asserted that the problem of "desertion" would only get worse after the first because of "the great facilities [for marronage] which will be afforded the praedials among their numerous liberated relations and friends for that purpose."[38]

By mid-1838, the threat of marronage and the problem of coping with alleged misclassifications were overwhelming the special magistrates. In March 1838, the new stipendiary magistrate for Bridgetown—the Afro-Antiguan journalist and abolitionist Henry Loving—reported that he already had 105 misclassification cases, of which he had so far managed to settle 57 (56 of them in the apprentices' favor). He expected the number of cases to rise because many praedial apprentices were afraid they would not be able to appeal their classifications after August 1, 1838. "Intense longing [for freedom]" he observed, "is the only motive by which the Slave of 1833 is guided at this moment." He spoke of a "feverish something [sic] pervading them to be changed into 'four year people,'" which would make it impossible for apprenticeship to endure even another year, let alone two.[39] In June 1838, under pressure from abolitionists, coupled with widely publicized re-

36. *Barbadian*, 21 November 1835.

37. CO 28/119, No. 143, MacGregor to Glenelg, 20 June 1837, enclosing monthly reports for June 1837, District A, Rural Division.

38. PP 1837–1838. vol. 48, *Report on Negro Education,* MacGregor to Glenelg, 1 January 1838.

39. CO 28/122, No. 108, MacGregor to Glenelg, 12 May 1838, enclosing monthly reports for March 1838, District A, Town Division.

ports of the abuse of the system, the British government forced colonial assembles to pass legislation terminating apprenticeship in August.[40]

GENDER, OCCUPATION, AND THE IMPACT OF EMANCIPATION

The lives of free people of color during slavery foreshadowed the trends for former slaves during apprenticeship. Nevertheless, many free Afro-Barbadians had ambivalent feelings about emancipation. For many free people of color apprentices were their friends, neighbors and family members. Additionally, the legislature's repressive efforts to control apprentices and freedpeople created common ground for resistance. Yet slave emancipation created difficulties for free people of color because of the loss of their enslaved property and because of economic competition from the newly freed population.

In 1837 American abolitionists Thome and Kimball visited the West Indies to observe apprenticeship. They met a number of government officials, stipendiary magistrates, and several free men and women of color. The abolitionists commented that, until recently, free Afro-Caribbean people were generally "indifferent" or even "hostile" toward emancipation. Thome and Kimball got a firsthand taste of this hostility when they met "a colored lady of good appearance and ladylike manners" in Morant Bay, Jamaica. She rapidly disabused them of their misconception that, as a person of color, she would support emancipation. "No American white lady" they wrote, "could speak more disparagingly of the niggers, than did this recreant descendant of the negro race. They did no work, they stole, were insolent, insubordinate, and what not." She was herself a slave owner and depended entirely upon hired out slave labor for her income. She told them bitterly, "I can't tell what will become of us after 1840. Our Negroes will be taken away from us—we shall find no work to do ourselves—we shall all have to beg, and who shall we beg from? *All will be beggars, and we must starve!*"[41]

Whether free Afro-Barbadians concurred or disagreed with this assessment of emancipation, there were few whose lives were not materially affected by it.

40. Woodville Marshall, "The Termination of the Apprenticeship in Barbados and the Windward Islands: An Essay in Colonial Administration and Politics," *JCH* 2 (May 1971): 39; James Williams, *A Narrative of Events, since the First of August, 1834, by James Williams, an Apprenticed Labourer in Jamaica*, ed. Diana Paton (Durham, N.C.: Duke University Press, 2001).

41. Thome and Kimball, *Emancipation in the West Indies*, 76 and 93–94.

Many Afro-Barbadian slave owners were among the large number of people for whom, like the Jamaican woman from Morant Bay, emancipation meant almost certain impoverishment.[42] Many landless slave owners, particularly white and Afro-Barbadian women, relied entirely upon their apprentices' labor for survival. For nonwhite female slave owners in a marginal economic position, legal status was the only distinction separating them from slaves, and slave labor the only barrier between them and poverty. Several owned small shops but much of their income derived from hiring out their slaves.

The case of a "coloured Lady," brought before stipendiary magistrate Colthurst by one of her female domestics for brutality, illustrates the loss of income and social status that emancipation entailed for some slaveholding women. Her partner, a colonel in the militia, had died and left her "besides other property, the services of eight or ten slaves, now apprentices." She kept a small liquor store near to St. Ann's military garrison. When Colthurst, amused by her pompous behavior, sarcastically referred to her as "the queen of Sheba," the following exchange took place:

> "Sir," said she, "I tell you I am neither a princess nor a queen." "Then," said I, "what are you?" "What am I, why I am Mrs. Colonel , by the by." "Good," said I, "now Mrs. Colonel , by the by, are you guilty of the charge your apprentice has made against you? . . . "I am, your Worship, but I am a hasty person, and was bred in slavery, and so was the poor dear Colonel, who always left the punishment of his slaves to me for seventeen years." "Well, madam," said I, "that will do. I should be sorry to detain you longer. I must, as the law directs, liberate your maid forthwith." "Sir," said madam, by the by, rising with a manner that really alarmed me, "you mean to free the hussy?" "Yes," said I, "I most certainly will, and that without delay." The maid cried out: "I am no more hussy than you." It was then high time to put an end to the scene by ordering madam by the by instantly to leave the court, at the same time directing her maid to come to me the following morning for her discharge.[43]

42. *Barbadian*, 30 July 1834.

43. Colthurst, *Colthurst Journal*, 122–123, cited in Melanie Newton, "'New Ideas of Correctness': Gender, Amelioration and Emancipation in Barbados, 1810s–1850s," *Slavery and Abolition* 21, no. 3 (2000): 94–124.

"Mrs. Colonel," accustomed to brutalizing her slaves with impunity, was now just another Afro-Barbadian shopkeeper. Her maid could insult her publicly and still walk away with her freedom. It is unlikely that "Mrs. Colonel" was actually married, since a white Barbadian militiaman married to a woman of color would never have made the rank of officer. She therefore did not have the status of widow to help her maintain her social standing.

In 1837 Thome and Kimball witnessed another Bridgetown case, also involving a "colored lady" and her domestic. The employer presented a list of charges of "insubordination" against her apprentice, including "wiping her greasy fingers" on the employer's gown, deliberately working slowly and saying, so her mistress could hear, that she could not wait to be free. The magistrate sentenced the domestic to four days' solitary confinement but agreed to release her into her mistress' service at the mistress' request.[44] During slavery, domestics had often employed such acts of defiance in the hope that owners would hire them out or allow them to find a new owner. Apprentices continued to use these tactics, hoping that employers would manumit them just to be rid of them.[45] Even so, this mistress probably could not face the social degradation of surviving without a domestic, and possibly could not afford to pay for one.

By contrast, for free Afro-Barbadian men, apprenticeship created employment opportunities previously reserved for white men, such as jobs in estate management. During apprenticeship there was nothing extraordinary about free men of color, included former slaves, holding positions of estate authority as managers, overseers and bookkeepers. The diary of the Moravian missionary at Mount Tabor in St. John referred often to a "coloured" man named Joe Redland, who was either manager or bookkeeper at nearby Redland estate. The fact that Joe's surname was Redland indicates that he previously had no surname and had once been a slave on the very estate where he now held a management position.[46] This trend apparently outraged some whites, for in December of 1833 a passerby found an anonymous letter lying by a road addressed to one Robert Jordan, the black submanager of the Codrington estates. The author pretended to be an apprentice or free Afro-Barbadian accomplice with whom Jordan was plotting rebellion. The governor

44. Thome and Kimball, *Emancipation in the West Indies,* 67.

45. CO 28/122, No. 60, MacGregor to Glenelg, 20 March 1838, enclosing monthly reports for February 1838, District A, Town Division.

46. Moravian Diary, 16 September and 18 December 1836.

suspected that a white person, angered at the appointment of an Afro-Barbadian to such a position, had written the letter hoping to implicate Jordan.[47]

Overall, the social and economic effects of losing slave labor were less dire for landless Afro-Barbadians than for landless whites. Men and women of African descent, both slave and free, had come to monopolize most areas of skilled wage labor and small business activity. Thome and Kimball observed that most of Bridgetown's merchants were "colored." Some of the town's "most popular instructors" were Afro-Barbadian men and women. They even asserted that the "most efficient and enterprising mechanics of the city are colored and black men. There is scarcely any line of business which is not either shared or engrossed by colored persons."[48]

URBAN TRADE AND COMPETITION FOR NONAGRICULTURAL LABOR

Urban free Afro-Barbadian workers now faced competition from former slaves determined to engage in petty trade or enter the ranks of the urban laboring class. The encroachment of former slaves on the trades, huckstering, shopkeeping, domestic work, and sewing threatened to depress wages in these occupations. The *Barbadian* reported in September 1834 that Bridgetown was being "deluged with tradesmen of every description, who are starving each other."[49]

The actual number of those who migrated to Bridgetown or took up regular employment there is uncertain, but even before emancipation white and Afro-Barbadian merchants and tradesmen saw former slaves as a threat to public order and public morals and called for the establishment of an urban police force to control them.[50] Early in 1834 Joseph Thorne, John Montefiore, Joseph Kennedy, William B. Nunes, Benjamin W. Massiah, and William S. Wilkey—Afro-Barbadian merchants, civil rights campaigners, and, in some cases, slave owners—joined white Bridgetown merchants in signing petitions expressing their willingness to

47. CO 28/113, No. 1, Smith to Stanley, 8 January 1834. See also chapter 8, p. 287.

48. Thome and Kimball, *Emancipation in the West Indies,* 76.

49. *Barbadian,* 20 September 1834.

50. A 1787 act had given magistrates the power to designate constables for the execution of writs and similar duties but there was no police force in the island. In 1813 St. Michael Vestry was authorized to raise money for a Bridgetown night watch but this order was not enforced until 1826, when the vestry created a constabulary of 24 men and placed street lights around the capital. Levy, "Barbados," 337.

pay taxes for an improved police force to deal with the anticipated problem of increased former slave migration to Bridgetown.[51] On this issue urban merchants and planter-legislators agreed and, later that year, the legislature passed an act establishing a Bridgetown police force. Similar acts were passed during apprenticeship to establish police forces in the rural districts, as well as Speightstown in St. Peter and Holetown in St. James parish.[52] The Bridgetown police act is particularly illustrative of the panic with which elites viewed the possibility of rural migration to the city. Very little of the act actually discussed the structure of the police force. Most of it was dedicated to an astonishingly detailed description of the business and social activities of urban apprentices and free Afro-Barbadians, which the act gave the St. Michael Vestry extensive powers to regulate.[53]

Bridgetown's working-class free people of color were caught by the tide of repressive legislation intended to stop the flow of people from the countryside. In

51. *Barbadian*, 8 January and 26 February 1834.

52. CO 30/21, No. 558, "An Act for the Establishment of Rules and Regulations for . . . the Rural Police of this Island . . . ," passed 1 July 1834; No. 560, "An Act to establish a Police in Bridge-Town, in the Parish of Saint Michael," passed 29 July, 1834; CO 30/22, No. 622, "An Act for the establishment of a police force in Speights Town and in the Hole Town," passed 28 March 1837.

53. The police act gave the vestry full power to pass ordinances "relative to . . . all offences, evils, and inconveniences whatsoever in the said Town, or in the Streets, Squares, or places therein, or within the Careenage or Mole-Head, relative to the exercising, using, and carrying on of dangerous, noisome, or offensive Trades of every kind in particular Streets, or places, in the said Town; relative to Markets in the said Town (but not to extend to regulating or ascertaining the price of any commodity or article of provision which may be brought to sale within the said Town) . . . relative to all suspicious persons loitering about the Town in the day or night, and who can give no good account of themselves; relative to Taverns, Grog-shops, Punch or Tippling-houses, Retailers of Liquors of every description, Hawkers, Pedlers, Hucksters, Porters, and Boatmen, and to the fixing and regulating the rates at which Licenses may be granted to them respectively, by the Justices of the Peace regulating and appointed to carry this Act into effect; relative to forestalling and regrating; relative to the assize of Bread; relative to putrid, damaged, or decayed Provisions and commodities of every kind; relative to the building of Houses within the limits of Bridge-Town, materials of which such Houses shall be constructed, so as to render the same less liable to take fire; relative to decayed Buildings, and vacant spots of Land; and to all other nuisances; relative to Hogs, Dogs, and Goats, going at large, or otherwise, being in the said Town . . . relative to the dispersing of all Mobs, and for the punishment of all indecorous Swearing, Quarrelling, or improper behaviour in the Streets of the said Town; relative to the enforcing due observance of the Sabbath; relative to trafficking in the Streets; and relative to any matter or thing whatsoever, which may concern the good government and Police of the said Town." "An Act to establish a Police in Bridge-Town, in the Parish of Saint Michael," 29 July 1834, in *The Public Acts in Force, passed by the legislature of Barbados, from the First of William IV* . . . (Bridgetown: House of Assembly, 1836), 39.

November 1835 the legislature passed an act authorizing the enclosure of the Bridgetown market place, which had a lengthy appendix of bylaws for the "good government" of the capital, all targeting specific everyday activities of laboring-class Afro-Barbadians, slave and free. These included "An Ordinance Relative to idle, disorderly, and suspicious Persons," "An Ordinance relative to Porters, Carters, Boatmen and Labourers," "An Ordinance regulating the time for bringing Provisions, Poultry, Guinea-Grass, and other articles from the country-side into Bridge-Town," "An Ordinance relative to hogs, goats and sheep going at large in the streets," and "An Ordinance relative to the dispersing of all Mobs, and the punishment of all indecorous behaviour within the limits of the Town."[54]

The most controversial of the bylaws, the "Ordinance Regulating the building of Houses," outlined new codes designed to reduce the number of wooden dwellings in the city, and empowered the Bridgetown magistrates to barge into private homes and determine any repairs necessary to decrease the risk of fire. This ordinance was really a means of preventing new migrants from establishing themselves in the city, especially in neighborhoods outside of already existing "Negro" slums. In his report in support of this ordinance Attorney General Henry Sharpe noted that although an eighteenth-century building regulations act was still on the books, its provisions had been "for many years totally disregarded." As a result, "[b]uildings of a frail character and of very unsightly appearance have spread themselves in all parts of the Town," posing a fire hazard that, it would seem, had only now become apparent to the legislature. Sharpe alluded to the real motivation behind the law when he stated that uncontrolled urban residential expansion "afford[ed] numerous receptacles for abandoned and profligate characters. . . converting many parts of the Town into little else than negro settlements. . . . [The end of apprenticeship will] lead to an insecure and unlimited establishment of a large portion of the emancipated population in the principal Town."[55] In March 1838 the St. Peter Vestry, which was responsible for Speightstown, passed similar bylaws.[56]

The fire prevention bylaw provoked a storm of protest from city residents of all social backgrounds. Bridgetown homeowners and landlords were concerned that

54. *Barbadian,* 21 November 1835; CO 30/22, No. 579, passed 10 November 1835.

55. CO 28/117, No. 4, 13 January 1836, Smith to Glenelg, enclosing Attorney-General Henry Sharpe, "Observations upon certain Bye Laws ordinances and Regulations for the good Government of Bridge Town," 29 December 1835.

56. *Liberal,* 21 March 1838.

the regulations would lower the value of their property. In January 1836, Governor Smith informed the Colonial Office that white and Afro-Barbadian Bridgetown residents had called separate mass meetings in order to formulate protest petitions, but the organizers took the unprecedented step of combining them in order to compose a single petition. The meeting took place at the Bible Depository of the Auxiliary Bible Society of the Free People of Colour, which was often used by free Afro-Barbadians for political meetings.

The petitioners objected to various aspects of the bylaw, including the powers granted to the police to enter homes. Significantly, the petition also opposed another ordinance requiring that boatmen and porters have licenses.[57] The fact that the issue of licenses for working-class occupations was raised at the meeting reflects the presence of such workers, both free Afro-Barbadians and apprentices. Smith confirmed this when he refused to send the petition to the Colonial Office, claiming that there were no "respectable" people at the meeting and that even apprentices and children had signed the petition. According to Smith, far from being "a general Meeting, comprized [sic] of White, Black and Coloured, it was well known to be got up at the instigation of two or three violent young colored Men. . . . [T]here was not of any Color, one Person of considerable Property present, the Whites being low dissolute Persons, and every opulent Individual of the Black or Colored Class either declining to attend, or withdrawing when they witnessed the violence of the Meeting's Procedures."[58]

Samuel Jackman Prescod, who was now the editor of a recently founded newspaper called the *New Times*, had been elected chairman of the meeting, and he wrote a letter to the *West Indian* newspaper rejecting Smith's claim that only lower-class people were there.[59] Prescod declared that nearly three hundred whites, some of them significant property owners, had been present. The meeting did attract both whites and Afro-Barbadians; of the twenty-one names mentioned in Smith's letter to the Colonial Office sixteen were men of color and five were white. However, most of the men known to have attended the meeting appear to have been laboring class or petty traders. Those who spoke out against

57. CO 28/117, No. 4, 13 January 1836, Smith to Glenelg, with enclosures.

58. Ibid.

59. The *New Times* was once owned by John Callaird, a man of color nearly deported a decade before for his part in the 1824 counteraddress controversy (see chapter 3, p. 83). Unfortunately, only one copy of the newspaper has survived.

the ordinances were neither wealthy nor previously prominent Afro-Barbadian men. In some cases, the meeting is the first or only time that their names appear in any surviving document. With the possible exception of Thomas Harris Jr., the other prominent figures at the meeting—Prescod, Benjamin Eversley, and John Callaird—were not at the time either particularly influential or wealthy men.[60]

Even if they opposed the details of the fire prevention ordinance, many elite men of color supported the underlying aim of the vestry's 1835 ordinances, which was to prevent urban migration of rural apprentices. Thomas J. Cummins, who was then a member of the St. Michael Vestry and one of only two vestrymen to vote against adopting the fire prevention ordinance, did not attend the meeting—nor did other prominent Afro-Barbadian political and civil rights agitators.[61] Neither does Cummins appear to have voted against the other ordinances, which, unlike the fire prevention ordinance, did not negatively affect the interests of urban property owners. At the same time, the meeting was partially successful as an attempt to establish a community of interests between less well-to-do urban whites and people of color, who were excluded from the political alliance of wealthy white and Afro-Barbadian Bridgetown merchants.

CHRISTIANIZING SLAVES

Apprenticeship brought new difficulties for free Afro-Barbadian men and women, but it also produced new opportunities for them. Popular education was among the most significant areas of civic involvement for free people of color during and after the apprenticeship period. Between 1835 and 1841 the British government gave an annual subsidy of thirty thousand pounds to a nondenominational trust called the Mico Charity and to various missionary societies for schools in the British Caribbean.[62] Apprentices were eager for the chance to educate their children. According to Colthurst, there were not enough schools to meet the enor-

60. CO 28/117, No. 4, Smith to Glenelg, 13 January 1836, with enclosures.

61. For the discussion of the circumstances of Cummins's election to the vestry, see chapter 6, p. 186, of the present volume.

62. CO 31/51, 26 January 1836; Carl Campbell, "Social and Economic Obstacles to the Development of Popular Education in Post-emancipation Jamaica, 1834–1865," in Beckles and Shepherd, eds., *Caribbean Freedom*, 262–268.

mous demand during apprenticeship. He noted that "a vast many [apprentices] hire their apprenticed children from their masters at a quarter-dollar a week, for the express purpose of sending them to school" and paid another quarter-dollar in school fees.[63]

An 1838 imperial report on education in the British Caribbean referred to the large pool of "respectable" white and Afro-Barbadian school teachers. Twelve male and fifteen female teachers of color worked in the island's Anglican schools. British abolitionists Joseph Sturge and Thomas Harvey, who visited Barbados during apprenticeship, referred to the existence of a number of schools for apprentices where the teachers were all men of color.[64] Many whites, free Afro-Barbadians, and apprentices used what little education they had to make a living running schools for apprentices and free children of color. The imperial education report also enumerated 13,869 children attending school, cautioning that those surveyed were less than a quarter of the island's schools. According to the report, there were "innumerable irregular channels through which desultory instruction is received by even the children and youth of the poorer classes, such as lessons given in the dwelling-houses of itinerant teachers."[65]

For some free people of color, teaching combined economic return with a political commitment to emancipation and the education of Afro-Caribbean children. In 1837, between his editorship of the *New Times* and the *Liberal* newspapers, Samuel Jackman Prescod announced the opening of his school for "young coloured boys," where "respectable" boys who moved to Bridgetown from rural areas would receive board on reasonable terms.[66] This was the only advertisement for Prescod's school, and, if he ever actually taught classes, the school was probably partly envisioned as a fund-raising venture for his own newspaper, the *Liberal*, which began publication later that year. Another man of color, a Methodist, began a school in 1833 in Nelson Street to teach the children whom he saw playing in the road outside his house how to read. The school was run

63. Colthurst, *Colthurst Journal*, 169 and 203; CO 28/119, No. 143, MacGregor to Glenelg, 20 June 1837, enclosing monthly reports of the stipendiary magistrates, No. 2, District A, Rural Division.

64. PP 1837–38, vol. 48, *Report on Negro Education*, 228–229; Joseph Sturge and Thomas Harvey, *The West Indies in 1837* (1838; reprint, London: Dawsons of Pall Mall, 1968), 130, 135 and 144–145.

65. PP 1837–38, vol. 48, *Report on Negro Education*, 228–229 and 256–257; Newton, "New Ideas of Correctness," 104.

66. *Barbadian*, 29 March 1837.

on charitable donations until 1837, when it was taken over by the Methodist Church.[67]

As Robin Blackburn argues the act of emancipation reflected popular displeasure with the aristocracy's assumption of its right to "untrammelled rule," but it was not necessarily a challenge to the principle that property conferred the right of political participation. Rather, mainstream abolitionists saw emancipation as "integral to a reformed and moralised version of the established order" in both Britain and the Caribbean.[68] Emancipation, literacy, and the Bible marched hand in hand, as amelioration and then emancipation provided missionaries with the opportunity for the mass education of slaves and free children of color.[69] The Bible was the principle instrument of instruction, and during apprenticeship, a teacher at an Anglican school in Barbados told Thome and Kimball that "the instructions of the school-room were carried to the homes of the children, and caught up by their parents."[70] Converting Afro-Caribbean people to Christianity was central to imperial efforts to constitute a new postslavery moral order while preserving as much as possible of the old social hierarchy.

Authorities viewed the patriarchal family, Christian marriage, and the suppression of illegitimacy and "polygamy" as central to the new moral order. Church, state, and press all used public display of what they considered to be respectable domestic conduct among former slaves as an incentive to others to marry. In 1833, in preparation for emancipation, the management of the Society for the Propagation of the Gospel's estates offered special allotments to married couples, gave them a day and a half off every week, and permitted wives not to come to work until nine o'clock in the morning. In August of that year, a visit by the bishop

67. The name of this Methodist schoolmaster is not known. PP 1837–38, vol. 48, *Report on Negro Education*, 256; Thome and Kimball, *Emancipation in the West Indies*, 71; Sturge and Harvey, *West Indies in 1837*, 148.

68. Blackburn, *Overthrow of Colonial Slavery*, 466.

69. Olwyn Blouet, "Education and Emancipation in Barbados, 1833–1846: A Study in Cultural Transference," *Ethnic and Racial Studies* 4, no. 2 (April 1981): 222; Shirley Gordon, "Schools of the Free," in Brian Moore and Swithin Wilmot, eds., *Before and after 1865: Education, Politics and Regionalism in the Caribbean* (Kingston: Ian Randle, 1998), 1–12.

70. Moravian Diary, 21 October 1826; Thome and Kimball, *Emancipation in the West Indies*, 71.

of the see occasioned a "public display" of the married couples. This was followed by the public signing of a symbolic "contract" between the estate attorney and the estate's married men, in which the men promised to "provide for ourselves, our wives, and children, food, clothing, and all the other necessaries of life."[71]

Friendly societies, formed after 1828 throughout the West Indies, were another site for white and Afro-Barbadian elites to display publicly their attempts to remake working-class Afro-Barbadians' domestic morals. In June 1835 the *Barbadian* carried a lengthy report on the three-hundred-member St. Mary's Male and Female Friendly Societies, which had been formed by the Afro-Barbadian St. Mary's Society for the Education of the Coloured Poor charity. The friendly societies held a sex-segregated procession through Bridgetown, joined by the children of the Colonial Charity School, to St. Michael Cathedral, where the Anglican bishop addressed them. One hundred and five of the societies' members were married men, and any man or woman found to be having a relationship out of wedlock was automatically expelled.[72]

The promotion of the patriarchal Christian family helped to produce normative discourses on public morality whose power derived as much from their role as social *ideals,* which few working-class people achieved or were expected to achieve, as from their influence on the actual behavior of the poor. In 1838, the *Barbadian* published a series of fictional "conversations" between a married apprenticed couple, John and Jane, and their local Anglican minister, allegedly for the instruction of former slaves in correct moral conduct. The articles were really for whites, since former slaves and free people of color were not the *Barbadian's* intended audience. These articles reassured whites that the newfound social respectability of their former legal subordinates could be compatible with a state of socioeconomic inequality. In the eyes of the editor, "respectable," patriarchal Christian family life provided a means by which even a common estate laborer could be a distinguished and respected member of society, but only if former slave parents cheerfully obeyed the authority of church, state, and estate and accepted their lot and that of their children to be field laborers:

71. CO 28/112, Miscellaneous Offices correspondence, No. 5977, Secretary of the SPG to George Lefevre, 28 December 1833, "Report Respecting the Negroes on the Codrington Estates," 1834; Extract of a letter from the Bishop, 30 August 1833; "Agreement between the Attorney and Negroes at Codrington," 16 August 1833.

72. *Barbadian,* 6, 10 June 1835 and 18 June 1836.

JOHN: . . . What difference is there between one labourer and another? Are they not all much alike?

MINISTER: . . . [I]t will make a great difference whether your children are brought up to be idle, or industrious; to be drunken and disorderly, or sober and well-behaved; to be half-naked, like savages, or all in rags, like paupers, or else like the children of respectable Christian parents, to be always decently clothed in proper and whole garments.

JANE: Oh! sir, as to that, I am sure our children have as good clothes as any children on the Estate, and they very often wear them at a funeral or so, or sometimes to go to Church.

MINISTER: Yes, *sometimes* to go to Church:—for I fear, Jane, your children have not been quite as regular at Church as I could wish them to have been, and as I hope they *will* be now. But do not mistake what I said about dress. I do not wish to see your children *fine*, but decent and respectable. . . . Nobody will respect you the more, but much less, for wearing *fine* clothes: but to see you and your children coming to Church plainly yet neatly dressed, will give everyone a good opinion of your industry, and motherly care of them; particularly if they find that, through the week also, they are never naked or ragged, but always respectable. Besides clothing, the state of your house should receive your attention. . . . Nothing makes a difference to any man, and particularly to a labouring man, more than a comfortable, happy home. It is the want of this that causes many a man, and many a child too, to become vicious and good for nothing. . . . There are few sights, John, equal to that of a Christian family, united in love and kindness to each other, and striving who shall do most to make the others happy.[73]

Behind the publication of such idealized representations lurked the unstated warning that any former slave who challenged planter authority deserved to feel the full weight of retribution from the planter state. In an earlier "conversation" the "Minister" had instructed "John" and "Jane" that parents who did not apprentice their children to the estates should expect harsh consequences.[74]

Elite Afro-Barbadian men used their own discourses of a new postslavery public morality against conservative whites in order to undermine racial discrimination, arguing that correct conduct conferred upon any man of property a social re-

73. *Barbadian,* 24 January 1838.
74. *Barbadian,* 3 January 1838.

spectability that entitled him to all the rights of citizenship. In March 1835 Prescod criticized the white police superintendent's conduct in a case that involved the unlawful detention of a boy (possibly apprenticed) who worked as a domestic in Prescod's household. The superintendent responded by referring to Prescod's illegitimate birth as the son of a white man and a free woman of color, deriding him as having "no claim to the name he assumes."[75] In his response, Prescod dismissed the commissioner's references to his birth and poured scorn on the notion of "respectability" as employed by the superintendent and elite whites in general. Prescod asserted that any man who consistently maintained a proper Christian demeanor could rightly claim to be a "gentleman":

> [O]nly *I* can forfeit—*my* claim to the title of gentleman! A claim which, bye the bye, I have, *despite my base birth,* dared to assume—which I have *hitherto* maintained and, God willing, *will* maintain during life—not by frothy declamations, not by mere *drivellings* about "respectability"—but by moral conduct, "by being *true* and *just* in ALL my dealings—by keeping my *hands* from *picking* and *stealing;* and my *tongue* from *evil speaking, lying,* and *slandering*—by keeping (or at any rate *endeavouring* to keep) my body in temperance, soberness, and chastity—by not *coveting,* nor desiring OTHER MEN'S GOODS," in short, by the general tenour [*sic*] of a life not disgracefully run through![76]

Nevertheless, the *Liberal*'s editors combined these progressive views with a class elitism that was typical of educated Afro-Barbadian men's attitudes toward women and former slaves. This combination of liberalism, patriarchy, and class paternalism was evident in the *Liberal*'s response to the legislature's 1836 "Act the better to regulate the sale of Goods, Wares and Merchandize by itinerant vendors." Part of the slew of authoritarian legislation passed during apprenticeship to control the urban activities of Afro-Barbadians, the act sought to curtail hucksters' activities by making it mandatory for itinerant hucksters to buy expensive government licenses.[77] The *Liberal* invoked a romantic image of the patriarchal family in

75. Hilton Vaughan Mss., "Prescod I: Letters, Speeches and Newspaper Articles, 1830–1838," BDA, enclosing letter from Prescod to the *Globe,* 9 March 1835, 11–13, and letter from superintendent Stephen Agard to the *Mercury,* 10 March 1835, 19–25; *Barbadian,* 11 March 1835.

76. *Barbadian,* 14 March 1835.

77. CO 30/22, No. 583, passed 16 August 1836.

attacking the law: "Some three of four years ago a poor woman, the wife of a poor mechanic, might assist her husband to maintain them, by a little petty traffic requiring a floating capital of one or two dollars. She must now obtain an annual licence for four or eight dollars, probably the whole of her profits!" This description both critiqued state efforts to undermine huckstering *and* minimized the importance of former slave women's entrepreneurship. The *Liberal* went further, arguing that the act was in fact a danger to public morality, because state repression of women's legitimate economic activities would force females to turn to "some less honorable profession, to which Legislative patrinage [sic] has not yet been extended."[78] This thinly veiled reference to prostitution echoed planters' antihuckster discourse, in which female itinerant vendors were represented as being one step removed from prostitutes.

Prescod's tone on the matter of former slaves' morality was so condescending that even the pro-planter *Barbadian* was impressed with his first article as editor of the *New Times* in 1836. Denouncing a proposal for a public lottery, Prescod argued that gambling by the elite was a bad example to the "lower orders" and exhorted the upper classes to smooth the transition from slavery to freedom by encouraging hard work and thrift among the poor:

> In these colonies especially—and at this moment above all others—it is the duty as it certainly is the interest of all, especially of the wealthy and great amongst us, to set a good example before the lower orders—To endeavour, by every means in their power, to raise the tone of religion and morals, and to promote honest and persevering industry amongst them, as the *only proper* means of bettering their condition in this life, and of purchasing eternal happiness in the next!! . . . [H]ow can we expect the lower classes amongst us to be proof against the vicious examples of those whom they have, from their infancy, been accustomed to look up to as their superiors in morals and intellect? With what justice can we make laws to punish them for those vices, which, if not sown by us, have, at least, been cherished and brought to maturity by the influences of our example?[79]

Well-to-do free people of color generally adhered to the ethnocentric view that the African-derived spiritual practices of former slaves and lower-class free Afro-

78. *Liberal*, 10 March 1838.
79. *Barbadian*, 4 May 1836, extract from the *New Times*.

Barbadians needed be suppressed. Stipendiary magistrate Colthurst spoke highly of the "coloured" lay preacher Joseph Thorne, who worked as an Anglican catechist on five plantations during the apprenticeship period, crediting him with putting "a final stop to the practice of oboe [Obeah]." Colthurst described an incident he witnessed on one estate, when Thorne, wielding a stick, violently dispersed a crowd of estate workers who were engaged in the "barbarous" practice of placing grave goods into the grave of a recently deceased member of their community. Such items were meant to accompany and nourish the dead on their journey in the afterlife. According to Colthurst, Thorne then used his stick to scatter and destroy the grave provisions.[80]

CHURCH, COMMUNITY, AND FAMILY LIFE

In theory, Christianity opened the possibilities of social equality to all, regardless of one's socioeconomic standing. After emancipation membership in a church became a defining mark of being free and a means to achieve social respectability. While baptism rates had been increasing since the early nineteenth century, they went into the thousands after 1834. In the Anglican parish records the names of former slaves, distinguished by the absence of surnames, appeared first in 1834 and rapidly became the majority, most of them mothers having children baptized.[81] Burial was transformed into a "Christian rite" after emancipation, as plantation burial grounds fell into disuse and burials in churchyards and chapels became the norm.[82] Former slaves also adopted many of the ceremonial customs associated with "respectable" Christian worship.[83]

Former slaves and free people of color were eager to be baptized but were se-

80. Colthurst, *Colthurst Journal*, 84. As Marshall points out, this was not an obeah ceremony. Slaves believed that the dead went on a journey. Patterson, *Sociology of Slavery*, 168.

81. RL 1/50A, BPL, Parochial Register—Baptisms Solemnized in the Parish of St. Thomas; the St. Thomas Sharon Moravian Church Book also shows that the majority of baptisms at Sharon between 1767 and 1839 were in the period between 1800 and 1839, particularly after the start of amelioration (baptism number 250 was in 1824). Only 122 out of 1,292 baptisms occurred before 1800. The most rapid increase was in the early to mid-1830s and during the apprenticeship period. Between 1831 and 1833, there were 238 baptisms, or more than one-fifth of the total.

82. Caldecott, *Church in the West Indies*, 109.

83. For example, in 1837 members of the congregation at the Sharon Moravian mission in St. Thomas proposed a subscription to pay for a hearse for funerals (Sharon Church Book, 1 January– 30 July 1837).

lective in their adoption of the "Christian" lifestyle being peddled by elites as
the proper way to live. The rapid increase in church membership among Afro-
Barbadians, usually the Anglican Church, during the apprenticeship period, was
facilitated by the Anglicans' relaxed admission policies. Unlike the Methodists and
the Moravians, who zealously screened applicants according to strict standards of
conduct, the Anglican clergy was, on the whole, more concerned with numbers
than individual behavior. In 1833 the Anglican rector of St. John's parish church
invited the slaves of the surrounding area to be baptized. The Moravian missionary in nearby Mount Tabor complained in his diary that "many of them went and
were baptised without having received any instruction previous to it; also some of
our candidates who had not Patience to wait any longer were induced to go with
the rest."[84] In 1837 the same missionary refused to baptize Fanny, an apprentice,
on the grounds that she led a "vicious life" and "used to come to her speaking de-
siring to be baptised without being willing to alter her conduct." Fanny went to
Bridgetown and was baptized an Anglican.[85]

The ease with which people could become Anglicans facilitated a process
whereby new converts could become Christian while comfortably continuing to
engage in practices that, according to the church, the state, and the upper classes,
were incompatible with Christianity. Thus while Christian baptisms and burials became the norm, polygamy and common-law unions continued. In 1838 the
Mount Tabor mission recorded seventeen as the highest annual number of marriages it had performed during apprenticeship. In 1835 there were no marriages
at all in the church, although hundreds of slaves signed up as candidates for baptism. That same year the missionary recorded a visit to the home of a free Afro-
Barbadian man whose apprentice was also his mistress. The missionary could not
decide whether to be dismayed or pleased when he arrived at the house one day to
find the mistress reading the Bible to the family.[86]

Even some members of the Afro-Barbadian elite were slow to adopt all of the
trappings of "respectable" Christianity. Although Christian marriage was a public
statement of good moral conduct and social respectability many prominent political and civil rights agitators were not baptized until well into their adulthood.
The wealthy black merchant London Bourne was married in an Anglican church

84. Moravian Diary, 1 January 1833.

85. Ibid., 9 August 1837.

86. Mount Tabor Moravian Church, List of Marriages in the Congregation, 1829–1839; Moravian
Diary, 14 February 1835.

in 1822, but he was not baptized Anglican until he was about thirty-one years old in 1824, six years after his manumission.[87] Prescod was a free thinker until the middle of the apprenticeship period, when he married a well-to-do woman of color, Katherine Cruden, and converted to the Church of England, which was the faith of most elite Afro-Barbadians.[88]

Reports from the middle of the apprenticeship period also indicate that friendly societies appealed most to comparatively comfortable members. In 1835 most of the St. Mary's Male and Female Friendly Societies' three hundred members were apprentices, but their ranks contained "a considerable number also of very respectable free persons." After a severe yellow fever epidemic in 1836 and 1837 it emerged that few members of the St. Mary's Friendly Society applied for aid, with the majority saying that they "did not absolutely require it." This revelation angered the Anglican bishop, who saw it as an indication that the society's members were "not of the poorest class."[89] Out of seventy-four members of the St. Mary's Male Friendly Society who signed an 1839 letter, forty-three can be positively identified as well-to-do men of color free before 1834. Of the remainder, twenty-one most likely were free before emancipation. Only ten of the signatories might have been apprentices or recently freed people.[90] Friendly societies' limited appeal probably stemmed from their strict regulations on marriage and general deportment. In 1836, according to the bishop, twenty-nine men had been expelled from the St. Mary's friendly society for living with women to whom they were not married.[91]

While Christian marriage and a legitimate birth for one's children were the pinnacle of respectability, an individual man or woman of color was unlikely to ostracized by others of the same social status for being in a relationship and for having children outside of marriage and it remained the norm for Afro-Barbadian mothers not to marry, even if they were in long-term relationships.[92] Decisions about marriage and families by and large reflected practical considerations and a process of cultural negotiation between Christian and African-Barbadian concep-

87. Karch, "Man for All Seasons," 3.

88. *Barbadian,* 9 September 1840; Vaughan, *Democrat,* 5 March 1971.

89. *Barbadian,* 10 June 1835 and 13 May 1837.

90. CO 28/129, Barbados Correspondence, No. 127, MacGregor to Russell, 17 December 1839, enclosing "An Address from certain Inhabitants of this Colony to the Reverend W. M. Harte"; Handler, Hughes, and Wiltshire, *Freedmen of Barbados,* 22.

91. *Barbadian,* 25 May 1836.

92. John Davy, *The West Indies before and since Emancipation, Comprising the Windward and Leeward Islands' Military Command* (London: N.p., 1854), 92–93.

tions of respectability, rather than a passive acceptance of British and elite Barbadian values.[93]

RACE, GENDER, AND THE SUPPRESSION OF "LICENTIOUSNESS"

During apprenticeship, elite whites and Afro-Barbadians used the press, the church, and missionary and philanthropy societies as arenas to demonstrate that their domestic respectability entitled themselves to public authority. For the white elite one of the most damaging aspects of abolitionism had been its condemnation of the "licentiousness" of West Indian society. The erosion of sympathy in Britain for the planter cause was clearly connected to abolitionists' arguments that white West Indians were morally bankrupt. It was certainly true that, during slavery, the right of white men to behave as badly they pleased affirmed white masculinity and racial supremacy. Abolitionist literature frequently contained gruesome depictions of drunkenness and acts of cruelty, especially rape and flogging, being committed against slaves, usually by white men.

Elite white men's philanthropic activities for poor whites and slaves during amelioration had been a first attempt to overcome such negative press. During apprenticeship elite white men took further steps to rehabilitate their public image and reassert their right to rule by establishing new codes of proper conduct for themselves. According to these new ideals of white male behavior, "respectable" Christian conduct, including a public repudiation of violence, hard drinking and promiscuity, was now as important for white men as for everyone else. This drive by white planters, clergymen and merchants to set high moral standards was also intended to preserve their dominance and keep Afro-Barbadian men politically subordinate, and white men excluded men of color from their civic activities. During apprenticeship temperance societies sprang up in several British Caribbean territories.[94] Elite whites and free people of color in some other islands organized these societies jointly but the members of the newly formed Barbados Temper-

93. Jean Besson, "Reputation and Respectability Reconsidered: A New Perspective on Afro-Caribbean Peasant Women," in Janet Momsen, ed., *Women and Change in the Caribbean: A Pan-Caribbean Perspective* (London: James Currey, 1993), 19; Diane Austin-Broos, "Redefining the Moral Order: Interpretations of Christianity in Postemancipation Jamaica," in Frank McGlynn and Seymour Drescher, eds., *The Meaning of Freedom: Economics, Politics, and Culture after Slavery* (Pittsburgh: University of Pittsburgh Press, 1992), 221–243.

94. Thome and Kimball, *Emancipation in the West Indies*, 21–22 (description of Antigua Temperance Society tea party); Mrs. Flannigan, *Antigua and the Antiguans; A Full Account of the Colony and its Inhabitants* . . . (1844; reprint, London: Spottiswoode, Ballantyne, 1967), 171–174.

ance Society in 1835 were all white planters, clergymen, and merchants. Although many prominent men of color espoused temperance views, they were not invited to join.[95]

After 1834 forms of gendered and interracial social interaction, especially sexual relations between white men and Afro-Barbadian women, which previously had received little public comment, now came under attack. During slavery white men's sexual access to the bodies of free and enslaved women of color, whether violent or consensual, was a means through which gender and racial inequity was constantly reaffirmed. During apprenticeship both white and Afro-Barbadian men attacked common-law interracial relationships as a danger to public morals. This condemnation of common-law interracial relationships reflected a wider "cult of domesticity" that privileged married status as the hallmark of respectability but it was also part of the political struggle between elite white men and free men of color. For whites, in the absence of a sociolegal system that guaranteed racial inequality and effectively proscribed interracial marriage, common-law relationships between white men and Afro-Barbadian women now became a route through which these women and their children might marry into the white community, contaminating "whiteness" and inheriting "white" property. For Afro-Barbadian men, the prevalence of white men's extramarital sexual intercourse with women of color was a challenge to their community and patriarchal authority and their control over "their" women. The confinement within marriage of the labor, sexuality, and reproductive capacity of Afro-Barbadian women was, in both symbolic and practical ways, central to Afro-Barbadian civil rights advocates' projection of themselves as respectable and politically responsible Christians.

After emancipation no white man, however high his social status, was above public condemnation for engaging in interracial sex with Afro-Barbadian women. In September 1841 the island's lieutenant governor held a "Dignity Ball" (a term for a private party at which prostitutes of color entertained upper-class men) at the governor's residence and invited a select group of white and nonwhite men. The white-owned and -edited *West Indian* newspaper was outraged that "WHITE persons, who are recognised in society as gentlemen have danced at Pilgrim [the gov-

---

95. Thome and Kimball, *Emancipation in the West Indies*, 26–27; *Barbadian*, 3 January 1835. Men of color who were abolitionists and supporters of temperance, such as Samuel Jackman Prescod, probably became involved in the international temperance movement, which had strong abolitionist ties. See Richard Blackett, *Building an Anti-Slavery Wall: Black Americans in the Atlantic Abolitionist Movement, 1830–1860* (Baton Rouge: Louisiana State University Press, 1983), 32–33.

ernor's residence] with women of impure character."[96] The *Barbadian* was equally shocked by the lieutenant governor's very public indiscretion and described the party as an "assembly of dissipated men—white, black and coloured—and coloured women of ill fame." Two years later the *Barbadian* vilified a white police officer after he was involved in a brawl at a "mulatto dance" he was attending.[97] The constant reiteration of the race of the men and women involved in such scandals was not a coincidence. For the white press similar parties at which only men of color cavorted with "impure" women would not have been an equal source of concern.

Thome and Kimball noted that everyone viewed the declining respectability of "concubinage" relationships between white men and women of color as a positive development. They observed that it was "the prevailing impression among whites, coloreds and blacks, that open licentiousness cannot long survive slavery." Interestingly, Afro-Barbadian men and women did not condemn interracial sexual relationships per se, only "concubinage" or extramarital relations. According to the two Americans, "The colored females are growing in self-respect, and are beginning to seek regular [married] connections with white men" rather than settling for "disreputable" common-law relationships. This suggests that, for free people of color, the legal circumstances of the match mattered more than the color of those involved.[98]

It is questionable whether apprenticeship and emancipation really reduced the numbers of "concubinage" relationships, or whether it just made them *publicly* unacceptable.[99] Still, for at least some of the Afro-Caribbean mistresses of white men, slave emancipation brought destitution as they were abandoned by the men who had supported them.[100] In 1838 the *Liberal* described the situation of an Afro-Barbadian woman from St. Peter named Molly Ann, abandoned by her white lover during apprenticeship. She was now too poor to support her child of

96. From the *West Indian,* quoted in the *Liberal,* 6 October 1841. In June 1841, Governor General Sir Evan MacGregor died and was replaced until 1842 by the lieutenant governor of Tobago, Maj. Gen. Henry Darling. Schomburgk, *History of Barbados,* 490–492.

97. *Barbadian,* 25 September 1841 and 15 November 1843. See Hawthorne, *Yarn of a Yankee Privateer,* 104.

98. Thome and Kimball, *Emancipation in the West Indies,* 79. See also 58.

99. U.S. journalist William Sewell, who visited the West Indies in the 1850s, argued that what was no longer openly sanctioned was now covertly tolerated. See William G. Sewell, *The Ordeal of Free Labour in the British West Indies* (1861; reprint, London: Frank Cass, 1968), 67–68.

100. Heuman, *Between Black and White,* 75; Lowes, "They Couldn't Mash Ants,'" 42.

this relationship, who died. The Anglican rector of St. Peter refused to bury the child because he had told her to break off the relationship and she had no money to pay for the burial. While the *Liberal* was appalled at the rector's callousness, and successfully demanded a public inquiry into the affair, Samuel Prescod observed somewhat coldly, "This woman belonged for some time to the class formerly so numerous, but, to the credit of the colony, now gradually disappearing, whose chief support was derived from the persons with whom they lived in a state of concubinage."[101]

In the early 1850s a British navy doctor who lived in the island commented on the lasting effects of this public distaste for drunkenness and interracial relationships, particularly those between white men and Afro-Barbadian women. He compared emancipation's impact on white men's behavior to the environmental after-effects of a hurricane:

> What the hurricane [of 1831] did for the physical atmosphere of Barbados, emancipation effected for its moral and domestic atmosphere, it purified that in a remarkable manner, and to the matron ladies and their daughters, always exemplarily correct, was an incalculable comfort. Licentiousness, whatever it might have been before, was almost entirely banished from society: young men no longer exposed to the same temptations as before, acquired new ideas of correctness and purer tastes and habits, all of an elevating kind favoring the development of the higher energies.[102]

Condemnation of interracial relations between white women and Afro-Barbadian men was far less common. It is possible that this was because such relationships were comparatively rare. Another explanation could be that white women who "betrayed" their race by engaging in sexual relations with men of color were not considered a threat to white property or racial purity, since they tended to have far less property and both they and their offspring were simply barred from the white community.[103]

101. *Liberal*, 27 June 1838.

102. Davy, *West Indies before and since Emancipation*, 74.

103. One rare example of such condemnation came from the Drax Hall plantation manager, who stated that he would evict "any white woman who cohabits with a color'd Man, now so common" from the estate. Records of Drax Hall Plantation, "Rules."

CONCLUSION

As a system of incomplete and unevenly distributed freedom, apprenticeship re-shaped labor relations and interactions between rural and urban life in Barbados. The period also unsettled the legal, socioeconomic, social and cultural boundaries between free people of color, slaves and white Barbadians. The end of slavery si-multaneously created economic possibilities for free people of color while also ex-posing them to competition from rural former slave immigrants to the island's towns and repression from the state. Many Afro-Barbadian slave owners, espe-cially women, faced an uncertain economic future. The apprenticeship period also ushered in a significant reordering of and contestation over Barbadians' under-standings of morality, respectability and "proper" Christianity conduct. Laboring-class Afro-Barbadians, both slave and free, contested efforts by both white and nonwhite elites to limit their possibilities for personal freedom and socioeconomic betterment and to remake their cultural practices and kin relationships. Even as elite Afro-Barbadians challenged traditional and racially exclusive definitions of respectability they also reinforced the class and gender inequities of Barbadian society. These dynamics formed the basis of social relations during apprentice-ship and in the early years of full freedom after 1838. Despite the planter state's efforts to maintain racial segregation and preserve the old plantocratic order, ap-prenticeship and the reconstitution of postemancipation social norms and insti-tutions opened the doors to an unprecedented level of involvement by free men of color in public life.

The Afro-Barbadian Bourgeois Public Sphere

W ITH the coming of emancipation, desegregation seemed a more realistic goal than it ever had during slavery. For the first time, during apprenticeship, elite Afro-Barbadian men publicly embraced emancipation as the moment of their freedom and former slaves as their "brethren," in some cases out of a sincere commitment to emancipation and, in others, as a convenient strategy to demonstrate to local whites and imperial authorities that they were the legitimate political representatives of a vast constituency of newly emancipated people. In keeping with the imperial government's view of free Afro-Caribbean people as an important aspect of the empire's strategy for managing the transition from slavery to freedom, the governors of Barbados during and immediately after apprenticeship selected a small number of wealthy men of color for political appointments. Nevertheless, despite imperial administrators' claims to support the desegregation of state institutions in the British Caribbean as part of their emancipation policy, most Afro-Barbadian men's hopes for political appointments were frustrated and very much contingent upon the whims of individual administrators and creole planter-politicians, who almost invariably blocked such appointments.

Still, elite men of color remained determined to translate their bourgeois respectability into political influence, and they continued their very public involvements with philanthropy and their petitioning campaigns to the local legislature and to the Crown while attempting to harness the popular support of a wider cross section of Afro-Barbadians. The most progressive wing of Afro-Barbadian reformist politics gained a new and powerful conduit through which to convey its political views to a wider public in Barbados and in Britain during apprenticeship, when, for the first time, newspapers owned and edited by people of color were founded in the island. The establishment of a printed media beyond the control of the local white creole elite transformed the terrain of local politics. The editors' advocacy of and frequent reporting on the struggles of rural apprentices and newly free estate workers created, for the first time, a tangible connection between rural laborers and the predominantly urban political world of elite free people of color. Their support for the struggles of the poor and underprivileged elevated the editors of these newspapers, who were young and previously relatively obscure figures, to the status of popular heroes who could claim widespread support among Afro-Barbadians and challenge the place of the merchant elite as the most influential voice in Afro-Barbadian politics. Still, while these newspapers became the platform for a wide range of reformist, plebian and radical politics, the editors were not themselves of laboring-class background, and their attitudes toward the laboring poor reflected their urban and bourgeois sensibilities.

A DANGEROUS INTELLIGENCE

The hypocrisy of the imperial government's attitude toward free Afro-Caribbean people was embodied in the person and politics of Governor Lionel Smith. Free Afro-Barbadians' initially high hopes for his tenure as governor were quickly disappointed. When he first arrived in the island, Smith gave his backing to the enfranchisement of a larger number of free people of color. By the middle of apprenticeship, however, less than two years after he first became governor, he had reconsidered his position. In 1835, rather than supporting the lowering of the franchise requirement for Afro-Barbadians to ten pounds, he instead recommended to the Colonial Office that the franchise qualification for white voters be increased to thirty pounds, where it currently stood for voters of color. Smith claimed in an 1835 dispatch that free Afro-Barbadians would accept a higher franchise qualification for everyone, so long as the principle of equality was respected: "[T]hey would be satisfied, even if it was raised to £40 or £50—all they maintain is, if we are British subjects, give us equal Rights; don't [sic] restrict us if we have Qualifications of property, Character, and Education, by Laws of complexion."[1]

Smith's change of heart was motivated by the realization that large numbers of former slaves might actually be able, by dint of hard work, to earn enough money to enter the ranks of property owners and qualify for the vote. He noted that "if

---

1. CO 28/115, No. 14, Smith to Aberdeen, 29 March 1835.

[the ten-pound franchise were] granted to all, there would be a mass of black Voters, when perfectly free, that would swamp all other Classes."[2] In other words, a lower electoral property requirement might end up making former slaves the most powerful voting bloc in the island, a scenario that neither Smith nor his superiors in Whitehall wished to see. Even if, as Glenelg put it in 1837, emancipation was supposed to give former slaves "personal freedom, in the full and unlimited sense of the term in which it is used in reference to the other subjects of the British Crown," "personal" freedom was not synonymous with political equality, in the view of Smith and the Colonial Office—former slaves certainly needed political representation but under no circumstances should they represent themselves.[3]

Smith had never expressed any intention of seeking the vote for former slaves, but his newfound hostility toward the enfranchisement of more free people of color requires some explanation, given his earlier eagerness to expand the political influence of "respectable" and educated Afro-Barbadian men as a means of pushing through imperial emancipation policies. It seems that Smith quickly came to be suspicious of the possibility that people of African descent might feel a sense of loyalty to each other that could compete with their loyalty to the empire. He was also unsettled by Afro-Barbadians' apparent belief that they *deserved* increases in civil rights, which were, in Smith's view, only a possibility because of the liberality of imperial officials like himself. By the middle of the apprenticeship period, his views on the political trustworthiness of all Afro-Caribbean people seem to have changed dramatically. In July 1836 Smith opposed a Colonial Office proposal to accept Afro–West Indians into the imperial army, in which Africans liberated from foreign slave ships already served. He argued that West Indians of color could not be relied upon to defend the interests of the empire, noting that "there is not in the whole Globe a more dissolute or indolent race of Men than the free Blacks of the West India Colonies. . . . I am positive they could never be depended on, if employed against their own Countrymen, whereas original Africans have the greatest contempt for them." Furthermore, although Smith thought that creoles were "more intelligent" than Africans, he saw in them "a dangerous intelligence,

2. Ibid.

3. Thomas Holt in Frederick Cooper, Rebecca Scott, and Thomas Holt, *Beyond Slavery: Explorations of Race, Labor, and Citizenship in Postemancipation Societies* (Chapel Hill: University of North Carolina, 2000), 34.

a rankling of hearts at inequality of condition, & unfounded notions of common rights."[4]

Clearly then, by the middle of apprenticeship, Smith had abandoned his earlier determination to, as he had put it in 1833, improve the political standing of the free Afro-Barbadian "castes." The only man of color whom Smith appointed to office in Barbados before he left the island in 1836 was Joseph Garraway, a Grenadian free man of color who became a stipendiary magistrate in Barbados in 1834. Garraway had previously held a low level royal appointment in the Grenadian Customs Office between 1832 and 1834, making him one of a small number of Afro-Caribbean men who received royal appointments during the last years of slavery.[5] In public, Smith expressed his wish to see some wealthy and educated men of color in positions of high office, but he did not appoint a single Afro-Barbadian to such a post during his term. Indeed, the only Barbadian of color whom he seemed to think worthy of such a position was Thomas J. Cummins, a figure noted before emancipation for his pro-planter and proslavery opinions. Smith's appointment was initially welcomed by free people of color and slaves in Barbados, but his vacillations made him extremely unpopular, and, according to abolitionists Sturge and Harvey, he left to take up a new post as governor of Jamaica in 1836 "amidst the execrations of the crowds of free blacks and apprentices assembled on the beach."[6]

THE AFRO-BARBADIAN PRESS

Although the desegregation of electoral politics was a primary goal of Afro-Barbadian civil rights campaigners, they had more immediate success with the printed media, an influential aspect of public life for those wishing to shape opinions in the colonies and in the metropole. Founded in 1836, the *New Times* was the island's first abolitionist newspaper and its first newspaper edited by Afro-Barbadians. Samuel Jackman Prescod was its first editor, and after he formed his own newspaper a year later, another Afro-Barbadian, Nathaniel Roach, took over

4. CO 28/117, No. 54, Smith to Glenelg, 31 July 1836 enclosing Smith to the Adjutant General of the Forces Horse Guards.

5. Cox, *Free Coloreds*, 108–109. For background information on Garraway and details of his 1834 appointment in Barbados, see the *Barbadian*, 2 November 1836. Of 119 special magistrates who served in Jamaica during apprenticeship, 7 were men of color. See Holt, *Problem of Freedom*, 58.

6. Sturge and Harvey, *West Indies in 1837*, xxxiv, quoted in Handler, *Unappropriated People*, 108.

the job. According to Hilton Vaughan, Roach was also a young man and the darling of the Afro-Barbadian old guard, which was suspicious of outsiders such as
Prescod. Vaughan alleges that, under Roach's "genteel guidance [the *New Times*]
quickly fell into public disfavour."[7] The founding of the *New Times* and the *Liberal*
secured the places of Prescod and co-owner Harris as the leading voices of a more
progressive wing in Afro-Barbadian politics. However, as radical as these men
were in the Barbadian context, they were far from embracing the most democratic
ideas circulating among abolitionists and people of color in the Atlantic world at
the time.

The *New Times* and the *Liberal* supported emancipation and demanded a wider
extension of the franchise to include at least some working-class people of color.
Neither Harris nor Prescod sought universal suffrage, instead demanding bourgeois political reform. They supported the lowering of the franchise qualification to ten pounds in order that "a number of the poor and middle classes of every
complexion be admitted to a share in legislation, as will make their voice to be respected."[8] Prescod argued that this change was also indispensable as an emancipation measure, stating that, without such reform, "in vain shall we expect justice
for the free laborer—in vain shall we expect him to be peaceful, or orderly, or contented: free men will never be contented with the treatment of slaves."[9]

Although both Prescod and Harris had been involved in the free Afro-Barbadian
civil rights movement since the amelioration era, there is no evidence that either
of them espoused abolitionist views prior to 1834. It is possible that these men
had abolitionist sympathies before emancipation but it was too dangerous to voice
them publicly. Prescod, his wife Katherine, Harris, and Roach had all lived in Europe, where Prescod and Harris, at least, had been influenced by and become involved in popular movements for domestic and imperial political reform. Thome
and Kimball met the Prescod and Harris families in 1837 and noted that Prescod
and his wife Katherine had been "liberally educated in England," a reference to
the political tenor of their schooling.[10] Harris certainly claimed that he had also

7. Vaughan, *Democrat*, 2 April 1971.

8. See speeches by Harris and Prescod at a franchise extension meeting reported in the *Liberal*,
23 January 1839.

9. *Liberal*, 10 March 1838.

10. Prescod left Barbados for England shortly before August 1834 in order to train as a lawyer, but
he fell ill and had to return to the island during the apprenticeship period. He never completed his legal training. Vaughan, *Democrat*, 28 May 1971.

spent time in France during the 1820s, and that, while in Europe, he had become involved with abolitionism. The late Hilton Vaughan argued that Prescod's anti-slavery views were the result of witnessing his great uncle, who was a slave, being driven to suicide by slavery while Beckles tentatively suggests that, sometime around emancipation, Prescod "became associated with anti-slavery opinions emanating from the slave yards."[11] However, despite the *Liberal's* support for and popularity among rural plantation workers, Prescod, like most free people of color, was a resident of Bridgetown, and his political and social connections appear to have been largely urban. There is no evidence that he had any regular contacts with estate workers in the countryside.

After their time in Europe, these four highly educated individuals were apparently stunned by the harshness of white creole racism when they returned to Barbados, an experience that perhaps led them to rethink their ideas about race, slavery, and their place in the world as people of African descent. According to Thome and Kimball, Prescod "had seen himself and his accomplished wife excluded from the society of whites, though keenly conscious of their capacity to move and shine in the most elevated social circles." Similarly, Harris alleged that, since his return to Barbados, he had "often found himself in court for his views." Although Prescod spoke "bitterly of the past" he expressed hope that racial prejudice would now diminish.[12] Additionally, Prescod was an avid reader of liberal political economic theory and foreign newspapers. Their high level of literacy and education would have given such people access to a world of new ideas circulating around the Atlantic world via the written word, making them part of a transnational political community of abolitionists, reformers, and educated people of African descent. Their political ideas owed at least as much to these transnational currents of intellectual thought as they did to local events.

In its editorials the *Liberal* newspaper challenged the discriminatory and elitist application of the island's laws, arguing that, in the eyes of the courts, that

---

11. Beckles, *History of Barbados,* 116; Hilton Vaughan, "Samuel Jackman Prescod: Eulogy," 2. Vaughan was referring to a speech made by Prescod and reported in the *Liberal* on January 23 1839, in which Prescod stated, "He had never directly in his person known Slavery. . . . He had seen one old man who loved him like a son, and whom he loved as a father; he had seen that old christian man . . . made to forget his God, and bring upon his grey hairs the odium of suicide; and that man was the brother of his grandmother"; Thome and Kimball, *Emancipation in the West Indies,* 74. See also Johnson, "Abolition of Chattel Slavery," 204.

12. Thome and Kimball, *Emancipation in the West Indies,* 72–75.

"which is *'proper spiritedness'* in one class (the wealthy whites), would be sedition in another (the poorwhites [sic]) and downright rebellion in a third (the colored and black)."[13] The *Liberal's* letters page became a forum for people who backed the newspaper's call for bourgeois reform. In 1839, a letter from a correspondent whose race was not specified argued that society's "middle orders," rather than the "excessively rich," should govern society. The writer argued that the rich could not be trusted to rule because they were too prone to "habits of gratification, of adulation, producing mental incapacity, and moral deadness. . . . Does not all history abound with the regulations which these men have made . . . to preserve in the hand of the rich all the high and lucrative posts of legislation and administration?"[14]

As had been the case during slavery, although most of the island's population could not read, information from newspapers traveled around the island via word of mouth and the *Liberal* became popular among rural field laborers, many of whom saw Harris and Prescod as their advocates. The *Liberal's* owners were particularly active opponents of apprenticeship and early postemancipation estate labor policies. As labor unrest and evictions increased during the early months of the postapprenticeship period, laborers would sometimes come to the *Liberal's* office in Bridgetown for help. In October 1838 the white-owned *Mercury* newspaper accused a group of laborers—who had told the *Mercury's* reporter that they had come to town to "get advice"—of "loitering" in Bridgetown. The *Liberal* retorted that the people in question were estate laborers from a rural St. Michael plantation, who had come to the *Liberal* for counsel in a wage dispute with their manager: "[T]hey came to us; and *at* our office, not 'patrolling the streets,' the wordy Editor of the *Mercury* saw them." The owners told the laborers of another estate where they could get work on better terms, and advised them to go back to their manager and use their knowledge of this better opportunity as a bargaining tool.[15] Such was the influence of the *Liberal* and the *New Times* that, in his speech during the debate about the colonial bill to end apprenticeship in April 1838, Solicitor General Clarke referred to these newspapers when he advised the House of Assembly not to assume that apprentices were ignorant of debates about emancipation in the Barbados legislature or the British Parliament. Besides the English

13. *Liberal*, 28 March 1838.
14. *Liberal*, 8 May 1839.
15. *Liberal*, 10 October 1838.

newspapers, he observed, "there is a press in this island which is devoted to their cause, which advocates all their rights—I wish I could say with a little more prudence."[16]

Prescod was the author of most, if not all, of the *Liberal*'s editorials. It is not clear whether co-owner Harris actually wrote anything, or how the staff of the newspaper was organized. His writings in the *Liberal* did much to consolidate Prescod's public position as a man of the people and the enemy of the colonial state. He became a member of the British Anti-Slavery Society, attending the important antislavery conference in Britain in 1840,[17] and the newspaper gave him a platform to publicize both his and Harris's abolitionist and antisegregationist activities, such as their annual antislavery dinners commemorating the end of apprenticeship.[18] Thus, in November 1838, Prescod and Harris hosted British abolitionist John Scoble's visit to the island, accompanying him on his visits to various plantations, and they organized an antislavery dinner in Scoble's honor at the St. Mary's Boys' School. Besides a number of whites and free Afro-Barbadians, former slaves also attended. When Prescod rose to speak, he was met (according to the newspaper of which he was himself the principal editor) with "wild cheering" and cries of "[W]e'll never desert him," "We'd sooner turn our backs on our fathers," and "[B]ut for him, we'd be worse than slaves."[19]

APPRENTICESHIP AND THE LIMITS OF DESEGREGATION

The founding of Afro-Barbadian owned and edited newspapers was one of a number of successes during apprenticeship in terms of the desegregation of public life. Upper-class white Barbadians sought to distance themselves publicly from the

16. CO 31/52, 24 April 1838.

17. William A. Green, *British Slave Emancipation: The Sugar Colonies and the Great Experiment, 1830–1865* (Oxford: Clarendon Press, 1976), 85; Handler, *Unappropriated People*, 105.

18. See reports of annual antislavery dinners in the *Liberal*, 4 August 1838, 3 August 1839, 5 August 1840, 3 August 1842, and 2 August 1843. Historians have associated such activities commemorating emancipation in the Caribbean with a much later period, particularly between the 1880s and the early twentieth century. See Barry Higman, "Remembering Slavery: The Rise, Decline and Revival of Emancipation Day in the English-speaking Caribbean," *Slavery and Abolition* 19, no. 1 (April 1998): 90–105.

19. CO 28/124, No. 340, MacGregor to Glenelg, 13 December 1838, enclosing correspondence between MacGregor, the Board of Gaol Commissioners and John Scoble, and extracts from the *Liberal*, 21 and 24 November 1838; *Liberal*, 1 December 1838.

virulent proslavery and racist rhetoric that had previously been so fundamental to white creole political identity. St. Michael Vestry reflected this trend, continuing to soften its once hostile position toward free black and colored philanthropy. In March 1834 the vestry increased its grant of £100 to the St. Mary's Society for the Education of the Coloured Poor and for Other Charitable Relief to £150, and gave the society £50 more to help build a school for children of color. The vestry went even further, bestowing semiofficial status on St. Mary's as a poor-relief organization by voting unanimously to appoint overseers from among the board of St. Mary's. These overseers would have powers similar to those of Poor Law overseers, but would have jurisdiction only over St. Mary's.[20]

The vestry's changing attitude toward Afro-Barbadian philanthropy reflected a rapid shift in attitudes among whites on the issue of emancipation. Although planters and the white press had fought emancipation, it rapidly became taboo during apprenticeship to express proslavery and racist views in public. In fact, whites suddenly went out of their way to disown slavery and the values associated with it. Less than a month after the start of apprenticeship, the *Barbadian,* a former bastion of antiabolitionism, referred to emancipation as "a blessed change for all" and expressed satisfaction "that we are no longer slave owners, nor slave dealers, and that absolute uncontrollable power is taken out of the hands of too many who abused it." The *Barbadian* even proclaimed that any "right-thinking man" must find it "the greatest comfort and consolation to know that the door is now more effectually opened for the admission of his brethren to all the glorious and inestimable blessings of religion, and the benefits of civilization."[21]

Similarly, in 1836 the white Ladies' Association for the Relief of the Sick and Indigent Poor of Bridgetown and its Environs made the entirely false claim that "the aid of this Institution has *ever been* administered to indigent sick individuals of every description, without any distinction whatever of sex, age, complexion, or nation and although they have not, hitherto, recorded the following regulation, they hope, from the nature of the Association, it has already been inferred."[22] By the middle of apprenticeship, planters were claiming that, deep down, they had never *really* supported slavery. In fact, former slave owners were fond of telling visitors that emancipation had also freed *them* from the "slavery" of owning other human beings. In 1837 Thome and Kimball spoke to a planter named in their book

20. Minutes of the St. Michael Vestry, 25 March 1834.
21. *Barbadian,* 23 August 1834.
22. *Barbadian,* 19 November 1836 (emphasis added).

as "Mr. C," who told them that emancipation "is as great a blessing to the master as to the slave. . . . [I]t was emancipation to me. . . . I felt myself, for the first time, a freeman on [August 1]." According to the two Americans, "Mr. C" claimed that he and many of his planter colleagues "had often wished for emancipation" but had not dared to admit it publicly.[23]

However genuine such sentiments might have been for some, the sudden clamor among white Barbadians to declare themselves abolitionists was a public relations exercise for the consumption of reading publics abroad, especially in Britain. It was also an acknowledgment of the new political climate of the early postemancipation era, when developments in the West Indies were intensely watched for signs of bad faith on the part of whites. Sharing one's private support for white supremacy and slavery with the wrong person and having such views widely publicized was politically unwise. Moreover, in reality, however much individual planters such as "Mr. C" might repudiate the values associated with slavery, the Barbadian regime continued to defend segregation in content, if not in name. St. Michael Vestry's generous nod in the direction of St. Mary's Society was also a convenient way to temporarily preserve the segregation of vestry services by paying St. Mary's a pittance to deal with the vast numbers of people of African descent who needed poor relief. Vestries sought to maintain separate seating in churches by expanding the area available to Afro-Barbadians but continued to use the pew rent system in order to exclude people of color from white areas.[24] People of color were important in education during the post-1834 period partly because both the vestries and the church maintained strict racial segregation among students and only allowed people of color to teach Afro-Barbadian children. Most parochial schools continued to be for white children only, and few parishes opened schools for children of color during and immediately after apprenticeship.[25]

Despite the success of some men of color, such as Cummins, in obtaining po-

23. Thome and Kimball, *Emancipation in the West Indies*, 55. Mr. C was James Chrichlow of Lears plantation. See *Liberal*, 29 August 1838.

24. Minutes of the Christ Church Vestry, 15 August 1833, 4 August 1834, 16 March 1837; Minutes of the St. George Vestry, 3 August 1835, 1 February, 18 April, and 1 August 1836. In 1840 the churchwarden of St. James forced a man of color to leave a pew leased to him by a white man who was temporarily away. *Liberal*, 4 April 1840.

25. Thome and Kimball, *Emancipation in the West Indies*, 71; Sturge and Harvey, *West Indies in 1837*, 144; Minutes of the St. Philip Vestry, 16 January 1837.

litical positions, the local legislature also continued to block the appointment of local men of color to high office. Now that it was no longer acceptable to exclude Afro-Barbadian men from political office explicitly on the basis of color, white colonial politicians adopted property ownership as a criterion, which served the same end. Very few Afro-Barbadian men, however wealthy, had property to equal that of the island's white landed elite. Just after the end of apprenticeship in 1838, Smith's successor, Governor Evan MacGregor, tried to appoint Thomas Cummins, who had already served a few years in the St. Michael Vestry, to the high office of magistrate and nominated him for the Legislative Council. Although, as he said, Cummins was "an opulent gentleman of color . . . whose manners and education, qualify him for the same rank," his nomination met with "considerable repugnance, on the part of several Members of Council to his nomination, when I made him a Magistrate." According to MacGregor, the council objected "on account, not of [Cummins's] complexion, but of his keeping a retail shop—and I have since, in vain, urged him to purchase a landed estate, in order to endeavour to be returned to the Assembly."[26] A few years later Cummins did succeed in being appointed to the council and becoming a magistrate, a development that was probably linked to his purchase of a landed estate.[27] Nevertheless, it is difficult to believe, given the lengths to which the legislature went to exclude people of color from public life, that his skin color was not a factor in the council's initial decision to block his appointment.

Some of the colonial state's attempts to maintain de facto racial segregation were unsuccessful. The legislature initially tried to keep people of color out of the police force being established to control the former slave population. In its first draft of the Bridgetown police bill, the House of Assembly inserted a clause preventing Afro-Barbadians from joining the police by making eligibility contingent upon voting qualifications, and excluding those enfranchised under the 1831 "Brown Privilege Bill." A committee of men of color sent the governor a petition of protest, and, on Smith's recommendation, the Colonial Office disallowed the bill.[28] The house had to amend the bill, opening the door for the participation of Afro-Barbadians in the police force. Almost from the very beginning of apprenticeship, one in three of the police constables in Bridgetown was a "coloured"

26. CO 28/123, Private, MacGregor to Glenelg, 8 September 1838.

27. On Cummins becoming a planter, see pp. 184, 269–270, of the present volume.

28. PP 1835, vol. 50, Papers . . . in explanation of the measures adopted . . . for giving effect to the act for the abolition of slavery, Glenelg to Smith, 20 June 1835, referring to 27 April 1835 address of free people of color on the Bridgetown Police Bill, 228–231; CO 31/52, 6 August 1835.

man.[29] Thome and Kimball visited District B police station, which had jurisdiction over the southwestern parish of Christ Church, and noted that all but "two or three" or the policemen there were men of color.[30] By 1839, a report on the racial and phenotypic composition of the national police force showed that of 162 constables in the island, 58 were "white," 56 were "coloured," and 58 were "black."[31] A planter testified before the 1842 imperial commission on the West Indies that the rural police force was almost entirely Afro-Barbadian.[32] With the disbandment of the militia tenancy in 1839, the militia—a potent symbol of racial prejudice and slavery—ceased to have any symbolic or actual relevance, and the predominantly Afro-Barbadian police force effectively replaced it.[33]

MEN OF COLOR IN POLITICS

Under Governor MacGregor, the demands of elite men of color for political appointments were satisfied to a limited degree. Several prominent men of color, among them Thomas J. Cummins and the Grenadian stipendiary magistrate Joseph Garraway, were appointed to three commissions of the peace, which toured the island in 1838 and 1839 explaining to apprentices their rights and duties under apprenticeship.[34] Surprisingly, the legislature raised no objections when, in late 1837, MacGregor appointed Henry Loving, the Afro-Antiguan abolitionist and journal-

29. PP 1835, vol. 50, *Papers . . . in Explanation of the Measures Adopted . . . for the Abolition of Slavery . . .*, Aberdeen to Smith, 10 January 1835, Glenelg to Smith, 20 June 1835, and Appendix A, "Return of the respective Numbers of White and Coloured Men, at present serving in the Bridge Town Police Establishment," 195–198.

30. Thome and Kimball, *Emancipation in the West Indies*, 67.

31. CO 28/129, No. 113, MacGregor to Russell, 8 November 1839, enclosure No. 1, "Return exhibiting the degrees of complexion of the Police Force, Barbados 30th October 1839."

32. PP 1842, vol. 13, *Report from the Select Committee on West India Colonies; together with the minutes of evidence, appendix, and index*, 12 May 1842, questions 1880–1884. The planter was George Carrington. This remained the case throughout the postemancipation period, see Barbados government, *Report of the Commission on Poor Relief* (Bridgetown, 1877), 11.

33. CO 28/128, No. 78, MacGregor to Normanby, 23 July 1839, laws No. 698, "An act to consolidate and amend the provisional Acts relating to the Militia of this Island and to provide for the better organization of the same," and No. 699, "An act to augment the number and increase the pay of the Police Force, and to consolidate the Laws relating thereto."

34. CO 28/119, No. 1, MacGregor to Glenelg, 2 January 1837; CO 28/123, No. 214, MacGregor to Glenelg, 11 August 1838, enclosure No. 11; *Barbadian*, 5 December 1838. The other Afro-Barbadian men on these commissions were Michael T Corbin, George Barclay, Robert Reece Sr., Robert Reece Jr., Thomas Ellis, and Valentine Wilkins.

ist, to the post of stipendiary magistrate in Barbados.[35] In 1838 the governor promoted Joseph Garraway to be a judge in the newly created assistant court of appeal, the highest level of the local judiciary, and a year later made him acting governor's private secretary.[36]

MacGregor also made *New Times* editor Nathaniel Roach the police magistrate for St. Lucy, a surprise decision that outraged the editor of the *Barbadian,* and probably many other whites as well.[37] In May 1839 MacGregor nominated, and the council approved, Nathaniel Roach and Joseph Thorne as "marriage officers" under the 1839 Marriage Act. It is not exactly clear what the position involved, but the new act was specifically designed to encourage Christian marriage among former slaves and people of color in general. It provided the assurance that, if couples now married, children born before the marriage would not suffer the legal disabilities associated with illegitimacy.[38]

Thomas J. Cummins's career was the most striking among Barbadian men of color. In 1839, after holding many minor civil service appointments and several years of being reelected to the St. Michael Vestry,[39] Governor MacGregor fi-

35. CO 28/119, No. 112, MacGregor to Glenelg, 19 May 1837; CO 28/120, No. 248, MacGregor to Glenelg, 30 October 1837; CO 28/123, No. 13, MacGregor to Glenelg, 27 January 1838; Loving had previously been superintendent of police and the governor's temporary private secretary in Antigua. Interestingly, he played a significant role in drafting Antigua's first Masters and Servants Act (see discussion of such acts in chapter 8, pp. 229–232), which was disallowed by the Colonial Office as being too harsh. After his posting in Barbados he was promoted to be the lieutenant governor's colonial secretary in Montserrat in early 1838 (CO 28/123, No. 24, MacGregor to Glenelg, 3 February 1838, and Lowes, "Peculiar Class," 146–147) but remained a stipendiary magistrate in Barbados until the end of apprenticeship. Governors could only recommend individuals to the Colonial Office for permanent appointment as stipendiary magistrates, while offering these men temporary appointments until the Colonial Office made a decision. I came across no instances in Barbados of governors' recommendations for the stipendiary magistracy being turned down by Whitehall.

36. CO 28/123, No. 164, MacGregor to Glenelg, 7 July 1838. In other Windward islands, the stipendiary magistrates stayed on after emancipation, but were transferred to new posts as police magistrates. However in Barbados, the preemancipation magistrates retained their judiciary power under the new title of police magistrate, and only three stipendiary magistrates were appointed to form the Assistant Court of Appeal; the earliest letter I have found signed by Garraway as acting private secretary was published in the *Barbadian,* 23 January 1839.

37. CO 28/127, No. 14, MacGregor to Glenelg, February 7 1839, and No. 67, MacGregor to Normanby, 14 May 1839; *Barbadian,* 8 May 1839.

38. *Liberal* and *Barbadian,* 13 March 1839.

39. By January 1836 Cummins was a member of St. Michael's vestry board. He was probably elected first in 1835, but the precise year of his first election is uncertain because the vestry records for 1834 through 1840 have been lost.

nally managed to get Cummins appointed to the Legislative Council and the post of magistrate for St. George parish, making him the first man of color to sit in the island's legislature. Between 1840 and 1842, he presided over the Court of Grand Sessions, the highest judicial appointment for a local magistrate. In 1841, he began his first of several terms as churchwarden of the St. Michael vestry, appointing a handful of other leading Afro-Barbadians—Valentine Wilkins, John Montefiore, and Thomas Ellis—to positions in the vestry's limited bureaucracy.[40]

The imperial government's interest in appointing men of color to positions of authority applied only if they had the right cultural capital and were deemed to be of acceptable socioeconomic status. Similarly, the well-to-do merchants, tradesmen, and planters who dominated the St. Michael electorate were unlikely to vote for working-class or politically progressive candidates of any color. It is therefore not surprising that all of the men appointed and elected to positions of authority were wealthy and well educated in comparison with other Afro-Barbadians. They also had to have acceptable political views. Despite the popularity and influence of the *Liberal,* Prescod was not nominated for a government post until 1860, by which time he had been an acknowledged senior figure in Barbadian politics for nearly two decades, and Harris, although nominated once for a magistrate's appointment, was passed over for the job.[41] Harris also ran for election to the St. Michael Vestry in 1842 but came in last.[42] With the exception of Nathaniel Roach, whose period as a supporter of popular causes was extremely brief, none of the men appointed or elected to political office had any strong association with the more progressive wing of antiracist and abolitionist politics in Barbados.

A background in antisegregationism or abolitionism may have been a political liability in postslavery Barbados, but those few successful Afro-Caribbean politicians who had such credentials were feted by people of color in the island. On the occasion of Roach's appointment to the magistracy, a group of men of color presented him with a letter of thanks, signed by 337 people, for "his unremitted exertions in behalf of the newly emancipated class; and also, his advocacy of the just claims of the oppressed *generally.*"[43] There were similar celebrations when stipen-

---

40. CO 31/55, Barbadoes Minutes of the Legislative Council, 1842–1855 (T. J. Cummins was listed as a member of Council for 1842–1849—his last meeting seems to have been April 3 1849); *Liberal,* 28 July 1842.

41. *Barbadian,* 9 October 1841. Prescod was elected to the House of Assembly in 1843 (see chapter 8, pp. 251–254) and was appointed as a judge on the assistant court of appeal in 1860.

42. *Barbadian,* 19 January 1842; *Liberal,* 15 January 1845.

43. *Liberal,* 30 January 1839.

diary magistrate Henry Loving was promoted to be the governor's colonial secretary in Montserrat. A deputation of "coloured gentlemen" presented Loving with one hundred guineas and a vote of thanks for his services as a "faithful uncompromising advocate of the rights of our long oppressed fellow descendants of Africa" and his devotion to the "coloured cause."[44]

By contrast, Afro-Barbadians greeted Thomas Cummins's political successes with silence, which is indicative of a speedy decline in his popularity. Although many people of color had rallied to his side when the legislature turned back his militia appointment in 1833, Cummins had since made it abundantly clear that he was not a man of the people. During apprenticeship he distanced himself from antisegregationist politics. His name all but disappeared from civil rights petitions, and he never attended any of the antislavery dinners organized by Prescod and Harris. There was also a marked lack of enthusiasm for Joseph Garraway, the other highly successful political appointee of color. When Garraway was appointed to the August 1838 Commission of the Peace during the labor unrest of the early postapprenticeship period, Prescod wrote that "the negroes do not know Mr. Garraway as a coloured man, and they are unlikely to place any confidence in him—although I am of opinion that he would do them every justice."[45] The fact that Garraway was the only man of color on the assistant court of appeal established in 1838 was seen as something of an insult. Thomas Harris argued that a "coloured committee" should have been appointed and suggested Joseph Thorne, London Bourne, Prescod, and, somewhat predictably, himself as suitable choices.[46] Although reputedly fair, Garraway had no history of antiracist political activity and his position as a stipendiary magistrate left him open to suspicion. Some Afro-Barbadians and abolitionists accused the stipendiary magistrates of being "greatly controlled by the planters. They associate with the planters, dine with the planters, lounge on the planters' sofas, and marry the planters' daughters."[47]

ABOLITIONISTS OF CONVENIENCE?

In spite of this limited political success Afro-Barbadian men found their hopes for political reform and desegregation continually frustrated during and imme-

44. *Liberal,* 22 August 1838. The merchants Thomas Harris, Valentine Wilkins, Joseph Thorne, London Bourne, Benjamin Massiah, and Edmund C. Haynes signed the tribute.

45. *Liberal,* 29 August 1838.

46. Ibid.

47. Thome and Kimball, *Emancipation in the West Indies,* 72–73; see also Sturge and Harvey, *West Indies in 1837,* 132. Garraway never married a planter's daughter.

diately after apprenticeship. The legislature showed no signs that it intended to give men of color equal access to the vote and the holding of political office. For ambitious Afro-Barbadian men, the only route to a political career at the end of the 1830s was either to be appointed to a post by the governor or to be elected to the St. Michael Vestry, both of which carried slim chances for success. Afro-Barbadians who sought election to the vestry relied on the votes of urban whites, who were reluctant to vote for men of color. Furthermore, white merchants might be willing to cooperate with men of color when it came to writing petitions and organizing philanthropic activities, but they still did not accept them as full so-cial equals and political partners. In January 1839 the all-white Bridgetown Com-mercial Hall, a merchants' club, blackballed the applications of two leading Afro-Barbadian merchants, John Montefiore and Thomas Griffith, for membership. The affair caused an uproar, with Governor MacGregor refusing to grant offi-cial recognition to the hall as long as "no mercantile gentlemen of the coloured body are members of the institution." The hall claimed that it had taken measures to make it more difficult for individual members to block applications by Afro-Barbadians but a month later the *Liberal* claimed that Afro-Barbadians continued to be rejected.[48]

Under such circumstances, many wealthy Afro-Barbadian merchants reconsid-ered their attitudes toward slave emancipation. Elite free men of color recognized that their struggle for the repeal of racially discriminatory laws benefited from the emancipation of slaves. By the middle of the apprenticeship period, even in-dividuals who had once been proslavery or had distanced themselves from aboli-tionism now publicly supported emancipation, claiming it as further justification for their civil rights demands. In 1837 Thome and Kimball met Joseph Thorne, his wife and two other "coloured gentlemen"—the Methodist minister Joseph Ham-ilton and Thomas J. Cummins—at Thorne's home. According to the two Ameri-cans, "All spoke with great gratitude of the downfall of slavery. It was not the slaves alone that were interested in that event. Political oppression, prejudice, and licen-tiousness had combined greatly to degrade the colored community, but these evils were now gradually lessening, and would soon wholly disappear after the final ex-tinction of slavery—the parent of them all."[49]

The merchant elite sought to rally the support of plebian Afro-Barbadians, in-cluding former slaves, and present itself as the leadership of an enlarged and united political constituency that needed political representation. Given the popularity of

48. *Barbadian,* 19 January 1839 and *Liberal,* 26 January and 2 February 1839.

49. Thome and Kimball, *Emancipation in the West Indies,* 74.

Prescod and the *Liberal,* civil rights campaigners who would normally have considered the *Liberal* too politically radical were now eager to associate with it. Support for the antislavery dinners organized by the *Liberal*'s owners became de rigueur for upperclass Bridgetown merchants of color. The merchant Joseph Kennedy's toast to Prescod at the *Liberal* owners' August 1839 dinner commemorating the end of slavery epitomized the changed attitude of members of the old elite. Kennedy, a former slave owner and longtime civil rights campaigner, admitted that he had once opposed Prescod because he thought his methods "ill-timed, but that was years ago now" and proclaimed that "so long as the colored classes were united and firm, nothing could prevent them from moving forward."[50] That year, at least eighteen Afro-Barbadian businessmen, including political moderates such as Kennedy, London Bourne, William Wilkey, Joseph Thorne, Andrew Fillan, and Edward W. Archer, closed their businesses in commemoration of emancipation day, and sold tickets for the dinner at their stores.[51]

These dinners helped to project a public image of Afro-Barbadians as being united, with slavery being the common enemy of the wealthiest person of color and the poorest former slave. The preservation of this appearance of unity of interest fundamentally depended on a denial of the fact that many preemancipation free people of color were newly minted abolitionists who had been, until a few years earlier, slave owners. The report of Prescod's speech at the August 1839 antislavery dinner illustrates how a highly selective memory of slavery was constructed as a means to promote racial solidarity in the postslavery era:

> [Prescod] needed not remind them of the indissoluble ties between them
> and the lately emancipated classes. Those were the stock from which they
> as branches had sprung, and in the degradation of that stock they had necessarily been degraded. They were now both free; and on the moral and social improvement of those brethren,—to effect which self-interest, properly understood, should now direct all their energies,—their own political
> advancement entirely depended. (Hear, hear, and applause.) He concluded

50. *Liberal,* 9 August 1839. Joseph Kennedy had been a member of the 1819 Alien Bill Committee although he refused to sign either the 1823 Belgrave address or the 1824 counteraddress. He was secretary of the Auxiliary Bible Society and a member of the board of directors of the St. Mary's Society. *Barbadian,* 22 August 1826, 27 September 1827, May 15 1833; Handler, Hughes, and Wiltshire, *Freedmen of Barbados,* 30.

51. *Liberal,* 20 and 27 July 1839.

with proposing "Our emancipated brethren; may their improvement keep pace with the wishes of their friends."—Drunk with cheers.[52]

During slavery, it would have been unthinkable for an educated Afro-Barbadian to celebrate publicly the blood ties between free people of color and slaves in this manner. A similar transformation took place with regards to civil rights campaigners' arguments for electoral reform. The broadening of the franchise, which many elite men of color had supported as a means of gaining protection *from* former slaves, was now promoted as a means to provide political representation *for* former slaves. In November 1838, at the dinner the *Liberal*'s owners organized in honor of abolitionist John Scoble, Scoble told the "pre-emancipation free people" in the audience, "They were the natural protectors of an immense class of their brethren. From their station, their characters, their influence, their knowledge, the lately emancipated slave looked up to them to secure him against the oppression of wrong doers." In response there were cries of "[W]e will do it," and Scoble "assured them of the cooperation of the British in this holy work." He concluded that, now that everyone in the colony was free, there was a need for "just and equal laws," in response to which someone shouted, "[W]e won't get it [*sic*], till we have an extension of the elective franchise!" Scoble's speeches indicate that at least some of those in attendance were former slaves, together with the "more respectable of the colored and black community" and "one or two liberal whites."[53]

Although prominent civil rights reformers of color saw electoral reform as the ticket to "just and equal laws," they were less than supportive of former slaves' own independent methods of defending their political and economic interests. In discussing the postemancipation political role of pre-1834 free people of color in Dominica, Michel-Rolph Trouillot notes the importance of distinguishing their demands for political and civil equality from a struggle for socioeconomic redistribution.[54] Like colonial officials and planters, elite Afro-Barbadians saw the survival of the sugar industry and the maintenance of economic stability as crucial to the interests of the country. Thome and Kimball summarized their discussion with Prescod, Harris, and Thorne about emancipation:

52. *Liberal*, 3 August 1839.

53. *Liberal*, 1 December 1838.

54. Michel-Rolph Trouillot, "The Inconvenience of Freedom: Free People of Color and the Political Aftermath of Slavery in Dominica and Saint-Domingue/Haiti," in McGlynn and Drescher, *Meaning of Freedom*, 162–175.

The gentlemen testified to the industry and subordination of the apprentices. They had improved the general cultivation of the island, and they were reaping for their masters greater crops than they did while slaves. The whole company united in saying that many blessings had already resulted from the abolition of slavery—imperfect as that abolition was. Real estate had advanced in value at least one third. The fear of insurrection had been removed; invasions of property, such as occurred during slavery, the firing of cane-fields . . . &c., were no longer apprehended.[55]

It is telling that these men should have been pleased about the increase in real estate prices, given that land in Barbados was already among the most expensive in the British Caribbean. This suggests that they did not have any interest in questioning the actual distribution of property in the island, which put former slaves at a severe disadvantage in their efforts to force planters to adopt more equitable labor policies. Furthermore, they viewed estate laborers' attacks on planters' property as vandalism rather than as an act of opposition by the dispossessed. During the rash of cane fires that occurred in the island between 1839 and 1840, the *Liberal* expressed pleasure that some laborers were helping to put the fires out, adding that the newspaper "trust[s] they know it is their duty" to help identify the culprits.[56]

Elite civil rights agitators often combined their commitment to reform and to philanthropy with very bourgeois dismissal of the realities of poverty. A pervasive ideology of self-help prevented many elite civil rights campaigners and philanthropists from supporting poor relief for anyone who was not practically starving. The *Liberal* argued that the exclusion of free people of color from vestry poor-relief services was the reason for their industriousness and argued that relief should be extended only to the "absolutely destitute."[57] In December 1838 the St. Mary's Society announced that it would no longer provide daily meals for poor children because of the "improved condition of the parents," a reference to emancipation that implied that freedom from slavery necessarily led to economic "improvement."[58] A year later the society announced that no one earning domestic servants' wages would be eligible for assistance.[59]

55. Thome and Kimball, *Emancipation in the West Indies*, 73.

56. *Liberal*, 25 September 1839.

57. *Liberal*, 17 March 1838.

58. *Liberal*, 29 December 1838.

59. *Barbadian*, 23 October 1839.

The *Liberal's* views on labor, as on all other matters, were entirely shaped by Prescod, who was consistent in his ideological commitment to classical social and economic liberalism. Like many abolitionists, Prescod was deeply committed to the ideas of free trade and free labor, opposing both market regulations and any controls on the labor market. Thus the *Liberal* opposed any efforts at "combination," or unionization, whether on the part of workers or employers. In an editorial opposing a planters' scheme to fix estate wages in the island at a rate beneficial to employers, the *Liberal* warned planters:

> To mention no other evil, it will be highly injudicious to set the laborer the example of combination to regulate what will best be regulated by circumstances, over which neither he nor his employer can have any possible controul [sic]. . . . We warn them that combinations on their part to lower wages, will most assuredly produce counter combinations among the laborers to raise wages.[60]

The newspaper encouraged estate laborers not to "combine" to oppose the plan, instead instructing them to look to the "middle classes" or "the respectable coloured community" to mediate in their struggle with planters and help direct their political activities.[61] The Colonial Office, the local government and the Afro-Barbadian elite all favored friendly societies as an alternative to combinations. In contrast to Britain, where unions often operated secretly under the guise of friendly societies,[62] friendly societies in early postslavery Barbados were firmly controlled by the white clergy, planters and merchants and, in the case of the St. Mary's friendly societies, the urban Afro-Barbadian elite. Even if former slaves accounted for most of the membership, they never sat on the societies' directorial boards or controlled their public relations activities and finances.

The *Liberal's* commitment to the idea that the market should be left to regulate matters stopped at the physical labor of women and girls outside the home. The confinement of female labor within the domestic sphere was thought to be worth the economic disruption to the sugar industry. Even though the owners recognized that economic circumstances would prevent many women from with-

60. *Liberal,* 26 May 1838.

61. Ibid.

62. Eric J. Evans, *The Forging of the Modern State: Early Industrial Britain, 1783–1870* (London: Longman, 1983), 158.

drawing into the home, they felt that economic activity on the part of such women should be limited to "assisting" their husbands. While huckstering might be appropriate work for women to supplement their husband's income, field labor was considered to be unfeminine. In 1839 the *Liberal* supported British abolitionists' argument that "negro females" should withdraw from field labor, adding, "We hope and trust that, whatever the consequences may be to "the crops," the negro laborers throughout the colonies will, ere long, insist on their wives and daughters keeping out of the field, except in reaping time to assist in the lighter works of harvest."[63]

CONCLUSION

As apprenticeship came to an end in 1838 elite Afro-Barbadian men found that emancipation had both raised and frustrated their hopes. Although the climate of reform and social change in the British Empire seemed to favor their civil rights cause they faced creole whites who by and large opposed the enfranchisement of blacks. Furthermore imperial officials who represented their best chance of support from above were reluctant to advance Afro-Barbadians' political careers out of fear of antagonizing the plantocracy, and sometimes out of a fundamental belief in the inferiority and untrustworthiness of the empire's Afro-Caribbean subjects. The emergence of an Afro-Barbadian press strengthened the public voice of antislavery and antiracism in the island and provided a bridge between elite and subaltern politics and between the worlds of urban bourgeois reformism and rural plantation life and struggles. Nevertheless, these realities remained distinct and efforts to create unity out of the diverse experiences and political aspirations of Afro-Barbadians remained fraught with tensions.

Afro-Barbadians drew on a long tradition in abolitionist and African diasporic thought to try to realize their political hopes and resolve—and, in many ways, suppress—tensions and differences among themselves. The civil rights struggle in Barbados gave rise to and was in turn shaped by intertwined discourses of nationhood—on one hand, about the African continent and, on the other, the British Empire—through which Afro-Barbadians sought to redefine their place in their own island and in the wider world in the aftermath of slavery. The next chapter will discuss the simultaneous articulation of African diasporic consciousness and imperial nationalism that became central to Afro-Barbadian politics in

63. *Liberal*, 30 March 1839.

the postapprenticeship era. These discourses offered an opportunity for Barbadian people of color to invoke a claim to imperial citizenship as a route to racial equality and a means to imagine themselves as part of a borderless nation of people of African descent, bound together by ties of blood and history. Afro-Barbadians sought to build a sense of both transatlantic and local unity that, in reality, they found difficult to attain.

7 / BETWEEN AFRICA AND THE EMPIRE

Diasporic Consciousness in Postemancipation Society

AFTER emancipation, elite Afro-Barbadians began to articulate publicly a politics of collectivity, which was based on a sense of themselves as members of a transatlantic African diaspora as well as equal subjects to whites within the British Empire. They adopted the emancipation of slaves as an event that also set them loose from bondage and sought a new political role for themselves as the legitimate political voice of all people of African descent in the island. Elite men of color saw themselves as the defenders of Africa in the British Empire and as the potential vanguard of British "civilization" on the African continent. This chapter examines the emergence of this simultaneously proimperial and "pan-African" political identity and illustrates its role as a "counterculture of modernity" and empire.[1]

As historical anthropologist Kevin Yelvington and others have argued, "race" and "blackness" were not "some essential and fixed entity, ready to be awakened and stirred."[2] Understanding how both racism and racial pride were constantly refashioned necessitates an approach that seeks to establish "the continuity between behavioral explanations sited at the individual level of human experience and

---

1. Gilroy, *Black Atlantic*, 1–40. I employ Gilroy's useful notion of the "counterculture of modernity" with several important caveats. I agree with Sidney Mintz's critique that Gilroy "ignores the historically-shaped differences within [the black diaspora] which make the thought of Black Brazilians, Jamaicans, Haitians, Cubans, and North Americans (for instance) different enough from one another to raise the question whether there is any single body to that uniqueness." Sidney Mintz, "Enduring Substances, Trying Theories: The Caribbean Region as *Oikomenê, Journal of the Royal Anthropological Institute* 2, no. 2 (1996): 299. A more trenchant and still relevant critique of bourgeois nationalism is in Frantz Fanon, *The Wretched of the Earth* (1961; reprint, London: Penguin Books, 1990), 119–165.

2. Quote from Kevin Yelvington, "The War in Ethiopia and Trinidad, 1935–1936," in Brereton and Yelvington, *Colonial Caribbean in Transition*, 189. See also Aline Helg, *Our Rightful Share: The Afro-Cuban Struggle for Equality, 1886–1912* (Chapel Hill: University of North Carolina Press, 1995), 13.

those at the level of society and social forces."[3] The intellectual and political currents that fostered abolitionism significantly reshaped attitudes about Africa, the British Empire, and the concept of "race" in Britain and its Caribbean territories. Afro-Barbadian racial consciousness in the postslavery era represented an attempt to give meaning to liberal ideas of freedom. This racial consciousness was used as a tool to further the political ambitions of middle- and upper-class people of African descent in the Caribbean. However, unlike pan-African political movements of the later nineteenth and twentieth centuries, the racial diasporic consciousness that elite Barbadians of color expressed in the era of slave emancipation was nationalist but *not* anti-imperialist. Afro-Barbadians racial consciousness combined imperial nationalism with a discourse of imperial civilizationalism. Elite reformers saw it as their special role as subjects of the British Empire to spread the light of capitalism and British culture to the unenlightened Afro-Barbadian working classes as well as to Africans. At the same time, these expressions of racial consciousness were a critique of mid-nineteenth-century Western European liberal imperialism and Eurocentrism.

The attempt to promote pride in African descent in emancipation era Barbados was also a way of sidestepping the fundamental differences in opinion and circumstances between Afro-Barbadians, which remained, and in some cases grew more significant, after the end of slavery. The role of many Afro-Barbadian men, such as police officers and estate constables, as the local arm of planter state power brought them into continuous conflict with other Afro-Barbadians. Additionally, slavery had left a legacy of profound shame and hostility toward Africa in the psyche of some African Caribbean people, which often surfaced in their dealings with the state and with each other.

ANTISLAVERY, EMPIRE, AND THE CIVILIZING MISSION

Slavery dehumanized people of African descent by constructing them as people without a past, and Africa, by extension, as a place where superstition ruled rather than religion, and myth instead of history.[4] According to one proslavery line of

3. Thomas Holt, "Marking: Race, Race-Making, and the Writing of History, *American Historical Review* 100, no. 1 (1995): 7.

4. See Alexander Saxton, *The Rise and Fall of the White Republic: Class Politics and Mass Culture in Nineteenth-Century America* (London: Verso, 1990), 14–15, cited in Joanne Pope Melish, *Disowning*

argument, plantation slavery might be harsh, but Africans enslaved in the New World would have been slaves in Africa anyway.[5] Slavery's supporters and detractors generally accepted the premise that a civilizational deficit separated Europe and Africa. Both saw Africa as uncivilized and prone to the depredations of slave trading because it was backward and therefore easy prey to the more advanced European powers.[6]

Ironically, as Ronald Robinson and John Gallagher have observed, "The stopping of the slave traffic involved the British in the affairs of the [West African] Coast far more than the trade itself had done." The slave trade's volume was greater after British slave emancipation than ever before, at the precise moment when the British humanitarian movement had enough political clout to "conscript their government into the anti-slaving crusade."[7] Schemes for promoting the "civilization" of Africa became an increasingly important aspect of British abolitionism from the late eighteenth century onward.[8] In 1788, the same year the first antislave trade bill was introduced and lost in the British Parliament, several leading British abolitionists established the West African port settlement of Sierra Leone. This was the first project to "repatriate" people of African descent from Europe and the Americas "back" to Africa, and the first time British subjects acquired land by treaty on the African continent.[9]

In 1808 the settlement was taken over by the British government, which fol-

---

Slavery: Gradual Emancipation and "Race" in New England, 1780–1860 (Ithaca: Cornell University Press, 1998), 5.

5. See, for example, Rev. H. E. Holder, *A Short Essay on the Subject of Negro Slavery, with a Particular Reference to the Island of Barbadoes* (London: Couchman and Fry, 1788), 13: "Slavery very extensively prevails in Africa: it should seem, then, that the transportation of Negroes, from Africa to the West-Indies, does not put them in a situation, *essentially,* different from that, in which they previously were."

6. Patrick Brantlinger, "Victorians and Africans: The Genealogy of the Myth of the Dark Continent," in Henry Louis Gates Jr., ed., *"Race," Writing and Difference* (Chicago: University of Chicago Press, 1986), 185.

7. Ronald Robinson and John Gallagher (with Alice Denny), *Africa and the Victorians: The Official Mind of Imperialism* (1961; reprint, Basingstoke: Macmillan, 1981), 27–28.

8. Ibid., 186–187 and 189. For a general discussion of "race" in imperial policy in the West Indies and India from the 1780s to the 1810s, see C. A. Bayly, *Imperial Meridian: The British Empire and the World, 1780–1830* (London: Longman, 1989), 147–155.

9. Brantlinger, "Victorians and Africans," 186; Christopher Fyfe, *A History of Sierra Leone* (London: Oxford University Press, 1962).

lowed its example, on a more limited scale, with the establishment of the Gambia and Gold Coast settlements for Africans liberated from foreign slave ships in 1816 and 1821, respectively. Such colonies were intended to be "bases from which legitimate commerce and civilisation would drive out the slave traffic."[10] They were supposed to illustrate to slave traders that the wage labor of free blacks was a viable alternative to slavery. The British abolitionists who initiated the Sierra Leone project thought that a British colony whose population was predominantly of African descent would be an effective means of gradually effecting the cultural transformations thought to be necessary to end slavery in Africa.[11] Colonization projects were also popular with white segregationists, particularly in the United States. In 1816 the predominantly white American Colonization Society (ACS) was established in New England, and in 1822 the ACS founded Liberia as a U.S. colony for the repatriation of free African Americans.[12] By contrast, the British Colonisation Society, founded in 1833, fell apart one year later, due, apparently, to lack of interest. Although British coastal settlements facilitated encroachment by explorers, missionaries and scientists, the racial segregationist associations of such schemes and the immense difficulties involved in administering Sierra Leone made the British government reluctant to support further expansion into Africa in the first half of the nineteenth century.[13]

Many leaders of the British abolitionist movement were also driven by a strong belief that Britain needed to "atone" for the sin of slavery in Africa and the West Indies. They viewed slavery as a stain on the national conscience, because Britain had risen to dominance on the backs of enslaved Africans and at the expense of the African continent.[14] In 1807 a group of influential abolitionists formed the African Institution, whose purpose was to raise public support for emancipation. In

10. Robinson and Gallagher, *Africa and the Victorians*, 28.

11. For descriptions of the composition of the early Sierra Leone population, see Ellen Gibson Wilson, *The Loyal Blacks* (New York: Capricorn Books, 1976), 311; Fyfe, *History of Sierra Leone*. See also Mavis Campbell, *Back to Africa: George Ross and the Maroons, from Nova Scotia to Sierra Leone* (New Jersey: Africa World Press, 1993).

12. Pope Melish, *Disowning Slavery*, 192–194.

13. Blackett, *Building an Anti-Slavery Wall*, 47–68, 78; Brantlinger, "Victorians and Africans," 185; on reluctance of the British government to expand into Africa during the period see Robinson and Gallagher, *Africa and the Victorians*, 27.

14. Boyd Hilton, *The Age of Atonement: The Influence of Evangelicalism on Social and Economic Thought, 1785–1865* (Oxford: Clarendon Press, 1988), 209; Robinson and Gallagher, *Africa and the Victorians*, 27.

an early pamphlet published under the institution's auspices, James Stephen, future legal advisor in the Colonial Office during the period of amelioration and slave emancipation, expressed the evangelical Christian view that Britain was in debt to Africa for its wealth: "It is false, that we promote wars, for the sake of our trade in Europe, but that we thus sin in Africa, is unquestionably true. . . . [I]f it be as the protector of the poor and the destitute, that God has entered into judgment with us, we must I repeat, look to Africa, and to the West Indies, for the causes of his wrath."[15] While it would be simplistic to see such writings by key nineteenth-century political figures as a precursor to later British imperial policy, they contained justifications for both emancipation in the West Indies *and* for greater British intervention in Africa.[16]

FREE AFRO-BARBADIANS AND AFRICAN COLONIZATION SCHEMES

Just as imperial officials saw free Afro-Caribbean people as potential intermediaries between former slaves and planters, they also thought they might play a similar role in relations between Africans and the British Empire. The belief that people of African descent were somehow naturally inured to illnesses that decimated whites in Africa became unquestioned orthodoxy in British political circles in the early nineteenth century, and colonial officials and abolitionists became to consider seriously the possibility of employing Afro-Caribbean people as low-level imperial agents in Africa. In 1827 Bathurst sent a request to the governors of Jamaica and Barbados asking for men of color who had military experience, education, and "character" to fill petty officer positions in the British army in Sierra Leone and thereby "preserve the Lives of British Officers." Bathurst claimed that people of color had "Constitutions more congenial with that Climate" than whites. The Barbadian assembly opposed the proposal, saying that no local free people of color would want to "relinquish the advantages of their present Situation to go to Sierra Leone." However, the legislature was clearly uneasy about the possibilities for political advancement the empire might create for its Afro-Barbadian subjects, and chose not to publicize the employment offer. Per-

15. James Stephen, *New Reasons for Abolishing the Slave Trade; Being the last section of a larger work, now first published, entitled "The Dangers of the Country"* (London: J. Butterworth, 1807), 11 and 26–27.

16. See discussion of the connection between antislavery and British colonization of Africa in David Brion Davis, *Slavery and Human Progress* (New York: Oxford University Press, 1984), 231–315.

haps it did not feel quite confident of its claim that free men of color would refuse to go.[17]

Afro-Barbadians had a very ambivalent relationship with the African continent. By the time of emancipation, few had any personal memories or knowledge of Africa since only 2 percent of the slave population was African-born.
Given the overwhelming tendency for manumitted people to be creole rather
than African-born, the percentage of Africans was probably even lower among
free people of color.[18] Still, Afro-Barbadians, like their counterparts in slave societies elsewhere in the Americas, were keenly interested in Africa and African colonization projects. In 1834, when a ship of African American emigrants bound for
Liberia stopped to provision in the Bridgetown port, the *Barbadian* reported that
the "coloured portion of our community" donated thirty dollars in provisions to
the Liberian colonists.[19] This act by Barbadian free people of color may have been
an expression of African diasporic solidarity, but it was not necessarily an expression of abolitionist sentiment. The Liberian scheme was greeted with almost universal condemnation by African American abolitionists, who objected to the notion of "repatriation" as a thinly veiled segregationist attempt to whiten the United
States.[20]

For wealthy and educated men of color whose political ambitions were blocked
in the Caribbean, colonization schemes held out the possibility of establishing a
political career in Africa. As the British government did not go out of its way to
find appointments in the West Indies for any Caribbean-born subjects, Sierra Leone seemed to offer the best hope for Caribbean men of color to acquire positions of influence in imperial administration. Even this was an uncertain prospect, since the British government lacked a coherent West African policy and was
not keen on colonization schemes. Nothing came of the Colonial Office's sporadic
and half-hearted requests for governors in the West Indies to furnish lists of suitable men of color as candidates for West African government.[21]

17. CO 28/100, Private Warde to Horton, 20 January, and Private, 27 April 1827, enclosing Governor's Private Secretary to the Council, 30 January 1827.

18. Handler, Lange, and Riordan, *Plantation Slavery in Barbados*, 29; Watson, *Civilised Island*, 135.

19. *Barbadian*, 24 February 1834.

20. Support for African colonization only grew among black American abolitionists after Liberia
began independent in 1847, and after the passage of the 1850 Fugitive Slave Law. See Blackett, *Building
an Anti-Slavery Wall*, 68; Pope Melish, *Disowning Slavery*, 261–267.

21. CO 28/100, Private Warde to Horton, 20 January and Private, 27 April 1827; CO 28/139, No. 21,
MacGregor to Secretary of State for the Colonies Lord Russell, 26 February 1841.

The case of Charles Phipps, an Afro-Barbadian man free before 1834, is a good example of the desires that some men of color had for careers as imperial officials and of the difficulties they faced realizing these dreams. A teacher and philanthropist, Phipps was a fairly prominent individual, having served for many years as secretary of the Colonial Charity School and having been secretary of the Barbados Auxiliary Bible Society of the Free People of Colour.[22] In 1842 Governor Sir Charles Grey described him as "a coloured Gentleman of respectable appearance and demeanour" who had studied in Dublin, Ireland. Between 1837 and 1842 Phipps sent at least six unsuccessful petitions to the governor and the Colonial Office asking for an imperial appointment, perhaps as a magistrate or a provost marshal, in either another Caribbean island or Sierra Leone. In 1842 Governor Sir Charles Grey wrote to the secretary of state saying that Phipps's "station in Society, though quite respectable, does not adapt him to be added to the existing body of Magistrates in this Island" and despite his qualifications, it would be difficult to find a "suitable" appointment for him in Barbados. Grey and the island's attorney general thought that perhaps "something on the coast of Africa" or in another Caribbean colony regulating the immigration of laborers from Africa would be most suitable.[23] Had Phipps been white, his background would probably have inclined the governor and the Colonial Office more favorably to his request for some kind of post, although they might still have thought him insufficiently wealthy to be a magistrate.[24]

This desire for a role in the imperial civil service was probably an influential factor when, in 1841, a group of Afro-Barbadian merchants, along with a number of prominent white planters, merchants and clergymen, established the Barba-

22. *Barbadian*, 22 August 1826; Handler, Hughes, and Wiltshire, *Freedmen of Barbados*, 42.

23. CO 28/127, No. 39, 3 April 1839, MacGregor to Glenelg, enclosing petitions from Charles Phipps, referenced as No. 274, 5 December 1837, No. 205, 5 July 1838, and No. 247, 1 September 1838. Also enclosing No. 28, Glenelg to Macgregor, n.d, about Phipps. Later correspondence regarding Phipps and enclosing his petitions: CO 28/134, No. 92, MacGregor to Russell, 22 October 1840; CO 28/140, No. 20, Lieutenant-Governor Henry Darling to Secretary of State for the Colonies Lord Stanley, 22 October 1841; CO 28/144, No. 43, Grey to Stanley, 26 August 1842. After 1834, the imperial government experimented with a scheme of using Africans liberated from foreign slave ships as indentured laborers in former slave colonies that needed estate labor. See Shuler, *"Alas, Alas, Kongo."*

24. Like Phipps, very prominent free men of color elsewhere, such as Henry Loving, John Athill and Tyrrell Shervington of Antigua, found by the 1840s that imperial officials' earlier enthusiasm for them had waned and they "could only get so far in the civil establishment." Lowes, "Peculiar Class," 148.

dos auxiliary to the British Society for the Extinction of the Slave Trade and the
Civilization of Africa, also known as the Barbados Auxiliary Anti-Slavery Society.
Thomas Fowell Buxton, the leader of the antislavery lobby in the imperial Parliament, had founded the parent society in Britain in 1839. The Barbados Auxiliary Anti-Slavery Society held its first meeting at Joseph Thorne's home. Not surprisingly, Charles Phipps and Thomas Cummins, both very politically ambitious
men, were among the founders, along with two other prominent nonwhite merchants and philanthropists: the Methodist reverend Joseph Hamilton and Edward
Archer, a teacher and shopkeeper. Invoking the language of civilizationalism and
climatological concepts of race, the society's founders announced their intention
to lobby the Colonial Office to recruit Afro–West Indians in order to "civilize"
Africa, so that Europeans would not have to set foot on Africa's "pestilential"
shores.[25]

Yet there was more driving this imperial nationalism and the accompanying commitment to the civilization of Africa than just individual political opportunism. The sense of pride in being simultaneously descended from Africa and
subjects of Britain was not confined to the elite. In July 1839, 49 former slaves
signed an address to the queen, on behalf of 792 other emancipated people from
St. Thomas parish. The authors thanked the governor and the British Parliament
for freedom and expressed the wish that the "Omnipotent will Ever be that Friend
to Your Majesty as You have Been to the Unfortunate Sons of Affrica [sic]."[26]
As their political hopes in the Caribbean were repeatedly thwarted, many Afro-
Caribbean people came to feel that the situation for people of African descent
in the Americas would never improve until the slave trade was completely suppressed and the African continent was accepted by Europeans states as an equal
on the world's political stage. After emancipation, Barbadian free people of color
sought a new role in the civilizing mission of a rejuvenated British Empire as ex-
amples of what the cultural and political benefits of imperial liberalism and trade
could bring to Africa.

25. *Barbadian*, 3 July 1841; *Liberal*, 10 July 1841, 19 and 26 January 1842. The three other merchants
of color involved were Benjamin Massiah, Joseph Kennedy, and William Wilkey.

26. CO 28/128, No. 76, MacGregor to Lord Normanby, 16 July 1839, enclosing "An Address of
Your Majesty's dutiful and loyal Subjects the Lately Emancipated of the Parish of St. Thomas . . ."; see
a similar address from former slaves in CO 28/127, No. 49, MacGregor to Normanby, 23 April 1839, enclosing address of "the recently enfranchised portion of the black and coloured population of the parish of St. George . . ."

EMANCIPATION, BELONGING, AND DOUBLE CONSCIOUSNESS

It was in this context that elite men of color in Barbados turned their imaginations toward the idea of racial utopia in Africa. At the same time that Afro-Barbadians pursued the desegregation of public institutions in the island, many also drew inspiration from Haiti and repatriation projects to Africa, which aimed to establish free black polities for people of African descent from the diaspora. While the participation of local men of color in the Barbados Auxiliary Anti-Slavery Society might represent an element of opportunism on the part of elites looking for jobs in the empire, colonization schemes also offered the possibility of building a new life free from racial oppression. The *Liberal* lobbied for racial equality in Barbados but also printed regular articles about Haiti and Sierra Leone, holding these societies up as symbols of black autonomy and racial equality. Toasts to "the infant Haiti" were a regular feature at the antislavery dinners at the St. Mary's Boys' School.[27]

People of color in postemancipation Barbados forged a sense of political collectivity based on a notion of "belonging" to two larger transnational communities: the British Empire and the African continent. In this formulation of political and community identification, claiming full citizenship in the British imperial nation offered people of African descent the possibility of a central role in creating and sustaining the forces of "civilization" and "progress." As a source of collectivity and belonging that predated slavery, the idea of Africa offered a sense of rootedness and ancestral connection for historically uprooted people. Gilroy has adopted W. E. B. Du Bois's concept of "double consciousness" to examine the forms of African diasporic identification that emerged in the Atlantic world out of slavery, antislavery struggles and the experience of racial inequality. Drawing on Du Bois, Gilroy explores the political investments associated with the "double consciousness" of striving to be both "European and black" and asserts that, for many people of African descent, "occupying the space between [Europeanness and blackness]

27. See the *Liberal*, 3 August 1839, 5 August 1840, and 3 August 1842; articles titled "Communication with Hayti" and "Biographical Sketch of the Late Sir John Jeremie, Governor of Sierra Leone," *Liberal*, November 26 1842. On the importance of the "redemption of Africa" and the defense of African civilization in the Haitian Revolution and early national Haitian thought, see Gordon K. Lewis, *Main Currents in Caribbean Thought: The Historical Evolution of Caribbean Society in Its Ideological Aspects, 1492–1900* (Baltimore: Johns Hopkins University Press, 1983), 254–256.

or trying to demonstrate their continuity has been viewed as a provocative and even oppositional act of political insubordination."[28]

The *Liberal's* antislavery dinners exemplify the motivations for and tensions inherent within nineteenth-century Afro-Barbadian double consciousness. At these events civil rights campaigners expressed their sense of themselves as simultaneously the cultural and political progeny of Europe and the "descendants of Africa." Samuel Jackman Prescod argued that Europe's exploitative slave-trading relationship with Africa was largely responsible for Africans' economic and cultural underdevelopment. Yet he also assumed that European Christianity, science and culture were superior to anything currently existing in Africa and that people of color in the British colonies were culturally superior to their contemporaries in Africa. Thus the regeneration of Africa would have to come from the outside forces of "legitimate" trade with Europe and the spread of the "advantages of civilization" from Europe to Africa. At the 1838 dinner in abolitionist John Scoble's honor, Prescod announced a toast to "the speedy civilization of Africa," his "motherland" and theirs, and argued that

[before] the white man would give up his notions of exclusive humanity . . . Africa must enjoy all the advantages of civilization. The light of the gospel must spread into her deepest recesses, and the foot of the slave merchant must desert her shores. The European must seek these shores to carry improvements to her children, and not to render her barbarism more barbarous—her mental darkness more impervious, by the damning influences of a traffic in human souls. . . . For until they [people of color in Barbados] could point to Africa, with the same feelings of pride, with the same degree of exultation, with which the white man, now pointed to Europe, and say, behold our Mother country—until they could do this, they must be satisfied to be still a degraded people, although revelling in wealth and comforts.

He then made his toast, which was "drunk with enthusiastic applause" by the audience.[29]

28. W. E. B. Du Bois, *The Souls of Black Folk* (1903; reprint, New York: Modern Library, 2003), 5; Gilroy, *Black Atlantic*, 1.

29. *Liberal*, 1 December 1838.

Prescod's faith in imperial liberalism and "legitimate trade" as forces that could "civilize" Africans and create equal relations between Africa and Britain echoed and was likely inspired by the thinking of the renowned eighteenth-century African-born abolitionist Olaudah Equiano, who initially argued in favor of the Sierra Leone project in 1789 on the grounds that a "System of Commerce once being established in Africa, the Demand for Manufactories will most rapidly augment, as the native Inhabitants will insensibly adopt our Fashions, Manners, Customs, etc. etc. . . . In proportion to the Civilization, so will be the Consumption of British Manufactures."[30] Prescod's speech, like Equiano's writings, illustrates the uncertain political implications of proimperial African diasporic consciousness. While Prescod accused Europeans of having retarded African development, he accepted the notion that Africans had to become students in the school of Western European "progress." Prescod, unlike, for example, the other men of his class who formed the Barbados Auxiliary Anti-Slavery Society, does not appear to have imagined that Europe should establish colonial control over the African continent— his desire to hold Africa up as the motherland of people of color on equal par to Europe's role for Europeans suggests the opposite. However Prescod's hope to see Christianity spread in Africa and to see European states use their might to drive slave merchants from the continent's shores indicates support for a far more invasive European role in Africa in the name of "civilization."

Some Afro-Barbadians asserted a new political role for British Caribbean people of color, arguing that it was their special role to be in the vanguard of Europe's modernization project on the "benighted" African continent. At the same time, many sought to challenge European cultural arrogance, arguing that the slave trade obscured the existence of great and ancient civilizations in Africa. In an 1841 letter, an anonymous contributor to the *Liberal*, who wrote as "Africanus," expressed his view of the special mission of the British Empire's black and colored subjects, to whom he referred as the "children of Africa in the Colonies":

There is a rumour afloat of a scheme of the British people, for the civilization of Africa. As this century is marked by a spirit of enterprize [sic], and the energies of the British people, pent up for years, now seek an outlet in philanthropic acts to benighted Africa. . . .

30. Cited in Campbell, *Back to Africa*, viii–x. Equiano eventually withdrew his support for the project.

How exalted ought to be the emotions of gratitude, in the breast of every descendant of Africa, to the British nation, that so disinterestedly, so humanely, extends the hand of succour to the sons of that despised land, with a view of raising them to a station among the civilised nations of the earth!

It is necessary for the practical success of the scheme, that the children of Africa in the Colonies should lend their zealous co operation in this gigantic undertaking. . . . [I]t is not unreasonable to infer, from instances afforded by history, that the vast unexplored continent of Africa may contain nations who have arrived at a high degree of civilisation. . . . Considering the high civilization of Africa in ages long past, and that there was the birth place of Literature and Science, and Art,—there is nothing in the least unreasonable in the idea, in the far regions of that vast continent, another China might be concealed from the vision of the great European nations, who at present consider themselves the Monopolisers of learning and science.[31]

This statement may have been a celebration of the presumed cultural superiority of nineteenth-century Europe, but it also challenged the racial hierarchies of European imperialism and colonial West Indian society. "Africanus" suggested that by going to Africa, people of color would uncover African civilizations, which might be, as he implies through his comparison with China, older than anything Europe had to offer. Thus the letter sought to contextualize European civilization as a relative newcomer in human history while presenting Africa as a place that, although once great, could only now revive and rediscover its ancient greatness through outside influence from the African-descended beneficiaries of the younger, more vigorous European legacy. Clifford Geertz observes that this tension between "essentialism" and "epochalism"—the uneasy pairing of apparently competing claims to a proud but stagnating "tradition" and a modernity associated with both inequality and "progress"—is strongly associated with racial and nationalist movements in contexts of colonial subjugation.[32]

"Africanus" invoked the history of forced migration, which had led to the scattering of people of African ancestry around the Atlantic world as a source of political adaptability, cultural strength and transcontinental solidarity. For "Af-

31. *Liberal,* 17 February 1841.
32. Clifford Geertz, *The Interpretation of Cultures* (London: Fontana Press, 1973), 240–241.

ricanus," it did not matter where in the world people of African descent found themselves—the shared fact of African ancestry created a basis of solidarity that superceded all differences of culture, language and local history. In his view the British civilizing mission was reinforced by the righteousness of the quest by Africans in the Americas for a homeland. Whatever Africanus's assumptions about the superiority of modern-day Europe and Europeans over Africa and Africans, his idealized vision of this unified yet diverse African diasporic nation-without-a-state was a far cry from British authorities' paternalistic dismissal of blacks' ability to exercise political autonomy:

> Our mental powers, although shackled by fetters of slavery, have not been extirpated. . . . If political equality is denied us in that land which gave us birth, by those in whom rests the power to bestow it—how are we to obtain it? There are but two courses: either by fighting our way to it, as the braver spirits among us are doing—bringing all our moral energies to the good work, or by seeking it (those who can seek) on other and more auspicious shores, leaving the land of our birth—that land which is dear to our hearts, to be tilled by the tyrants who claim it as their own. We are not borne down by the paltry considerations of locality. No! Wherever our species is found, there we instinctively feel to be our home, because with them we are identified; and if some of us perish through the baleful influence of climate, in our attempts to build for ourselves a temple of liberty, we will die with the consoling reflection that our race will reap the benefits of our martyrdom in their cause. When we raise our voices in that cause, we awaken a responsive chord in the breast of the negro in every part of the world. The differences of language occasioned by particular localities, are not sufficient to obliterate from our minds the identity of our origin.[33]

Africanus's writing illustrates how the dream of migrating to Africa to establish a utopian community for people of Africans in the diaspora grew out of the struggle for civil rights in "the land of his birth" as an alternative solution should the problem of racism in Barbados prove to be insurmountable. His words also reveal the inherent tensions between his diasporic consciousness and his imperial nationalism. His arguments proceeded from the unspoken presupposition that loy-

33. *Liberal,* 10 February 1841.

alty to the empire might be contingent upon the British government's willingness and ability to guarantee equality for its subjects of African descent somewhere in the world. He hinted at the politically revolutionary possibility that people of African descent did not necessarily need to wait for British or other European imperial sanction to move elsewhere to establish their utopia, they could simply go wherever their "species," meaning people of African origin, already had roots and settle there without the support or permission of the imperial government.

At the same time, "Africanus" assumed that people of African descent would naturally be welcomed as long-lost relatives wherever they went, including Africa, and that such colonization could never lead to relations of domination. This idealized vision had already proven to be greatly at odds with the reality of colonization schemes on the African continent.[34] In the same vein, one can only imagine the consequences had anyone acted on an 1839 suggestion, made by the Irish abolitionist MP Daniel O'Connell to the radical Quaker abolitionist Joseph Sturge, that the "waste territory of Mexico" be used as a "Free State for British coloured subjects." The *Liberal* reprinted O'Connell's proposal and expressed its wholehearted approval of the idea.[35]

COLOR-BLIND JUSTICE AND THE SONS OF AFRIC

Afro-Barbadian civil rights campaigners' most immediate and urgent hope was that the end of slavery would usher in a new era of racial equality in Barbados itself. People of color, both former slaves and preemancipation free people, venerated British law. They hoped that the British government would bring racially neutral justice to the island, and that British judicial officers would rise above the color prejudice that motivated white creole administrators. Afro-Barbadians' fraught interactions with the postemancipation judicial system are evidence of this respect for and belief in the antiracist potential of imperial judicial and political institutions. Rather than dismissing the courts as a place where they could not expect justice, people of color in the West Indies were active participants in the court system. Diana Paton has noted that court cases in postemancipation Jamaica invariably attracted a large public audience. In the early years of freedom Afro-Jamaicans, while critical of the colonial justice system, were willing to use

34. Campbell, *Back to Africa.*
35. *Liberal,* 16 October 1839.

the courts, including against each other.[36] Descriptions of courtroom scenes in Barbados after emancipation also indicate that people came to court to insist by their presence that justice be served, and not just to witness the spectacle.[37] Apprenticeship gave former slaves their first opportunity to prosecute their erstwhile owners for crimes and to obtain redress. One planter complained that his apprentices would "always hold him to the letter of the law, and [were] ready to arraign him before the special magistrate for every infraction of it on his part, however trifling."[38] In 1836 stipendiary magistrate Colthurst noted, "When the negroes see even-handed justice given to all, they express great astonishment; they stare and exclaim 'white man upon tread mill too.'"[39]

The 1838 court case against Gunning Best, a man of color free before emancipation and a *Liberal* reporter, illustrates the popular view that it was the role of the common law to be the impartial arbiter between white and nonwhite Barbadians. The Court of Grand Sessions convicted Best of assaulting a police officer. It is highly likely that the case was a trumped up charge to punish Best for his political views. During the proceedings, Best argued that the solicitor general and the magistrate had conspired to exclude witnesses vital to his defense. In sentencing him to hard labor and fines totaling more than one hundred pounds, the magistrate displayed his bias by describing Best as "a most quarrelsome and violent individual: he had formerly been in the Police; and it was not, as he [Magistrate Gill] believed for *good* conduct, that he had to leave it." During the same session of the court, two white men were convicted of the manslaughter of an apprentice but were sentenced without hard labor. The differences in the outcome of the two cases provoked a petition from a group of men of color to Governor MacGregor in which they compared Best's treatment to that of the white defendants: "These [the white men] were brought to the Bar of *Justice*, Arraigned for manslaughter, *they shot the*

---

36. Diana Paton, *No Bond but the Law: Punishment, Race, and Gender in Jamaican State Formation, 1780–1870* (Durham, N.C.: Duke University Press, 2004), 156–190.

37. For example, throughout 1839 several laborers took employers to court for pay they said they were owed. In one particular case involving a group of laborers from Salter's plantation, St. George, who said the attorney owed them money, there was outrage when the magistrates found for the defendant: "This decision seemed to create great dissatisfaction, and on the complainant's [*sic*] quitting the Court and informing their friends (of whom we reckon no less than 30) of the issue of the trial, the commotion was so great, that the Magistrate left his seat, and desired an Officer to disperse them." *Liberal*, 24 April 1839. See also *Barbadian*, 24 March 1849.

38. Thome and Kimball, *Emancipation in the West Indies*, 63.

39. Colthurst, *Colthurst Journal*, 119.

sons of Afric, they *shed blood*—Best, in the *discharge* of *his duty,* as a Reporter for the 'Liberal' paper, after being struck by a police Officer, *merely defended himself.*"[40] During his trial, Best and a group of other men of color formed the Barbados Political Union Society, whose mission was to "defend and protect the rights of the poor." The society does not seem to have survived very long, as this is the only reference made to it. However its existence indicates that civil rights campaigners saw themselves as the defenders of both the disenfranchised and the rule of British law in the island.[41]

Even as Afro-Barbadians appealed to British imperial institutions and governance for justice, imperial support for the cause of racial equality in the Caribbean was waning. Once the legislative framework of racial slavery was dismantled and the most obviously discriminatory laws had been repealed, the imperial government saw itself as having no further proactive role to play in regulating race relations in the Caribbean. Governor MacGregor exemplified the imperial view that the postemancipation state was de jure racially blind. After August 1838, he began to distance himself from demands from Afro-Barbadians that he had a duty to protect and expand the civil rights of people of color. Like the legislature, he used the language of class and property to justify the fact that so few Afro-Barbadians ever received political appointments, arguing that "no political privileges are withheld from any portion of the population, the Question is, in fact, rather one of *Station,* than of *Color.*" He suggested that to appoint men of color of little property to government posts would be racist, saying that "the whites protest against the elevation of persons, merely because they are of colour, to high offices, which would not be conferred on white Candidates of equal merit, and of the same rank in life."[42]

MacGregor argued that men of color who raised the issue of racial discrimination were in fact perpetuating racism. In December 1838, writing on the governor's behalf in his capacity as the governor's acting private secretary, the Afro-Grenadian Joseph Garraway informed the petitioners who accused the presiding

40. CO 28/124, No. 355, MacGregor to Glenelg, 13 December 1838, enclosure B, No. 1. The signatories to the petition were *New Times* editor Nathaniel Roach, John Arthur Chase, who had been considered one of the ringleaders of the 1824 counteraddress; Benjamin C. Eversley, who had signed the 1811 petition, James Reed, who had supported Prescod's 6 May 1833 petition, and Charles R. Arthur. Biographical information from Handler, Hughes, and Wiltshire, *Freedmen of Barbados.*

41. *Liberal,* 3 October 1838.

42. CO 28/123, Private, MacGregor to Glenelg, 8 September 1838.

magistrate and the solicitor general of racism in Gunning Best's trial of the governor's "regret that you should therein, have alluded to distinctions of Class, fortunately no longer recognized by law—and the unkind remembrance of which . . . seems, in this Colony, to be Sedulously perpetuated,—rather by the injudicious measures of certain descendants of Africa,—than by the proceedings of their White Brethren and Fellow Subjects."[43]

Such views made MacGregor unpopular among people of color, but his attitudes reflected the increasingly racist political climate in Britain.[44] While the British government may have been unwilling to push the political claims of free people of color, it was ready to step in if the result of leaving race relations to sort themselves out would be former slaves' control of the state. The British government was disturbed by postemancipation socioeconomic trends in the Caribbean, particularly in Jamaica, where, the sugar industry was collapsing while the Afro-Jamaican electorate grew. In Jamaica, where an acre of land cost between four and twenty pounds (compared with between sixty and two hundred pounds in Barbados), the number of freeholders went from around 2,000 in 1838, to 27,379 in 1845, and would climb to about 50,000 by 1861.[45]

The changing nature of the electorate was reflected in the Jamaican House of Assembly, in which, after 1837, the number of Afro-Jamaican representatives steadily increased.[46] In the first years of emancipation, all the nonwhite assemblymen in Jamaica were wealthy and educated, and a few were even planters.[47] However, as W. P. Morrell states (referring to Jamaica), the British government feared that "white ascendancy in the West Indies would ultimately lead to a black ascendency worse than itself." In other words, the British government was afraid that former slaves and free people of color would gain control of the island's political institutions, a situation it assumed would lead to race war. The Whig administration therefore took action in 1839 to try to forestall the political consequences of Afro-Jamaican political dominance, and introduced a bill to suspend the island's

43. CO 28/124, No. 355, MacGregor to Glenelg, 22 December 1838, enclosing Garraway, Governor's Acting Private Secretary, 14 December 1838.

44. According to Levy, MacGregor's death in 1841 "was regarded as a great loss by the whites but was scarcely noticed by the blacks." Levy, *Emancipation, Sugar, and Federalism*, 86. On the racist turn in British public life during this period, see Hall, *Civilising Subjects*, 338–379.

45. Bolland, "Systems of Domination," 111.

46. Heuman, *Between Black and White*, 100–103.

47. Ibid., 61.

constitution for five years as a precursor to abolishing the Jamaican legislature. Faced with overwhelming parliamentary opposition to the measure, Lord Melbourne's administration resigned. Although the "bedchamber crisis" brought the Whig government back to power, the Whigs abandoned their policy of intervention in West Indian affairs in favor of conciliation of, and cooperation with, the plantocracy. The official view on race and politics was clear: planter oligarchy was acceptable, but a former-slave democracy was not.[48]

REGIONALISM AND MULTIRACIALISM

While civil rights campaigners pursued reform strategies based on Afro-Barbadian solidarity and appeals to imperial justice, they sought to build strategic political alliances at a number of different levels. Prescod, as usual, was the most innovative in this regard, building on his experiences with sympathetic middle-class whites he had come to know during the apprenticeship period in campaigns against the Bridgetown ordinances of 1835 and the continuing campaign for separate representation for the capital city in the House of Assembly. In 1840 Prescod organized the Liberal Party, a loose biracial coalition that resembled the powerful and much older Jamaican Town Party, consisting of white and Afro-Barbadian merchants and small white planters, who challenged planters for seats in the House of Assembly. Most of the party's candidates seem, however, to have been white. Prescod argued that he decided to widen his base of support to include white men because the "struggle between ancient exclusiveness and modern equality in civil and political affairs is not a struggle between white and coloured, but between the poor and middle class of *all complexions* and the assumptions of the wealthy few."[49] Prescod would lead the Liberal Party for the next two decades and, as will be discussed in subsequent chapters, its course would reveal both the significant strengths and the profound weaknesses of his, as well as other well-to-do Afro-Barbadian progressives,' political vision for postslavery society.

48. W. P. Morrell, *British Colonial Policy in the Age of Peel and Russell* (London: Clarendon Press, 1930), 152–153. See also Blackburn, *Overthrow of Colonial Slavery,* 461; Holt, *Problem of Freedom,* 215–261; Douglas Hall, *Free Jamaica, 1838–1865: An Economic History* (London: Caribbean Universities Press, 1969), 3–8; Richard Lobdell, "British Officials and the West Indian Peasantry, 1842–1938," in Malcolm Cross and Gad Heuman, eds., *Labour in the Caribbean: From Emancipation to Independence* (London: Macmillan Caribbean, 1992), 195–207.

49. Beckles, *History of Barbados,* 120; Woodville Marshall, "The Prescod Reform Programme," unpublished article (cited with permission of the author), n.d., 7–9.

That same year Prescod tried to develop a regional political framework for Afro-Caribbean activists, forming the Colonial Coloured Union, an abortive political association whose aim was equality for "black and mulatto men" throughout the West Indies.[50] Although this organization never got off the ground, it represented an unprecedented level of federalism in popular anglophone Caribbean politics. The union was intended to have branches in every territory of the West Indies, and the imperial government was so afraid of its "subversive potential" that it increased its surveillance of Prescod.[51] Despite the ultimate failure of the union, its conceptualization does seem to have been based on some level of preexisting regional interactions between Afro-Caribbean civil rights agitators. Prescod's wife Katherine Cruden probably played a key role in the establishment of the union. She was Antiguan born, and it would likely have been through her that Prescod made and maintained contact with radicals of color from Leeward territories.[52] Prescod also maintained contacts in the Windward Caribbean. The *Liberal* published letters from people of African descent elsewhere in the Caribbean, including radical letters from a group of people of color from the nearby island of Trinidad who went under the nom de plume The Six of Us. This group, as well as a local man of color who wrote under the name "Claudius," cautioned people of color against believing that whites were now their friends and political allies. The Six of Us did not support the idea of any kind of political alliance with West Indian whites and expressed their "surprise, and indeed . . . regret, that some otherwise well informed members of the coloured body are so weak as to swallow the common place, and now hackneyed, statements of our natural enemies that 'all old prejudices are now abolished' and 'the law makes no distinction'!" "Claudius" was even less charitable, arguing that any "coloured persons" who were satisfied with their current civil and political status were either of "weak intellect" or "foolish."[53]

These writers made it abundantly clear that their demands for political equality and the racial integration of the institutions of the state were based on abstract principles of justice and equality rather than any secret longing for "social intercourse" with whites. Writing in support of Prescod's Colonial Colored Union, "Claudius" vilified white newspaper editors in the island, notably the ultraconservative Abel Clinckett, editor of the *Barbadian*, who had attacked the Union

50. *Liberal*, 19 September 1840.

51. Marshall, "Prescod Reform Programme," 7.

52. Vaughan, *Democrat*, 9 April and 14 May 1971.

53. *Liberal*, 9 and 12 September 1840.

as antiwhite, and suggested that people of color boycott Clinckett's newspaper. "Claudius" said that, although he was not prejudiced against whites, and saw them as "one of the families of the human race, and therefore equal to ourselves in capacity, moral and physical" no one should believe that people of color were "over ambitious to throw open our drawing rooms to them, or to enter theirs."[54] Such negative sentiments about social interactions with whites would indicate that not all Afro-Barbadian radical reformers saw lower-class and bourgeois whites as potential political allies against the plantocracy.

Those who professed themselves to be racially conscious remained determinedly silent about slavery and their own past relationships to it. One of the few to raise this taboo subject was John Richard Belgrave, a man who described himself as a "poor coloured man." In an 1841 letter, which was published, interestingly, in the *Barbadian,* Belgrave wrote a unique and astonishingly subtle analysis of how class, race, and a refusal, on the part of many whites and people of color, to reflect constructively on the past combined to shape postemancipation politics in the island:

> I the undersigned with the warmest feelings of love towards my brothering [*sic*: brethren]; more especially my poor class. Now my brothering you that have tasted of Slavery, were we persecuted by the white Inhabitants alone or was it every one that was capable of owning a Slave. Now my brothering as far as my judgment extends every man had his original faults, and so we are faulty to this day, I know that God suffer'd slavery or it would not have been in existance for what reason I do not know, but I know that it is by the same Lord have delivered us and no one else. . . . [W]e ought not to be revengeful, for vengeance belongeth to God. . . . [N]ow my brothering, I speak of those that have tasted of Slavery have you never known a Collard [*sic*: coloured] person possessing wealth and have taken their own Brother, Sister, Niece, Nephew, Cousin, or else, and made merchandize of them as well as any White person would. . . . [N]ow we are a Jealous race for if a man is placed in any Public Situation he is sanctioned with many evils, when many of you perhaps would not exercise it with a pure conscience, you all have so much to say about a White Man and yet you never feel yourselves any way aggrandized except you are seen in their Company,

54. *Liberal,* 9 and 12 September 1840. See similar language in articles in early postemancipation Afro-Cuban newspapers, cited in Helg, *Our Rightful Share,* 39.

for I have heard the argument that a Man have used to his Collard Brothering, and then to hear him when he gets before two or three white men if
they will be seen with him, his argument is as different, as a Stone to a bit
of Cheese, I have heard them. . . . I am a poor my Brothering, no wealth, no
voice. . . . [A]nd my Brothering of the higher Class if any of you are thinking of your forefathers doings I beseech you to with draw your minds from
it, and be contented for the great change that God has been pleased to
make . . . we may enjoy that peace that do not exist among us now, to the
satisfaction of our future days, and let God be praised.[55]

Belgrave's letter is remarkable for the author's careful specifications of his use
of the term "Brethren" to refer to people of his "race"; to those of his own socioeconomic background, whether "white" or "black"; or to all Barbadians, regardless of race or class status. In one sense, Belgrave's use of the term is biblical, indicating his belief in the existence of a human family, but in his reference to people
of color as "a Jealous race," he employs clear concepts of racial difference. The letter is also important as a rare postemancipation admission of the fact that some
people of color had also been slave owners. It was at once a call to racial, class, and
country solidarity, based on a shared past of the experience of living in a slave society and a call for sober reflection and reconciliation in order to achieve a more
just postemancipation social and political arrangement for all dispossessed people.
There was no response to his letter in any of the island's newspapers.

THE LIMITS OF SOLIDARITY AND
THE INTERNALIZATION OF RACISM

However sincere expressions of racial solidarity and African diasporic pride may
have been, many people of African descent had a troubled relationship with their
African heritage as well as a material interest in the institutions of state repression that were mobilized after emancipation against the newly freed. The participation of people of African descent in the new police force in particular systematically undermined the rhetoric of racial solidarity. While Afro-Barbadian civil
rights campaigners were demanding that men of African descent be given equal
opportunities to whites in the constabulary, police constables were busily acquir-

55. *Barbadian*, 19 December 1840.

ing a reputation for extreme brutality against former slaves and people of African descent in general.

From its inception, it was clear that the police force was essentially a modernized version of the militia, developed specifically to help the plantocracy maintain control over the postemancipation laboring population. In 1834 members of the Moravian congregation at Mount Tabor told the missionary that they were afraid to come to prayer meetings because of the danger of being arrested by the police "who had treaded [sic] several very roughly." This harassment occurred even though the local stipendiary magistrate had instructed the police not to prevent people from going to church.[56] Accusations also reached the imperial government that the police were conducting illegal floggings of apprentices.[57] In 1834, the Colonial Office received an anonymous letter from an individual claiming to be a Barbadian apprentice, the only extant letter ever sent to Whitehall by either a slave or apprentice from the Caribbean. The author begged the secretary of state to curb the excesses of the police: "[T]here is a Police framed but the men acts in a most in humane manner rushing into mens house beating them and Cutting them a Country Policemen killed a poor apprentice Struck him to the heart and he dyed and it was said it was all in self defence a poor Black Woman in a Pregnant state was kicked in the Belly and sevearly beaten by him and laid out Dead."[58] After apprenticeship there were several court cases in which the police were found to have falsified reports and assaulted prisoners, and there were instances of laborers dying under suspicious circumstances in both urban and rural jails.[59]

Since the majority of constables in the police force by 1839 were men of color, it seems rather unlikely that only white officers abused their power. The only brutality case in which the race of the police officer was specifically mentioned was the 1838 case involving Gunning Best. The officer who prosecuted Best, whom Best accused of assaulting him and targeting him for arrest on political grounds, was himself Afro-Barbadian.[60] Ironically, although the inclusion of men of color on the force was hailed as a victory against racism, the police were accused of par-

56. Moravian Diary, 5 October 1834.

57. See CO 28/115, No. 9, Smith to Aberdeen, 14 March 1835, enclosing documents concerning the case of a runaway apprentice named Eliza.

58. CO 28/114, Alphabetized correspondence ("A"), unnumbered, Anonymous, Barbados, 1 October 1834.

59. *Liberal* 27 April 1839; letter from "Aristides," 12 June 1839, 16 March 1842.

60. CO 28/124, No. 355, MacGregor to Glenelg, 13 December 1838, enclosure B.

ticipating in the maintenance of illegal racial segregation. In March 1839 Benjamin Goodridge, a white political ally of Prescod's from Speightstown, wrote to the *Liberal* saying that the police had turned people of color away from a concert, and had physically assaulted those who resisted.[61]

Male apprentices who had been part of the favored stratum of plantation slaves mirrored the role of police officers as the arms of state repression. After 1834 the state provided a means through which some estate headmen acquired even more coercive physical authority over others as an extension of the policing and surveillance power of the postemancipation state. The rural police force was assisted after 1834 by a network of "estate constables," male apprentices selected to help the police keep the peace on a particular estate. In nearly all cases, these "constables" were former headmen, particularly slave drivers. Although it was illegal for drivers—now called "superintendents"—to carry whips into the field, estate constables were issued with batons, like the police, and it emerged during apprenticeship that many constable-headmen were carrying their batons into the fields with them to supervise the work of field laborers. Estate constables also carried out evictions of estate laborers from their homes during and immediately after apprenticeship.[62]

As a result, relations between headmen and field laborers after emancipation were sometimes extremely sour. In 1834, the missionary at Mount Tabor noticed that the laborers at one of the estates in the neighborhood refused to come to hear him when he visited, because he held his meetings in the driver's house. He sent word to them "that I would keep the meeting under the tree before their Master's house, [which] met their approbation very much, tho the driver did not seem to like it, but we had a larger company this time than before."[63] During a particularly acrimonious field laborers' strike in August 1838 at a St. George estate, magistrates, policemen, and the estate constables converged on the scene of the strike and threatened to evict the strikers. According to the estate attorney, the laborers

61. *Liberal*, 13 March 1839.

62. CO 28/127, number missing, MacGregor to Glenelg, 26 March 1839, enclosing No. 6, Governor's circular to the special magistrates, 18 February 1839, and No. 7, Nathaniel Roach, police magistrate for St. Lucy, to Joseph Garraway, Governor's Private Secretary, 23 February 1839; Governor's correspondence to the special justices, 5 July and 23 Sept, 1837; *Liberal*, report on the case of Molly Cuffy, 13 March 1839; See also *Liberal*, 17 July 1839, case of Fanny Rowe, laborer, against John Sue, driver and estate constable.

63. Moravian Diary, 19 October 1834.

told the magistrates they had no right to interfere, and "as for the rural constables, if one of them spoke and demanded silence, or in any way attempted to exercise his authority, the clamour was so great that it was impossible for any one to demand silence in the Queen's name so as to be heard."[64] The practice of appointing former slave drivers as estate constables proved so disruptive that, in March 1839, the governor instructed police magistrates not to allow drivers to become constables, although it is unclear if this order had any effect.[65]

Perhaps one of the most tragic legacies of slavery was the fact that many people of African descent had deeply internalized negative attitudes about their own blackness. In 1835, for example, an estate constable arrested an apprentice accused of stealing canes and brought him before stipendiary magistrate Colthurst. The constable, whom Colthurst described as an "old negro man," told him that the apprentice was a disreputable character, and added, "Massa, massa, Major, dat man is not belong to de property—he is bad man, he only dare two, three days ago—de damn black nigger."[66] This internalization of racism combined with a well-placed distrust of state authorities to make some former slaves wary of people of African descent who held positions of authority over them. White police magistrates frequently alleged that laborers preferred white to nonwhite employers and had more confidence in whites in positions of authority than men of color.[67] While such claims should not be accepted without question, they are supported by an incident from 1841, when a crowd of people of color gathered to witness a black porter or boatman named Cox resisting arrest by a black police officer. A witness testified in court that, as the black policeman dragged Cox through Trafalgar Square in the center of Bridgetown, Cox declared that he "would not go to the Station-house with any black villain of a Policeman" and that he only stopped resisting when a white officer turned up.[68]

Some of the prominent pre-1834 free men of color who sought to promote ra-

64. CO 28/123, No. 220, MacGregor to Glenelg, 22 August 1838, enclosure No. 2, James Henry Went, Justice of the Peace, to MacGregor, 16 August 1838.

65. CO 28/127, date missing, MacGregor to Glenelg, 26 March 1839, enclosing No. 8, Joseph Garraway, Acting Private Secretary, to magistrates, 15 March 1839.

66. Colthurst, *Colthurst Journal*, 104–106.

67. See, for example, PP 1842, vol. 29, *Papers Relative to the West Indies, 1841–42. Jamaica and Barbados*, "Questions for Quarterly Reply from the Police Magistracy . . . 1840": 1 January to 31 March, No. 2, St. James, and No. 4, St. John; 1 April to 30 June, No. 11, Rural St. Michael; 1 July to 30 September 1840, No. 8, St. Joseph; *Liberal*, 22 January 1840.

68. *Liberal*, 22 September 1841.

cial solidarity and pride in their African origins also exhibited a profound sense of shame about cultural practices associated with Africa. Colthurst's description of Thorne's aggressive dispersal of a group of apprentices assembled for an African-inspired Barbadian slave burial ceremony, described in chapter 5, seems almost visceral, and one might suggest that his assault on the burial ceremony was rooted in a deeper sense of personal shame at his own origins in a community that indulged in such forms of cultural expression. Thorne's later political career and that of many other elite Afro-Barbadians, which are discussed in the final chapters of this book, suggests that such internal identity conflicts might have been a force guiding their attitudes toward former slaves and toward their own African heritage.

The hue of one's skin color was not as politically significant among Afro-Barbadians as it was in most other Caribbean societies. Yet in Barbados, as elsewhere in the Americas after slavery, Afro-Barbadians' sense of "collective identity . . . did not exclude personal distinctions based on color and ethnicity."[69] Despite attempts to promote racial pride among people of color, many Afro-Barbadians had internalized negative attitudes about dark skin color as a signifier of a connection with Africa that was too close for comfort. Regardless of their wealth and social status, Afro-Barbadians were expected—frequently by other people of color—to show deference to those of lighter complexion. In August 1842 several hundred people of color attacked the home of Afro-Barbadian merchant London Bourne after he charged one of his shop assistants, a light-complexioned man of color named John Piper, with theft. Bourne, who had been enslaved until 1818, was a keen supporter of schemes for colonization and "civilization" in West Africa, and in the 1850s he became one of the principle organizers of an Anglican mission to part of what is now the Gambia.[70] In 1859 he was described as "a man of unmixed African blood," which suggests that he was of very dark complexion.[71]

69. Quote from Helg, *Our Rightful Share*, 40.

70. See Bishop's Court records, microfilms BS 33–38, particularly BS 38 (BPL); CO 28/173, No. 73, Colebrooke to Grey, 29 November 1850, enclosing Bishop of Barbados to Colebrooke, 28 November 1850, enclosure No. 4, "Proposed Mission from the Church of the West Indies to Western Africa" (Barbados: Barbadian Office, 1850). Thomas J. Cummins, John Montefiore, and London Bourne were members of the committee for this project. See also Karch, "Man for All Seasons," 21–31. In his will Bourne left an annual sum of five pounds, to be paid for the next five years, to the British and Foreign Anti-Slavery Society and the mission he had helped to establish in the Rio Pongas region of the Gambia. See Will of London Bourne, BDA.

71. Karch, "Man for All Seasons," 19.

Some of Bourne's neighbors, themselves people of color, apparently either participated in the attack or refused to help the police sent to disperse it. In an editorial on the 1842 incident the *Liberal* expressed outrage that anyone in the island would "openly riot" for the principle "that fair complexion and respectability, real or presumed, are to be a passport to impunity from crime, when the party injured happens to be a black man! And that black men and women, above all others, should be the fools to be led away by this preposterous notion to commit a breach of the law and expose themselves to its penalties, is evidence of their zealous sincerity."[72]

The crowd threw stones at the house and threatened to kill Bourne's son, who had testified against Piper, referring to Bourne as a "Barbadian Congo" and his son as "the congo son."[73] Caribbean lexicographer Richard Allsopp describes the term "Congo" in the West Indies as a derogatory expression for a "person who is black, whose standard of living is of the lowest, speech uneducated and language rough, and who is also considered basically stupid and ignorant." Many creole slaves in the anglophone Caribbean, who comprised over 90 percent of the Barbadian slave population by the end of the eighteenth century, apparently held Africans brought from the Congo in low regard, associating them with a "stigma of stupidity."[74] The use of this term during the 1842 riot indicates how deeply ingrained negative attitudes toward Africa were among some people of African descent in Barbados, and the prevalence of the view that, as a man of darker color than Piper, Bourne had no right to prosecute him.

CONCLUSION

Afro-Barbadians of the early postemancipation era sought to reimagine Britishness as an expansive and inclusive basis for claims to citizenship and equality within the empire. Their reconceptualization of what it meant to be British challenged both the Little Englandism and parochialism of the creole plantocracy and the dismissal and distrust of Africans' and blacks' political capacities, which emanated from Britain. They invoked Africa both to claim a place as agents, rather than just objects, in the British Empire's civilizing mission as well as to assert

72. *Liberal*, 20 August 1842.

73. *Liberal*, 3 September 1842; see also reports in the *Barbadian*, 20 and 27 August 1842.

74. Richard Allsopp, *Dictionary of Caribbean English Usage* (New York: Oxford University Press, 1996), 167.

their sense of solidarity with people of African descent elsewhere in the Atlantic world. This imperial nationalism was informed by their faith that British legislative and judicial institutions, trade and foreign policy would promote and guarantee the roll back of racially discriminatory practices in the Caribbean, while also suppressing the slave trade and engaging with Africa and Africans as equals. Many Afro-Barbadians saw a role for themselves on the continent as both long-lost siblings and would-be "civilizers." For them, a "mission" to Africa offered the possibility of creating a political community where they might enjoy the equality that eluded them in the Caribbean.

These invocations of Britishness and Africanness were also a means through which Afro-Barbadians tried to form themselves into a united community out of the profoundly divided and divisive past of slavery. Appealing to such a transnational language of collectivity deferred the unresolved issue of what basis actually existed within the Barbadian context for political unity. While the passing of slavery in some ways removed significant sources of division—between slave owners and the enslaved, free and unfree—other sources of discord remained, such as class and gender inequality, cultural distinctions, a lack of sustained communication between rural workers and elite urban reformers and fundamentally different visions of what desegregation entailed and how far political and social reform should go.

Even before the end of apprenticeship it was rapidly becoming clear that Afro-Barbadians had diverse and frequently conflicting ideological positions regarding the structure of postemancipation society. It was one thing to invoke the language of imperial citizenship and African diasporic solidarity in order to highlight the importance of one's group to the empire. It was quite another matter to agree on who should actually have the rights of citizenship—particularly the right to vote and hold elective office—in Barbados and what the place of former slaves should be in the postslavery order of things. As the next chapter illustrates, the questions of labor and citizenship would severely test Afro-Barbadian efforts to unite against racial discrimination and unravel the threads of political solidarity that optimism about emancipation had helped to create among them.

PART THREE

This then, is the end of his striving: to be a co-worker in the kingdom of culture, to escape both death and isolation, to husband and use his best powers and his latent genius. These powers of body and mind have in the past been strangely wasted, dispersed, or forgotten. The shadow of a mighty Negro past flits through the tale of Ethiopia the Shadowy and of Egypt the Sphinx. Throughout history, the powers of single black men flash here and there like falling stars, and die sometimes before the world has rightly gauged their brightness.

—W. E. B. DU BOIS, *The Souls of Black Folk*

8 / THE EMIGRATION DEBATE
AND POSTEMANCIPATION POLITICS

I n September 1840, during a speech at a dinner in his honor, Samuel Jackman Prescod asked those in attendance to reflect on an issue that had been central to the Afro-Barbadian civil rights struggle. "Why should it be called liberality, and so much credit assumed for the act," he asked, "when a black or coloured man [is] appointed to fill a public situation[?]"[1] Prescod's bitterness reflected the reality that, within a few years of the end of apprenticeship, the colonial regime, which for so long had been loath to appoint people of color to official posts, was now successfully using such appointments to undermine the tenuous and fleeting political solidarity that Afro-Barbadian civil rights campaigners had forged during apprenticeship. Men of color who previously had been allies turned against each other in public fashion, the divisions between them carefully nurtured by the government.

The source of the crisis in Afro-Barbadian politics was much deeper than a problem of official meddling. Their disagreements arose from fundamentally different ideological views of the meaning of freedom after slavery, as they took opposite sides in the debate over how to resolve the widespread labor unrest of the early postapprenticeship years. Between 1838 and the early 1840s, the Barbadian countryside hemorrhaged people, as rural laborers fled before planters' increasingly draconian labor policies. Estate workers did not just leave the countryside— many left the island altogether, taking advantage of labor shortages in neighboring Caribbean territories to escape the repressive atmosphere of Barbados. Movement had always been one of the key ways in which Afro-Barbadians exercised freedom and demonstrated their opposition to state and planter authorities. The early post-slavery wave of emigration posed a serious threat to planters' cherished control over a captive labor force and to their political and economic power.

The debate over emigration in the postemancipation British Caribbean divided the forces of reform in the British Empire at all levels. In Britain, the issue

1. *Liberal,* 19 September 1840.

proved devastating for the antislavery movement, already in decline in the face of rising antiblack sentiment. In Barbados, the issue of emigration fatally undermined the already fractious Afro-Barbadian civil rights struggle. In the end, the losers in this battle were not the elite, most of whom would see their hopes for political influence fulfilled, but the majority of working-class Afro-Barbadians who had hoped emancipation would lead to meaningful political and economic change.

THE CRISIS IN CARIBBEAN AGRICULTURE

The abolition of slavery contributed to one of the worst economic crises in the history of British Caribbean plantation agriculture. By the 1820s the price of sugar from the British West Indies had gone into a seemingly irreversible decline. Saint Domingue, the greatest eighteenth-century threat to the British Caribbean sugar industry, had been replaced by even more daunting competition from Cuba and Brazil.[2] A similar crisis struck other important West Indian export crops, such as coffee and cotton, the latter a crop vital for the survival of small landholders.[3] After the long cycle of declining prices and political controversy over slavery, creditors lost confidence in British West Indian agriculture and demanded loan repayments while refusing to extend further credit.[4] Planters also faced a new challenge from the advocates of free trade in Britain, who supported popular demands for the end of tariff protection for agricultural products such as sugar and corn, which, free traders argued, kept prices for these necessary items artificially high.[5]

2. Between 1820 and 1860 Cuba's annual sugar exports rose from 43,119 tons to 447,000, while Brazil's grew from 75,000 to 82,000 between 1820 and 1839 but afterward tended to fluctuate a great deal from year to year. See Deerr, *History of Sugar*, 1:131. See also Burn, *Emancipation and Apprenticeship*, 337 and 368–369; Watts, *West Indies*, 300.

3. Burn, *Emancipation and Apprenticeship*, 23–24; Richard Lobdell, "Patterns of Investment and Sources of Credit in the British West Indian Sugar Industry, 1838–1897," in Beckles and Shepherd, ed., *Caribbean Freedom*, 319.

4. Lobdell, "Patterns of Investment," 320–321; Butler, *Economics of Emancipation*, 64–68; Richard Pares, *A West India Fortune* (London: Longmans, Green, 1950), 261.

5. Beginning in 1663, sugar entering Britain from its Caribbean colonies was taxed at a lower rate than sugar from elsewhere. Since the 1790s there had been pressure from abolitionists and parliamentarians with financial interests in India to equalize the sugar duties. Noel Deerr, *History of Sugar*, vol. 2 (London: Chapman and Hall, 1950), 427–448; Holt, *Problem of Freedom*, 202–213; Levy, *Emancipation, Sugar, and Federalism*, 99; Lowell J. Ragatz, *The Fall of the Planter Class in the British Caribbean, 1763–1833: A Study in Economic and Social History* (New York: Century, 1928), 104, 204–212, and 361; Eric Williams, *Capitalism and Slavery* (London: Andre Deutsch, 1964), 134–196.

Emancipation also presented the likely prospect of a Caribbean-wide labor shortage, particularly in Trinidad, British Guiana, and Jamaica.[6] Planters in territories facing estate labor crises experimented with indentured immigration schemes to obtain laborers from elsewhere.[7] By contrast, as Beckles asserts, Barbadian planters' near total domination of land and political power led to a "situation whereby after emancipation a workforce which did not own homes, or have access to land, was created with a inbuilt dependency on the plantation. . . . The system provided planters with an adequate supply of labour, and afforded them considerable control over that labour."[8] That being said, planters' power to determine the conditions of labor in Barbados had limits. Planters from Trinidad and British Guiana set their sights on the large labor force of their neighbor, Barbados, which, with more than eighty-two thousand slaves and an estimated population density of five hundred enslaved people per square mile in 1834, had the second largest and most dense slave population in the Caribbean.[9]

Imperial officials were enthusiastic about the prospect of redistributing some of Barbados's former slave population to other parts of the Caribbean where labor was required. In 1833 Governor Smith described the island as "dreadfully overpeopled. . . . It is most desirable to encourage emigration—Trinidad and Demerara would be the best points."[10] Barbadian planters, however, had others plans: They wanted to maintain a labor reserve to ensure themselves of an adequate supply of workers and to keep wages down.[11] In response to the threat from British Guiana and Trinidad, the legislature quickly passed the 1836 "Act to regulate the Emigration of Laborers from this Island." The House of Assembly claimed that local

6. Emmanuel Riviere, "Labour Shortage in the British West Indies after Emancipation," *JCH* 4 (May 1972): 1–30.

7. Green, *British Slave Emancipation*, 245–251, 269–270; Mahdavi Kale, *Fragments of Empire: Capital, Slavery and Indian Indentured Labor Migration in the British Caribbean* (Philadelphia: University of Pennsylvania Press, 1998); Levy, *Sugar, Emancipation and Federalism*, 80; Brian Moore, *Race, Power and Social Segmentation in Colonial Society: Guyana after Slavery, 1838–1891* (New York: Gordon and Breach Science, 1987), 31–47; Brinsley Samaroo, "Two Abolitions: African Slavery and East Indian Indentureship," in David Dabydeen and Brinsley Samaroo, *Across the Dark Waters: Ethnicity and Indian identity in the Caribbean* (London: Macmillan Caribbean, 1996), 25–41; Shuler, *"Alas, Alas, Kongo."*

8. Beckles, *History of Barbados*, 110–111.

9. Jamaica had the largest slave population at 311,070, with an estimated 74 slaves per square mile, and Trinidad, with 20,657 emancipated people, had a former slave population density of 12 per square mile. St. Kitts had the second highest density, with 314 slaves per square mile, and a slave population of 19,780. Green, *British Slave Emancipation*, 193.

10. CO 28/111, General, unnumbered, Smith to Stanley, 8 July 1833.

11. Mary Chamberlain, *Narratives of Exile and Return* (London: Macmillan Caribbean, 1997), 21.

"crimps," as emigration agents were called, were buying laborers' remaining apprenticeship then forcing them to sign three-year contracts for work in British Guiana. Besides reflecting planters' worries about losing laborers, the act was motivated by racism and parsimony, as the legislature did not want to have any Afro-Barbadian children, whose parents had emigrated, for whom the vestries might have to care.[12]

The legislature was also concerned about losing rural labor to the island's towns and to itinerant occupations such as artisanal work and huckstering. To counteract this danger, a new poor law, passed a few months before the 1836 emigration act, gave the vestries power to expel illegitimate children whose parents dwelt outside of the parish, so that the vestries would not have to assume financial responsibility for them after emancipation.[13] This act was designed to discourage laborers from moving from parish to parish or from the countryside to towns in search of work. In 1835 the legislature passed acts increasing the tax on huckstering, and instituted a system of licenses for various types of nonagricultural labor.[14] As former slaves established rum shops and small retail stores during apprenticeship, the legislature also increased the cost of a license to sell alcohol from five to ten pounds.[15]

The legislature was keen to prevent the migration of rural agricultural workers, but it would have been pleased to rid the island of large numbers of working-class people in other types of employment. The 1836 antiemigration act was quite specific about targeting agricultural laborers, but it kept the possibility of emigration open for paupers and nonagricultural workers. The legislature considered urban working-class Afro-Barbadians to be a particular nuisance because they competed with white workers and merchants and represented, in the legislature's opinion, a threat to public order. Planters viewed artisans, hucksters, domestics, and urban people of color as a potentially destabilizing force and a dangerous example for rural field apprentices. The *Barbadian* likely reflected white elite opinion when

12. CO 28/117, No. 50, Smith to Glenelg, 26 July 1836.

13. CO 28/117, No. 24, Smith to Glenelg, 13 April 1836, enclosing Attorney General Henry Sharpe to Smith, 26 March 1836, re: "An Act to confer settlement or right of Paupers to dwell immoveably in some one particular parish of this island"; CO 30/22, No. 194, passed 6 March 1836.

14. See chapter 5, pp. 158, 164–165.

15. CO 30/22, No. 587, "An Act for amending and continuing in Force An Act entitled An Act for laying a Tax on Licenses to be granted for the retailing of Rum, Brandy, Gin and other Liquors . . . ," passed 15 December 1835.

the editor wrote enthusiastically about the emigration of skilled workers to Liberia and published advertisements requesting skilled tradespeople for British Guiana while supporting legislation restricting the emigration of field laborers.[16]

LABOR LEGISLATION AND RURAL UNREST

In order to convince laborers to remain on their estates, planters made improvements to the quality of housing and increased the amount of land estates allotted for homes, with each dwelling accompanied by a plot of usually less than a quarter of an acre. This apparent generosity, however, was tied to a decidedly coercive employment policy. The 1836 antiemigration act was merely the first of a slew of repressive pieces of legislation designed to enhance the ability of planters and the colonial state to control the movements of former slaves and limit their alternatives to estate labor once apprenticeship ended. Planter dominance was based on what came to be known variously as the wage-rent, located laborer, or tenantry system. The 1838 "Act to regulate the Hiring of Servants," the legislation that sanctioned this island-wide policy, was meant to be the centerpiece of postemancipation labor legislation.[17] Under this act, five days of continuous labor on one estate was deemed to constitute a binding contract for one year. Either side could break this "contract" with one month's notice, but workers on the estate had to work exclusively and continuously for the estate from which they rented their homes and land. Failure to do so was a breach of contract, and tenants faced heavy fines, possible eviction, or imprisonment, while employers faced nominal monetary fines.[18]

Planters' almost total control of the island's land, the legislature and the judiciary gave them enormous power to force people to rent from and work exclusively for them or run afoul of the law and face fines, imprisonment and destitution. The vagrancy act buttressed the power of the Masters and Servants Act by out-

16. *Barbadian*, 24 February 1834 and 10 August 1836.

17. CO 28/123, No. 165, MacGregor to Glenelg, 8 July 1838, enclosure No. 2, "An Act to regulate the Hiring of Servants, and for the more expeditious recovery of Wages by them." This law was also known as the "Masters and Servants Act."

18. CO 28/122, No. 220, MacGregor to Glenelg, 22 August 1838, enclosure No. 7, MacGregor to Commissioners of the Peace (Parry, Maxwell, and Garraway), 18 August 1838; Beckles, *History of Barbados*, 109; Bentley Gibbs, "The Establishment of the Tenantry System in Barbados" in Woodville Marshall, ed., *Emancipation II: Aspects of the Post-slavery Experience in Barbados* (Bridgetown: National Cultural Foundation and Department of History, UWI, Cave Hill, 1987), 27–33.

lawing any form of employment not licensed by the colonial state, and increasing the state's control over occupations that conferred too much freedom to "wander." Furthermore any man who deserted his wife and children could now face imprisonment, as did anyone who did not rent a house on an estate, lived in a house rented by someone else, gambled or played cards by a road, or carried a weapon. Estate constables were empowered to take anyone thought to be violating the provisions of the act before a magistrate. The "bastardy" act denied poor relief to any person who had not been resident in a parish for one year, another means of forcing laborers to abide by the Masters and Servants Act. Finally, the riot act gave police and magistrates the right to deem any gathering of more than twelve people a riot and made those who disobeyed orders to disperse subject to transportation or imprisonment, which effectively made all strikes or protests illegal.[19] After apprenticeship, local magistrates regained almost total jurisdiction over labor law, replacing the stipendiary magistrates of the apprenticeship period as the arbiters of labor disputes. Even though most of the stipendiary magistrates in Barbados had interpreted the law in ways favorable to the plantocracy, planters still considered them an annoyance. Only three former stipendiary magistrates remained in the island as the judges of the newly created court of appeal.[20]

This repressive legal apparatus contributed to an ideal climate for labor conflict and apprenticeship came to an end amid strikes, evictions, and violent confrontations between laborers on one side and estate authorities, estate constables, the police force, and magistrates on the other.[21] Between July and October 1838

19. See CO 28/123, No. 165, MacGregor to Glenelg, 8 July 1838, enclosure No. 4, "An Act to punish and suppress Vagrancy, and to determine who are Vagrants, Rogues, and Vagabonds, and incorrigible Rogues and Vagabonds"; CO 28/123, No. 165, MacGregor to Glenelg, July 8 1838, enclosure No. 5, "An Act for the government and better ordering of the Poor in this Island, and the prevention of Bastardy," and No. 6, "An act for preventing Tumult and Riotous Assemblies, and for the more speedy and effectual punishing of the Rioters." Although these laws stirred controversy in Britain, they closely resembled metropolitan laws against vagrancy and squatting. Blackburn, *Overthrow of Colonial Slavery*, 461.

20. CO 28/122, No. 220, MacGregor to Glenelg, 22 August 1838, enclosure No. 2, Police Magistrate James Henry Went to MacGregor, 16 August 1838.

21. Jean Besson, "Freedom and Community: The British West Indies," in McGlynn and Drescher, *The Meaning of Freedom*, 184–187; Gad Heuman, "Riots and Resistance in the Caribbean at the Moment of Full Freedom in the Anglophone Caribbean," *Slavery and Abolition* 21, no. 2 (August 2000): 135–149; Woodville Marshall, "'We Be Wise to Many More Tings': Blacks' Hopes and Expectations of Emancipation," in Beckles and Shepherd, eds., *Caribbean Freedom*, 12–20; Michel-Rolph Trouillot, "Labour

newspapers in Barbados carried reports of strikes and evictions throughout the island. Laborers refused to accept a system that forced all members of a family and residents of a house to work permanently for the estate where they resided. They wanted to combine the minimum amount of labor required to retain their homes on estates with other types of more lucrative and autonomous economic activity. Laborers wanted access to land on which to grow marketable provisions. Many also wished to send their children to school, or train them in more profitable and respected types of work.[22] Furthermore, they wanted the right to seek work on the open market, and to sell their labor to the highest bidder. Planters thought this was all most unreasonable, particularly since laborers' homes and land belonged to the estates.

In the unsettled circumstances of the early postapprenticeship period, laborers were able to take advantage of differences in wages from one estate to another. Planters attempted to coerce estate laborers to accept salaries of two bits a day, but in many instances, their efforts only resulted in the loss of part of their labor force. At Maxwell plantation in Christ Church, where the owner had freed his apprentices in June and started paying them three bits a day, he announced in August that he would reduce their pay to two bits. He informed them that if they did not agree they could leave, which "most of the young men that had no connection on the estate" promptly did.[23] Some of the smaller estates lost entire gangs of laborers and were forced to offer higher wages.[24] Magistrates interpreted the Masters and Servants Act as strictly as possible in order to prevent laborers from leaving their employers to search for work on the open market. For example, in August a mason from one estate was fined more than twenty pounds for telling two women whom he met on a road, and who had left another plantation, that there was work available on his.[25]

The Colonial Office disallowed the 1838 Masters and Servants Act and va-

---

and Emancipation in Dominica: Contribution to a Debate," *Caribbean Quarterly* 30, nos. 3–4 (1984): 73–84.

22. See, for example, *Barbadian,* 15 August and 26 September 1838; Marshall, "Rock Hall," 23–24.

23. *Liberal,* 19 August 1838. Two bits was the equivalent of a quarter of a dollar. The Spanish silver dollar was the principle form of currency used throughout much of the anglophone Caribbean at the time of emancipation.

24. Letter from "A Justice of the Peace," *Barbadian,* 15 August 1838.

25. *Liberal,* 25 August 1838.

grancy act, which eased tensions to some degree and temporarily created greater space for negotiation between workers and employers.[26] But in 1840 the legislature passed new versions of both acts that were little different from their predecessors. In the wake of the 1839 Jamaican constitutional crisis, which brought down the Whig government in Britain, imperial officials were far less committed to supporting former slaves against the West Indian plantocracy, and the new laws received royal assent. The 1840 Masters and Servants Act came to be known as the Contract Act, and as with that of 1838, located laborers could be sentenced to jail for breach of contract, although the sentences were reduced. Contracts between laborers and employers could not generally be for a period of longer than one month—but located laborers who refused to sign them were subject to immediate eviction and employers had the power to decide what happened to the crops the laborers had planted. Laborers who quit the estate lost all rights to their crops. Additionally, anyone found guilty of "enticing" a laborer away from his/her previous employer could be fined ten pounds.[27] Based as it still was on the principle that occupancy of a house was contingent on full-time labor on an estate, the act sparked widespread strikes and acts of sabotage. According to the *Barbadian*, ninety estates had lost their entire labor forces by the beginning of February 1840 and there were twenty-seven cane fires in January.[28]

THE IMPACT OF RURAL RESISTANCE ON NONAGRICULTURAL WORKERS

In response to the efforts of the legislature, magistrates and estate authorities to prevent laborers from "wandering," former slaves drew on the experience of slavery to circumvent the provisions of postemancipation labor legislation, using family and community relations to help them evade contracts. Like maroons during slavery, many people secretly lived with relatives and friends in estate villages, and worked illegally as hucksters or in other forms of itinerant labor. Others, unknown to estate authorities, slept in their houses on estates and worked elsewhere

26. Gibbs, "Establishment of the Tenantry System," 37; Levy, *Emancipation, Sugar, and Federalism*, 101; Governor's circular to the magistrates, 30 October 1839.

27. CO 28/133, No. 6, MacGregor to Russell, 23 January 1840; Gibbs, "Establishment of the Tenantry System," 34–35.

28. *Barbadian*, 18 January 1840; *Liberal*, 8 February 1840; Gibbs, "Establishment of the Tenantry System," 38.

during the day.[29] As soon as the Contract Act was passed in 1840, magistrates' reports alluded to the appearance of independent itinerant field labor gangs, composed mainly of young men, who roamed the countryside selling their labor on different estates each day, working on a task-work basis for a higher rate of pay than resident first gang laborers. In 1840 the St. John magistrate argued that a "system of independent jobbing is rapidly growing out of the present state of things, and, by these independent gangs, a great portion of the most laborious work is performed."[30]

Repressive labor conditions in rural areas also encouraged further rural-urban migration, another tendency authorities had intended to prevent. Once they reached the towns, migrants disappeared among the masses of other people of color already there. In 1840 the magistrate for St. Peter, where Speightstown was located, recommended further legislation regulating occupations connected with the island's ports because "at this time, those who perform these occupations are frequently found to belong to that class of agricultural laborers who had quitted the country . . . and their connexion with the country, added to the fact of their being unknown in the town, render their detection and apprehension difficult."[31] Speightstown's city limits were eventually extended because of "the vastly increased habitations and streets annexed thereto which are not included in the local rates of the said Town."[32]

Although there were undoubtedly numerous women who left field labor for the towns, most were men, and in 1838 the *Barbadian* complained about the "great number of able-bodied young men from the country [who] are now thronging the town, and foolishly offered themselves, without procuring any characters, as grooms, coachmen, cooks, &c. Grooming horses is the occupation which these chaps chiefly desire." The editor mentioned the case of one young man who applied for a job as a coachman, but confessed when questioned that he had in fact been a pig-driver. The newspaper bemoaned the fact that "[e]very day brings a fresh accession of these skulkers from the country to town" and that the vagrancy

29. *Barbadian*, August 15 1838; PP 1840, vol. 35, pt. 2, No. 19, "Second Series of Questions . . . [and] Answers relative to the working of the Free System in Barbados," reply from St. Lucy, Question 17, 160.

30. PP 1842, vol. 29, "General reports for 1840," St. John, 127–133.

31. PP 1840, vol. 35, pt. 2, No. 19, "Second Series of Questions . . . [and] Answers relative to the working of the Free System in Barbados," reply of the magistrate for St. Peter, 36th question, 154.

32. CO 30/23, No. 794, "An Act to extend the limits of the Town called Speights Town, in the Parish of St. Peter," passed 14 February 1843.

act, which was supposed to have prevented this phenomenon, "seems to be already a dead letter."[33]

As had been the case during apprenticeship, laws passed to curb migrants' access to alternative occupations negatively affected the livelihood of those already employed in various kinds of skilled and independent urban labor. In 1842 St. Michael Vestry extended the scope of the 1835 Bridgetown bylaws to discourage rural-urban migration. The new ordinances instructed Bridgetown magistrates to report annually on the number of licenses issued to porters, boatmen, and carters and revoke the licenses of any person convicted of theft. They made it illegal for anyone to "manufacture or fire any cask or Casks in any of the Streets, lanes, or alleys of the said Town," which suggests that rural migrants were setting themselves up as artisans in the streets, competing with the businesses of established urban tradesmen. The amendments also authorized magistrates to confiscate sheep, hogs or butchers' meat brought from the country to the town, until they were certain that the alleged owners had "come by them honestly," suggesting an increase in huckster traffic from the countryside. This provision was aimed at laborers who stole livestock from their plantations and took it to the urban markets.[34] The following year the ordinances were extended to Speightstown and Holetown.[35]

AFRO-BARBADIANS AND EMIGRATION

For the increasing number of disaffected laborers, urban paupers, hucksters, domestics, and skilled tradespeople, emigrating to another Caribbean island was one more step in a series of mobile strategies for escaping the net of labor repression in postemancipation Barbados.[36] Barbadians, including skilled slaves, had a history of emigration to neighboring colonies, and there was a constant traffic back and forth between the countries of the Windward Caribbean. Despite the absence of emigration agents for St. Lucia or Dominica in Barbados, Barbadian domestics and artisans regularly went to work there for short periods and then returned to

33. *Barbadian*, 15 August 1838.

34. Minutes of the St. Michael Vestry, 17 October 1842. For a discussion of state regulation of the activities of people of colour in urban areas see Pedro Welch, "Notes from the Underground: Postemancipation Adjustments in Bridgetown, Barbados," unpublished seminar paper, UWI Cave Hill, c. 1994.

35. CO 31/53, 12 January 1843.

36. PP 1846, vol. 28, *Papers . . . Relating to the Labouring Population of the British Colonies*, Sir Charles Grey to Lord Stanley, 4 September 1845, enclosing "Statistical Summary for the Parish of St. John."

Barbados.[37] Many Barbadians also had relatives in British Guiana and Trinidad. In 1839 the agent employed by planters in Demerara to recruit Barbadian laborers for that colony observed that "a very large proportion of the Mechanics, Hucksters, and Domestics [in Demerara], are natives of [Barbados]" who communicated frequently with their relatives back in Barbados "by letters, by presents, and by visits." The existence of such family connections continually drew people to these territories in search of work opportunities such as those their kin had found.[38]

While the greatest demand in Trinidad and Guiana was for agricultural labor, both planters and the legislatures in these two territories advertised in Barbados for everyone from agricultural laborers to headmen, policemen, and tradesmen.[39] Although many Barbadians went to British Guiana and Trinidad to work on plantations, many also went hoping to find nonagricultural work, particularly in the towns. Thus while Guianese and Trinidadian planters did succeed in obtaining estate workers from Barbados, they often found that the Barbadians who arrived were seeking what they could not find back at home: skilled jobs in towns, not estate work. Much of the emigration between Barbados and its southern neighbors was merely a redistribution of some the urban population of one territory to others. In 1840 the St. Peter magistrate commented that the "idlers and the petty thieves who exist in the towns and their neighbourhood . . . would not be readily induced to undertake the toil of agricultural labor in the colonies of Demerara and Berbice; with such persons, therefore, the emigration crimps have not reaped a harvest for themselves by their artful practices, that have too fatally succeeded with the deluded agricultural population."[40] The same magistrate mentioned that many of those who had left the island from St. Peter were fishermen, porters, and hucksters. These were occupations in which free blacks and coloreds had been concentrated, and it is likely that free people of color, as well as skilled former slaves, were among these "idlers and petty thieves."[41]

37. PP 1842, vol. 29, *Papers Relative to the West Indies*, "Quarterly Reports," 1 October–31 December 1840, No. 12; Barbados government, *Report on the Commission for Poor Relief* (Bridgetown, 1877), 31–32.

38. *Liberal*, 9 October 1839. Approximately twenty-eight thousand Barbadians emigrated to British Guiana from Barbados between 1838 and 1918. Klein, *African Slavery*, 137.

39. See advertisements in the *Liberal*, 14 July 1838, 22 August, 22 September, 10 and 31 October 1838.

40. PP 1842, vol. 29, *Papers Relative to the West Indies*, "Quarterly reply from the Police Magistracy . . ." 1 October–31 December 1840, No. 6, St. Peter.

41. PP 1842, vol. 29, *Papers Relative to the West Indies*, "Quarterly reply from the Police Magistracy . . . ," 1 April–30 June 1840, No. 6, St. Peter.

In fact, the few extant records listing the occupations of those whose applications for emigration were granted show that most were artisans or domestics. It should be noted, however, that this gives no indication of how many actually applied.[42] In 1841 Prescod, who was acting as the emigration agent for Trinidad, published a notice stating that he had received too many requests to emigrate from tradesmen and domestics. He informed the public that only those accustomed to doing fieldwork on an estate, or those willing do this if other employment was unavailable, should apply.[43]

One historian has claimed that Barbadian workers showed no "enthusiasm" for emigration, despite their difficult circumstances, as they were too "attached to their country, proud of their British heritage, and scornful of other places in the West Indies."[44] On the contrary, laborers displayed little evidence of a reluctance to leave Barbados and work abroad. In fact, they were using the threat of emigration as a bargaining tool in labor disputes, according to one rural magistrate, who noted that "if the Labourers on the Estates are not allowed to work when they please, where they please, and as little as they please for a full day's pay, they openly threaten those who rebuke them, that they will go to Demerara."[45] A letter writer in the *Liberal* estimated that by 1840, more than two thousand laborers had gone to Demerara, listing several plantations that had lost nearly their entire labor force through emigration.[46]

Magistrates suspected that illegal emigration was continual during the 1840s. In 1842 the St. Andrew magistrate reported his suspicion that many migrants "have been clandestinely conveyed away without any reference to me."[47] The magistrate for rural St. Michael shared these concerns. He had signed 115 applications

---

42. Minutes of the St. John Vestry, copies of six emigration certificates dated 3 May 1838–19 February 1840, four of them "artificiers" and two "labourers," all male; 20 February–29 February 1840, seven certificates grants to five men and two women. Men listed as "artificiers" and "labourers," but no breakdown of this number, women's occupations not given; CO 28/128, No. 111, MacGregor to Russell, 26 October 1839, enclosure No. 15, "Return of Emigrants from the Island of Barbados for British Guiana, between the 4th of September and 25th of October, 1839," from Francis Sheridan, Colonial Secretary, 25 October 1839: two women, a domestic and a washerwoman, three male domestics and artisans, two male field laborers.

43. *Liberal*, 3 February 1841.

44. Levy, *Emancipation, Sugar, and Federalism*, 101.

45. CO 28/134, No. 103, MacGregor to Russell, 11 November 1840, with enclosures from the Assistant Court of Appeal and the police magistrates, St. Andrew, 30 June 1840.

46. *Liberal*, 29 July 1840.

47. PP 1842, vol. 29, *Papers Relative to the West Indies*, "Quarterly Reports," 1 July–30 September 1840, No. 10, St. Andrew.

for emigration between April and June 1840 but suspected illegal emigration was continuing "to an alarming extent." He recommended that all ships carrying migrants be checked for stowaways, because "almost every vessell that leaves with 'emigrants,' carries away a considerable number without tickets."[48] The harbor master of the Bridgetown port admitted that the ships carrying emigrants were so crowded that it would be easy for people without tickets to slip on board.[49]

The number of emigrants to the tiny island of Tobago during the 1840s was significant enough to draw attention. At the opening of the court of grand sessions in 1849, the Tobago chief justice attributed the increasing restlessness among estate laborers to "the introduction of *barbadian* Immigrants," claiming that there had been an "influx of worthless people from Barbados, who have completely changed the character of the Tobago peasantry."[50] Emigrants often conceived of their journey as a seasonal migration, and part of the attraction of emigration agents' offers was the promise of a paid return passage in a few months, but it was estimated in 1842 that about 90 percent of the three to four thousand who had left since 1838 had not returned.[51]

Many of those who left seeking nonagricultural work were destined to be disappointed. In 1840, the *Liberal* published a letter sent by a woman in Demerara to her Barbadian nephew. The woman told him that Barbadians who went to Guiana did well if they could find work in the towns, but could not adjust to the arduous labor demanded on British Guianese plantations. She claimed that many who could find no work in Georgetown were seen "crying in the streets."[52] The following year, the *Barbadian* expressed its surprise that

48. PP 1842, vol. 29, *Papers Relative to the West Indies*, "Quarterly Reports," 1 April–30 June 1840, No. 11, St. Michael rural.

49. CO 28/133, No. 26, MacGregor to Russell, 21 March 1840, enclosing J. J. Evelyn, Harbour Master, to Garraway, Governor's Private Secretary, 16 March 1840.

50. *Barbadian*, 20 October 1849.

51. Governor's circular to magistrates, 24 February 1840; *Liberal*, 18 April and 17 June 1840; PP 1842, vol. 13, *Report from the Select Committee*, 148; PP 1842, vol. 29, *Papers Relative to the West Indies*, "Questions [and Answers] for Quarterly Reply from the Police Magistrates of the Island of Barbados," 1 April–30 June 1840, 96–97; Levy, *Emancipation, Sugar, and Federalism*, 81–83 and 102; Bruce M. Taylor, *Black Labor and White Power in Post-Emancipation Barbados: A Study of Changing Relationships* (New York: Current Bibliography on African Affairs, 1973), 185–187. Trevor Marshall estimates that between 1834 and 1850, five to eight thousand left the island. Trevor Marshall, "Post-emancipation Adjustments in Barbados, 1838–1876," in Alvin O. Thompson, ed., *Emancipation I: A Series of Lectures to Commemorate the 150th Anniversary of Emancipation* (Barbados: National Cultural Foundation and the History Department, UWI, Cave Hill, 1984), 97.

52. *Liberal*, 14 March 1840.

our negroes still emigrate to British Guiana, though information reaches this island by every opportunity of great numbers of those who have gone before them, wandering about the streets of Georgetown, without employment. . . . [T]he Demerara Editors of papers, out of sheer spite to us, are continually boasting over us that our labourers are pouring into the colony.[53]

In 1839 the legislature passed two harsh antiemigration laws in order to strengthen the 1836 legislation. The first act prevented the "clandestine deportation" of anyone under sixteen years of age, as well as those under twenty-one who were apprenticed to a trade. This latter provision was intended to stop the emigration of young men who claimed to be skilled tradesmen, but who were, in fact, former field laborers. It also increased the penalties for those convicted of acting as emigration "crimps." The second act stipulated that anyone seeking to emigrate had to prove that they would leave no elderly, young, and infirm family members behind them (the 1836 act had outlawed emigration only for those with dependents under fourteen years of age). As with the 1836 act, any applicants for emigration had to obtain permission from the parish churchwarden and a magistrate.[54] These acts made it difficult for anyone, including skilled preemancipation free people of color, paupers, and skilled former slaves, to emigrate legally.[55] By the mid-1840s magistrates were receiving very few applications for emigration, and while illegal emigration was still a concern, the authorities were no longer worried that it would lead to a decrease in the size of the labor force.[56]

EMIGRATION AND AFRO-BARBADIAN POLITICS

The issue of emigration turned out to be the nemesis of the racial solidarity movement. The right of former slaves to dispose of their labor wherever they pleased, even if this were to the detriment of the local sugar industry, irrevocably divided

53. *Barbadian,* 4 September 1841.

54. CO 30/22, No. 597, 19 July 1836, "An Act to regulate the emigration of labourers from this Island; CO 30/22, No. 706, 19 December 1839, "An Act entitled an Act to amend an Act to regulate the emigration of labourers from this island"; CO 30/22, No. 696, 16 April 1839, "An Act to prevent the clandestine deportation of young persons from this island."

55. Welch, "Notes from the Underground," 19–20.

56. Anon., *The Sugar Question: Being a digest of the evidence taken before the committee on sugar and coffee plantations* (London: Smith, Elder, 1848), 6.

Afro-Barbadian civil rights campaigners. From 1838 to the early 1840s, while some people of color free before 1834 defied the antiemigration legislation and supported the rights of former slaves to freedom of movement, others sided with the plantocracy and its efforts to maintain firm control over rural labor.

The support of the *Liberal* and the *New Times* for contract labor emigration grew out of their principled opposition to postemancipation labor laws. Both objected to the Masters and Servants Act, described by *New Times* editor Nathaniel Roach in 1838 as an "EXECRABLE LAW."[57] In the first months of emancipation, both newspapers offered advice to would-be emigrants in their offices.[58] Prescod opposed any attempt to regulate the labor market, and although he had reservations about labor migration schemes, he argued that former slaves had the right to migrate if they wished. He blamed employers' repressive policies for rural unrest and laborers' growing desire to emigrate and promoted emigration as the only way to stop planters' interference with the free movement of labor.[59] The Afro-Barbadian press became the platform for political opponents of the rural labor regime. For example, in March 1839 a correspondent calling himself "A Labouring Man" addressed a letter to rural laborers, advising them, "Whatever you attempt . . . let it be *together. Move in a body,* and move in a body *out of this country,* if you can."[60]

However, in late 1838, Nathaniel Roach was made magistrate of the northern country parish of St. Lucy, where there were many large plantations. On taking office, he reversed his earlier opposition to the contract and emigration laws. The *Barbadian* mocked Roach's "utter astonishment, wonder, and what not, at the disgraceful conduct of the negroes in that district [St. Lucy]" and blamed both Roach's newspaper and the *Liberal* for "sowing the seeds of discontent" among their rural "brethren of African descent."[61] The *Barbadian* also suggested that the journalists at the *New Times* and the *Liberal* were driven by political ambition because the editors were excluded from public office. In a editorial on Prescod's 1840 Colonial Coloured Union, part of whose mandate was to challenge the labor legislation being passed throughout the British Caribbean, the editor wrote, "Roach's foul mouth was stopped, and his mischief-making pen arrested by his appointment to

57. *Barbadian,* 8 May 1839.
58. *Barbadian,* 22 September 1838.
59. *Liberal,* 15 July 1840.
60. *Liberal,* 6 March 1839.
61. *Barbadian,* 8 May 1839.

the office of Police Magistrate—but Prescod, disappointed in his ambitious views, has taken good care to fan the dying embers of political discontent."[62]

The few men of color elected or appointed to office certainly tended to distance themselves from demands for political reform and racial desegregation once they got into office. For example, in October 1838 St. Michael vestryman Thomas J. Cummins, then still the only man of color in an elected office, apparently voted in favor of a motion that would have had the effect of excluding Afro-Barbadians from a new public lunatic asylum being contemplated by the vestry. Cummins's vote provoked an angry response. A correspondent to the *Liberal* pointed out that Cummins's decision was inconsistent, "especially when he or any relation of his would be debarred from this whited sepulchre."[63] Shortly afterward, Cummins admitted that his vestry votes were influenced by careerist considerations. At a franchise extension meeting organized by Prescod and Harris in January 1839, Cummins was asked to explain to the audience why he had adopted the majority position of the St. Michael Vestry board during that's year's vestry elections and supported a conservative white candidate over Thomas Harris. "I am aware that my tenure is by permission of the Vestry, and that were I to incur their displeasure by opposing any of their views they might prevent my reelection," Cummins stated. He added that he supported franchise extension as his best hope of "retaining my seat in the Vestry in opposition to the caprice of the old members."[64]

At that meeting, Prescod publicly accused Roach of having been "bought" by the plantocracy with his appointment to the magistracy. The meeting was called to elect a committee to lobby the legislature and the imperial government to lower the franchise requirement, and although Cummins was elected, Roach, who held an equally prestigious political post as magistrate and had stronger credentials as a civil rights reformer, was not even invited to attend.[65] In August Prescod wrote a letter to the *British Emancipator* accusing the governor and Roach of having conspired to undermine the Afro-Barbadian press. He repeated his claim that MacGregor had bribed Roach with his appointment in exchange for Roach agreeing to end his association with the *New Times*, an accusation Roach denied.[66]

The split between Prescod, Harris, and Roach further factionalized Afro-

62. Quote from *Barbadian*, 29 July 1840; Levy, *Emancipation, Sugar, and Federalism*, 83–84.
63. *Liberal*, 31 October 1838.
64. *Liberal*, 23 January 1839.
65. *Liberal*, 23 and 26 January 1839.
66. *Liberal*, 7 and 21 August 1839.

Barbadian oppositional politics. At the January meeting, speeches by Prescod's supporters were interrupted by supporters of Roach, who saw Roach's exclusion from the committee as an insult. By 1839 Prescod's editorship of the *Liberal*, and his aggressive stand on the issue of rural labor relations, had made him simultaneously the most controversial and most popular public figure in the island. Many elite franchise reformers feared that Prescod's methods, and his popularity among the urban poor and rural laborers, would damage the credibility of the franchise reform movement. At the meeting, one of his supporters felt compelled to publicly dismiss claims that Prescod "had not the support of the respectable colored community" and that "it was only the lower orders, the rabble, who viewed his conduct with approbation."[67]

Despite the tensions that surfaced at the meeting, twenty-four men of color who attended were elected to an Elective Franchise Committee, with a mandate to petition the legislature and the governor for franchise reform. The committee represented what was to be a short-lived truce between Prescod's faction, who wanted a significant lowering of the franchise requirement, and conservative and wealthier Afro-Barbadian men who would benefit from a more limited reform. In February 1839 the committee sent a petition to the legislature and the governor requesting extension of the suffrage, but without specifying what that new requirement should be.[68]

DIVIDE AND RULE

The emigration issue irreconcilably divided the different political factions among free people of color between 1839 and 1840. The catalyst for the crisis came in September 1839, when a new agent for British Guiana, Thomas Day, arrived in Barbados. Day was unlike previous agents, who had conducted their operations discreetly. According to the governor, upon his arrival, Day made it known that he

67. *Liberal*, 23 January 1839.

68. There were twenty-five men elected in total. B. F. B. Goodridge, who was white, was one of Prescod's supporters. Of the men elected, Anthony Barclay, John Reed, William F. Lynch, Henry Hawkesworth, and William F. Thomas supported Prescod. See CO 28/129, No. 26, MacGregor to Russell, 18 March 1841, enclosure No. 5, magistrates Tinling, Sealy, and Cummins. The other men elected were London Bourne, Valentine Wilkins, Joseph Kennedy, Joseph Hamilton, Andrew Fillan, William Seon, Edmund C. Haynes, William S. Wilkey, Thomas J. Cummins, Samuel J. Collymore, Robert H. Ashby, Benjamin Massiah, Benjamin Norville, William Thomas, Joseph Thorne, James F. Reed, George R. Sealy, William H. Austin, and Prescod. *Liberal*, 26 January 1839.

had a "higher motive" for being an agent, namely, "to raise the wages of Labor in Barbados which he considered himself in condition to prove too low."[69] Whether or not Day's political claims were genuine, his statements endeared him to the editors of the *Liberal* and earned him the wrath of the governor, legislature, and planters. Day quickly set to work discrediting the Barbados antiemigration acts, sending petitions to the Colonial Office outlining their injustice and unconstitutionality.[70] In articles, editorials, and advertisements, Day and the *Liberal* conducted a vigorous emigration campaign. In 1840 Thomas Harris even took a trip to British Guiana, paid for by several British Guianese planters, in order to refute claims that the working conditions there were poor.[71]

Within a month of Day's arrival, the governor anxiously requested that the island's magistrates locate his "co-adjutors" and "emissaries," who were "seducing" laborers from their districts to go to British Guiana.[72] The governor took action to counteract the threat from Day and the *Liberal,* nominating Joseph Thorne, the former slave and Anglican lay catechist, to the newly created position of assistant harbor master. Thorne's task was to spot agricultural laborers who came to the harbor with emigration certificates, and to convince them to remain. Although there are no recorded statements of Thorne's views on emigration prior to his appointment, MacGregor was apparently aware of his opposition to indentured emigration. The governor, who disapproved of appointing men on the basis of color, clearly felt that the labor crisis was a special circumstance, describing Thorne to the Colonial Office as "a very worthy Member of the Colored Body,—deservedly possessing the confidence of the Agricultural Laborers."[73]

Thorne, who seems never to have left Barbados in his life, opposed emigration on the grounds that the climate of British Guiana was dangerous for Barbadians and the emigration of laborers from Barbados would affect the island's prosperity.[74] When he learned that the imperial government had disallowed a recent British Guiana emigration act, Thorne approved the decision, stating that "it

69. Governor's correspondence with magistrates, 2 September 1839; CO 28/128, No. 95, MacGregor to Normanby, 19 September 1839.

70. CO 28/128, No. 102, MacGregor to Normanby, 9 October 1839, enclosure No. 7, Memorial of Thomas Day, 19 September 1839.

71. *Liberal,* 18 April 1840; *Barbadian,* 2 May 1840.

72. Governor's circulars to magistrates, No. 20, 20 September 1839.

73. CO 28/128, No. 95, MacGregor to Normanby, 19 September 1839.

74. CO 28/133, No. 26, MacGregor to Russell, 21 March 1840, enclosure D, Joseph Thorne to Joseph Garraway, 21 March 1840.

would be highly prejudicial to the Laborer, as the Proprietor, had [Day] succeeded in drawing the Laborers away from a healthy to an unhealthy Colony. . . . I shall not cease to advise all whom I may hear of, to remain in their native Country, as, in my Opinion, we can find ample employment for them all."[75] The *Liberal* and Day accused Thorne and other government officials of coercing would-be emigrants into remaining in the island. Day charged Thorne with lying to laborers who came to the port, telling them, for example, that slavery still existed in British Guiana. Both he and Prescod produced statements from laborers accusing Thorne and the magistrates of colluding against laborers who applied for emigration certificates.[76] Thorne, like the *Liberal* editors, believed he was acting in the laborers' interests. He freely admitted that he advised all potential emigrants not to go to British Guiana as contract workers, and, in the following statement, invoked abolitionism to justify his behavior:

> I have advised them not to go, and will continue to do so whether they hear or whether they forbear. And in so doing, I am borne out by one of the best friends that the negro race ever had, namely, Mr. [John] Scoble; and upon the authority of that gentleman, and many others who have resided there, and have seen the labour to be performed in that Colony, and what is to be done here, also from what I have seen written in the *Liberal* from time to time, I feel justified as a man of colour to give them advice which I have done and will continue to do.[77]

In March 1840 the legislature moved to close off the loopholes in previous anti-emigration acts in order to make it more difficult for emigration agents to operate, or for plantation workers passing themselves off as domestics and artisans to leave the island. The more important of the two acts made it illegal to grant emigration

75. CO 28/128, No. 95, MacGregor to Normanby, 19 September 1839, enclosure No. 17, Thorne to Garraway, 24 September 1839.

76. *Liberal*, 12 October 1839; CO 28/129, No. 131, MacGregor to Russell, 20 December 1839, enclosure No. 1, Meeting of the Court of Error, 3 December 1839.

77. *Liberal*, 16 October 1839. Thorne either misunderstood or deliberately misrepresented Scoble's views on migrant labour. Scoble actually supported labour migration from Barbados as a population control measure. He stated two years later than Barbados could spare five to eight thousand labourers for emigration. PP 1842, vol. 13, *Report from the Select Committee*, 10 June 1842, Question 4299. On Scoble's opposition to the use of indentured laborers from India in the Caribbean, see Kale, *Fragments of Empire*, 32–35.

certificates to an individual if any member of her/his family was known to object, and anyone who "encouraged" another person to emigrate was liable to prosecution and to a fine of ten pounds for every person she or he encouraged to leave. Furthermore, all emigration agents had to be sanctioned by the Barbadian government, a rather unlikely prospect. The second act more clearly defined and expanded the authority of the assistant harbor master, and increased the governor's power to issue emergency decrees to prevent emigration.[78] In early April an Afro-Barbadian Bridgetown shopkeeper was convicted under the act of being an emigration agent, simply for saying to a pauper whom she passed on the street that he would be better off in "Demerary."[79] A St. Philip man of color was even fined fifty pounds for renting his cart to laborers who used it to travel to Bridgetown in order to board a ship for Demerara.[80] Day and another Guiana agent who had an office in Speightstown were prosecuted and heavily fined.[81] The second act allowed the government to impose a smallpox quarantine on British Guiana. In 1842 the British Guianese government was still protesting against the quarantine restrictions, saying that, without it, laborers from Barbados would have been flocking to their shores.[82]

The *Liberal* immediately dubbed the first of the two acts the Gagging Act (act. no. 720), because it made it illegal even to voice a positive opinion about emigration. The act did nothing to improve relations between the editors and Thomas Cummins, by now a member of council and the magistrate for St. George, in which capacity he did his best to discredit the supporters of emigration. Cummins reported that laborers would be less restive if they were "left to themselves, and not interfered with by those interested and self-constituted emigration agents and their emissaries, who now infest our land."[83] The *Liberal* retorted that, as a man of

78. CO 28/133, No. 26, MacGregor to Russell, 21 March 1840, enclosing "An Act to amend . . . an act to prevent the clandestine deportation of young Persons from this Island, and to protect the Laborers in this Island from . . . Emigration agents" and "An Act to empower the Governor . . . to make such regulations as he shall deem expedient . . . and to appoint an Assistant Harbour Master to see such regulations carried into effect. . . ."

79. *Liberal*, 1 April 1840 and CO 28/139, No. 25, MacGregor to Russell, 17 March 1841.

80. *Liberal*, 18 April 1840. The Court of Appeal reduced the fine to twenty-five pounds.

81. CO 28/134, No. 35, MacGregor to Russell, 9 April 1840, enclosure B, police magistrate of St. Philip to Garraway, 3 April 1840.

82. *Barbadian*, 2 February 1842.

83. PP 1842, vol. 29, *Papers Relative to the West Indies*, "Quarterly Reply . . . ," 1 January–31 March 1840, No. 3, St. George.

color, Cummins should have resigned from the council in protest at the passage of the act.[84]

Afro-Barbadian public opinion was so divided over act no. 720 that in 1840, a *Liberal* correspondent writing under the pseudonym "Ignatius Sancho," a good indication that he was a man of color, pleaded with people of color to forget their differences and unite.[85] On March 23 the Barbados Auxiliary Anti-Slavery Society met to draw up a resolution regarding the act. The society's membership was largely Afro-Barbadian, with a committee of twelve men of color, but Solicitor General Clarke and one or two white clergymen and planters were also members.[86] At the meeting Clarke introduced motions to adopt the British Anti-Slavery Society's condemnation of indentured emigration and a motion stating that "this meeting deems emigration inimical to the true interests of the labouring population of Barbados." With the exception of Prescod, the committee—among them, inexplicably, Harris—voted in favor. However, seven members of the committee, including Prescod and Harris, issued a counterstatement, saying that they owed it to themselves and "to their laboring brethren, and to the Country" to condemn the 1840 act as it would only worsen social relations in the island. After the meeting the *Liberal* distributed handbills in Bridgetown condemning the act, on behalf of the society.[87]

It is likely that most working-class Afro-Barbadians agreed with Prescod's stance and that the members of the Barbados Anti-Slavery Society who sided with the solicitor general did not really reflect popular sentiment. Nevertheless, the division in the Anti-Slavery Society had lasting and damaging consequences for the forces of desegregation and popular politics in the island. In the aftermath of the society's meeting, MacGregor blamed preemancipation free people of color for their continuing political marginalization and dismissed them as an insignificant political force. In a somewhat smug tone, he informed the secretary of state that

84. *Liberal,* 18 April 1840.

85. *Liberal,* 7 March 1840.

86. *Barbadian,* 28 March 1840. The committee consisted of Samuel Prescod, Thomas Harris, Edmund C. Haynes, S. B. Arthur, Henry Pinheiro, Edward W. Archer, Henry Hawkesworth, W. R. Haynes, Joseph Kennedy, London Bourne, Samuel J. Prescod, Joseph Hamilton, and Anthony Barclay. Also present were an Anglican clergyman and a planter named Wiltshire Stanton Austin, who chaired the meeting, and Solicitor General R. B. Clarke.

87. CO 28/134, No. 35, MacGregor to Russell, 9 April 1840. Joseph Thorne, London Bourne, and Joseph Kennedy voted against the counterstatement; Pinheiro and Arthur abstained.

although no impediment, even when emanating from the Coloured Body themselves,—as in the Case of the Auxiliary Anti-Slavery Society—will alter or induce me to discontinue my steady, although quiet exertions in contributing towards their further elevation, I much fear that the political partizanship [sic], in which they have imprudently allowed themselves to be involved, may retard that amicable intercourse with their White Brethren which has of late been gradually gaining ground.[88]

The governor and other emigration opponents took the opportunity presented by the internal rift to characterize Prescod publicly as a hypocrite. The disagreement was a minor victory for Afro-Barbadian elites who opposed both Prescod and labor emigration. In his correspondence with the secretary of state, MacGregor referred to the "perverse inconsistency" of Prescod's behavior and asserted that his conduct had led to uneasiness among other people of colour such as "the universally respected Joseph Thorne."[89] Thorne himself supported this statement, and in December 1841 he wrote:

The ascendancy acquired over the minds of the people was both great and general, and I regret to say that the press, advocating the case of Mr. Day by false representations, has contributed greatly towards inducing many to leave the island. And I cannot help adding that the editor of the *Liberal* stated publicly that he did so because he thought the emigration law restrictive, although he had previously declared that the emigration system was the worst thing that could happen to the labourer of this island, and he believed that three out of every four would die; this he stated openly at a public meeting.[90]

In 1840 Thorne, who had been elected in 1839 to Prescod's Elective Franchise Committee, switched sides, and campaigned for Solicitor General Clarke in the latter's bid to be returned as the representative for St. Michael parish, once

88. CO 28/134, No. 35, MacGregor to Russell, 9 April 1840.

89. Ibid.

90. PP 1842, vol. 29, *Papers Relative to the West Indies*, "General Reports for 1840," Thorne to Felix Bedingfeld, Governor's Private Secretary, 11 December 1841, 131–132. I found no other reference to this alleged statement by Prescod.

Bridgetown merchants had collectively endorsed Clarke as their candidate.[91] During the 1840 elections Thorne's support for Clarke provoked a sarcastic comment from an anonymous writer, who hinted that Thorne's decision might earn him an appointment to the magistracy, where he might at last "reserve the exercise of his powerful and extensive influence, among the colored classes, for a more propitious cause."[92] Thorne's involvement in Clarke's campaign probably helped him in his later successful bid to become the second man of color elected to the St. Michael vestry board.

THE FAILURE OF FRANCHISE REFORM

The final blow for the forces of racial solidarity and progressivism came when the judiciary and the solicitor general colluded with a group of estate headmen and conservative elite men of color to shut down the *Liberal*. In late 1840, Frederick Watts, the magistrate for St. George, sued Prescod for libel after Prescod wrote a scathing comment accusing him of being a tool of the planters. Watts got a group of fifty-four estate headmen from the parish to sign their Xs to an address contradicting Prescod's claims and take it to the governor "on behalf" of all the laborers from St. George.[93] Prescod dismissed the delegation as consisting of "the favourite tools (superintendants and drivers) of the [planters]," who assisted employers in "oppressing the labourers."[94]

Prescod's libel trial was a major public event, which lasted from December 1840 to January 1841. During the trial some of the headmen confessed that they could not read and were not certain what they had signed. Others said they had signed because they felt they had no choice, or, in rare cases, denied having signed the address in the first place. Several, however, were fully aware of what they had signed, and one "under Manager" named Robert Jordon[95] admitted that he had not

91. *Barbadian*, 3 June 1840.

92. *Liberal*, 3 June 1840.

93. *Liberal*, 16 November 1839; *Barbadian*, 20 November 1839; CO 28/133, No. 9, MacGregor to Russell, 24 January 1840, enclosure C, "Address from the Laborers of the Parish of St. George"; CO 28/134, No. 118, MacGregor to Russell, 26 December 1840, enclosing the *West Indian*, 21 December 1840, report on the proceedings of the court of grand sessions.

94. *Liberal*, 20 November 1839 and 20 February 1841; *British Anti-Slavery Reporter*, February 12 1840.

95. See reference to Robert Jordan, possibly same individual, in chapter 5, pp. 154–155.

consulted the laborers from his estate before signing the statement. "They knew nothing about it," Jordan declared. "I did not mention the Address to them—I only questioned them relative to their condition, and I considered that sufficient to authorize me to go to the Governor. . . . I thought I had a right to sign it." Many signed in order to deny Prescod's claim that the laborers in their district were being oppressed. One of the leaders of the deputation, a man named Cushey Alleyne, said that he had been told that Prescod had called laborers "savages" and he felt that such a statement "could only have been written by one of their worst enemies." Another headman, Tobias Went, was quoted in the *Anti-Slavery Reporter* as having said he would not have signed the address had he known it was directed against Prescod, but in court he denied making this statement. Altogether, their testimony illustrated that fear and self-interest had been stronger motivations than any sense of solidarity with an advocate of laborers' interests, such as Prescod, or any sense of injustice regarding the harsh conditions of rural life.[96]

In a bitter irony, colonial administrators used the trial, which was intended to silence the most eloquent voice of antiracism in the island, to demonstrate their commitment to desegregation to the Colonial Office. "[B]y an unprecedented coincidence," as MacGregor informed his superiors in Whitehall, "several respectable coloured and black gentlemen served in the Grand Jury, and . . . that Individual occupying from his Station, as Member of Council, the first rank amongst the descendants of Africa, in Barbados, presided, during the Sessions in the high and honourable Office of Chief Justice." MacGregor was referring to the fact that Thomas Cummins was chief justice of the 1840–1841 court of grand sessions—the first time an Afro-Barbadian had filled that post—and presided over Prescod's trial. Three men of color—Joseph Kennedy, Henry Brathwaite, and Henry Wilkins— sat on the jury that sentenced Prescod to five months in prison and fined him two hundred pounds.[97] The presence of men of color on the jury and on the bench was not, in fact, a coincidence but a thin disguise for the fact that this was a political and racially motivated trial. The harshness of the fine and jail term suggests that the jury was collaborating in a state-orchestrated attempt to silence the *Liberal*. During the proceedings, Prescod argued that the court was prejudiced against him because he was a man of color, a claim Solicitor General Clarke described as

96. *Liberal,* 12 February 1840 and 20 February 1841; *British Anti-Slavery Reporter,* 12 February 1840.

97. CO 28/134, No. 119, MacGregor to Russell, 26 December 1840, enclosing MacGregor to the Provost Marshal General, 24 December 1840.

nonsense, since such distinctions had been abolished along with slavery. Clarke added that Prescod and others like him were responsible for any lingering racial divisions.[98] Governor MacGregor pardoned Prescod and released him from jail, allegedly on the grounds that it was Prescod's first conviction and a prison term would be injurious to his health. Such a display of apparent mercy was an astute political move, since it was certainly not in the interests of the colonial adminis-tration to incur the wrath of the population by keeping the island's most popular public figure in jail and making a martyr of him.[99] The trial confirmed Prescod's popularity with the Afro-Barbadian majority of Bridgetown, and upon his release, Prescod was greeted at his home by "an immense number of the inhabitants of the town" and was "heartily cheered by the assembled multitude."[100] Prescod's legal problems had no immediate effect on the *Liberal*'s opposition to the conditions of rural labor, and the next year he served as the emigration agent for Trinidad.[101]

Nevertheless, 1840 was a major turning point in Prescod's political career. With the founding of the Liberal Party later that year he began to invest more of his energy in party politics and the struggle for franchise reform and less and less directly in questions of the dynamics of labor. The Liberals were a coalition of vari-ous interest groups: privileged and working-class Afro-Barbadians and people of color free before 1834 as well as former slaves, urban merchants, and liberal white planters. However much all of these groups might agree on the need for reform they had rather divergent views as to what kinds of reform were most urgently re-quired. The party's platform in the early 1840s focused mainly on public sector reform and retrenchment. Its principle objectives included economy in public spending and greater public accountability for the finances of the colonial state through annual budgets, professional audits and a system of tender for public works projects and a reduction in taxes. The major social reform proposal was state support for elementary education to be paid for by a reduction in the size of the police force. Finally, and most important, the Liberals sought franchise re-form in order to reduce political corruption and ensure the election of a more rep-

98. CO 28/134, No. 119, MacGregor to Russell, 26 December 1840, enclosing *West Indian,* 21 De-cember 1840.

99. CO 28/135, No. 119, MacGregor to Russell, 26 December 1840, cited in George Belle, "Samuel Jackman Prescod," in Glenford Howe and Don Marshall, eds., *The Empowering Impulse: The Nationalist Tradition of Barbados* (Kingston: Canoe Press, 2001), 92.

100. *Liberal,* 26 December 1840.

101. *Liberal,* 3 February 1841; CO 28/139, No. 25, MacGregor to Russell, 17 March 1841.

resentative and responsible assembly.[102] While this was certainly not a conservative political program, it was a centrist and far more strategic approach, whether in comparison to the political positions Prescod had adopted earlier in his life or in comparison to contemporary radical political movements, such as Chartism or socialism.

Despite Prescod's pardon, 1840 also represented a defeat for the struggle by progressive and working-class Afro-Barbadians for access to the rights of citizenship and a meaningful desegregation of the electoral process. That year the legislature finally passed a new electoral franchise bill setting the qualification for all male Barbadians at a house value of twenty pounds or five acres of freehold land. On one hand the reform was a victory for the principle of racial equality, since the qualification was now equal regardless of color, and the bill created a separate constituency for Bridgetown, which was a victory for urban politics. However, few potential voters of color owned five acres of land, and very few owned their homes at all, much less homes worth twenty pounds. The bill even disenfranchised a significant number of whites.[103]

What remained of the Elective Franchise Committee held a last emergency public meeting to oppose the act, arguing that a tax-based franchise of two pounds and ten shillings would have redressed the imbalance against the "respectable shopkeepers and tradespeople" excluded by the new act.[104] Prescod petitioned the Colonial Office on the committee's behalf, arguing that the new bill would in fact significantly decrease the size of the electorate. He further asserted that the act, although it did not state it openly, discriminated against Afro-Barbadians. Secretary of State for the Colonies Lord John Russell was favorable to his petition, and initially disallowed the act. However, shortly thereafter, the imperial government of Sir Robert Peel replaced the Whig administration in which Russell served. In the wake of the Jamaican constitutional crisis, the new secretary of state, Lord Stanley, the man who had drafted the act of emancipation, was determined to pursue a less

102. Marshall, "Prescod Reform Programme," 11–12.

103. Of the island's 1,874 registered landowners in 1841, 668 owned five acres or less of property. Most of the island's 383 female landowners, who could not vote, would have been in this category, along with many of the poor whites. See CO 28/140, No. 27, Lieutenant Governor H. C. Darling to Stanley, 28 October 1841, enclosing "Report of the Joint Committee of the [Council and Assembly] . . . ," 16 October 1841.

104. CO 28/140, No. 27, Darling to Stanley, enclosing Prescod to Russell, 13 July 1840.

confrontational policy toward West Indian planters. Stanley reversed Russell's decision, and the act came into force in November 1842 with minor revisions.[105]

The *Barbadian* hailed the bill as a victory for the legislature over Prescod and his "thirteen hundred tinkers, shoemakers, and tailors."[106] In fact, the new franchise act changed little. The electorate now numbered roughly eleven hundred, just over four hundred of whom were in St. Michael, which was more or less the same as before.[107] The bill made the greatest difference in St. Michael, where during the 1840s the urban elite of color became influential in the politics of Bridgetown and St. Michael, with the backing of white and nonwhite merchants and artisans. During the 1840s, men of color had some success in the elections for St. Michael Vestry. Besides Cummins, Joseph Thorne also became churchwarden of the vestry many times, beginning in 1844. On several occasions during the 1840s, of an average of eighteen candidates for sixteen vestry seats, at least four of five merchants of color ran for the vestry, with Cummins, Thorne, Valentine Wilkins, and William S. Wilkey being the most successful at the polls.[108]

Prescod's essentially bourgeois views on franchise reform and economic policy attracted urban merchants. When the new franchise act was brought into operation, a group of white and Afro-Barbadian Bridgetown merchants urged Prescod to run for one of the two newly created Bridgetown seats as the merchants' candidate, and he agreed to do so "expressly on the consideration that he was to receive support from that class of voters."[109] His decision to participate formally in politics clearly affected the content of his newspaper. The *Liberal* still published articles on matters pertaining to the rights of laborers, but noticeably less frequently,

---

105. CO 28/137, Correspondence with Mr. Prescod, No. 1255, Prescod to Lord John Russell, n.d.; CO 28/140, No. 27, Darling to Stanley, enclosing Prescod to Russell, 13 July 1840; CO 30/23, No. 727, "An Act to amend the Representation of the People, and to declare who shall be liable to serve on Juries . . . ," passed 29 April 1840; Levy, *Emancipation, Sugar, and Federalism*, 56–57; Schomburgk, *History of Barbados*, 488.

106. *Barbadian*, 19 February 1942.

107. PP 1845, vol. 31, *Copies of the last Census taken in each of the British West Indian Islands and in British Guiana . . . together with any Information subsequently received . . . relative to the Number of the Emancipated Negroes who have become Freeholders . . .*, Grey to Stanley, 4 September 1845, "Questions [for] the . . . Magistrates," No. 11, Bridgetown.

108. *Liberal*, 15 January 1840; *Barbadian*, 19 January 1842, 12 January 1848, 17 and 20 January 1849.

109. *Liberal*, 18 February 1843.

and the Liberal Party was careful to avoid the issue of race in political campaigning. Its candidates relied on the votes of white merchants and, in rural areas where they had less success, white planters and small farmers. In an election notice describing his 1843 political platform, Prescod outlined his laissez-faire liberal and utilitarian principles, declaring, "As regards my politics . . . I need only state here that freedom, full and unrestrained, in all things, is the rule; limitations and restrictions the exception. My object, the greatest possible good to the greatest possible number." He added that the rich had no right to oppress the poor, that trade "flourished best when least meddled with" and that he supported education for all people.[110] Such principles, although progressive, were vague enough to appeal equally to urban merchants, wealthy but liberal whites, and the small minority of people of color and former slaves who could vote. Prescod and his running mate, a white man named B. L. Trimingham, were opposed by two conservative candidates, one of them being Henry Sharpe. Merchants endorsed Prescod, and he won the election with 185 votes, becoming the first man of color to sit in the House of Assembly. Sharpe won the other seat, placing second with 168 votes, the other conservative candidate third, and Trimingham last.[111]

Support for the Liberal Party consolidated the racial integration of elite merchant politics, first nurtured by common support for electoral reform during the early apprenticeship period. In 1844, to commemorate the anniversary of his election, a delegation of merchants, both white and Afro-Barbadian, gave Prescod three hundred dollars to buy a printing press. In accepting the gift, Prescod stated that the delegation's composition, in which "every shade of complexion from pure white to pure black" was represented, assured him that "the greatest and most formidable obstacle of all has been surmounted. We are no longer a white, or a black, or a coloured party, struggling, as a class, for class privileges. We are a body of free men, labouring to free the institutions of our country from the blight of corruption which hangs festering over them, engendering all sorts of maladies in our public affairs."[112]

The diversity of this delegation notwithstanding, the race and class divisions that characterized Bridgetown life were as evident in the elections of 1843 as they had been in 1834. The atmosphere of celebration among people of color that had surrounded Sharpe's candidacy in 1834 now characterized Prescod's campaign.

110. *Liberal*, 31 May and 3 June 1843.
111. *Liberal*, 7 June 1843.
112. *Liberal*, 12 June 1844.

Between 1834 and 1843 Sharpe had ceased to consider himself a "liberal," a decision that greatly improved his relations with the legislature as attorney general and destroyed his popularity with the Afro-Barbadian laboring classes.[113] According to Governor Sir Charles Grey, Prescod's victory gave "great pleasure to the numerous class of colored inhabitants."[114] Prescod's campaign provided a vehicle for the urban poor to express their hostility toward the wealthy, and various reports mentioned that Sharpe and the other conservative candidate were hissed at in the streets and greeted with cheers of "Prescod forever!" While campaigning, Sharpe's wife rebuked Prescod's Afro-Barbadian political supporters for being "turncoats."[115] Although the *Liberal* asserted that "some of the most respectable Merchants" were among those celebrating in the streets after Prescod's victory, during the election the following year, a journalist from another newspaper contrasted Prescod's and Sharpe's followers in class terms, sarcastically referring to Prescod's "radicals" as

> [d]emagogue brawlers, without a doubloon that they could honestly call their own. . . . *Jobbers*—metamorphosed into Patriots and *Economists* . . . [whereas Sharpe's supporters are] gentlemen, the *Elite* of the wealth and respectability of the city; Gentlemen—five of whom shipped last year fully *five-sixths* of the whole staple crop of this sugar producing colony; and two of whom probably contribute to the Treasury of this Island fully as large a sum as the grand total of the Radical faction all put together. . . . [The Liberals/Radicals are] paupers, the large majority of them—with nothing to lose, and every thing to hope for in the event of their succeeding in upsetting the old constitution of the Colony . . . [and introducing a] *mobocracy* in to the House of Assembly.[116]

Prescod's campaign and election in 1843 illustrate how much the Afro-Barbadian merchant elite distanced itself from the overt discussions of racial discrimination that had characterized its public discourse in the first few years of emancipation. His decision to run was publicly endorsed in a letter from a group of fifteen leading Bridgetown residents, at least nine of them merchants of color.

113. *Liberal*, 22 July 1843.
114. CO 28/156, No. 47, Grey to Stanley, 17 June 1843.
115. *Liberal*, 7, 17, and 21 June 1843, letter from "Pliny."
116. *Liberal*, 27 July 1844, letter titled "The Globe's say."

However, in contrast to the tone of the racial equality agitation of the 1830s, they made no reference to color, or to the importance of having a man of color in the legislature. Instead, they thanked him as merchants for "the zeal and ability which you have displayed on all occasions connected with the general welfare of the Island, more especially on those relating to Trade and Commerce."[117] This reluctance to make overt references to race was also evident in the decision by the St. Mary's Society for the Education of the Coloured Poor to drop the word "Coloured" from its name during the 1840s. Despite the name change, the society still provided relief exclusively to impoverished people of color, and its governing board consisted of sixteen "gentlemen of colour," along with the Anglican bishop, the parish rector, and the curate of St. Mary's Church.[118]

It was also some years before Prescod was free from the accusation that his supporters were not "respectable," and although he was backed politically by a wide cross-section of people, there were social divisions between them. Of those who signed the 1843 address to Prescod, only Anthony Barclay, a shopkeeper, attended a dinner held in early August to celebrate jointly Prescod's election and the anniversary of emancipation, possibly the last such event commemorating the end of slavery until the twentieth century.[119] Some of those who spoke, such as Barclay and another man named Edward Archer, were longtime philanthropists and participants in the struggle for political and civil equality. However, not even the few wealthy and leading merchants who had previously participated in these dinners, such as Joseph Kennedy, were present.[120] These elite men may have been unwilling to socialize with the small artisans and shopkeepers who supported Prescod.

Despite the festive mood surrounding Prescod's election, less than 1 percent of the population could vote in 1843. Conservative politicians and the planter press still had good reason to fear the democratic potential of the crowds who assembled during the 1843 election. Yet in the aftermath of the 1842 franchise bill, the crowd represented a force far less immediately threatening to the established order than the throngs of working-class people and slaves who had flocked to the hustings at

117. *Liberal,* 22 February 1843.

118. Minutes of the St. Michael Vestry, 18 November 1845.

119. Higman asserts that on the jubilee of emancipation in 1888, Barbadian planters "were joined by black and coloured leaders in promoting a collective forgetting." Higman, "Remembering Slavery," 92.

120. *Liberal,* 2 August 1843.

the St. Michael church to support Henry Sharpe in his more progressive days, on the eve of emancipation just nine years earlier.

CONCLUSION

Within a decade of emancipation the radical and lower-class struggle that had sought to shape the politics of racial liberation in a more democratic fashion was systematically undermined by the combined efforts of the imperial government, the local aristocracy and members of the Afro-Barbadian elite. The debate over the freedom of movement of the rural laboring population proved to be the undoing of efforts to unite Afro-Barbadians against racial discrimination in the early postslavery years. When the long-wished-for reform of the franchise law did take place it once again excluded the overwhelming majority of Barbadians, both of African and European descent, from the rights of citizenship. Demanding that elite men of color like Cummins, Prescod, and Thorne be admitted into the highest circles of colonial politics was central to popular hopes for change, yet for most people of color this demand remained symbolic of more radical, democratic desires. By accepting a few elite men of color into the political fold without making fundamental changes, the imperial and colonial regimes ensured that the political momentum of radical reformers was arrested while the exclusion of the majority from public life was reaffirmed.

I N 1843, during the first elections for the Barbados House of Assembly under the 1842 franchise law, an aspiring politician named John Inniss sued William Clarke, the police magistrate of the district of rural St. Michael, for electoral fraud and lost. Inniss, a white Barbadian, was challenging the incumbents, both planters, for the district's two legislative seats and was running as part of a slate of "liberal" candidates led by Samuel Jackman Prescod. The lawsuit centred around John Millington, an Afro-Barbadian man who had qualified for the vote under the new twenty-pound franchise qualification. Clarke was so sure that he controlled Millington's vote that he had assured one of the planter candidates, John Packer, that he could depend upon it. During the campaign Packer's brother came round to see Millington and was outraged when Millington informed him that he planned to vote liberal. Packer went to Clarke's office, knowing that Clarke "still held great influence over [Millington] . . . to get him to exercise that influence on behalf of his brother."[1]

Clarke visited Millington and demanded that he vote for either Packer or John Bovell, the other planter candidate. Millington testified that he told Clarke "that I was sorry to be obliged, for the first time, since I had ceased to be his slave, to refuse compliance with his request; but I had already promised to give my vote to Mr. Prescod. . . . I was a poor man and had resolved to give it [my vote] on the other side." At this point, Clarke threatened Millington, insinuating that, if Millington kept insisting that he would vote for the liberals, Clarke would disenfranchise him by having his property valued at less than twenty pounds and make any future dealings with the state difficult for Millington. Faced with the wrath of Packer and Clarke and fearing the consequences of his political decision, Millington tried to convince Packer that he had not fully understood the significance of his vote:

1. *Liberal*, 3 and 7 June 1843.

He told me that one who had a house rated at the annual value of £20 was entitled to vote. I said I was very glad of that, for, if he would but dismount and look at my house, he would find it far from being worth £20 a year, as it was "merely a skeleton," and as I did not wish to offend any one, I would send and beg Mr. Prescod to excuse me, and vote on neither side. Mr. Packer told me that if I did as I said, he considered that I would be looked upon as a better man for it, for I would then offend neither party.

In the end Bovell and Packer were returned to the House of Assembly with seventy-nine and seventy-three votes, respectively, while Inniss, with fifty-three votes, placed third. Millington did not vote.[2]

This instance in which the coercive power of the colonial state and individual planters reinforced each other and were brought to bear against this Afro-Barbadian in order to disenfranchise him and silence opposition is illustrative of a wider postslavery reality in Barbados. By the 1840s, the dust of emancipation settled to reveal that, in the absence of any fundamental economic transformations, it was nearly impossible to challenge the planter oligarchy effectively. The passage of the 1842 franchise act, the entrenchment of a harsh rural labor regime, and the legislature's almost total elimination of the emigration option reaffirmed the power of the plantocracy and the exclusion of the Afro-Barbadian majority from political and economic influence.

On one level, this backlash against reform was not unique to Barbados or other areas of the Caribbean. It was equally a feature of politics across the Atlantic in Britain at the end of the 1840s where, less than two decades after mass mobilization for emancipation and the reform of parliament, Chartism, and anti-slavery were in retreat while "working class Liberalism" and popular racism were ascendant. The rise of racial and economic determinism in British politics led, in the 1840s and 1850s, to the steady withdrawal of imperial support for policies and institutions that had helped Afro-Caribbean people to evade planter coercion.[3]

2. Ibid.

3. Eugene Biagini and Alastair Reid, eds., *Currents of Radicalism: Popular Radicalism, Organised Labour and Party Politics in Britain, 1850–1914* (Cambridge: Cambridge University Press, 1991), introduction, 10; Hall, *Civilising Subjects*, 338–379.

During apprenticeship, white Barbadian elites had been eager to disown slavery, to represent—and re-present—themselves as advocates of social equality, and
to downplay the racism that shaped colonial state policy and social relations. By
contrast, less than a decade later, elite whites felt comfortable engaging publicly in
racist discourses that reclaimed slavery as, in many ways, a golden age of white supremacy, expressed through romanticized images of slavery's disenfranchisement
of Afro-Barbadian men and the sexual exploitation and subordination of Afro-
Barbadian women. This discursive rehabilitation of slavery was especially evident
in one of the earliest works of fiction from the mid-nineteenth-century British Caribbean, the 1842 novel *Creoleana: Or, Social and Domestic Scenes and Incidents in
Barbados in Days of Yore* written by J. W. Orderson, a male member of the Barbadian planter class. As Edward Said has argued, the "main battle in imperialism is
over land, of course; but when it came to who owned the land, who had the right
to settle and work on it, who kept it going, who won it back, and who now plans its
future—these issues were reflected, contested, and even for a time decided in narrative." *Creoleana,* no less than similarly racist and proslavery fiction and nonfic-
tion writings then being produced in Britain, represented the resurgence of elite
and conservative values in Britain and in the Caribbean, an effort by planters and
their metropolitan sympathizers to "block other narratives" of postemancipation
society.[4]

The class, gender, and racial ideology that informed *Creoleana* also guided the
economic, labor, and social policies of the plantocracy and the planter state. As imperial policy and growing competition from slave-grown sugar sparked a long period of economic crisis for the British Caribbean sugar industry, Barbadian planters used their nearly total domination of political and economic power to force the
Afro-Barbadian poor to shoulder the burden of economic hardship. The political
success of a small number of men of color, including a progressive and antiracist
reformer such as Prescod, during the 1840s and 1850s did little to blunt the effects of state and planter coercion. The political careers of prominent elite people
of color flourished under oligarchic rule. Ultimately, they participated in the in-
stitutionalization and containment of demands for radical political change that
had predated emancipation. As the possibilities for social, political and economic
change in Barbados grew increasingly remote, many working-class people of color
once again turned their attention to the African continent, viewing emigration as

4. Edward W. Said, *Culture and Imperialism* (Vintage: London, 1993), xiii.

the agents of the British Empire in Africa as a means to escape planter hegemony in the Caribbean.[5]

As the example of the Barclay family illustrates, West Africans of Barbadian background brought with them all of the contradictions of Afro-Barbadians' anti-slavery, diasporic, and civilizationist thinking about Africa. The Barclays would play a crucial and ambivalent role in West Africa as simultaneously the agents of colonization, carried out by migrants of color from the Americas, and opponents of imperialism on the African continent.

GENDERING THE DISCOURSE OF REACTION

In the postslavery era, as had been the case during slavery, stereotyped and sexualized representations of women of color, especially the "mulatto" woman, often served as the means through which white reactionaries expressed both antiblack sentiment and fear of racial "amalgamation." After slavery, such representations were also a means to glorify the days of slavery as a time of order when everyone could be more easily kept in their "proper" place, and when people of color who sought "improper" relations with people above their station in life could be punished almost with impunity. Under cover of this revision of the past, such representations became a veiled reflection of and blueprint for race relations in the postslavery period.

Orderson's *Creoleana* was a prime example of this gendered and sexualized expression of racist hostility. Orderson was the former editor and son of the founder of the *Mercury* newspaper, the first newspaper in the island, which enjoyed a publication run of more than half a century. He had also been a planter and was a well-respected member of planter society. *Creoleana* was set in late-eighteenth-century Barbados and was simultaneously a revision of slavery and a moral reformist tale to guide behavior in postemancipation society. Orderson's fictional work offers rare insight into the normative elite public discourse concerning sexual, familial, and financial relations between whites and nonwhites in the 1840s. What at first appears to be simply a mediocre and rather forgettable tale becomes, when understood in the context of social relations in slave and postemancipation society, a sinister commentary on race, class, and gender relations. Published in the same year the planter state's exclusionary new franchise act

5. For a brief analysis of *Creoleana* in the wider context of eighteenth- and nineteenth-century writing against the "mulatto" in the Caribbean, see Lewis, *Main Currents in Caribbean Thought*, 232–236.

went into effect—cutting all but 1 percent of the island's population out of the political process and ensuring the continued dominance of the plantocracy— *Creoleana* represented the resurgence of planter confidence as the forces of plebian resistance, bourgeois reformism, and antiracist activism were temporarily vanquished.

The novel tells the fictional tale of one Mr. Fairfield, a self-made merchant-cum-planter, who, in his younger days, maintained an "unhallowed connexion" with a slave woman, a relationship that resulted in the birth of a daughter, Lucy. Shortly after the girl was born, Fairfield "became more than ever anxious to enter into the matrimonial state and determined to shake off his illicit connexion." He freed his "paramour," gave her an annuity, and by her consent took away their infant daughter and placed her "under the care of a respectable matron," who raised her. He himself married a "respectable" white woman and had a white daughter, Caroline. When both girls were around seventeen years old, Fairfield brought his mixed-race daughter into his home as the maidservant for Caroline. Lucy did not know who her real father was and had no recollection of her mother, who had, rather conveniently, died of "rapid consumption soon after her emancipation." In the end, Caroline married a successful young creole named John Goldacre. Lucy, by contrast, foolishly rejected the marriage proposal of an "exemplary" young free black artisan named Joe Pollard, who, through "honest industry," which earned him the "esteem" of the neighborhood gentry, had made enough to buy five acres of land, a "neat" cottage, and a few slaves. Lucy secretly became the mistress of a Scottish libertine and conman named Mr. Mac Flashby. Lucy came to her senses but too late; Pollard learned of her past relations with Flashby and withdrew his proposal. Lucy gave birth to a stillborn and illegitimate mixed-race child and died shortly thereafter.[6]

The novel is an especially transparent allegory of white men's desire to erase both the dangerous figures of the "hybrid" and "impure" Afro-Barbadian woman, who subverted legal, socioeconomic, and racial boundaries, and the politically aggressive and ambitious free man of color. "Illicit" sexual relations between white men and women of color—even those that led to the birth of mixed-race children—were acknowledged as a rite of passage in the life of a young white Barbadian man during slavery, which could be tolerated so long as he never married

6. On African American emigration to the Caribbean and Africa in this period, see R. J. M. Blackett, "The Hamic Connection: African-Americans and the Caribbean, 1820–1865," in Moore and Wilmot, eds., *Before and after 1865*, 317–329.

his Afro-Barbadian mistress, and eventually produced legitimate white heirs. The novel at once brought together white men's fantasy of making such women disappear after emancipation and their wish to reimagine slave society as a relatively benign system of race and class paternalism. Free men of color such as Pollard knew their place, had no political aspirations, and sought only to marry women of their own color. White Barbadian men like Fairfield bestowed chivalry upon their slave mistresses by manumitting them and raising their mixed-race offspring but never by elevating them to the status of wife or publicly acknowledged progeny. Only an outsider like Mac Flashby would dare to violate the proper code of white male conduct and make promises of marriage and security he never intended to keep. Mixed-race children, like Lucy, remained in slavery, were servile, made no financial or other claims upon their white fathers, and accepted gratefully the second-class status given to them by these fathers.

It is also revealing that Orderson made Pollard a slave owner, a deliberate acknowledgment that some free people of color had owned slaves, a fact that, after emancipation, many Afro-Barbadians free before 1834 sought to downplay. While Pollard's slave ownership was arguably a more honest representation of the lives of some free people of color during slavery, it indicates Orderson's virulent hostility toward the racial politics of the postemancipation period. He trivialized the effects of slavery and racial subordination on the lives and economic prospects of free people of color, making Pollard unusually prosperous (although, significantly, with too few acres of land to vote under the old franchise law). Orderson set up Pollard as a "good" man of color, isolated from any political community of free people of color—Pollard and Lucy are the only free Afro-Barbadian characters in the novel—and loyal and subservient to whites.

Perhaps the most discursively violent aspect of the novel is that Orderson managed to kill off all of the Afro-Barbadian female characters and their children. It is significant that Lucy's mother died of consumption immediately after her emancipation, while Lucy died having given birth to a stillborn child, suggesting that Orderson posited a direct connection between Afro-Barbadian women's sexual and racial promiscuity, and physical infirmity in these women and their offspring. Consumption was a disease popularly associated with sexual promiscuity in women. The mother's quick death immediately after her manumission is reminiscent of the postemancipation outcry against Afro-Barbadian women who had been the free mistresses of white men during slavery. With the death of this character, Orderson expressed a desire for these women to cease to disturb the domestic peace of their white lovers after freedom, erasing them from both the island's slaveholding past and from postslavery society. In Orderson's moral order, women like Lucy and her mother, along with their offspring, paid for their immoral interracial and extramarital sexual relations with their lives.

Lucy's stillborn child, the offspring of a mixed-race woman and a white man, was a social aberration for whom there was no place in Orderson's imagination, lest it grow up to pass for white, thereby polluting whiteness and endangering white property. The sanctity of white purity, marriage and landed property after emancipation were embodied in the characters of John Goldacre and Caroline Fairfield, who stood for a new postemancipation generation of white creoles coming of age in the aftermath of slavery. Their lives, property, and offspring would, Orderson envisioned, be unsullied by the sins of their white fathers and unperturbed by mixed-race female relatives such as Lucy or her children, whom Orderson wrote out of existence.

CAPTIVE LABOR AND THE GROWTH

OF THE NONAGRICULTURAL SECTOR

Creoleana was the fictional counterpart of a repressive postslavery political and socioeconomic reality for most Afro-Barbadians. By the mid-1840s, the labor fluctuations caused by the early movement of rural laborers away from estate work had slowed, and the labor market was stagnating. The 1844 census of the island shows that 48 percent of working adults—25 percent of the total population—performed nonagricultural work in 1844. This percentage, like the distribution of property, remained more or less the same for decades, even though the population grew.[7] Although planters in Barbados, as elsewhere, complained in the early 1840s that they could not get former field laborers to work regularly on the estates, Barbadian laborers still did more hours of estate labor a week on average than workers elsewhere in the Caribbean.[8] Planters were aware that there were more people

---

7. According to the 1876 census, 27 percent of the total population were adults who worked in agriculture, while the total population reached over 162,000. George Belle, "The Abortive Revolution of 1876 in Barbados," in Beckles and Shepherd, *Caribbean Freedom*, 181.

8. PP 1842, vol. 13, *Report from the Select Committee*, Testimony of William Sharpe, 12 May 1842, Questions 1515–1548; PP 1842, vol. 29, Darling to Russell, 19 September 1841, "Questions . . . directed by Lord John Russell," No. 3, St. Andrew, 31 July 1841.

in Barbados than there was work to employ them all, but justified the legislature's antiemigration stance on the grounds that "a redundant population" was necessary for the affordable cultivation of sugar.[9]

The harsh labor regime that would define the island for generations to come was firmly entrenched by the mid-1840s, as the island slipped into an economic depression that would last, almost without interruption, until the close of the century. In contrast to many other Caribbean territories sugar production continued to increase in Barbados during the 1840s and 1850s at the expense of the island's overworked estate labor force, which saw its real wages and living conditions worsen over time. Between 1842 and 1852, the average price paid for Barbadian sugar fell by half, and planters responded by increasing the workload of estate laborers while cutting salaries. Although wages gradually returned to pre-1846 levels after 1848, food prices continued to rise. By the end of the 1840s, Barbadian laborers had the lowest real incomes in the British Caribbean.[10]

In 1845 the imperial Parliament passed a measure that spelled economic disaster for the Afro-Caribbean poor and decisively signaled the end of its commitment to the great social project of emancipation. The 1845 Sugar Duties Act, under which the duty on foreign sugar imported into the British market was reduced annually and finally abolished in 1854, removed tariff protection for British Caribbean sugar and opened the British domestic market to sugar grown anywhere in the world, including slaveholding states. Even before the act was passed, slave-grown sugar was entering the British imperial market. In a bitter irony, British Caribbean colonies exported all of their sugar to the metropole and had to import sugar for domestic consumption, which was often slave grown.[11] The Sugar Duties Act contributed to a financial crisis in the British Caribbean, which was compounded in 1847 when the West India Bank, one of a number of banking institutions established by Caribbean planters after emancipation to help finance estate operations, went bankrupt. When the bank collapsed it took with it the entire revenue of the Barbadian state, which was invested there, nearly bringing

9. PP 1842, vol. 29, *Papers Relative to the West Indies,* "Quarterly Reports," 1 July–30 September 1840, No. 8, St. Joseph.

10. Deerr, *History of Sugar* 2:194; Green, *British Slave Emancipation,* 231 and 247; Levy, *Emancipation, Sugar, and Federalism,* 112–114.

11. *Liberal,* 17 November 1841.

the country to an economic standstill.[12] Wage payments stopped, and many laborers had to rely entirely on their tiny garden plots for subsistence. Several vestries ran out of money, and planters stopped paying their debts to urban merchant houses.[13]

Economic crisis for workers in Barbados did not mean the same for the island's planters, whose profits were not seriously affected until the next major international depression of the 1880s and 1890s. The Barbadian colonial government and individual planters responded to the crisis of the 1840s by shifting the economic burden away from landowners onto merchants and consumers in the form of wage reductions and taxation. To cut the island's budget deficit in 1840, the colonial government imposed the first of a number of consumption and trade taxes, charging duty on all imported merchandise. Bridgetown merchants protested that the taxes would force them to raise prices, thereby reducing the buying power of their customers and imposing an additional burden on the working poor, but to no avail. When the tariff reduction began in 1846, planters lowered resident estate workers' wages to one shilling and three pence—even as low as seven pence at one point—making wages in Barbados among the lowest in the British Caribbean.[14]

The legislature also largely ignored the growing problem of poverty and unemployment, preferring to leave welfare provision to vestries, private philanthropists and the church.[15] In both countryside and town, the problem of unemployment and underemployment worsened in the 1840s. In August 1845 the vestry of St. Philip met to discuss a report from the poor law overseers that described the "general Poor" of the parish as being in a state of "Actual starvation." The vestry responded by giving the overseers the meagre sum of $120 to buy provisions for those who could not afford them.[16] St. Michael was one of few parishes whose vestry listed names of both white and Afro-Barbadian paupers, and in 1845 there were 1,123 people officially classed as paupers in Bridgetown, which only included those

---

12. Lobdell, "Patterns of Investment," 321. The Jamaican Planter's Bank and thirteen West Indian merchant houses also failed that year. Deerr, *History of Sugar* 2:438.

13. CO 28/167, No. 80, Governor William Reid to Secretary of State Earl Grey, 7 December 1847.

14. Levy, *Emancipation, Sugar, and Federalism,* 96 and 109–113; Riviere, "Labour Shortage," 29; *Sugar Question,* 7 and 9.

15. Richard Carter, "Public Amenities After Emancipation," 49–69; Leonard Fletcher, "The Evolution of Poor Relief in Barbados, 1838–1900," *JCH* 53, no. 2 (1992): 171–207.

16. Minutes of the St. Philip Vestry, 14 August 1845.

who received poor relief.[17] Despite growing urban poverty, town life still offered marginally better possibilities than life as a rural laborer, and people continued to move to towns. The *Barbadian* complained in 1849 that Bridgetown was "infested with crowds of young persons, most of them having been formerly slaves, as well as others who have been born since the abolition of slavery, who are in a state of shocking demoralization." The paper's editor claimed they took every opportunity to steal and referred to cases of "highway robbery," a possible indication to a more sympathetic observer of the extent of people's desperation.[18]

The climate of imperial disinterest and economic crisis negatively affected Afro-Barbadians' lives in other ways. In 1840, the new conservative imperial administration announced that it would gradually phase out the imperial grant that supported thousands of schools for children of color across the West Indies. The Barbadian planter-state refused to fill the gap, only agreeing in 1846 to grant £750 a year for the next three years to the Church of England to fund its schools. To cope with the grant reduction, most schools raised fees, and parents, unable to pay, began to withdraw their children from school. In April 1842 there were 3,356 pupils in the island's Anglican schools; three years later the number had fallen to 2,975. Although there were many children of color in private schools or schools sponsored by other Christian denominations, no inquiry was conducted into the grant reduction's impact on these schools, nor did the legislature grant these schools funding to make up for the cuts.[19]

The decline in government support for education affected the rural poor far more than urban workers or well-to-do Afro-Barbadians. In 1846 nearly all of the island's rural magistrates reported that the number of children in schools was decreasing as parents were forced to withdraw them and send them to work as agricultural laborers. In contrast, the Bridgetown magistrate replied that the employment of children in the city was "unattended (as far as we have observed) by a

17. PP 1846, vol. 28, *Papers . . . Relating to the Labouring Population of the British Colonies*, Grey to Stanley, 4 September 1845, enclosing "Questions [for] the . . . Magistrates," No. 12, Bridgetown.

18. *Barbadian*, 22 August 1849.

19. CO 30/24, No. 876, "An Act authorizing quarterly payments for a limited period from the public towards the moral and religious education of the people of this island," passed 14 July 1846; CO 31/56, 1 July 1846. Prescod voted against this bill because it only assisted Anglican schools, but was the only member of the House to oppose it. See also p. 1846, vol. 28, *Papers . . . relating to the Labouring Population of the British Colonies*, 164–165, No. 4, Grey to Gladstone, March 23 1846, enclosing Bishop of Barbados to Grey, 29 December 1845.

corresponding decrease or increase of those at school."[20] Wealthier free people of color were also unaffected, and in 1848 the *Barbadian* noted how "very gratifying" it was to see "gentlemen of the coloured community sending their sons to England to receive liberal educations" in fields such as divinity, medicine and law. In the late 1850s, for example, Joseph Thorne's son received the first Island Scholarship from Codrington College and went to study divinity at King's College, London.[21] The newspaper acknowledged that few people of color could afford this yet rebuked white and Afro-Barbadian laboring-class parents because they "refused" to pay for their children's education.[22]

With few opportunities available to them for economic betterment, the majority of Afro-Barbadians were destined to remain a permanent underclass. Very few of those emancipated in 1838 ever acquired land, and those who did come to own land usually owned very little of it. In 1840 there were 934 freeholds of fewer than ten acres, most of which predated emancipation.[23] In the exceptional cases in which former slaves bought property, it was rarely more than one or two acres, usually not enough to meet the franchise requirement.[24] In 1849 there were 1,469 people owning one to five acres of land, a number that had increased to 2,098 by 1875, less than 1.5 percent of the total population in both cases. The growth in the number of small landholders during this period was mainly due to the subdivision of inherited plots, rather than the acquisition of new land.[25] By 1850 "the plantation's land monopoly was still unbroken, and this, combined with a rising demand for land by ex-slaves, ensured the persistence of high land prices."[26]

20. PP 1846, vol. 28, *Papers . . . Relating to the Labouring Population of the British Colonies*, Grey to Stanley, 4 September 1845, enclosing "Questions [for] the . . . Magistrates," No. 12, Bridgetown.

21. *Barbadian*, 29 July 1857.

22. *Barbadian*, 19 July 1848 and 28 March 1849.

23. CO 28/140, No. 27, Darling to Stanley, 28 October 1841, enclosing "Report of the Joint Committee"; Watts, *West Indies*, 330. Janet Momsen states that there were 1,367 freeholds of less than ten acres in 1840, but the source of this figure is unclear. See Momsen, *Post-emancipation Rural Settlement in Barbados* (Newcastle-upon-Tyne: University of Newcastle upon Tyne, 1988), 1.

24. PP 1845, vol. 31, *Copies of the last Census taken*, Grey to Stanley, 4 September 1845, enclosing "Questions [for] the . . . Magistrates," Nos. 1–12; PP 1846, vol. 28, *Papers . . . Relating to the Labouring Population of the British Colonies*, magistrates' reports for October 1844 to June 1845.

25. Marshall, "Rock Hall, St. Thomas: The Search for the First Free Village in Barbados," paper presented at the 14th ACH Conference, Georgetown, Guyana, 1977, 37.

26. Woodville Marshall, "Villages and Plantation Sub-Division," in Marshall, *Emancipation III: Aspects of the Post-Slavery Experience in Barbados* (Bridgetown: National Cultural Foundation and Department of History, UWI, 1988), 8.

The economic situation of the majority of Afro-Barbadians deteriorated steadily. Matters reached their nadir in 1854, when a devastating cholera epidemic killed about one-fifth of the population within a few months. Faced with such a calamity, the colonial government was forced to admit that poverty and poor living conditions, particularly in the continually expanding Bridgetown slums, were the root cause of the rapid spread and devastating impact of the epidemic.[27] The colonial state slowly and reluctantly began to expand its role as a provider of social services. However such changes were limited, and the state made no attempt to keep pace with the growing poverty rate.[28]

AFRO-BARBADIANS AND FORMAL POLITICS

The failure to redistribute wealth was reflected in the political system. During the first four decades after emancipation, the percentage of eligible voters remained virtually unchanged at about 1 percent of the population.[29] Prescod and the Liberals fought tenaciously to have the franchise law reformed and to get Liberal candidates into the House of Assembly, with Prescod again setting up franchise reform committees in 1849 and 1856. The 1840s and early 1850s were the high watermark in terms of the possibility of influencing the political system through the ballot since, after that point, the number of small property owners who qualified for the vote declined. This was mainly due to the division of smallholdings among descendants.

Woodville Marshall's research into the free village community of Rock Hall in St. Thomas very clearly illustrates this trend in landownership, as well as its political consequences. While the establishment of free villages was a widespread phenomenon in other parts of the British Caribbean after emancipation, it was

27. CO 28/181, No. 74, Governor Colebrooke to Grey, 27 November 1854, enclosing a "General Report on the Condition of Bridgetown."

28. Fletcher, "Evolution of Poor Relief," 173–176.

29. Between 1842 and 1854, the electorate went from only about 1,100 to 1,444, although the population exploded from an estimated 103,000 just before emancipation to 152,722. By 1876, when the population was 162,042, there were just 1,644 voters, of whom 613 were in St. Michael parish. See Belle, "The Abortive Revolution," 181; Levy, *Emancipation, Sugar, and Federalism*, 119. As no census of the entire population was taken in 1834, the 1834 population figure is based on varying estimates for 1829 of between 101,288 and 103,983. See David Gobert and Jerome Handler, trans., "Barbados in the Apprenticeship Period: The Report of a French colonial official [April 1836], *JBMHS* 36, no. 2 (1979): 111; and Schomburgk, *History of Barbados*, 86.

highly unusual in Barbados, where land was too expensive and difficult to acquire in small plots, and where former slaves lacked the support of nonconformist missionaries with the resources to help groups of them purchase land. Rock Hall, the island's first free village, was established in the early 1840s by former slaves who were in the unusual position of having the money to purchase land. It is likely that most of the original landowners were former slaves from Mount Wilton plantation whose owner, Reynold Alleyne Ellcock, bequeathed them money in his will—a fact that may have precipitated his grisly murder at the hands of a number of his slaves, who all knew of the bequest, in 1821. The bequest was not paid until after emancipation, when eighty-three claimants received eighty-five pounds each. Many claimants used the money to buy land in the nearby subdivisions of Rock Hall and Bridgefield (seventy pounds in the case of those who bought an acre of land in Rock Hall), both of which became free villages.

The unusual presence of villages such as Rock Hall and Bridgefield in St. Thomas made them vital to the Liberal Party's most serious bid to challenge planter power in the House of Assembly. In the 1849 elections, on the back of a concerted voter registration campaign and a major mobilization of Afro-Barbadian voter power, the Liberals managed to defeat incumbent planter candidates in St. Michael and St. Thomas parishes. The voter registration campaign of 1848 probably explains why the electorate in St. Thomas increased from forty-three to seventy-four in a matter of months. Twelve men from Rock Hall were among twenty-one registered voters from St. Thomas who supported Liberal candidates Haynes Gibbs Bayley and Joseph Yearwood against the planters James Sarsfield Bascom and John Grant. Only one vote separated frontrunner Bayley from Bascom and Grant, and after the House of Assembly investigated the qualifications of the voters, the vote of one Rock Hall resident was thrown out on the grounds that he did not meet the franchise qualification. Since this man had voted for Bayley, a by-election took place in April 1849. Bascom and Grant now ran against the Liberal team of Bayley and Nathaniel Forte but, in the face of a well-organized block of Liberal electoral support, withdrew at the last minute, leaving Bayley and Forte the winners. By contrast, only eleven Rock Hall villagers qualified for the vote in 1868, and only four—three of whom had voted Liberal in 1849—were registered voters. This decrease reflected the steady fragmentation of farm lots, many of which had been one acre in size, into "virtual house-spots" as the original owners died and passed the land on to their descendants.[30]

30. On the Ellcock bequest, the formation of Rock Hall, and the 1849 election, see Marshall, "Rock Hall," 9ff.

The economic conditions of the 1840s put a ceiling on social mobility for the working poor, and further widened the socioeconomic gap between rich and poor Afro-Barbadians. Urban merchants continued to be the core of the elite of color, both in terms of social and financial status. For a generation they remained, almost to a man, the same individuals who had constituted the free Afro-Barbadian elite during the final years of slavery. All of those men who held elected or appointed political positions up to the mid-1850s were people of color free before 1834, and nearly all of them had earned their wealth as merchants.[31] In the 1850s Nathaniel Roach became a judge in the neighboring colony of Grenada, and his name was floated as a possible replacement for Joseph Garraway as a court of appeal judge when the latter died in 1853.[32] Until his death in 1871 Prescod remained the only man of color to be elected to the House of Assembly in the lower house of the Barbadian legislature. A second Afro-Barbadian, a protégé of Prescod named Conrad Reeves, would not be elected to the legislature until 1874. By contrast, at the end of the 1840s, there were thirteen representatives of color in the Jamaican house of assembly and, during the 1850s, tradesmen and small shopkeepers were being elected to the Jamaican lower house.[33]

The entry of some elite men of color into the ranks of the Barbadian landed aristocracy served to legitimize a social order that still privileged a few wealthy whites at the expense of the majority of Afro-Barbadians and whites. Some merchants of color, notably John Montefiore, London Bourne, and possibly Thomas J. Cummins, became planters themselves between the 1840s and 1860s. In the early 1840s, Montefiore bought the 149-acre Neal's plantation in St. Michael, and Davy noted that there were other men of color who became substantial property owners after emancipation. He observed that these "respectable men . . . were it not for their color, could have been in no way distinguished from other proprietors."[34] Some of those who managed to penetrate the highest circles of politics and property ownership found a degree of social acceptance in elite white circles that would have been unthinkable before emancipation. Thomas J. Cummins, for ex-

31. One exception was Thomas Ellis, a planter of color who ran unsuccessfully as a conservative candidate in the House of Assembly elections from a St. Peter seat against a white Liberal Party candidate in 1843. *Liberal,* 24 June 1843.

32. *Barbadian,* 14 December 1853.

33. Heuman, *Between Black and White,* 61–75 and 147–148.

34. Minutes of the St. Michael Vestry, 24 March 1842; BMHS Catalogue of Barbadian Estates; *List of Property Owners of One Acre or More, 1842,* BDA; Will of London Bourne, BDA; Davy, *West Indies before and since Emancipation,* 80.

ample, crowned his political success by joining the large and influential St. Philip's District Agricultural Society, a planter association and a bastion of conservatism.[35] In 1841, having become a magistrate, Cummins would refer derisively, in a communication with the Colonial Office, to Prescod's supporters as being from among "the lower orders of Tradesmen . . . whose names, but not their rank or occupation, frequently appear in his paper either as Memorialists or Orators." Among these lower order tradesmen were individuals with whom Cummins had once been willing to associate, when he was still struggling to be elected or appointed to office.[36]

Despite the tendency of men of color to distance themselves from antiracist politics once in office, the presence of Afro-Barbadians in high political offices did have some impact on the state's racial segregation policies, particularly in the St. Michael vestry. During the 1840s and 1850s, under the influence of men of color, the vestry assumed a greater responsibility for poor relief for people of color. In 1841, during Thomas Cummins's tenure as churchwarden, the vestry gave £1,150 to the St. Mary's Society, more than to any other charitable organization, including the Ladies Association. The fact that Cummins was then also the secretary of St. Mary's probably had some bearing on this decision.[37] By 1845–1846, when there were at least five men of color out of sixteen vestrymen, and Joseph Thorne was churchwarden, there had been a further shift in vestry policy. At the request of the St. Mary's Society, the vestry assumed responsibility for the Society's poor relief asylum and for its pensioners on the grounds that "the relief of the colored poor [is] now more a parochial concern, than as it was [sic] formerly dependent upon the voluntary exertions of individuals asserting themselves for that purpose."[38]

Vestrymen of color also challenged racial segregation in the vestry's educa-

35. PP 1846, vol. 28, Papers . . . Relating to the Labouring Population of the British Colonies, Grey to Stanley 4 September 1845, enclosure No. 1, "Questions [for] the . . . Magistrates, No. 1, St. Philip, "Fifth Annual Report of the St. Philip's District Agricultural Society of Barbados, for the Year 1844." Cummins also became the magistrate for Bridgetown, the most important judicial post beneath that of court of appeal judge, in 1849. Barbadian, 14 April 1849.

36. CO 28/139, No. 26, MacGregor to Russell, 18 March 1841, enclosure No. 5, Police Magistrates Tinling, Sealy and Cummins, Commission of Inquiry into the case of Frederick Watts v. Samuel Jackman Prescod, 13 March 1841.

37. CO 28/164, No. 27, Grey to Secretary of State W. E. Gladstone, 25 July 1846, enclosing Joseph Thorne, Churchwarden, St. Michael, 18 November 1845; Liberal, 26 July 1838.

38. CO 31/43, 13 May 1845; St. Michael Vestry, 13 March 1846.

tional services. In 1851, when Joseph Thorne was once again churchwarden, he seconded a motion making the continuation of the Central School's grant conditional upon the vestry being able to select 10 boys for the school, a method of forcing the school's trustees to accept pupils of color. Even though the trustees agreed, the vestry still redistributed some of the money it provided for parish education from the Central School to other schools for children of color.[39] In 1853 several members of the vestry tried to delay making a decision on renewing the salary of Edward Archer, the teacher of the St. Mary's Society Boys' School. Thorne, still the churchwarden, put his foot down, saying that the school was "as important to the parish as the Central School" and the decision should be taken immediately. Archer's salary was renewed.[40]

Prescod took a somewhat different view of the issue of poor relief from that of the St. Michael vestrymen of color. Like them he opposed the racial segregation of state charity, and argued that, if vestries provided poor relief for whites, then they should also offer it to people of color.[41] However, he did not support the idea of government accepting a greater role as a provider of social services. In 1842, when a planter, who was also a Liberal Party candidate, published a political platform advocating greater legislative responsibility for poor relief, Prescod opposed the proposal, arguing, on the basis of classical liberal principles, that poor relief provision was properly a private matter and that public charity would "stifle every manly sentiment of independence—every enobling [sic] aspiration by which the human mind is prompted to struggle on against surrounding difficulties on the way to improvement. . . . [It would be a] grievous wrong done to the really industrious and provident, by forcibly taking from them to bestow upon the idle and improvident."[42] In Prescod's view, free movement of labor, rather than state intervention, was the solution to the problem of poverty. He argued that the number of paupers in the island was increasing because planters continued to prevent emigration, and he described emigration as "the only safety valve for the evils under which our Peasantry are now groaning."[43] Even so, Prescod stopped publicly advo-

39. Minutes of the St. Michael Vestry, 1 May and 19 July 1853.

40. *Barbadian*, 6 April 1853.

41. *Liberal*, 17 March 1838.

42. *Liberal*, 14 December 1842.

43. CO 28/134, No. 35, MacGregor to Russell, 9 April 1840, enclosure D No. 3, Minutes of the Barbados Auxiliary British and Foreign Anti-Slavery Society . . . 23rd March 1840"; *Liberal*, 9 December 1840.

cating emigration after his election, probably out of political prudence and possibly because it was a hopeless cause, given the antiemigration laws. His record in the House of Assembly indicates that he remained consistent in his liberal economic views and his support for merchants' interests, advocating lower taxes and reduced state spending as an answer to the island's dire financial woes during the 1840s.[44]

Afro-Barbadian women were almost completely excluded from civic and economic life beyond involvement in charities and church activities. There are no recorded references to women of color speaking at Afro-Barbadian political meetings. It may be that women *were* present at civil rights meetings but were either not permitted to speak or men did not consider their contributions important enough to be recorded. For elite women of color, charitable work provided a modicum of space for independent community activity, for interactions with other women and the poor from a position of authority, and for the development and display of organizing skills. Yet philanthropy also represented the domestication of elite women of color. "Christian" philanthropic work for former slaves and the poor became the sine qua non of respectability for upper-class free women of color and women who took part in such charitable work were held up by prominent nonwhite men as models for others to follow.

The case of Sarah Hope, the daughter of a prominent free man of color named Thomas G. Hope, sums up the ambivalence of the public persona that female Afro-Barbadian philanthropists assumed. When she died in 1838, the *Liberal* praised Hope for her philanthropic work and for having devoted herself "to her service and the good of her fellow creatures." According to the *Liberal*, Sarah Hope was actively involved in organizing Sunday and Evening Schools, was "a strong supporter of that useful body, the Friendly Society," was secretary of the Bible Society, was one of the principal organizers of the choir at St. Paul's Anglican church and had been a member of "the Committee for furnishing ready-made clothes to the poor and indigent." The *Liberal* lamented that, with her death, "the poor have lost an invaluable friend and supporter; her charities being those of the true Christian— secretly and unostentaciously [sic] bestowed."[45] Sarah's charitable activities likely gave her a platform from which she commanded community authority and respect. Given the vital importance of philanthropy to the political designs of free men of color, women like Sarah would also have shaped the direction of both

44. See, for example, CO 31/53, 3 October 1843, 13 May 1845, and 9 May 1848.
45. *Liberal*, 12 May 1838.

philanthropic and political developments among Afro-Barbadians. At the same time, the ease with which this obituary condensed her life into a public symbol of "proper" Afro-Barbadian womanhood encapsulates the limits of the ability of female philanthropists to mold their own public image. As Sarah Hope's life illustrates, charities and church activities became the only acceptable areas of public life for "respectable" women of color. Their involvement in these activities was neither "secret" nor "unostentacious"—it was a stage for parading the orderly gender relations of the Afro-Barbadian elite.

British medical officer John Davy, who traveled through the British Caribbean in the 1850s, noted that he could say little about upper-class and "half caste" women of color in Barbados because they were "so little in society. From the few opportunities I had of judging, they appeared inferior in manners, and greatly inferior in information to the men, the natural consequence of a more secluded life, and a more limited and imperfect education."[46] In 1844 a group of "Ladies" of color presented Prescod with three hundred dollars to celebrate his election victory, a rare reference to any involvement in politics on the part of elite females. The gift was presented before a delegation of businessmen who had supported Prescod's campaign. While the names of the businessmen were reported in the newspaper the names of the women were not, suggesting that the presentation was primarily a symbolic statement of the political strength and wealth of the Afro-Barbadian male merchant elite.[47]

EMIGRATION AND DISENFRANCHISEMENT

In the harsh political and socioeconomic climate of postslavery Barbados many Afro-Barbadians despaired of the possibility of change in the island and turned decisively away from the reformist struggles that had shaped their politics for decades. Large numbers came to see emigration, rather than reform, as the solution to their troubles. Toward the close of the 1840s the dream of Afro-Barbadian migration to Africa resurfaced, but the discourse of this new emigration movement was very different from that of the period between 1838 and the early 1840s. In the earlier period, Africa had served as a metaphor for the hope and great expectations that many elite Afro-Barbadians had of emancipation. West Africa had been a potential source of imperial employment for a small number of educated and politi-

46. Davy, *West Indies before and since Emancipation*, 81.

47. *Liberal*, 12 June 1844.

cally ambitious Afro-Barbadian men. By the late 1840s African emigration was still floated as an opportunity for Afro-Caribbean people to play a role in the empire's mission to spread Western civilization, commerce, and culture in Africa. However, such a mission to Africa was now a means of escape from crippling poverty and political and economic disenfranchisement in Barbados.

In late 1847 the Afro-Barbadian teacher and philanthropist Charles Phipps, who was still unsuccessfully petitioning the Colonial Office for a government post in West Africa, sent a new proposal to the secretary of state. He suggested that tradesmen and mechanics from Barbados be sent to Sierra Leone (accompanied by himself, it would seem) in order to teach the "natives" trades.[48] Later that year the Barbados Colonization Society was founded, and under the auspices of the society 103 Afro-Barbadians volunteered to emigrate to Africa to help the British government with "the suppression of the slave trade and the introduction of civilization into Africa." They claimed that they wished to help save British lives and were "actuated . . . by a consciousness of their physiological fitness for the Task they would undertake" because of their "constitutional congeniality to the African Climate." They were certain that "the knowledge and habits which they have acquired in a civilized community, must peculiarly fit them for carrying out the benevolent intentions of Government."[49]

Despite these expressions of concern for the lives of white Britons, a resolution passed at the inaugural meeting of the society bluntly admitted that the project was also a response to appalling living conditions in Barbados, which was "overstocked with inhabitants, who are increasing in such a rapid degree, that it will be morally impossible, in a short time, for them to find adequate employment, in fact, in the present depressed state of the Island, there are hundreds who are in this predicament, and who could well be spared." The organizers of the scheme were clearly hoping that such projects would become a long-term means of dealing with the pressing problem of poverty, pointing out that "said emigrants must ultimately benefit themselves as well as others, as the means will thus be afforded of effecting a mutual interchange of the already civilized to a place where civilization and industry are required."[50] The proposal was published in the newspapers and met with an overwhelming response. In October, 234 Afro-Barbadian men,

48. CO 28/169, Misc. No. 338, Barbados, 4 January 1848, containing petition of Charles Phipps to Earl Grey.

49. CO 28/168, No. 33, Reid to Earl Grey, 7 May 1848.

50. Ibid.

among them 120 married men who offered to emigrate with their families, signed a follow-up petition, making a total of 671 people who were prepared to emigrate immediately to West Africa. A detailed list of their occupations shows a variety of backgrounds, ranging from schoolteacher to "general agriculturalist," which perhaps referred to either an independent peasant farmer or an estate worker. Most of those listed claimed to be artisans.[51]

Lacking the money themselves for such an undertaking, this group appealed to the imperial government for assistance to help them emigrate, but the secretary of state for the colonies declined.[52] Despite this setback, Afro-Barbadians kept petitioning for government assistance to get out of the island. That same year, 965 tradesmen and mechanics, led by a politically vocal artisan of colour named Henry Dayrell, sent a new petition to the House of Assembly, also asking to be allowed to emigrate because of the depressed state of business but without specifying a destination.[53] The petition, which the house ignored, was one of the largest it had received on any subject since emancipation. It is likely that all of those who signed were Afro-Barbadian, since the organizers of the meeting at which the petition was discussed were criticized in the press for not inviting any white people.[54]

Unknown to those seeking emigration to Africa, some of the Barbadians who had been transported to Sierra Leone after the 1816 rebellion were simultaneously trying to return home. Although they had eventually assimilated into the community in Sierra Leone and a number had become successful, an 1827 imperial report observed that, among the Barbadian Sierra Leonians "there was by no means that

51. The occupations were 1 draper, 3 storekeepers, 12 schoolmasters, 45 cabinet makers, 49 tailors, 1 architect, 4 millwrights, 14 wheelwrights, 20 carpenters, 18 shoemakers, 6 turners, 1 newspaper reporter, 4 masons, 4 clerks, 1 saddler, 5 upholsterers, 4 blacksmiths, 2 druggists, 1 farrier, 3 coopers, 2 shipwrights, 1 gold and silversmith, 1 hairdresser, 1 sailmaker, 1 butcher, 1 baker, 1 registered tailor, 20 agriculturalists, 1 bookbinder, 1 coach panelist, 5 fishermen, 3 net makers, 1 plumber and coppersmith, 2 mattress makers, and 1 general agriculturalist. See CO 28/169, Misc., unnumbered, Charles Phipps and Edward Archer to Grey, 9 October 1848.

52. CO 28/169, No. 10, Earl Grey to Governor William Colebrooke, 22 November 1848.

53. CO 31/56, 11 April 1848.

54. *Barbadian,* 28 February 1848. This was an entirely separate group from the Colonization Society. Dayrell, who had until recently been a member of the Barbados Colonization Society and had initially supported the colonization scheme, left after a rumor spread that the society's scheme "intended establishing a republican government so soon as they got to Africa." *Barbadian,* correspondence between Dayrell and Charles Phipps and Edward Archer of the Barbadian Colonization Society, 1, 5, 8, 21, and 26 July 1848.

decided expression of satisfaction which perhaps many would have expected." In 1841, perhaps prompted by the opportunity to return to a Barbados now free from slavery, a group of them petitioned the Colonial Office to be repatriated to Barbados. The Colonial Office offered to send them to Jamaica, hoping that they would join indentured workers there who had been brought in to alleviate the island's crippling labor shortage, but the petitioners refused and an unspecified number of them eventually returned to the island.[55]

Despite the failure of these emigration proposals, the struggle to build lives and communities in West Africa where Afro-Barbadians and their descendants could be the authors of their own fate and shape the future of the African continent continued. Afro-Barbadians were centrally involved in organizing an Anglican mission from Barbados to the Rio Pongas area of West Africa in what is now Gambia, which was established in 1855.[56] The mission survived for almost a century, and over the course of its existence a succession of Afro-Caribbean missionaries trained at Codrington College lived, worked, and, in some cases, died there, seeking to Christianize the predominantly Muslim population. Their experience there was, however, marked by constant struggle; the Rio Pongas mission was hampered by the racism of the Church of England hierarchy, which consistently devalued the work of missionaries of color, as well as by Afro–West Indian missionaries' own civilizationalist attitude toward the local population and Africans who worked for the mission.[57] Also, at the close of the American Civil War in 1865, the American Colonization Society, with whom Barbadian colonization activists had close contacts, granted ten thousand dollars to assist "in furtherance of Barbadian Liberian Emigration," which one newspaper in Barbados described as "a scheme so benevolent to an Island so overpopulated as Barbadoes." The money enabled 346 Barbadians of color to emigrate to Liberia later that year on a ship carrying predominantly African American emigrants.[58]

55. Blyden, *West Indians in West Africa*, 37.

56. See Bishop's Court records, microfilms BS 33–38, particularly BS 38, BPL; CO 28/173, No. 73, Colebrooke to Grey, 29 November 1850, enclosing Bishop of Barbados to Colebrooke, 28 November 1850, enclosure No. 4, "Proposed Mission from the Church of the West Indies to Western Africa" (Barbados: Barbadian Office, 1850). Thomas J. Cummins, John Montefiore, and London Bourne were members of the committee for this project. See also, recently, Karch, "Man for All Seasons," 21–31.

57. See Bakary Gibba, "The West Indian Missionaries and the Rio Pongas Mission in West Africa, 1850–1950" (Ph.D. diss., University of Toronto, forthcoming).

58. "Extracts from the *Times*, February 1865, *JBMHS* 30 (1976–77), quoted in Karch, "Man for All Seasons," 27–28.

FROM BRIDGETOWN TO MONROVIA

Among those new Barbadian arrivals to Liberia in 1865 was the Barclay family, consisting of Bridgetown shopkeeper Anthony Barclay Jr., his wife Sarah, and their twelve children. Barclay Jr. had been politically active in Barbados since at least 1833, when he supported a motion by Prescod to criticize the House of Assembly for continuing to block the enfranchisement of free people of color. His father, Anthony Barclay, had also been a minor figure in the civil rights struggle, signing the 1811 petitions and the 1824 apology for the counteraddress. Barclay Jr. and his wife settled in Monrovia and went on to raise one of the most prominent West Indian political families in early-twentieth-century Liberia. The tenth of their children, Arthur Barclay, born in Barbados in July 1854, was president of Liberia from 1904 to 1912. Another son, Ernest J. Barclay, became secretary of state, and Ernest's son, Edwin Barclay, was president of the republic from 1930 to 1944.[59] The Barclays and their descendants were in many ways the fulfillment of the vision of "Africanus," the 1841 correspondent to the *Liberal* who had dreamed of the possibilities for Afro–West Indians who went to Africa.[60] Just as "Africanus" had suggested, once the British Empire showed itself to be uninterested in facilitating the "return" of its black subjects to Africa, the Barclays took the radical step of turning their backs on the empire altogether and going to Africa without the sanction of the imperial government. Furthermore, as powerful individuals in Liberia's political history they brought to their relations with indigenous Africans both the Afro-Caribbean version of the imperial "civilizing mission" and the determination of many Afro–West Indians to defend the African continent politically from European imperialism.

Arthur Barclay was Liberia's last foreign-born president, all of his predecessors having begun their lives in the United States. Like them, his leadership of the country reflected his perspective as a Liberian born on the other side of the Atlantic. He took over a country troubled since its founding in 1822 by uncertainty over its borders, tense relations between black colonists from the Americas and indigenous African communities, the continuation of domestic slavery, and threats to the republic's sovereignty from Western colonial powers, especially Britain,

59. Charles Morrow Wilson, *Liberia: Black Africa in Microcosm* (New York: Harper & Row, 1971), 106–109, 120ff.; Nathaniel R. Richardson, *Liberia's Past and Present* (London: Diplomatic Press and Publishing, 1959), 117–127, 143–159.

60. See chapter 7, pp. 206–209.

France, and the United States. Barclay's inaugural speech offers key insights into Afro-Barbadian migrants' understandings of the meaning of freedom, nation, citizenship, and community as these terms applied to Africans. He set his government the task of regularizing relations between Liberia's "civilised population" and its "natives." In particular, the indigenous populations of the coastal regions within Liberia's borders were to be "organised as soon as possible into townships" with a chief chosen and commissioned by the government, a policy similar to that pursued in the late nineteenth and early twentieth centuries by the U.S. and Canadian federal governments, as they consolidated the power of North American settler society. Barclay's proposals created new forms of chiefly authority that were not organic to indigenous communities and better served the interests of the colonizing state in its dealings with indigenous populations.

Within the townships each man was to be assigned twenty-five acres of land. Women, it appears, were not eligible for such grants. Furthermore, while the Liberian government would protect indigenous rights to the use and occupancy of township lands, these lands were to be held in common, not by individuals, and the land could not be sold without the written consent of the Liberian government. In language reminiscent of the British government's attitude toward the political capabilities of former West Indian slaves in the 1830s, Barclay noted that the inhabitants of the townships "would not of course possess the right of suffrage." Two-thirds of the male inhabitants of a township could apply for permission to divide up the land into individual freehold lots, and these freeholders would then acquire the right to vote based on their ownership of land. However, the final decision to grant suffrage rested with the Liberian government, and if "the community appeared not sufficiently advanced for the step, the petition might be refused." Barclay also had plans to put the "native population" to use in military service and proposed dividing it "into two classes—the more spirited tribes will furnish fighters, and the tribes who are unwarlike, military laborers and carriers."

In common with former leaders of Liberia and missionaries in both the West Indies and Africa, Barclay was deeply concerned about the perceived dysfunctionality of African societies, especially polygamy and domestic slavery. He was optimistic that the "problem" of polygamy was slowly disappearing, as "the West African native is gradually becoming monogamic." He was willing to consider passing legislation to increase the "fixed and superior" position of the first wife within the polygamous family, but as a rule, he noted, polygamy "ought to be tolerated [as] but a stage in the social development of communities [which will] gradually disappear as the native communities advance in civilization, and with the increase of sound moral and religious ideas." Barclay pledged to abolish domestic slavery "in a just and equitable manner," using government funds to compensate the owner for the loss of their enslaved property. In an echo of the apprenticeship system of the British Caribbean, Barclay felt that former slaves, for whom the government had paid compensation, would then owe the Liberian government for their freedom. He wanted his government to "take the freedman and his family, if any, under its protection, and hire him out for a limited period, receiving a portion of his wages against the expenditure incurred, until the debt is paid." The government should also resettle many former slaves on small plots of public land where their labor could be more "advantageously utilized by artisans and farmers." It is unclear how much say the newly freed were supposed to have in either this resettlement plan or the "advantageous" disposal of their labor.[61]

Arthur Barclay also fought to prevent the United States, France, Germany, and Britain from successfully using the republic's growing debt problem as an excuse to take official control of the country's finances, as the United States did across the Atlantic in the Dominican Republic and Haiti in 1905 and 1907. But his efforts faltered in the face of a concerted effort by western governments and lending agencies to force Liberia into a financial crisis, and he left office in the middle of ongoing negotiations with the administration of William Howard Taft in the United States over a massive loan at high interest. Although the loan of 1.7 million dollars in 1912 arguably "saved Liberia from outright backruptcy and literal foreclosure," in the long run it probably increased Liberia's dependence on Western financial assistance. It also came with very long strings attached; the terms to which Barclay and his successor in office had to agree allowed the U.S., British, French, and German governments to appoint receivers general for Liberia (with a larger salary than the republic's president), giving them an unprecedented level of control over the country's finances.[62]

The political career of Arthur Barclay's nephew Edwin was similarly marked

61. Richardson, *Liberia's Past and Present*, 117–123.
62. Wilson, *Liberia*, 106–109.

by political battles over slavery and forced labor in Liberia and efforts to deal with the "resentment" of indigenous people. Edwin Barclay also faced the trials of the Great Depression and World War II and an attempt, spearheaded by Britain and the United States, to turn Liberia from an independent state and a member of the League of Nations into a league mandate. The younger Barclay began his term as president facing one of the most serious threats to Liberia's sovereignty since its independence in 1847. Throughout the 1920s, when Edwin Barclay was Liberian secretary of state, British and American officials insisted that Liberia actually *apply* to the League of Nations for the removal of its independent status because of the alleged existence of slavery in Liberia and the republic's failure to meet its international debt payments. Edwin Barclay's predecessor as president, another Liberian of West Indian ancestry named Charles King, appointed an international commission of inquiry into the issue of slave labor that included the elderly Arthur Barclay. The commission examined and refuted the claims in its 1930 report, but the scandal precipitated King's resignation and Edwin Barclay became acting president in December 1930. He was confirmed as president after bitter and intensely fought elections in 1831, but Britain and the United States initially refused to recognize the new government, still insisting that Liberia should willingly forfeit its sovereignty.[63]

As secretary of state in the 1920s, Edwin Barclay negotiated with Marcus Garvey and representatives of his Universal Negro Improvement Association about the mass immigration of 30,000 African Americans (many of them West Indian migrants to the United States) to Liberia. According to one historian of Liberia, King and Barclay were "pure" blacks from the Caribbean and therefore "did not share the prejudices of the paler Americo-Liberians" who dominated the country economically and politically and feared the political impact Garvey and his supporters might have on Liberia. Arguably, had events on the other side of the Atlantic taken a different turn, Barclay might have facilitated the mass migration of blacks from the United States (many of them West Indian born) into Liberia in the 1920s and 1930s. But once news reached Liberia in 1924 of the disastrous collapse of the Black Star Line and the charges against Garvey for mail fraud, Barclay and King withdrew their support for the project, and Barclay wrote on behalf of the

63. Richardson, *Liberia's Past and Present*, 143–146; Richard West, *Back to Africa: A History of Sierra Leone and Liberia* (New York: Hold, Rinehart, and Winston, 1970), 307–312.

government to state that it was "irrevocably opposed . . . to the incendiary policy of the Universal Negro Improvement Association," which would threaten Liberia's relations with Britain and France, the imperial states that controlled all of Liberia's neighbors.[64]

CONCLUSION

The generations of Afro-Barbadians who lived through the turbulent final decades of slavery and early postslavery society had high hopes that emancipation would usher in a period of significant political and socioeconomic change. However, a combination of transatlantic and local economic forces—notably changes in the world sugar market, the decline in imperial support for the reconstruction of the postemancipation Caribbean, and the repressive policies of the Barbadian plantocracy—helped shut down these hopes. Nevertheless, the struggle by Afro-Barbadians, whether free or enslaved before 1834, for equality of opportunity with whites and for respect and recognition from metropolitan Britain would go on both in the island and on the African continent. While the Barclays and hundreds of others sought their fortunes in Liberia, those who stayed in Barbados also fought to transform the island's social, economic, and political landscape and remake it in the interests of the Afro-Barbadian majority. In 1876 the island was shaken by a popular rebellion in favor of a political federation of Barbados and the other islands of the Windward Caribbean, which could have facilitated Afro-Barbadian migration and significantly weakened planter control. In a letter to the governor, who had outraged the local plantocracy by advocating the plan, an Afro-Barbadian man from St. Philip wrote on behalf of the poor and disenfranchised of his area to express his support for the governor and for confederation. In his letter one hears the echoes of the imperial nationalism, racial consciousness, populism, and antielitism that had been the hallmark of plebian Afro-Barbadian politics for much of the century:

My deer Sir we has made up in our mines from seeing the white people is so much against Confedoractions which is for our good to raise up a rebellion on the eveinin afater ester against them so you but stand pun we side

64. West, *Back to Africa*, 269–272.

with the sogers. . . . [I]f it is tru it will bring you in truble we shant do it but you no when the white people ses the firs—they gets very friton it will do good on that nite as the people will be in a good temper so tel us if the sogers will fite for us.[65]

65. Belle, "The Abortive Revolution," 189.

T HIS study is an effort to grapple with the complexities of Afro-Caribbean people's relationship with the process of slave emancipation and to think historically about contemporary political discourses and the modern public sphere in the postcolonial Caribbean. The analysis signposts the wider implications of the study of slavery and emancipation and the place of race, nation, nationalism and gender as tools of historical analysis and forms of social identity. One should always be mindful of the dangers of making the study of slave emancipation into "the servant of present needs," as historian of British slave emancipation William A. Green once termed it.[1] Nevertheless, there are significant and intriguing resonances between the concerns and struggles of Afro-Barbadians in the age of emancipation and the challenges that face Afro-Barbadians, as well as other communities across the Anglophone Caribbean, in our own time. These similarities were crystalized by the Barbadian government's 1998 declaration of ten "National Heroes," among whom were two free people of color discussed in this book, Afro-Barbadian Methodist Sarah Ann Gill and journalist and politician Samuel Jackman Prescod. This is not the place to debate whether or not these individuals deserve to be national heroes—or even why it was suddenly considered important to *have* national heroes. What is in question is the manner in which Gill and Prescod were represented in this official commemoration process.

In the government's booklet on *Our National Heroes* Prescod is described as someone who "gave a voice to the dispossessed and the marginalized when they did not have one, and who broke down the barricades of Parliamentary segregation, creating the aperture through which all the rest of us have followed. . . . [He] had a futuristic vision of the importance of training the masses in the business of self-government" and earned the title "counsellor" and "adviser" from the people.[2] Sarah Ann Gill also is eulogized:

1. William A. Green, "The Creolization of Caribbean History: A Critique of Dialectical Analysis," in Beckles and Shepherd, *Caribbean Freedom,* 28.

2. Barbados Government Information Service (GIS), *Our National Heroes* (Bridgetown: GIS, 1998), 10.

Widowed early and a woman alone, fighting for religious freedom, the rights of the individual, and, in a most dangerous age, representing and radiating the indomitable spirit of Barbadian womanhood. . . . By her faith, her courage, her charity and nobility she altered the course of history. She symbolises the faith, strength and courage of Barbadian women through history, and the great rock of Christian faith they built, on which our lives are based.[3]

These official eulogies are a crude reflection of the relatively small body of historiographical writing on Afro-Barbadian political activity in the era of slave emancipation and they fairly cry out for analysis. They contain echoes and reverberations of the normative gender and class discourses that shaped elite representations of "correct" bourgeois Afro-Barbadian masculinity and femininity during the era of emancipation.

Sarah Ann Gill is the only "national heroine," and in *Our National Heroes* she is *Mrs.* Sarah Ann Gill, "widowed early, and a woman alone"—the only one of the national heroes whose marital status has been provided. This is reminiscent of the privileging of marital status among elite Afro-Barbadian philanthropist women during the early nineteenth century, distancing themselves from less "respectable" and unmarried women in the public domain.[4] Gill's entry into the sphere of public life is justified by the fact that as a "woman alone," she had no one to protect her from the planter state. The reference to her widowhood renders her involvement in a public political struggle respectable because she crossed the line between involvement in "nonpolitical" church and missionary activity, areas of civic engagement that are still considered "respectable" and appropriate for Afro-Barbadian women, into the sphere of politics. Gill's religiosity and that of other Afro-Barbadian women is marked as the "rock" on which the "lives" of generations of Barbadians have been built. Such language resonates with the idea of her as a maternal figure, casting her in the role of a spiritual Christian mother to the nation and a symbol of proper bourgeois motherhood for other women. This description of Gill reflects the fact that, despite the high political profile of Afro-Barbadian women and the recent increase in the number of women occupying powerful positions in formal party politics, women in politics are still treated by male public commentators as suspect and public speculation about the respect-

3. Ibid., 23.
4. See chapter 3, pp. 99–100.

ability and orderliness of their private sexual conduct and domestic arrangements remains rife.

In the case of Prescod, this gendered and patriarchal commemoration is taken directly from the work of historians, who have presented him to the public as a patriarchal figure for the modern nation-state and for the Afro-Barbadian "masses." Indeed, Prescod has long been claimed as a "proto" nationalist; he was recently incorporated in a collection of essays on the "nationalist tradition" in Barbados.[5] Writing about him has very much followed a "great-man" approach to historical inquiry, in which he alone is an individual, leading nameless, faceless, and voiceless masses on to liberation. The fact that Prescod, in an age of democratic revolutions, was expressly *not* a democrat and did not support universal manhood suffrage (there is no evidence that he wished to "train" the masses to govern themselves) has been ignored.

Such representations, in which the complex world view of free people of color is reduced to part of the story of a nation coming into being, can severely limit efforts to engage critically with the Afro-Barbadian past. Like other Afro-Barbadians of their time—and probably many Barbadians until independence—Gill and Prescod saw themselves as black Britons. Prescod's African diasporic consciousness was certainly a forerunner of Caribbean pan-Africanism but he and other Afro-Barbadians invoked Africa as much to claim full rights as equal citizens to whites within the British empire as they did to assert their sense of solidarity with people of African descent elsewhere in the Atlantic world. This imperial nationalism was an articulation of Britishness and a demand that the British Empire accord the same rights to its nonwhite subjects as it did to those of European descent. If we dismiss this aspect of their consciousness because it sits uncomfortably with our sense of place in the world, then we cannot fully understand them and their struggles.

This research questions historiographical trends that would seek to easily fit nineteenth-century Afro-Barbadian political consciousness into positivist historical narratives about the development of a "Barbadian nationalist enterprise."[6] The representation of Prescod as a nationalist constructs understandings of the present in ways that serve the interests of political elites who have inherited the run-

5. See Howe and Marshall, *The Empowering Impulse*, especially vii, and Belle, "Samuel Jackman Prescod," in Howe and Marshall, *The Empowering Impulse*, 56–102.

6. See Howe and Marshall, *Empowering Impulse*, vii.

ning of the former colonial state. The image of Prescod as a nationalist leader of the laboring poor fits neatly within the twentieth-century official history of decolonization, when a political class of Afro-Barbadian professionals rose to power as labor leaders on the shoulders of popular revolt a century after emancipation.[7] To reread what has been described in this book as Barbadian "nationalism"—a concept Gill and Prescod probably could not even have imagined—as opposed to a radical Barbadian, Caribbean and African diasporic reformulation of British imperial identity, is to write history backward, to entirely misinterpret the political aspirations of people of color in Barbados during this period, and to miss the nuances of their political worldviews. Understanding the complexities and conflicts of their perspectives, including the profoundly pro-British and African diasporic consciousness described in this work, may enhance our knowledge of the genealogy of late-eighteenth- and early-twentieth-century political ideologies, such as pan-Africanism and anti-imperialism.[8]

While this study is strongly critical of efforts to force nineteenth-century Afro-Barbadian articulations of racial consciousness into a nationalist paradigm, it is perhaps salient to remember C. L. R. James's 1938 observation that the road to West Indian national identity lies through Africa.[9] This is especially the case in a country such as Barbados, where the population has remained for centuries over 80 percent of African descent. Just as abolitionists of the 1830s and 1840s judged emancipation as a "success" or "failure" based on the willingness of Afro-Caribbean people to accept their place at the bottom of the socioeconomic hierarchy, people of African descent considered that the metropole had to pass the "test" of freedom by living up to its promises of African empowerment on the continent and in the Caribbean. The central place of Africa in Afro-Barbadians' early-

7. O. Nigel Bolland, The Politics of Labour in the British Caribbean: The Social Origins of Authoritarianism and Democracy in the Labour Movement (Kingston: Ian Randle, 2001), 549–564.

8. For an example of such a genealogical excavation see discussion of the role of Marcus Garvey's father in the Underhill Meetings in the months before the Morant Bay Rebellion in John Henrick Clarke and Amy Jacques Garvey, Marcus Garvey and the Vision of Africa (New York, Vintage Books, 1974), 30, cited in Sheller, Democracy after Slavery, 238–240. See the excellent discussion of the ideology of proimperialism and Britishness in the reactions of West Indian volunteers and black radicals such as Marcus Garvey to World War I in C. L. R. James, Beyond a Boundary (1963; reprint, New York: Pantheon Books, 1984) and Winston James, Holding Aloft the Banner of Ethiopia: Caribbean Radicalism in Early Twentieth Century America (London: Verso, 1998), 52–69.

9. See James, Black Jacobins, 402.

nineteenth-century loyalty to the British empire rested on a sense of the empire's indebtedness, both to them and to the African continent.

Implicitly, then, there was a certain contractual element to Afro-Caribbean imperial loyalties, a contingency clause that depended on whether or not Britain appeared to abiding by a mandate of atonement bequeathed to it by its history as one of the world's most prolific enslaving states. Given this contingency, it is no surprise that support for the empire began to unravel in the early twentieth century and that Britain's repudiation of its perceived duty to defend the freedom of Africans on the continent and in the diaspora played a central role. In the 1930s, when Britain's support for the Italian invasion of Ethiopia coincided with the one-hundredth anniversary of slave emancipation and the hardships of the Great Depression, the empire was rocked by violent popular uprisings throughout the British Caribbean, including protests in Barbados in 1937.[10] The generation of black and mixed-race middle-class professional leaders, who rose to prominence in Barbados and across the soon-to-be-former British Caribbean out of the ashes of these popular rebellions, were arguably the political descendants of the bourgeois-elite of color of a century before. The mid-twentieth century would witness the consolidation of a bourgeois-led Barbadian nationalist project that, even if it did not completely reject the symbols and institutions of the empire, certainly encompassed a critique of the assumed right of British rule.

The processes of revolution, reform, and slave emancipation and the new debates and challenges that arose as a result laid the foundations of public life in the modern Caribbean and, indeed, throughout the Atlantic world. Abolitionism and emancipation opened up great social and political debates, which have surfaced repeatedly in the postslavery Atlantic world. The challenge of forging a civil rights agenda that could unite people of African descent across race, class, and gender lines—and of confronting the limits of race as a basis for political mobilization—would be revisited across the Atlantic world, most famously in the U.S. civil rights movement and the antiapartheid movement in South Africa. The failure of liberal imperial claims that the former slaveholding state could provide equality of opportunity and equality before the law laid the groundwork for late-twentieth-century debates about social welfare policy and affirmative action. Already at the time of emancipation it was questionable whether any social redress was possible without a serious engagement at the state level with the institutionalized legacy of slavery.

10. Bolland, *Politics of Labour*, 212–378.

As Jacqui Alexander has illustrated, the question of the role of class, gender, and race in determining access to citizenship in the Caribbean, which was raised by the long process of slavery's demise, also remains unresolved.[11]

What responsibility do former slaveholding states, including the British government and governments of recently independent states such as Barbados, have to correct the historical wrong of slavery and the abandonment of serious efforts at socioeconomic reform after emancipation? One example of a response to this question was the massive expansion of social services in Barbados after decolonization. Successive governments invested heavily in education, housing, health care and welfare provision to address the appalling inequalities of race and economic status for which Barbados was notorious. Yet this transformation of the colonial administration into a version of the mid-twentieth-century welfare state, a process that continued after decolonization, also represented a fear of racial conflict and tension as well as an effort to manage public discussions and debate about race and class inequality. Although the white planter-merchant oligarchy was thrown out of the political arena by universal suffrage and the place of sugar in the national economy has declined, the oligarchy has retained its place as the most economically powerful sector of Barbadian society. Sugar has been replaced by tourism as the major engine of the national economy, but as many scholars have illustrated, the Caribbean's tourism-driven economies retain many of the socioeconomic features of the plantation system that they have ostensibly replaced.

While most Barbadians have heard of Samuel Jackman Prescod (and now, thanks to her elevation to the status of "national heroine," Sarah Ann Gill), most of the people and events discussed in this book have long passed out of popular memory. Yet the echoes of Barbadians' long struggle to come to terms with slavery, its demise, and the reconstitution of postslavery society can be heard in every aspect of life in the island. The lessons of the past are profound, especially in a world currently hurtling down the path of economic determinism, neoliberal conservatism and a withdrawal of the state from the arena of social welfare policy. These are policies that, as this book and others have shown, did much to undermine the

---

11. M. Jacqui Alexander, "Not Just (Any) Body Can Be a Citizen: The Politics of Law, Sexuality and Postcoloniality in Trinidad and Tobago and the Bahamas," *Feminist Review* 48 (Autumn 1994): 5–23; M. Jacqui Alexander, "Erotic Autonomy as a Politics of Decolonization: An Anatomy of Feminist and State Practice in the Bahamas Tourist Economy," in M. Jacqui Alexander and Chandra Talpade Mohanty, *Feminist Genealogies, Colonial Legacies, Democratic Futures* (New York: Routledge, 1997), 63–100.

transformative potential of emancipation. At the dawn of the twenty-first century, governments, some public intellectuals, and (often self-appointed) community leaders in Barbados are trying to accommodate themselves and their constituents to the "new reality" of free trade, as though the Caribbean had not seen such things, and their consequences, before. If they could speak directly to us, the Afro-Barbadian civil rights campaigners of the age of emancipation might have something to say about this. They might remind us that, however significant the political differences between them and however much some of them wished to forget their past complicity with enslavement, they generally understood that racial slavery was the silent referent in all struggles to define the meaning of freedom in the Atlantic world. At stake in the current debate—no less that at the time of emancipation—are fundamental issues of social sustainability, survival, political access, and democratic possibility. The current resurgence of dehumanizing, market-driven and neoimperial ideology has taken place in large part because emancipation failed to live up to the expectations of many former slaves and free people of color. Emancipation—its triumphs, failures, and unresolved tensions—is present and living history, and we forget this fact at our peril.

Records of the Colonial Office, National Archives, Kew Gardens, London

CO 28/85–181. Barbados, Original Correspondence, 1816–1854.

CO 30/20–25. Barbados, Acts, 1814–1856.

CO 31/47–58. Barbados, Sessional Papers, 1816–1863.

CO 318/52–62, 76, 80, 116. West Indies, Original Correspondence, 1816–1833.

CO 33/1–4, 9–12, 33–64. Barbados, Miscellanea, 1829–1854.

T 71/520, 521, 533, 536, 544, 546, 547, 548, 549, 552. Barbados Slave Registries, 1817–1832.

Manuscripts and Private Papers

Abstracts of cases against apprentice and free labourers (5), 1837–1838. BPL.

Colleton Plantation Journal and Ledger, 1818–1844. BMHS.

Governor's Circulars to Magistrates, 1836–1847. BPL.

Governor's Correspondence to Special and General Magistrates, 1836–1838. BPL.

Governor's Correspondence with Assistant Court of Appeal, 1838–1841. BPL.

Governor's Messages, 1836–1840. BPL.

Hilton Vaughan Mss. "Prescod I: Letters, Speeches and Newspaper Articles, 1830–1838." BDA.

Nathaniel Lucas Mss. Microfilm 17. BPL.

Newcastle and Bissex Hill Plantation Journals. BMHS.

Newton Estate Papers. UWI, Cave Hill, Barbados.

Records of Boarders and Turners Hall Plantations in the Fitzherbert Papers. D239M/E20455–20485, 20486–20617. BDA.

Records of Drax Hall Plantation. Z9/11/ 4–27. BDA.

Sir Robert Peel Mss. British Library Additional Mss. 40.651. British Library.

Parish Government Records

Minutes of the Christ Church Vestry, 22 August 1831–26 November 1842, 9 Jan 1843–28 March 1867.

Minutes of the St. George Vestry, 8 January 1816–23 August 1856.

Minutes of the St. John Vestry, Minute Books. 1792–1820, 1829–1863.

Minutes of the St. Lucy Vestry, 1846–1875.

Minutes of the St. Michael Vestry, March 1823–July 1834, 24 September 1840–26 May 1848, 5 July 1849–6 January 1853, 17 January 1853–11 December 1857.

Minutes of the St. Philip Vestry, 25 March 1794–19 December 1835, 18 January 1836–17 December 1856.

Minutes of the St. Thomas Vestry, 1843–1874.

Records of the Anglican and Moravian Churches

Board of Education Minute Books, November 1850–13 March 1860.

Clifton Hill Church Book, 1837–1948. Microfilm BS 69. BPL.

Diary of the Negro Congregation at Mount Tabor Moravian Church, St. John. 1826–1854. Microfilm BS 59. BPL.

Mount Tabor Church Book of Baptisms, 1826–1860. Microfilm BS 58. BPL.

Mount Tabor Moravian Church Miscellaneous Documents, 1825–1912. Microfilm BS 58. BPL.

Mount Tabor Moravian Church Book, 1828–1860. Microfilm BS 53. BPL.

Mount Tabor Conference Books, 1837–1858. Microfilm BS. 64. BPL.

RL 1/50A, Parochial Register—Baptisms Solemnized in the Parish of St. Thomas. BDA.

Sharon Church Book, 1769–1854. Microfilm BS 57 and 58, BPL.

Newspapers and Serials

Barbadian. 1824–1856. BPL.

Barbados Globe and Demerara Advocate. 1829. CO 33/1. National Archives.

Barbados Mercury and Bridgetown Gazette. 24 November 1812–23 January 1816, microfilm R. 23; 23 January 1816–1819, microfilm R. 24; 1 May 1819–May 1824, microfilm R. 25 and R. 26. BPL.

Democrat. 1970–1971. BDA.

Liberal. 1837–1854. BPL and National Archives.

British Anti-Slavery Reporter. 1840.

Estate Catalogues

Catalogue of Barbadian Estates. BMHS.

List of Property Owners of One Acre or More, 1842. BDA.

British Parliamentary Papers

PP 1816, vol. 19. *Colonial Laws Respecting Slaves.*

PP 1817, vol. 17. *Additional Colonial Laws Respecting Slaves, 1816–1817.*

PP 1823, vol. 18. *Acts of Colonial Legislatures for Registry of Slaves.*

PP 1823, vol. 18. *Slave Population: Papers and Returns.*

PP 1823, vol. 23. *Papers relating to the Treatment of Slaves in the Colonies; viz. Acts of Colonial Legislatures, 1818–1823.*

PP 1824, vol. 24. *Papers . . . in explanation of the Measures adopted . . . for the melioration of the con-dition of the slave population . . . in the West Indies.*

PP 1824, vol. 24. *Returns of the . . . Slave Population in each of His Majesty's Colonies in the West In-dies; distinguishing the Males and Females. . . .*

PP 1825, vol. 15. *First report of the Commissioner of Inquiry into the administration of civil and criminal justice in the West Indies.*

PP 1826, vol. 26. *Colonial Population.*

PP 1826, vol. 28. *Slave Population.*

PP 1826, vol. 28. *Slave Population. Further Papers relating to the Slave Population of British Posses-sions in the West Indies and South America.*

PP 1826, vol. 29. *Papers containing abstracts of acts passed by the legislatures of the West India colo-nies, since the 15th May, 1823, for improving the condition of slaves.*

PP 1826–1827, vol. 25. *Papers . . . in explanation of the measures adopted . . . for the amelioration of the condition of the slave population in . . . the West Indies.*

PP 1826–1827, vol. 26. *Papers relating to the slave population in the West Indies.*

PP 1828, vol. 25. *Slave population.*

PP 1828, vol. 27. *Papers in explanation of the measures adopted . . . for the melioration of the condition of the slave population . . . in the West Indies.*

PP 1829, vol. 25. *Papers . . . in explanation of the measures adopted . . . for the melioration of the con-dition of the slave population in the West Indies.*

PP 1830, vol. 21. *Slave population in the colonies.*

PP 1830–1831, vol. 16. *Papers . . . in explanation of the measures adopted . . . for the melioration of the condition of the slave population in . . . the West Indies.*

PP 1831, vol. 19. *Colonies: population, trade etc.*

PP 1831, vol. 19. *Slave emancipation: crown slaves.*

PP 1831–1832, vol. 20. *Report from select committee on the extinction of slavery throughout the Brit-ish dominions.*

PP 1831–1832, vol. 31. *West Indies—toleration laws.*

PP 1831–1832, vol. 46. *Papers . . . in explanation of the measures adopted for the melioration of the condition of the slave population in . . . the West Indies.*

PP 1831–1832, vol. 47. *Slave laws, Barbadoes.*

PP 1831–1832, vol. 47. *Slave population. Extracts from returns.*

PP 1833, vol. 26. *Slave population (slave registries).*

PP 1835, vol. 50. *Papers . . . in explanation of the measures adopted . . . for giving effect to the act for the abolition of slavery.*

PP 1837–1838, vol. 48. *Report on Negro Education, Windward and Leeward Islands.*

PP 1840, vol. 35, part 2. *Second Series of Questions . . . [and] Answers relative to the working of the Free System in Barbados.*

PP 1842, vol. 13. *Report from the Select Committee on West India Colonies; together with the minutes of evidence, appendix, and index.*

PP 1842, vol. 29. *Papers Relative to the West Indies, 1841–42. Jamaica and Barbados.*

PP 1845, vol. 31. *Copies of the last Census taken in each of the British West Indian Islands and in British Guiana . . . together with any Information subsequently received . . . relative to the Number of the Emancipated Negroes who have become Freeholders. . . .*

PP 1846, vol. 28. *Papers . . . relating to the Labouring Population of the British Colonies.*

Published Primary Sources

Anon. "Remarks on the Insurrection in Barbadoes, and the Bill for the Registration of Slaves." *Christian Observer* 15, no. 6 (June 1816): 403–414.

——. *The Sugar Question: Being a digest of the evidence taken before the committee on sugar and coffee plantations.* London: Smith, Elder, 1848.

Barbados Council. *Report of a Committee of the Council of Barbadoes, appointed to inquire into the actual condition of the Slaves in this Island. . . .* London: N.p., 1824.

Barbados government. *Report of the Commission on Poor Relief.* Bridgetown, 1877.

Barbados Government Information Service (GIS). *Our National Heroes.* Bridgetown: GIS, 1998.

Barbados House of Assembly. *The Public Acts in Force, Passed by the Legislature of Barbados, from the First of William IV. . . .* Bridgetown: House of Assembly, 1836.

——. *Report of a Select Committee of the House of Assembly appointed to enquire into the origin, causes, and progress, of the late Insurrection.* Bridgetown: T. Cadell and W. Davies, 1818.

Bayley, F. W. N. *Four Years' Residence in the West Indies, during the years 1826, 7, 8 and 9.* London: William Kidd, 1833.

British Parliament. *The Statutes of the United Kingdom of Great Britain and Ireland,* 1 and 2 Victoria, 1837–1838.

Coleridge, H. N. *Six Months in the West Indies, in 1825.* London: N.p., 1826.

Colthurst, John Bowen. *The Colthurst Journal: Journal of a Special Magistrate in the Islands of Barbados and St. Vincent, July 1835–September 1838.* Edited by Woodville Marshall. New York: KTO Press, 1977.

Davy, John. *The West Indies before and since Emancipation, Comprising the Windward and Leeward Islands' Military Command.* London: N.p., 1854.

Dickson, William. *Letters on Slavery . . . to which are added, Addresses to the Whites, and the Free Negroes of Barbadoes.* London: J. Philips, 1789.

Dwarris, Fortunatus. *Substance of the Three Reports of the Commissioner of Inquiry into the Administration of Civil and Criminal Justice in the West Indies, extracted from the Parliamentary Papers. . . .* London: Joseph Butterworth and Son, 1827.

Flannigan, Mrs. *Antigua and the Antiguans; A Full Account of the Colony and Its Inhabitants . . . from the time of the Caribs to the present day. . . . Also an impartial view of slavery and the free labour system. . . .* 1844. Reprint, London: Spottiswoode, Ballantyne, 1967.

Gobert, David, and Jerome Handler, eds. and trans. "Barbados in the Apprenticeship Period: The Report of a French Colonial Official [April 1836]." *JBMHS* 36, no. 2 (1979): 108–128.

Hall, Richard. *Acts, passed in the island of Barbados. . . .* London: R. Hall, 1764.

Hawthorne, Nathaniel, ed. *The Yarn of a Yankee Privateer.* New York: Funk and Wagnall's, 1926.

Hazlitt, William. *The Spirit of the Age; or, Contemporary Portraits.* Edited by E. D. Mackerness. 1825. Reprint, Plymouth: Northcote House, 1991.

Holder, Rev. H. E. *A Short Essay on the Subject of Negro Slavery, with a Particular Reference to the Island of Barbadoes.* London: Couchman and Fry, 1788.

Lascelles, Edwin, James Colleton, Edward Drax, Francis Ford, John Brathwaite, John Walter, William Thorpe Holder, James Holder, and Philip Gibbes. *Instructions for the Management of a Plantation in Barbadoes and for the Treatment of Negroes, &tc.* London: N.p., 1786.

Lloyd, William Lloyd. *Letter from the West Indies, During a Visit of 1836, and the spring of 1837.* London: N.p., 1839.

Orderson, J. W. *Creoleana: or Social and Domestic Scenes and Incidents in Barbados in Days of Yore.* London: Saunders and Otley, 1842.

Parliament, House of Commons. *An Authentic Report of the Debate in the House of Commons, June the 23rd, 1825, on Mr. Buxton's Motion Relative to the Demolition of the Methodist Chapel and Mission House in Barbadoes, and the Expulsion of Mr. Shrewsbury, a Wesleyan Missionary, from That Island.* London: J. Hatchard and Son, 1825.

Poyer, John. *The History of Barbados, from the First Discovery of the Island, in the year 1605, till the Accession of Lord Seaforth, 1801.* London: Printed for J. Mawman, 1808.

Schomburgk, Robert H. *The History of Barbados.* London: Longman, Brown, Green and Longmans, 1848.

Sewell, William G. *The Ordeal of Free Labour in the British West Indies.* 1861. Reprint, London: Frank Cass, 1968.

Statutes of the United Kingdom of Great Britain and Ireland, 3 and 4 William IV. London: Parliament Commons, 1833.

Stephen, James. *New Reasons for Abolishing the Slave Trade; Being the Last Section of a Larger Work, Now First Published, entitled "The Dangers of the Country."* London: J. Butterworth, 1807.

Sturge, Joseph, and Thomas Harvey. *The West Indies in 1837.* 1838. Reprint, London: Dawsons of Pall Mall, 1968.

Thome, J. A. S., and J. H. Kimball. *Emancipation in the West Indies: A Six Months' Tour of Antigua, Barbados and Jamaica in the Year 1837.* New York: American Anti-Slavery Society, 1838.

Williams, James. *A Narrative of Events, since the First of August, 1834, by James Williams, an Apprenticed Labourer in Jamaica.* Edited by Diana Paton. Durham, N.C.: Duke University Press, 2001.

Secondary Sources

Alexander, M. Jacqui. "Not Just (Any) Body Can Be a Citizen: The Politics of Law, Sexuality and Postcoloniality in Trinidad and Tobago and the Bahamas." *Feminist Review* 48 (Autumn 1994): 5–23.

———. "Erotic Autonomy as a Politics of Decolonization: An Anatomy of Feminist and State Practice in the Bahamas Tourist Economy." In M. Jacqui Alexander and Chandra Talpade Mohanty, eds., *Feminist Genealogies, Colonial Legacies, Democratic Futures*, 63–100. New York: Routledge, 1997.

Allsopp, Richard. *Dictionary of Caribbean English Usage*. New York: Oxford University Press, 1996.

Anderson, Benedict. *Imagined Communities: Reflections on the Origin and Spread of Nationalism*. London: Verso, 1983.

Austin-Broos, Diane. "Redefining the Moral Order: Interpretations of Christianity in Post-emancipation Jamaica." In McGlynn and Drescher, *Meaning of Freedom*. 221–243.

Bayly, C. A. *Imperial Meridian: The British Empire and the World, 1780–1830*. London: Longman, 1989.

Beckles, Hilary. "Land Distribution and Class Formation in Barbados, 1630–1700: The Rise of a Wage Proletariat." *JBMHS* 36, no. 2 (1980): 126–143.

———. *Black Rebellion in Barbados: the Struggle Against Slavery, 1627–1838*. Bridgetown: Antilles Publications, 1984.

———. "On the Backs of Blacks: The Barbados Free-Coloureds' Pursuit of Civil Rights and the 1816 Slave Rebellion." *Immigrants and Minorities* 3, no. 2 (July 1984): 167–188.

———. "From Land to Sea: Runaway Barbados Slaves and Servants, 1630–1700." *Slavery and Abolition* 6, no. 3 (1985): 79–94.

———. "The Slave-Drivers' War: Bussa and the 1816 Barbados Slave Rebellion." *Boletín de estudios latinoamericanos y del Caribe* 39 (December 1985): 85–110.

———. "Black over White: The 'Poor White' Problem in Barbados Slave Society." *Immigrants and Minorities* 7, no. 1 (1988): 1–15.

———. "Slaves and the Internal Market Economy of Barbados: A Perspective on Non-Violent Resistance." Paper presented at the 20th ACH conference, University of the Virgin Islands, U.S. Virgin Islands, 1988.

———. *Natural Rebels: A Social History of Enslaved Black Women in Barbados*. London: Zed Books, 1989.

———. *White Servitude and Black Slavery in Barbados, 1627–1715*. Knoxville: University of Tennessee Press, 1989.

———. *A History of Barbados: From Amerindian Settlement to Nation-State*. Cambridge: Cambridge University Press, 1990.

———. "White Women and Slavery in the British Caribbean." In Beckles and Shepherd, *Caribbean Slavery in the Atlantic World*. 659–669.

Beckles, Hilary, and Andrew Downes. "The Economics of the Transition to the Black Labour System in Barbados, 1630–1680." In Beckles and Shepherd, *Caribbean Slavery in the Atlantic World*. 239–252.

Beckles, Hilary, and Verene Shepherd, eds. *Caribbean Freedom: Economy and Society from Emancipation to the Present*. Kingston: Ian Randle, 1993.

————. *Caribbean Slavery in the Atlantic World: A Student Reader.* Kingston: Ian Randle, 2000.

Beckles, Hilary, and Karl Watson. "Social Protest and Labour Bargaining: The Changing Nature of Slaves' Responses to Plantation Life in Eighteenth-Century Barbados." *Slavery and Abolition* 8, no. 3 (1987): 272–293.

Belle, George. "The Abortive Revolution of 1876 in Barbados." In Beckles and Shepherd, *Caribbean Freedom.* 181–191.

————. "Samuel Jackman Prescod." In Howe and Marshall, *Empowering Impulse.* 56–102.

Benjamin, Walter. *Illuminations: Essays and Reflections.* Edited by Hannah Arendt. New York: Schocken Books, 1968.

Bennett, J. Harry. *Bondsmen and Bishops: Slavery and Apprenticeship on the Codrington Plantations of Barbados, 1710–1838.* Berkeley and Los Angeles: University of California Press, 1958.

Berlin, Ira. *Slaves without Masters: The Free Negro in the Antebellum South.* New York: New Press, 1974.

Besson, Jean. "Freedom and Community: The British West Indies." In McGlynn and Drescher, *Meaning of Freedom.* 183–219.

————. "Reputation and Respectability Reconsidered: A New Perspective on Afro-Caribbean Peasant Women." In Janet Momsen, ed., *Women and Change in the Caribbean: A Pan-Caribbean Perspective,* 15–37. London: James Currey, 1993.

Bhabha, Homi. "Of Mimicry and Man." In Stoler and Cooper, *Tensions of Empire.* 152–160.

Biagini, Eugene, and Alastair Reid, eds. *Currents of Radicalism: Popular Radicalism, Organised Labour and Party Politics in Britain, 1850–1914.* Cambridge: Cambridge University Press, 1991.

Bilby, Kenneth, and J. S. Handler. "Obeah: Healing and Protection in West Indian Slave Life." *JCH* 38 (2004): 153–183.

Blackburn, Robin. *The Overthrow of Colonial Slavery: 1776–1848.* London: Verso, 1988.

————. *The Making of New World Slavery: From the Baroque to the Modern, 1492–1800.* London: Verso, 1997.

Blackett, Richard. *Building an Anti-Slavery Wall: Black Americans in the Atlantic Abolitionist Movement, 1830–1860.* Baton Rouge: Louisiana State University Press, 1983.

Blackett, R. J. M. "The Hamic Connection: African-Americans and the Caribbean, 1820–1865." In Brian Moore and Swithin Wilmot, eds., *Before and after 1865: Education, Politics and Regionalism in the Caribbean,* 317–329. Kingston: Ian Randle, 1998.

Blouet, Olwyn. "Education and Emancipation in Barbados, 1833–1846: A Study in Cultural Transference." *Ethnic and Racial Studies* 4, no. 2 (April 1981): 222–235.

Blyden, Nemata. *West Indians in West Africa: The African Diaspora in Reverse.* Rochester, N.Y.: University of Rochester Press, 2000.

Bolland, O. Nigel. "Systems of Domination after Slavery: The Control of Land and Labour in the British West Indies After 1838." In Beckles and Shepherd, *Caribbean Freedom.* 107–123.

————. "Proto-Proletarians? Slave Wages in the Americas." In Turner, *Chattel Slaves.* 126–138.

————. *The Politics of Labour in the British Caribbean: The Social Origins of Authoritarianism and Democracy in the Labour Movement.* Kingston: Ian Randle, 2001.

Brantlinger, Patrick. "Victorians and Africans: The Genealogy of the Myth of the Dark Continent." In Henry Louis Gates Jr., ed., *"Race," Writing and Difference*, 185–122. Chicago: University of Chicago Press, 1986.

Brathwaite, Edward. *The Development of Creole Society in Jamaica, 1770–1820*. Oxford: Clarendon Press, 1971.

Brereton, Bridget. "Family Strategies, Gender and the Shift to Wage Labour in the British Caribbean." In Brereton and Yelvington, *Colonial Caribbean in Transition*. 77–107.

Brereton, Bridget, and Kevin Yelvington, eds. *The Colonial Caribbean in Transition: Essays on Postemancipation Social and Cultural History*. Gainesville: University Press of Florida, 1999.

Bridenbaugh, Carl, and Roberta Bridenbaugh. *No Peace Beyond the Line: The English in the Caribbean, 1624–1690*. New York: Oxford University Press, 1972.

Buckley, Roger Norman. *Slaves in Red Coats: The British West India Regiments, 1795–1815*. New
Haven: Yale University Press, 1979.

Burn, W. L. *Emancipation and Apprenticeship in the British West Indies*. London: Jonathan Cape,
1937.

Burnard, Trevor. "A Failed Settler Society: Marriage and Demographic Failure in Early Jamaica."
Journal of Social History 28, no. 1 (Fall 1994): 63–83.

Burnett, D. Graham. *Masters of All They Surveyed: Exploration, Geography, and a British El Dorado*.
Chicago: University of Chicago Press, 2000.

Burton, Richard D. E. *Afro-Creole: Power, Opposition, and Play in the Caribbean*. Ithaca: Cornell
University Press, 1997.

Butler, Kathleen Mary. *The Economics of Emancipation: Jamaica and Barbados, 1823–1843*. Chapel
Hill: University of North Carolina Press, 1995.

Butler, Mary. "Mortality and Labour on the Codrington Estate, Barbados." *JCH* 19, no. 1 (May
1984): 48–67.

Caldecott, A. *The Church in the West Indies*. London: Society for Propagating Christian Knowledge, 1898.

Calhoun, Craig, ed. *Habermas and the Public Sphere*. Cambridge, Mass.: MIT Press, 1992.

Campbell, Carl. *Cedulants and Capitulants: The Politics of the Coloured Opposition in the Slave Society of Trinidad, 1783–1838*. Port-of-Spain: Paria Publishing, 1992.

———. "Social and Economic Obstacles to the Development of Popular Education in Postemancipation Jamaica, 1834–1865." In Beckles and Shepherd, *Caribbean Freedom*. 262–
268.

———. "Trinidad's Free Coloureds in Comparative Caribbean Perspectives." In Beckles and Shepherd, *Caribbean Slavery in the Atlantic World*. 597–612.

Campbell, Mavis. *The Dynamics of Change in Slave Society: A Socio-political History of the Free Coloreds of Jamaica, 1800–1865*. London: Associated University Presses, 1976.

———. *Back to Africa: George Ross and the Maroons, from Nova Scotia to Sierra Leone*. Lawrenceville,
N.J.: Africa World Press, 1993.

Carter, Richard. "Public Amenities after Emancipation." In Marshall, *Emancipation II*, 49–69.

Chamberlain, Mary. *Narratives of Exile and Return.* London: Macmillan Caribbean, 1997.

Cohen, David, and Jack Greene. *Neither Slave nor Free: The Freedmen of African Descent in the Slave Societies of the New World.* Baltimore: Johns Hopkins University Press, 1972.

Connell, Neville. "Hotel Keepers and Hotels in Barbados." *JBMHS* 33, no. 4 (1970): 162–185.

Cooper, Frederick, Rebecca Scott, and Thomas Holt. *Beyond Slavery: Explorations of Race, Labor, and Citizenship in Postemancipation Societies.* Chapel Hill: University of North Carolina, 2000.

Cox, Edward L. *Free Coloreds in the Slave Societies of St. Kitts and Grenada.* Knoxville: University of Tennessee Press, 1984.

Craton, Michael. *Testing the Chains: Resistance to Slavery in the British West Indies.* Ithaca: Cornell University Press, 1982.

———. *Empire, Enslavement, and Freedom in the Caribbean.* Kingston: Ian Randle, 1997.

Davidoff, Leonore, and Catherine Hall. *Family Fortunes: Men and Women of the English Middle Class.* London: Routledge, 1987.

Davis, David Brion. *The Problem of Slavery in the Age of Revolution, 1770–1823.* Ithaca: Cornell University Press, 1975.

———. *Slavery and Human Progress.* New York: Oxford University Press, 1984.

de Barros, Juanita. *Order and Place in a Colonial City: Patterns of Struggle and Resistance in Georgetown, British Guiana, 1889–1924.* Montreal: McGill-Queen's University Press, 2003.

Deerr, Noel. *The History of Sugar.* Vols. 1 and 2. London: Chapman and Hall, 1949 and 1950.

Díaz, María Elena. *The Virgin, the King, and the Royal Slaves of El Cobre: Negotiating Freedom in Colonial Cuba, 1670–1780.* Stanford: Stanford University Press, 2000.

Dubois, Laurent. *A Colony of Citizens: Revolution and Slave Emancipation in the French Caribbean, 1787–1804.* Chapel Hill: University of North Carolina Press, 2004.

Du Bois, W. E. B. *The Souls of Black Folk.* 1903. Reprint, New York: Modern Library, 2003.

Dunn, Richard S. *Sugar and Slaves: The Rise of the Planter Class in the English West Indies, 1624–1713.* Chapel Hill: University of North Carolina Press, 1972.

Eudell, Thomas. *The Political Languages of Emancipation in the British Caribbean and the U.S. South.* Chapel Hill: University of North Carolina Press, 2002.

Evans, Eric J. *The Forging of the Modern State: Early Industrial Britain, 1783–1870.* London: Longman, 1983.

Fanon, Frantz. *The Wretched of the Earth.* 1961. Reprint, London: Penguin Books, 1990.

Ferguson, Moira. *The Hart Sisters: Early African Caribbean Writers, Evangelicals, and Radicals.* Lincoln: University of Nebraska Press, 1993.

Fick, Carolyn E. *The Making of Haiti: The Saint Domingue Revolution from Below.* Knoxville: University of Tennessee Press, 1990.

Fletcher, Leonard P. "The Evolution of Poor Relief in Barbados, 1838–1900." *JCH* 53, no. 2 (1992): 171–207.

Foner, Laura. "The Free People of Color in Louisiana and St. Domingue." *JSH* 3, no. 3 (1970): 406–430.

Forde-Jones, Cecily. "Mapping Racial Boundaries: Gender, Race, and Poor Relief in Barbadian Plantation Society." *Journal of Women's History* 10, no. 3 (Autumn 1998): 9–31.

Fyfe, Christopher. *A History of Sierra Leone.* London: Oxford University Press, 1962.

Garrigus, John D. "Redrawing the Color Line: Gender and the Social Construction of Race in Pre-Revolutionary Haiti." *JCH* 30, nos. 1 and 2 (1996): 28–50.

Gaspar, Barry David, and David Geggus, eds. *A Turbulent Time: The French Revolution and the Greater Caribbean.* Bloomington: Indiana University Press, 1997.

Gaspar, Barry David, and Darlene Clark Hine, eds. *More than Chattel: Black Women and Slavery in the Americas.* Bloomington: Indiana University Press, 1996.

Geertz, Clifford. *The Interpretation of Cultures.* London: Fontana Press 1973.

Geggus, David. "The Slaves and Free Coloreds of Martinique during the Age of the French and Haitian Revolutions: Three Moments of Resistance." In Paquette and Engerman, *Lesser Antilles in the Age of European Expansion.* 280–301.

Gibba, Bakary. "The West Indian Missionaries and the Rio Pongas Mission in West Africa, 1850–1950." Ph.D. diss., University of Toronto. Forthcoming.

Gibbs, Bentley. "The Establishment of the Tenantry System in Barbados." In Marshall, *Emancipation II,* 27–33.

Gibson Wilson, Ellen. *The Loyal Blacks.* New York: Capricorn Books, 1976.

Gilmore, John. "Episcopacy, Emancipation and Evangelization: Aspects of the History of the Church of England in the British West Indies." PhD. diss., Cambridge University, 1984.

Gilroy, Paul. *The Black Atlantic: Modernity and Double Consciousness.* Cambridge: Harvard University Press, 1993.

Gordon, Shirley. "Schools of the Free." In Brian Moore and Swithin Wilmot, eds., *Before and after 1865: Education, Politics and Regionalism in the Caribbean,* 1–12. Kingston: Ian Randle, 1998.

Goveia, Elsa. *The West Indian Slave Laws of the 18th Century.* Barbados: Caribbean Universities Press, 1970.

Gragg, Larry. *Englishmen Transplanted: The English Colonization of Barbados, 1627–1660.* Oxford: Oxford University Press, 2003.

Gray White, Deborah. *Too Heavy a Load: Black Women in Defense of Themselves, 1894–1994.* New York: W. W. Norton, 1999.

Green, William. *British Slave Emancipation: The Sugar Colonies and the Great Experiment, 1830–1865.* Oxford: Clarendon Press, 1976.

———. "The Creolization of Caribbean History: A Critique of Dialectical Analysis." In Beckles and Shepherd, *Caribbean Freedom.* 28–40.

Greene, Jack. "Changing Identity in the British Caribbean: Barbados as a Case Study." In Nicholas Canny and Anthony Pagden, eds., *Colonial Identity in the Atlantic World.* Princeton: Princeton University Press, 1987.

Habermas, Jürgen. *The Structural Transformation of the Public Sphere.* Cambridge, Mass.: MIT Press, 1989.

Hall, Catherine. *White, Male, and Middle Class: Explorations in Feminism and History*. Cambridge: Polity, 1992.

———. *Civilising Subjects: Metropole and Colony in the English Imagination, 1830–1867*. Chicago: University of Chicago Press, 2002.

Hall, Douglas. *Free Jamaica, 1838–1865: An Economic History*. London: Caribbean Universities Press, 1969.

Hall, Neville. "Law and Society in Barbados at the Turn of the Nineteenth Century." *JCH* 5 (1972): 20–45.

Handler, Jerome S. *The Unappropriated People: Freedmen in the Slave Society of Barbados*. Baltimore: Johns Hopkins University Press, 1974.

———. "Joseph Rachell and Rachael Pringle-Polgreen: Petty Entrepreneurs." In Sweet and Nash, *Struggle and Survival in Colonial America*, 276–291.

———. "Freedmen and Slaves in the Barbados Militia." *JCH* 19 (1984): 1–25.

———. "Escaping Slavery in a Caribbean Plantation Society: Marronage in Barbados, 1650–1830s." *New West Indian Guide/Nieuwe West-Indische Gids* 71 (1997): 183–225.

Handler, Jerome, and Charlotte Frisbie. "Aspects of Slave Life in Barbados: Music and Its Cultural Context." *Caribbean Studies* 11, no. 4 (January 1972): 5–46.

Handler, Jerome, Frederick Lange, and R. V. Riordan. *Plantation Slavery in Barbados: An Archeological and Historical Investigation*. Cambridge: Harvard University Press, 1978.

Handler, Jerome, Ronald Hughes, and Ernest M. Wiltshire. *Freedmen of Barbados: Names and Notes for Genealogical and Family History Research*. Charlottesville: Virginia Foundation for the Humanities and Public Policy, 1999.

Handler, Jerome S., and Arnold Sio. "Barbados." In Cohen and Greene, *Neither Slave nor Free*. 214–257.

Hanger, Kimberly S. "Patronage, Property and Persistence." In Landers, *Against the Odds*. 44–64.

Hartman, Saidiya V. *Scenes of Subjection: Terror, Slavery and Self-making in Nineteenth Century America*. New York: Oxford University Press, 1997.

Helg, Aline. *Our Rightful Share: The Afro-Cuban Struggle for Equality, 1886–1912*. Chapel Hill: University of North Carolina Press, 1995.

Henshall-Momsen, Janet. "Gender Roles in Caribbean Agricultural Labour." In Cross and Heuman, *Labour in the Caribbean*, 141–157.

Heuman, Gad. *Between Black and White: Race, Politics, and the Free Coloreds of Jamaica, 1792–1865*. Oxford: Greenwood Press, 1981.

———. "Runaway Slaves in Nineteenth Century Barbados." *Slavery and Abolition* 6, no. 3 (December 1985): 95–111.

———. "Riots and Resistance in the Caribbean at the Moment of Full Freedom in the Anglophone Caribbean." *Slavery and Abolition* 21, no. 2 (August 2000): 135–149.

Higman, Barry. *Slave Population and Economy in Jamaica, 1807–1834*. 1976. Reprint, Kingston: Press, 1995.

——. *Slave Populations of the British Caribbean, 1807–1834.* 1984. Reprint, Kingston: Press, University of the West Indies, 1995.

——. "Remembering Slavery: The Rise, Decline and Revival of Emancipation Day in the English-speaking Caribbean." *Slavery and Abolition* 19, no. 1 (April 1998): 90–105.

Hilton, Boyd. *The Age of Atonement: The Influence of Evangelicalism on Social and Economic Thought, 1785–1865.* Oxford: Clarendon Press, 1988.

Hoetink, Harry. "Surinam and Curaçao." In Cohen and Greene, *Neither Slave nor Free.* 64–84.

Holt, Thomas. *The Problem of Freedom: Race, Labor, and Politics in Jamaica and Britain, 1832–1938.* Kingston: Ian Randle, 1992.

——. "Marking: Race, Race-Making, and the Writing of History. *American Historical Review* 100, no. 1 (1995): 1–20.

Honeychurch, Lennox. *The Dominica Story: A History of the Island.* London: Macmillan Education, 1995.

Howe, Glenford, and Don Marshall, eds. *The Empowering Impulse: The Nationalist Tradition of Barbados.* Barbados: Canoe Press, 2001.

Hünefeldt, Christine. *Paying the Price of Freedom: Family and Labor among Lima's Slaves, 1800–1854.* Berkeley: University of California Press, 1994.

James, C. L. R. *The Black Jacobins: Toussaint L'Ouverture and the San Domingo Revolution.* 1938. Reprint, Penguin Books, 2001.

——. *Beyond a Boundary.* 1963. Reprint, New York: Pantheon Books, 1984.

James, Winston. *Holding Aloft the Banner of Ethiopia: Caribbean Radicalism in Early Twentieth-Century America.* London: Verso, 1998.

Jennings, Lawrence C. *French Anti-Slavery: The Movement for the Abolition of Slavery in France.* Cambridge: Cambridge University Press, 2000.

Johnson, Alana. "The Abolition of Chattel Slavery in Barbados, 1833–1876." Ph.D. thesis, Cambridge University, 1994.

Jordan, Winthrop D. *White Over Black: American Attitudes towards the Negro, 1550–1812.* Chapel Hill: University of North Carolina Press, 1968.

Kale, Mahdavi. *Fragments of Empire: Capital, Slavery and Indian Indentured Labor Migration in the British Caribbean.* Philadelphia: University of Pennsylvania Press, 1998.

Karasch, Mary. *Slave Life in Rio de Janeiro, 1808–1850.* Princeton: Princeton University Press, 1987.

Karch, Cecilia. "A Man for All Seasons: London Bourne." *JBMHS* 45 (1999): 1–35.

Kerr, Paulette. "Victims or Strategists? Female Lodging-House Keepers in Jamaica." In Verene Shepherd, Bridget Brereton, and Barbara Bailey, eds., *Engendering History: Caribbean Women in Historical Perspective,* 197–212. Kingston: Ian Randle, 1995.

King, Stewart. *Blue Coat or Powdered Wig: Free People of Color in Pre-revolutionary St. Domingue.* Athens: University of Georgia Press, 2001.

Klein, Herbert. "The Colored Freedmen in Brazilian Slave Society." *JSH* 3 (1969): 30–52.

Klein, Herbert S. *African Slavery in Latin America and the Caribbean*. New York: Oxford University Press, 1986.

Knight, Franklin, and Peggy Liss, eds. *Atlantic Port Cities: Economy, Culture, and Society in the Atlantic World, 1650–1850*. Knoxville: University of Tennessee Press, 1991.

Lack, Paul D. "An Urban Slave Community: Little Rock, 1831–1862." *Arkansas Historical Quarterly* 4, no. 3 (1982): 258–287.

Lambert, David. "'True Lovers of Religion': Methodist Persecution and White Resistance to Anti-Slavery in Barbados, 1823–1825." *Journal of Historical Geography* 8, no. 2 (2002): 216–236.

Landers, Jane, ed. *Against the Odds: Free Blacks in the Slave Societies of the Americas*. London: Frank Cass, 1996.

Lazarus Black, Mindie. *Legitimate Acts and Illegal Encounters: Law and Society in Antigua and Barbuda*. Washington, D.C.: Smithsonian Institute Press, 1994.

Levy, Claude. "Barbados: The Last Years of Slavery, 1823–1833." *Journal of Negro History* 44, no. 4 (October 1959): 308–347.

———. *Emancipation, Sugar, and Federalism: Barbados and the British West Indies*. Gainesville: University Presses of Florida, 1980.

Lewis, A. K. O. "The Moravian Mission in Barbados 1816–1886: A Study of the Historical Context and Theological Significance of a Minority Church among an Oppressed People." Ph.D. thesis, University of Birmingham, 1983.

Lewis, Andrew. "'An Incendiary Press': British West Indian Newspapers during the Struggle for Abolition." *Slavery and Abolition* 16, no. 3 (December 1985): 346–361.

Lewis, Gordon K. *Main Currents in Caribbean Thought: The Historical Evolution of Caribbean Society in Its Ideological Aspects, 1492–1900*. Baltimore: Johns Hopkins University Press, 1983.

Lobdell, Richard. "British Officials and the West Indian Peasantry, 1842–1938." In Malcolm Cross and Gad Heuman, eds., *Labour in the Caribbean: From Emancipation to Independence*, 195–207. London: Macmillan Caribbean, 1992.

———. "Patterns of Investment and Sources of Credit in the British West Indian Sugar Industry, 1838–1897." In Beckles and Shepherd, *Caribbean Freedom*. 319–329.

Lowes, Susan. "The Peculiar Class: The Formation, Collapse, and Reformation of the Middle Class in Antigua, West Indies, 1834–1940." Ph.D. diss., Columbia University, 1994.

———. "'They Couldn't Mash Ants': The Decline of the White and Non-White Elites in Antigua, 1834–1900." In Karen Fog Olwig, ed., *Small Islands, Large Questions: Society, Culture and Resistance in the Post-Emancipation Caribbean*, 31–52. London: Frank Cass, 1995.

Luster, Robert. *The Amelioration of the Slaves in the British Empire, 1790–1833*. New York: Peter Lang, 1995.

Marshall, Trevor. "Post-Emancipation Adjustments in Barbados, 1838–1876." In Alvin O. Thompson, ed., *Emancipation I: A Series of Lectures to Commemorate the 150th Anniversary of Emancipation*. Bridgetown: National Cultural Foundation and Department of History, UWI, 1986.

Marshall, Woodville K. *Emancipation II: Aspects of the Post-Slavery Experience in Barbados; Lec-*

tures Commemorating the 150th Anniversary of Emancipation, Delivered in February and March 1986. Bridgetown: National Cultural Foundation and Department of History, UWI, 1987.

———. *Emancipation III: Aspects of the Post-Slavery Experience of Barbados; Lectures Commemorating the 150th Anniversary of Emancipation, Delivered in February and March 1987.* Bridgetown, National Cultural Foundation and Department of History, UWI, 1988.

———. "Rock Hall, St. Thomas: A Free Village in Barbados." *JCH* 41, nos. 1 and 2 (2007): 1–50.

———. "Rock Hall, St. Thomas: The Search for the First Free Village in Barbados." Paper presented at the 14th annual ACH Conference, Georgetown, Guyana, 1977.

———. "The Termination of the Apprenticeship in Barbados and the Windward Islands: An Essay in Colonial Administration and Politics." *JCH* 2 (May 1971): 1–45.

———. "Villages and Plantation Sub-Division." In Marshall, *Emancipation III*, 1–19.

———. "'We Be Wise to Many More Tings': Blacks' Hopes and Expectations of Emancipation." In Beckles and Shepherd, *Caribbean Freedom*. 12–20.

Mathieson, William. *British Slavery and Its Abolition, 1823–1838.* London: Longmans, Green, 1926.

McCusker J., and R. Menard. *The Economy of British America, 1607–1789.* 1985. Reprint, Chapel Hill: University of North Carolina Press, 1991.

McDonald, Roderick A. *The Economy and Material Culture of Slaves: Goods and Chattels on the Sugar Plantations of Jamaica and Louisiana.* Baton Rouge: Louisiana State University Press, 1993.

McGlynn, Frank, and Seymour Drescher, eds. *The Meaning of Freedom: Economics, Politics, and Culture after Slavery.* Pittsburgh: University of Pittsburgh Press, 1992.

Midgley, Clare. *Women against Slavery: The British Campaigns.* London: Routledge, 1992.

Mintz, Sidney. *Sweetness and Power: The Place of Sugar in Modern History.* New York: Penguin Books, 1985.

———. "Enduring Substances, Trying Theories: The Caribbean Region as *Oikomenê, Journal of the Royal Anthropological Institute* 2, no. 2 (June 1996): 289–311.

Mintz, Sidney, and Douglas Hall. *The Origins of the Jamaican Internal Marketing System.* Yale University Publications in Anthropology 57. New Haven, 1960.

Mintz, Sidney, and Richard Price. *An Anthropological Approach to the Afro-American Past: A Caribbean Perspective.* Philadelphia: Institute for the Study of Human Issues, 1976.

Moitt, Bernard. *Women and Slavery in the French Antilles, 1635–1848.* Bloomington: Indiana University Press, 2001.

Momsen, Janet. *Post-emancipation Rural Settlement in Barbados.* Newcastle-upon-Tyne: University of Newcastle, 1988.

Moore, Brian. *Race, Power and Social Segmentation in Colonial Society: Guyana after Slavery, 1838–1891.* New York: Gordon and Breach Science, 1987.

Morgan, Jennifer L. *Laboring Women: Reproduction and Gender in New World Slavery.* Philadelphia: University of Pennsylvania Press, 2004.

Morgan, Philip D. *Slave Counterpoint: Black Culture in the Eighteenth-Century Chesapeake and Lowcountry.* Chapel Hill: University of North Carolina Press, 1998.

Morrell, W. P. *British Colonial Policy in the Age of Peel and Russell*. London: Clarendon Press, 1930.

Morrissey, Marietta. "Women's Work, Family Formation, and Reproduction among Caribbean Slaves." In Beckles and Shepherd, *Caribbean Slavery in the Atlantic World*. 670–682.

Mullin, Michael. "Slave Economic Strategies: Food, Markets and Property." In Turner, *From Chattel Slaves to Wage Slaves*. 68–78.

Newton, Melanie. "'New Ideas of Correctness': Gender, Amelioration and Emancipation in Barbados, 1810s–1850s." *Slavery and Abolition* 21, no. 3 (2000): 94–124.

———. "The King v. Robert James, A Slave, for Rape: Inequality, Gender and British Slave Emancipation, 1823–1833." *Comparative Studies in Society and History* 47, no. 3 (2005): 583–610.

———. "Philanthropy, Gender and the Production of Public Life in Barbados, c1790–c1850." In Pamela Scully and Diana Paton, eds., *Gender and Slave Emancipation in the Atlantic World*, 225–246. Durham, N.C.: Duke University Press, 2005.

Oldfield, J. R. *Popular Politics and British Anti-Slavery: The Mobilisation of Public Opinion against the Slave Trade*. Manchester: Manchester University Press, 1995.

Paquette, Robert L., and Stanley L. Engerman, eds. *The Lesser Antilles in the Age of European Expansion*. Gainesville: University Press of Florida, 1996.

Pares, Richard. *A West India Fortune*. London: Longmans, Green, 1950.

Paton, Diana. "Decency, Dependence and the Lash: Gender and the British Debate over Slave Emancipation, 1830–34." *Slavery and Abolition* 17, no. 3 (December 1996): 163–184.

———. *No Bond but the Law: Punishment, Race, and Gender in Jamaican State Formation, 1780–1870*. Durham, N.C.: Duke University Press, 2004.

Patterson, Orlando. *The Sociology of Slavery: An Analysis of the Origins, Development and Structure of Negro Slave Society in Jamaica*. London: MacGibbon and Kee, 1969.

Peabody, Sue. *"There Are No Slaves in France": The Political Culture of Race and Slavery in the Ancien Régime*. New York: Oxford University Press, 1996.

Pérotin-Dumon, Anne. "Free Coloreds and Slaves in Revolutionary Guadeloupe: Politics and Political Consciousness." In Paquette and Engerman, *Lesser Antilles in the Age of European Expansion*. 259–279.

Pope Melish, Joanne. *Disowning Slavery: Gradual Emancipation and "Race" in New England, 1780–1860*. Ithaca: Cornell University Press, 1998.

Prakash, Gyan. *After Colonialism: Imperial Histories and Postcolonial Displacements*. Princeton: Princeton University Press, 1995.

Puckrein, Gary. *Little England: Plantation Society and Anglo-Barbadian Politics, 1627–1700*. New York: New York University Press, 1984.

Ragatz, Lowell J. *The Fall of the Planter Class in the British Caribbean, 1763–1833: A Study in Economic and Social History*. New York: Century, 1928.

Richardson, Nathaniel R. *Liberia's Past and Present*. London: Diplomatic Press and Publishing, 1959.

Riviere, Emmanuel. "Labour Shortage in the British West Indies after Emancipation." *JCH* 4 (May 1972): 1–30.

Robinson, Ronald, and John Gallagher (with Alice Denny). *Africa and the Victorians: The Official Mind of Imperialism.* 1961. Reprint, Basingstoke: MacMillan, 1981.

Ryan, Mary. "Gender and Public Access: Nineteenth-Century America." In Calhoun, *Habermas and the Public Sphere.* 259–288.

Said, Edward W. *Culture and Imperialism.* Vintage: London, 1993.

Samaroo, Brinsley. "Two Abolitions: African Slavery and East Indian Indentureship." In David Dabydeen and Brinsley Samaroo, eds., *Across the Dark Waters: Ethnicity and Indian Identity in the Caribbean,* 25–41. London: Macmillan Caribbean, 1996.

Schmidt-Nowara, Christopher. *Empire and Antislavery.* Pittsburgh: University of Pittsburgh Press, 1999.

Scott, Julius Sherrard III. "The Common Wind: Currents of Afro-American Communication in the Era of the Haitian Revolution." Ph.D. diss., Duke University, 1987.

Scott, Rebecca. *Slave Emancipation in Cuba: The Transition to Free Labor, 1860–1899.* Princeton: Princeton University Press, 1985.

Scully, Pamela. *Liberating the Family? Gender and British Slave Emancipation in the Rural Western Cape, 1823–1853.* Oxford: James Currey, 1997.

Sheller, Mimi. "Quasheba, Mother, Queen: Black Women's Public Leadership and Political Protest in Post-Emancipation Jamaica, 1834–65." *Slavery and Abolition* 19, no. 3 (December 1998): 90–117.

———. *Democracy after Slavery: Black Publics and Peasant Radicalism in Haiti and Jamaica.* London: Macmillan Education, 2000.

Sheppard, Jill. *The "Redlegs" of Barbados: Their Origins and History.* New York: KTO Press, 1977.

Shuler, Monica. *"Alas, Alas, Kongo": A Social History of Indentured African Immigration into Jamaica, 1841–1865.* Baltimore: Johns Hopkins University Press, 1980.

Singh Mehta, Uday. *Liberalism and Empire: A Study in Nineteenth-Century British Liberal Thought.* Chicago: University of Chicago Press, 1999.

Sio, Arnold. "Race, Colour and Miscegenation: The Free Coloured of Jamaica and Barbados." *Caribbean Studies* 16, no. 1 (1976): 5–21.

———. "Marginality and Free Coloured Identity in Caribbean Slave Society." In Beckles and Shepherd, *Caribbean Slave Society and Economy,* 150–159.

Small, Stephen. "Racial Group Boundaries and Identities: People of 'Mixed Race' in Slavery across the Americas." *Slavery and Abolition* 15, no. 3 (1994): 17–37.

Socolow, Susan. "Economic Roles of the Free Women of Color of Cap Français." In Gaspar and Clark Hine, *More than Chattel.* 279–297.

Stanley, Amy Dru. *From Bondage to Contract: Wage Labor, Marriage, and the Market in the Age of Emancipation.* Cambridge: Cambridge University Press, 1998.

Starkey, Otis. *The Economic Geography of Barbados: A Study of the Relationship between Environmental Variations and Economic Development.* New York: Columbia University Press, 1939.

Stoler, Ann Laura. *Race and the Education of Desire: Foucault's* History of Sexuality *and the Colonial Order of Things.* Durham, N.C.: Duke University Press, 1995.

Stoler, Ann Laura, and Frederick Cooper. *Tensions of Empire: Colonial Cultures in a Bourgeois World.* Berkeley and Los Angeles: University of California Press, 1997.

Sweet. D. G., and G. B. Nash, eds. *Struggle and Survival in Colonial America.* Berkeley and Los Angeles: University of California Press, 1981.

Taylor, Bruce M. *Black Labor and White Power in Post-Emancipation Barbados: A Study of Changing Relationships.* New York: Current Bibliography on African Affairs, 1973.

Thomas, Nicholas. *Colonialism's Culture: Anthropology, Travel, and Government.* Cambridge: Polity, 1994.

Thornton, John. "'I Am the Subject of the King of Congo': African Political Ideology and the Haitian Revolution." *Journal of World History* 4, no. 2 (1993): 181–214.

Titus, Noel. *The Development of Methodism in Barbados.* Bern: Peter Lang, 1993.

Trouillot, Michel-Rolph. "Labour and Emancipation in Dominica: Contribution to a Debate." *Caribbean Quarterly* 30, nos. 3–4 (1984): 73–84.

———. "The Inconvenience of Freedom: Free People of Color and the Political Aftermath of Slavery in Dominica and Saint-Domingue/Haiti." In McGlynn and Drescher, *Meaning of Freedom.* 147–182.

Turner, Mary. *Slaves and Missionaries: The Disintegration of Jamaican Slave Society, 1787–1834.* Urbana: University of Illinois Press, 1982.

———, ed. *From Chattel Slaves to Wage Slaves: The Dynamics of Labour Bargaining in the Americas.* London: James Currey, 1995.

Vaughan, Hilton. "Samuel Jackman Prescod: Eulogy delivered on the occasion of the centenary of his death, Sunday, 26th September, 1971." Unpublished manuscript. Barbados, BDA, 1971.

Viotti da Costa, Emilia. *Crowns of Glory, Tears of Blood: The Demerara Slave Rebellion of 1823.* New York: Oxford University Press, 1994.

Wade, Richard. *Slavery in the Cities: The South, 1820–1860.* London: Oxford University Press, 1964.

Ward, J. R. *British West Indian Slavery, 1750–1834: The Process of Amelioration.* Oxford: Clarendon Press, 1988.

Watson, Karl. *The Civilised Island Barbados A Social History, 1750–1816.* Bridgetown: Graphic Printers, 1979.

———. "Salmagundis vs. Pumpkins: White Politics and Creole Consciousness in Barbadian Slave Society, 1800–34." In Howard Johnson and Karl Watson, *The White Minority in the Caribbean,* 17–31. Oxford: James Currey, 1998.

Watts, David. *The West Indies: Patterns of Development, Culture and Environmental Change since 1492.* Cambridge: Cambridge University Press, 1987.

Welch, Pedro. "Notes from the Underground: Post-emancipation Adjustments in Bridgetown, Barbados." Unpublished seminar paper, UWI, Cave Hill, Barbados, c. 1994.

———. "'Crimps and Captains': Displays of Self Expression among Freed Coloured Women, Barbados, 1750–1834." *Journal of Social Sciences* 4, no. 2 (December 1997): 89–113.

———. *Slave Society in the City: Bridgetown, Barbados, 1680–1834.* Kingston: Ian Randle, 2003.

Welch, Pedro, and Richard Goodridge. *"Red" and Black over White: Free Coloured Women in Pre-Emancipation Barbados.* Bridgetown: Carib Research and Publications, 2000.

Wells, A. F., and D. Wells. *Friendly Societies in the West Indies: Report on a Survey by A. F. and D. Wells.* London: HMSO, 1953.

West, Richard. *Back to Africa: A History of Sierra Leone and Liberia.* New York: Hold, Rinehart, and Winston, 1970.

Williams, Eric. *Capitalism and Slavery.* London: Andre Deutsch, 1964.

Wilson, Charles Morrow. *Liberia: Black Africa in Microcosm.* New York: Harper & Row, 1971.

Wrong, Hume. *Government of the West Indies.* Oxford: Clarendon Press, 1923.

Yelvington, Kevin. "The War in Ethiopia and Trinidad, 1935–1936." In Brereton and Yelvington, *Colonial Caribbean in Transition.* 189–225.

Jordan, Samuel and Renn, 78n66
Jordan, Thomas, 78n66, 84–85
Jordan, Winthrop D., 63
Justice system, 65, 125–129, 209–213, 210n37, 230.
    See also Court testimony

Kennedy, Joseph: and Alien Bill Committee, 78n66,
    190n50; and Barbados Auxiliary Anti-Slavery
    Society, 203n25; on emancipation, 190; and po-
    lice petition, 155–156; and populist politics,
    133; on Prescod, 190; and Prescod's libel trial,
    248; as slave owner, 2, 2n2, 4; and St. Mary's
    Society, 104–105, 190n50
Kimball, Horace: on apprenticeship, 152, 154; on
    Bridgetown merchants, 155; on concubinage,
    171; on emancipation, 191–192; on planter's at-
    titude toward emancipation, 182–183; on po-
    lice, 185; on Prescod, 179; Thorne's meeting
    with, 62–63, 64n20, 189
King, Charles, 280–281
Klein, Herbert, 38n59

Ladies' Association for the Relief of the Sick and In-
    digent Poor, 111–112, 124, 182, 270
Lambert, David, 128
Landers, Jane, 38n59
Landownership: by former slaves, 266; as highly
    valued, 141; land prices in Barbados compared
    with other Caribbean territories, 150, 192, 212;
    petition of free Afro-Barbadians on, 66–67; by
    planters and slave owners, 30, 60; and political
    appointments, 184; statistics on, 266, 266n23;
    as voting requirement, 121–122, 134, 178, 250
Laws: Alien and Census Act/Alien Bill Commit-
    tee, 77–78, 78n66, 80, 82, 84–85; antiemigra-
    tion laws in postemancipation era, 227–229,
    238, 239, 242, 243–245, 263; Brown Privilege
    Bill, 121–122, 132, 184; Consolidated Slave Act,
    94–96; emancipation law, 141; franchise re-
    form, 120–122, 130, 132, 134, 176–177, 178, 191;
    on free Afro-Barbadians, 16, 41, 46–48, 59–60,
    66–67, 76–77, 78, 86, 89, 156, 156n53; on huck-
    stering, 92–93, 164–165, 228; labor legislation
    during postemancipation era, 229–232; mar-
    riage law, 186; Masters and Servants Act, 229–
    232, 239; on Obeah spirituality, 89; poor laws,
    228, 230; riot act, 230; on slavery, 27, 30, 36–37,
    46–48, 59–60, 76, 89, 92–96, 93n21; Sugar Du-
    ties Act (1845), 263; vagrancy law, 229–230. *See
    also* Barbados House of Assembly

Lewis, Daniel, 55
Lewis, Hannah, 61, 107
Liberal newspaper: on African diaspora, 206–209,
    277; and antislavery dinners, 181, 190–191, 205;
    on attack on Bourne's home, 221; Best as re-
    porter for, 210–211; on cane fires, 192; on Co-
    lonial Coloured Union, 214–215; on election of
    1843, 253; on emigration during postemanci-
    pation era, 236–239, 242–245; on female labor
    outside the home, 193–194; founding of, 178;
    on Franklyn's execution, 72; on Sarah Hope,
    272; huckstering law, 164–165; on labor, 193;
    on Mexico as free state for British people of
    color, 209; on patriarchal family, 164–165; on
    poor relief, 192; Prescod as editor of, 1, 13, 72,
    160, 164, 178–181, 187, 190, 241; on racial dis-
    crimination, 179–181, 218; on refusal to bury
    child of color, 172. *See also* Prescod, Samuel
    Jackman
Liberal Party, 213, 249–250, 252, 268, 271
Liberia, 12–13, 199, 201, 201n20, 277–281
Library Association, 107
Loving, Henry: as abolitionist and journalist, 2–4,
    124–125; career of, 186n35, 188; and imperial
    civil service, 202n24; as stipendiary magistrate
    in Barbados, 3, 151, 185–186, 188
Lucas, Nathaniel, 71
Lunatic asylum, 240
Lushington, Stephen, 99
Lyceum, 107, 108
Lynch, Hamlet, 86n88, 105–106
Lynch, Miss, 105
Lynch, Mrs. Hamlet, 105

MacGregor, Evan: and Cummins's appointment as
    magistrate and Legislative Council member,
    184, 186–187; and end of apprenticeship, 151;
    and justice system, 210–212; political appoint-
    ments of elite men of color by, 185–187; on pre-
    emancipation free people of color and Prescod,
    245–246; and Prescod's libel trial, 248–249;
    and Roach's appointment as magistrate, 240;
    and Thorne's appointment as assistant harbor
    master, 242
Manning, John S., 86n88
Manumission: and amelioration of slaves, 38n57,
    97–98; and apprenticeship, 141, 146–148;
    coartación (gradual manumission), 36; elimina-
    tion of fees for, 93n21, 97, 146; fees for, 37–38,
    52–53, 61, 76, 94, 97; by free Afro-Barbadians,